THE

JEWISH RELIGION

Printed in the U. S. A.

The
JEWISH RELIGION

By

Michael Friedlander, Ph.D.
Late Principal, Jews' College, London

---

*American edition, revised and enlarged, with a biography
of the author.*

Forword by

THEODOR H. GASTER, A.M. Ph.D.

Preface by

JOSHUA BLOCH, Ph.D. D.D.

NEW YORK
PARDES PUBLISHING HOUSE, Inc.
1946

Dr. M. FRIEDLÄNDER.

PREFACE.

In presenting this volume to the public the author does not claim much originality. He merely desires to reproduce the religious principles which were sown into his heart by his parents, ז״ל, and cultivated by the great teachers of Israel—the Prophets, the Soferim, and their successors—in order that the blessing which he himself has always derived from these principles may also be enjoyed by his brethren. The original sources of religious knowledge, viz., the Scriptures and Post-Biblical Jewish Literature, are of course accessible to all, and every one may sit at the feet of our great teachers and listen to their instruction. But there are many who are in need of assistance, who require the aid of an interpreter. The present volume is intended to render that assistance and to serve as such interpreter. The author therefore addresses himself to his brethren, especially to his disciples, in the words of an ancient teacher of the Mishnah (Aboth v. 25), "Turn it, and turn it over again;" and if he cannot add also "for everything is in it," he hopes that that which is in it will be found useful to those who seek religious knowledge, and that it will prove an incentive to many " to learn and teach, to heed and do, and to fulfil in love all the words of instruction in the Divine Law."

In conclusion, the author begs to thank the Rev. S. Singer for his assistance and his many valuable suggestions thewhile book was passing through the press

M. FRIEDLÄNDER.

JEWS' COLLEGE, 3 *Iyar* 5651.

PREFACE TO THE SECOND EDITION.

THE first edition being exhausted a second edition has been prepared. There is no cause for any change in the body of the book. Religion, both "Glaubenslehre" and "Pflichtenlehre," are given as objectively as possible, and the most rigid examination of all that is taught in "The Jewish Religion," discovered no misstatement. A few unimportant errors, which according to the Psalmist (Ps. xix) are excusable, are rectified in the list of Errata. Questions concerning religious principles which have arisen in the Community since the publication have been foreseen and dealt with according to Law and Tradition. A few notes are added in the second edition, where further elucidations seemed necessary. There is also appended the bibliography of text-books of Jewish Religion, an abstract of a paper on Religious Education, read before the Jews' College Literary Society, and the prayer which in the Spanish and Portuguese Synagogues is offered up by the Barmitzvah when called to the Law. The latter practice is worthy of imitation.

M. F.

London, Adar I., 5660.

FOREWORD

FOR MORE than half a century the present work has ranked
as a classic exposition of the beliefs and practises of Judaism.
It is not difficult to see why. The genius of this book is that
it cuts across doctrinal differences within the House of Israel
and avoids the divisiveness of conflicting ideologies and
approaches. What it expounds is neither Orthodox nor Conservative nor Reform Judaism but rather that basic traditional heritage which underlies them all and of which they
are but variant interpretations.

The author was what would be called today an orthodox
Jew, but he himself would probably have eschewed that
unfortunate term, with its suggestion of canonical authority
and dogmatic rigidity. The view upon which his entire
approach is predicated is that while revelation may be pro-
gressive and while interpretations may change in the light
of changing experiences, the thing revealed and interpreted,
its inherent inspiration and value, is necessarily constant and
permanent. To Friedlander, Torah and the Judaism which
issues from it are an expression of the inherent moral order
of the world, whose source is God; and it is in this sense
that they are, in their essence, both divine and immutable.
Accordingly, he is not concerned with discussing the particular forms of expression and the particular changes of
emphasis which they may assume when they come into contact with the varying experiences of successive generations
and the varying emergencies of different epochs; what con-

cerns him is the essential verity which underlies these manifold and variant expressions. To the rabbinic statement that the Torah was written in black flame upon white flame, Friedlander would have added that behind the many-colored glow lies the eternal fire of God. It is, indeed, this emphasis upon the eternal verities, this insistence that variety of emphasis and expression in no way affects constancy of essence, that constitutes the unique genius of Friedlander's presentation, and renders his volume an authoritative guide for all who would understand the basic meaning and message of Judaism.

An equally significant feature of the author's presentation is his insistence on traditional ceremony and observance as the indispensable vehicle of the Jewish way of life. In Friedlander's conception, the modern view that Judaism is a civilization and that the primary reason for maintaining its institutions is to preserve the integrity of that civilization and the cohesion of the group which embodies it, would have represented but half of the truth. To him the sole *raison d'etre* of Jewish existence was the realization and exemplification, through observance of the Torah, of what was in fact the inherent moral code of mankind. Ceremonies and observances were therefore more than mere picturesque expressions of a national culture; they were the means by which the divine dispensation was exemplified and concretized. If, as in so many instances, they commemorated specific events in the history of Israel, they were nevertheless more than national memorials; for the history so commemorated was but the career of a "people of priests and an holy nation" marching through the centuries to the Promised Land of the Kingdom of God.

Because its presentation of Judaism is thus rooted in what Solomon Schechter so luminously characterized as the concept of "catholic Israel," and because in the havoc of our time there is such imperative need for the reaffirmation of basic verities, as against "constructions" and "reinterpretations," the publication of this classic in an American edition is to be welcomed. As the grandson of Michael Friedlander ז״ל I deem it a special privilege to commend it to the American public.

THEODOR H. GASTER

Library of Congress
Washington, D.C.
June 17, 1946.

PREFACE TO AMERICAN EDITION

The Jewish Religion by Dr. Michael Friedlander serves as an excellent guide-book of Jewish belief and practice. Not only will rabbis and religious school teachers turn to its pages for guidance but the average reader seeking an authentic presentation of Jewish traditional teachings and practices will likewise find help in them. It is a work which presents the principles and practices of the Jewish religion in a manner at once authoritative and attractive. It offers a complete exposition of the principles and precepts of Judaism as a religious system. It treats of the laws and customs, as well as the foundations of Jewish ethics and religious practice as developed during the many centuries of Jewish experience. It casts light upon most of the religious practices of the Jewish home as well as on those ceremonies which characterize worship in the synagogue. It is a work which demonstrates that Judaism is a religion of daily life and not merely a formal creed, or a scheme of salvation for the Jew only. It is a practical religion not a theoretical sentimentalism. To be sure, it is a religion in which both conduct and doctrine have their respective places; righteous conduct is the aim and purpose of every ceremony and rite. Moreover, it shows that Judaism is a religion, not for Sabbath and holiday merely, but for every day. It certainly shows that Judaism is old but not antiquated. Though many handbooks on the Jewish religion have been written in the English language the presentation of traditional Judaism is introduced best in the present volume. This, in a large measure, accounts for its popularity. This, too, explains the fact that the book has gone through many editions in England and has been translated into German and published under the title *Die Jüdische Religion,* Frankfurt-a-M., 1922.

The appearance, at this time, of the American edition of *The Jewish Religion* by Dr. M. Friedlander will, no doubt, be fully appreciated now when the need for such a book is so keenly felt after the terrible upheaval and complete upsetting of many a moral and religious value. It should contribute to strengthen the faith which has weakened and the tradition which is apparently waning.

The volume is provided with a short biographical appreciation of the author and a tenderly written Foreword by his grandson, Dr. Theodor H. Gaster.

JOSHUA BLOCH

The New York Public Library
July 1, 1946

DR. MICHAEL FRIEDLANDER
(A biographical sketch)

No MAN ever lived a more harmonious life with the teachings and practices of the Faith of his Fathers as did the Reverend Dr. Michael Friedlander. The tenets of this Faith, its rites and ceremonies he so well described in his work on *The Jewish Religion,* a standard hand-book on the subject. Dr. Friedlander lived a blameless life. By his gentle character, his religious earnestness and his deep scholarship he lent distinction and inspiration to many of his faithful followers and disciples. His influence was great and abiding and his wide learning and enthusiasm for Jewish lore and literature gave no small measure of impetus to Jewish learning in English-speaking lands. He was endowed with many exalted qualities that distinguished him as a man, as a Jew, as a scholar, and, above all, as a great teacher in Israel.

Though modest and unassuming his personality and work have left a deep impress upon the religious fortunes of the Jewish community in English-speaking lands. Not a little of the love of Judaism manifested in those lands is, in no small degree, due to his exhortations and above all to the example he set. His was a life worthy of emulation.

Dr. Michael Friedlander was born at Jutroschin, Prussia, on April 29, 1833, and died in London, England, on December 10, 1910. His early education he received in his native city. It consisted of secular studies at the local Catholic elementary school and religious instruction obtained in the Jewish traditional manner at the *Cheder* and from his father who was a Talmudist, a Hebrew grammarian and an accomplished master of Hebrew style. He was a precocious boy and at quite an early age he began to impart knowledge to other children. In the year 1850, he went to Berlin to devote himself entirely to study. There he prepared himself for advanced studies. He entered the Gymnasium and pursued Hebrew and Rabbinic studies under the direction of the

Rabbis Jacob Joseph Oettinger and Elchanan Rosenstein. Upon completing his studies at the Gymnasium he matriculated, in 1856, in the university and specialized in the study of oriental and classical languages as well as in mathematics. In the year 1862, the University of Halle conferred upon him the degree of Doctor of Philosophy. While in Berlin, he was appointed principal of the Talmud school. His fame as a profound Hebraist and Talmudist as well as a classical and mathematical scholar became widely spread.

In the year 1865, he resigned his position as principal of the Talmud school in Berlin to accept a call to occupy the post of principal of Jews' College, London, England, in succession to Barnett Abrahams. An unsuccessful effort was made by Dr. Azriel Hildesheimer, the eminent leader of orthodox Jewry in Germany, to have him come back to Berlin in order to join the faculty of the Rabbiner Seminar. Dr. M. Friedlander preferred to remain in the capitol of Great Britain, where, in addition to his duties as Principal of Jews' College, he also played a potent role in various scholarly and literary endeavors. The Society for the Diffusion of Jewish Literature and the Society of Hebrew Literature gained his special devotion. For the latter he translated and edited (1) *The Commentary of Ibn Ezra on Isaiah;* (2) *An Essay on the Writings of Ibn Ezra;* and (3) an English translation from the original Arabic, with notes, of *The Guide for the Perplexed* by Moses Maimonides, a work that has gone through many editions.

Dr. M. Friedlander was active in Jewish communal affairs in Great Britain. He was a member of the Council of the United Synagogue and of the Board of Management of the Central Synagogue in London. He was a member of the Board of Deputies of British Jews, a member of the Executive Committee of the Jewish Historical Society of England as well as the Honorary Chairman of the Union of Jewish Literary Societies.

In the year 1907 when he retired from the arduous post of Principal of Jews' College, Dr. Michael Friedlander completed forty-two years of service to the Anglo-Jewish community. They were years filled with loyalty and earnestness devoted entirely to the cause of his people and his Faith. During the years of his active life, especially in the discharge of his duties as head of the largest Jewish theological seminary maintained by British Jewry, he, no doubt, more than once, encountered grave difficulties. In coping with them and in the endeavor to discharge his high responsibilities he was always sustained by a deep sense of personal duty. By his sincere piety, by his labors in the field of Jewish learning, by his many lovable qualities, primarily by his humility and kindness, he succeeded in winning the regard and affection of his disciples and friends. His influence has been exercised on, and felt by, several generations of preachers and teachers in English-speaking Jewry, who, after passing from his care have issued forth to lead in the intellectual and moral struggles of the Jewish community of the whole English-speaking world in its continual, although at times unconscious, striving towards the ideal. In that capacity Dr. Michael Friedlander had in his hands the formation, to a considerable extent, of the characters of the spokesmen of the Jewry in the British Empire, of the representatives of the Jewish community before the eyes of its Christian neighbors.

The scholarly works which Dr. Michael Friedlander left behind him testify to the depth and breadth of his learning. Dr. Israel Abrahams, who was first his pupil and later his colleague, gave testimony to the versatility of Dr. Friedlander in the following words: "He seemed to us to know everything—he was certainly a first-rate classic, a fine mathematician with inborn gifts of originality, and, of course, he was learned in Hebrew and Rabbinics." At Jews' College he taught not only theology and biblical and rabbinical exegesis and Jewish history and Talmud but mathematics and, on occasions, classics and even Arabic as well. His learning was phenomenal, not only in those subjects which he was particularly called upon to impart to his pupils, but in many and in most diversified branches of knowledge. In fact, his knowledge was encyclopedic. It was as deep as it was universal. For years his knowledge of astronomy enabled him to supply the tables of nightfall in all parts of England for Valentine's Almanac as well as for his own work on the Jewish calendar.

In addition to his several publications enumerated above Dr. M. Friedlander was also the author of *The Book of Isaiah,* an Anglican version amended according to the commentary of Abraham Ibn Ezra. He edited *The Jewish Family Bible* in English and Hebrew. The English text consisted of the Anglican version which he revised in order to make it conform to the traditional Jewish interpretation of Sacred Scriptures. It was widely used in English-speaking Jewish communities. He was also the author of two books on Judaism, they are: *The Jewish Religion* and the *Text Book of the Jewish Religion,* specially designed for use in Jewish religious schools. He contributed many articles to such learned publications as the *Jewish Quarterly Review, Dictionary of National Biography* and other publications. Numerous papers and special lectures which he delivered have appeared separately.

Dr. Michael Friedlander's sincere piety as a Jew was of that modest and unassuming type which bears unmistakably the stamp of sincerity and of a profound conviction which pervades the whole man. Of his own orthodox views and practices he was consistently tenacious. He led a religious life scrupulously observant. Dr. Moses Gaster, the distinguished Haham of the Spanish and Portuguese congregation of London, speaks of his father-in-law as "a great Jew, great in his wisdom, great in his piety, great in his learning, and great in his meekness." He was a truly pious son of Israel, a devout servant of God and of his people. He served them well with all his heart, with all his spirit and with all his might.

CONTENTS.

—————

CONTENTS.

THE JEWISH RELIGION.

INTRODUCTION.

" Man is the most privileged of creatures ; he has been made in the image of God. His privilege is still further enhanced by the fact that he has been made aware of his distinction" (Aboth iii. 14). There is in man a consciousness or feeling of a certain relation between him and a superior Being, on whose Will his own existence depends. This consciousness is the basis of religion, but is not religion itself. It is the influence which this feeling exercises over man's actions and conduct in life that forms the essence of religion. When man begins to feel that he is responsible for his actions to a higher Being, and forms his actions in harmony with this feeling, he may be called religious. Two elements must therefore be distinguished in religion : the notion of man's dependence on and responsibility to a superior Being, and the influence of this notion on his actions: religious belief and religious practice, or faith and duty. Religious belief or faith, in its most simple and most general form, may be said to be common almost to all mankind ; and in the great variety of faiths, produced by

A

various circumstances and experiences, this simple idea
may easily be detected as the fundamental principle
of all of them. The same can be said with regard
to religious practice. There are certain fundamental
principles of duty which are recognised and adopted
by the most diverse religious sects; they form, as it
were, the common stem from which a large number of
branches spring forth in all directions. These branches
diverge more and more the larger they grow and the
more numerous they become.

Judaism is one of these various religions. It has
been the source of most of the religions of the civilised
world, and is destined to become, in its simplest principles, the universal religion.

What is Judaism? or what does Judaism teach its
adherents to believe, and what does it teach them to
do? The answers to these two questions form the
main subject of every book on our holy religion. The
answer to the first question must include our doctrine
about God, His attributes, His relation to the material
world, and especially to man; the mission of man, his
hopes and fears. The answer to the second question
must include our duties toward God, toward our fellow-
men, and toward ourselves. Both answers must be
based on that which we are taught in the Holy Writings, and especially in the Torah. Recourse may be
had to philosophic speculation, to which, indeed, the
first question peculiarly invites, but the result must be
rectified by the teaching of the Torah.

In accordance with the maxim, "The secret things
belong to the Lord our God; but those things which
are revealed belong unto us and to our children for

ever : *that we may do all the words of this Law,"* abstruse metaphysical disquisitions about the essence and the attributes of the Divine Being will be avoided in the present work, as also every attempt at proving, philosophically or mathematically, truths which have been revealed unto us in a supernatural way.[1] But the simple truths taught in the Holy Writings and explained by our sages will be expounded, the different opinions about them will be examined, and it will be shown that these truths are not contradicted by common sense or by the results of scientific research.

The second question, however, What does Judaism teach us to do? refers to "the things which are revealed," and must be treated more fully. Care will be taken, as far as possible, that nothing be omitted that is required for the right understanding and the correct estimate of our religious duties.

[1] When our great theologians, Saadiah, Bachya, Maimonides, Albo, &c., considered it necessary to write long and abstruse metaphysical essays in order to firmly establish certain truths, it was done rather for the purpose of combating the views of opponent theologians than for the instruction of the multitude, and it may fairly be said that Maimonides has done far greater service to his brethren by the composition of a systematic code of laws than by his philosophical "Guide." The former, the *Mishneh-Torah,* never fails to enlighten those who seek in it enlightenment with regard to some religious duty, whilst the "Guide" would scarcely relieve any one of his perplexities in matters of religious belief. There is a saying in the Talmud Jerus. (Chagigah, ch. i.), "Would that they had forgotten me, and kept my commandments!" or, in other words, "Theologians would do better if they were less eager to investigate into the essence of God and His attributes, and were more anxious to study and to do God's commandments." Instead of devoting their chief attention to the knowledge and the practice of the Law, they waste their energy and their time in attempts to solve problems to which the human mind is unequal (S. Plessner, Religions—Unterricht, p. xxxviii.).

Religion therefore includes two elements: faith and practice. In religious life, as well as in the teaching of religion, both elements are equally essential; faith without religious practice does not suffice, nor the latter without faith. We are accustomed to look upon certain dogmas as fundamental, and certain practices as essential, and are therefore prone to renounce beliefs which are not fundamental in our eyes, and to abandon such religious practice as seems to us less essential. Hence the frequent inquiry as to what is the minimum of belief, and what the minimum degree of conformity to the Law, that Judaism demands. But in reality there can be no compromise in religion, whether in matters of faith or of practice. Convinced of a certain number of truths, it is impossible for us to abandon any of them without being false to ourselves; being convinced of the binding character of certain religious commands and prohibitions, it would be perverse to pronounce at the same time part of them as superfluous. *Judaism is the adherence to the truths taught in the Holy Law, and the faithful obedience to its precepts.*

The principal Hebrew equivalents for the modern term "Religion," תורה and אמונה, confirm this view. In the Bible תורה signifies "instruction," and is applied to the teaching of religious truth, as well as to that of religious precepts. The same is the case with the second term אמונה which signifies "firmness," "perseverance," or "permanence," and is used of "consistency" in faith as well as of conscientiousness in the practice of the Divine ordinances.[1]

---

[1] Post-biblical authors frequently employ the term אמונה in the sense of *religious belief*, and תורה in the sense of *religious duties;* the equivalent for *religion* is דת.

I.

OUR CREED.

———

INTRODUCTION.

FAITH is the implicit and absolute belief in the truth of the communication made to us and in the trustworthiness of him who makes it to us. The child has faith in its parents that their wishes or commands are for its good; the pupil in his teachers that they impart correct knowledge; we have faith in our friends that they have no intention to deceive us; in the men of science and learning that the results of their researches may be accepted as well established. In all these cases the faith is but imperfect and of a relative and temporary character. Time, investigation, and extended observation and knowledge may either confirm the contents of our faith or may convince us that we have been in error. This is not the case with religious faith. It keeps within the boundaries of its own domain and does not encroach on that of the senses and of reason. Whatever can be known by means of scientific research and thorough investigation we need not accept on faith. Religion —I have, of course, our own religion, the Jewish, in mind — does not only not forbid such examination, but even encourages it. Thus we read in the Book of Proverbs, " A fool believeth every word, but the prudent man looketh well to his going" (xiv. 15). For this purpose God has given us intellectual faculties that we should employ them in our search for truth. At the same time, however, He has set limits to our faculties, and there are things which are beyond these limits, being *nistaroth*, "things hidden" from our senses, whose existence has been made known to us through the grace of God, by such means as His infinite wisdom determined. We search and investigate, examine and demonstrate, within the sphere of our senses ; but all that is beyond their reach belongs to the *nistaroth*, the knowledge of which can only be imparted to us directly by the Almighty, or indirectly by those to whom they have been communicated by Him. Our belief with regard to these *nistaroth* may be supported or strengthened by philosophical or dialectical arguments, but can never be proved by mathematical or logical demonstration.

The sources from which we derive our knowledge of these *nistaroth* are *Revelation* and *Tradition*. God *reveals* things otherwise unknown to man to such persons or to such a generation as His wisdom chooses, and from those thus privileged the knowledge spreads to the rest of mankind by means of *Tradition.* In addition to these two sources there is a third one in ourselves: God implanted in our souls certain ideas common to all of us as essential elements of our inner life, and these ideas form to some extent the basis of our faith. Such is, *e.g.*, the idea of an all-powerful Being, God, who is the source and origin of everything in existence.

There is no real conflict between faith and reason. It may sometimes seem as if there were such a conflict, and we then naturally begin to doubt. In such cases the truth of our faith may be doubted, but the correctness of our reasoning is no less subject to doubt. We may have erroneously included in our faith beliefs which do not belong to it, and on becoming aware that they are contrary to reason, we cast them aside without the least injury to our faith. On the other hand, our reason is not perfect; we frequently discover mistakes in our arguments and conclusions, and reject opinions which we hitherto have considered as firmly established.

Through patient and thorough investigation of our doubts, without over-estimation of our reasoning faculties, we shall be able to settle the seeming conflict between reason and faith in a satisfactory manner. The examination of our doubts will prove that none of the truths which the Almighty revealed to mankind are contrary to reason.

In this way we are enabled to separate from our faith all elements that in reality are foreign to it; we shall be able to distinguish between faith and superstition. The latter consists of erroneous notions and beliefs which can be tested and subjected to the ordinary means of inquiry. Superstition is not tolerated by true religion; strict adherence to the teachings of our holy religion is the best check to superstitious beliefs.

The importance which the Bible attaches to implicit faith in God and His word may be gathered from the following passages :—

" And *he* (Abraham) *believed in the Lord,* and He reckoned it to him as righteousness " (Gen. xv. 6).

The Hebrew for " righteousness " is in the original צדקה which is used in the Bible as the sum-total of everything good and noble in man's life.

When the Israelites had crossed the Red Sea, it is said of them : " And Israel saw the great work which the Lord did upon the Egyptians, and the people feared the Lord : and *they believed in the Lord,* and in Moses His servant " (Exod. xiv. 3 1).

Again, when Moses and Aaron had sinned at the waters of Meribah by striking the rock instead of speaking to it, they were rebuked for want of אמונה " faith," in the following words : " Because *ye believed not in me* (לא האמנתם בי) to sanctify me in the eyes of the children of Israel, therefore ye shall not bring this assembly into the land which I have given them " (Numb. xx. 1 2).

When Moses in his song האזינו blamed the Israelites for their evil doings, he called them " children in whom there is no *faith* " אמון (Deut. xxxii. 20).

King Jehoshaphat, addressing the army before the battle, says : " Have *faith* in the Lord and you will be safe ; have confidence in His prophets and you will succeed " (2 Chron. xx. 20).

In the same sense Isaiah says to King Ahaz : " If you have no *faith,* surely you will not be safe " (Isa. vii. 9).

Also Jeremiah, speaking of Israel's disobedience to the word of God, exclaims : " *The faith,* האמונה *is perished,* and it is cut off from their mouth " (Jer. vii. 28).

The prophet Habakkuk, praying to God for an explanation why evil-doers succeed and prosper, receives the divine answer : " The righteous shall live *by his faith* " וצדיק באמונתו יחיה (Hab. ii. 4) ; and when Hosea predicts the future redemption of Israel, he tells them in the name of God, " And I will betroth thee unto me *by faith* " וארשתיך לי באמונה (Hos. ii. 22).

Our teachers, the sages and rabbis, who succeeded the prophets, have been equally emphatic in commending religious faith. The following are a few of their sayings concerning faith :—

" Great is the merit of faith. Through their faith in the Creator of the universe the Israelites were inspired by the holy spirit, and were enabled to sing praises to the Lord." " Faith in the Lord was the source of all the temporal and eternal blessings which were bestowed upon Abraham ; it gave him the enjoyment of this world and the world to come." " When the Psalmist says : ' This gate leads to the Lord ; righteous people (צדיקים) shall come in through it,' he denoted by the term ' righteous ' *those who possess faith in God*" (Yalkut on Ex. xiv. 31).

In spite of the fact that the Torah and the prophets most emphatically declare *faith* אמונה to be a very essential element in Judaism, it does not seem to have the same importance in the writings of Jewish theologians and philosophers, some of whom have endeavoured to substitute reasoning and logical arguments for simple faith, and to rebuild upon scientific research the religious edifice erected on the foundation of faith. The following are the utterances of the principal Jewish theologians since the close of the Talmud on the relation between faith and reason :—

The Gaon Saadiah of Fayyum wrote a book **On**

creeds and religious beliefs (אמאנאת ואעתקאד־אמונות ודעות). In the Introduction to this work the philosopher describes the causes of human error and doubt, and assumes four classes of believers. There are, first, those who recognise the truth found by them, cling to it, and are happy in it. There are, secondly, those who have the true principle before them, but do not recognise it, doubt its correctness, and abandon it again. The third class includes those who adopt an opinion without having recognised it as true; they mistake falsehood for truth. The last division consists of those who form no definite opinion, but remain continually in an unsettled state of mind. Saadiah is anxious to see at least his co-religionists in the first class, and his work was intended to help them towards this end.

According to Saadiah, belief or faith must be an integral part of our soul; the various truths which form the faith are stored up in the soul as in a repository, completely ready for use whenever required. It is, however, possible that we store up opinions as true which are false. Tests must be applied to each opinion in order to ascertain its right character. Three of the tests are of a general nature, but the fourth has its force only for us, the believers in the truth of the Holy Writings. The first three tests will show us whether a certain opinion is confirmed or contradicted by our senses, by our innate ideas, or by our logical reasoning. In addition to these we possess a fourth test in the trustworthy communication (הגדה הנאמנת), i.e., the contents of Holy Writ and Tradition. Holy Writ recognises the necessity of the three general tests, and frequently exhorts us to apply them. On the other hand, Saadiah is convinced that the contents of Holy Writ and Tradition are never contradicted, but in many cases are confirmed by these tests. Such confirmation is in reality superfluous; but the human mind feels more at ease when it finds that the teaching of Holy Writ is supported by other proofs. Besides, attacks on the Bible come frequently from these tests, and it is therefore useful to learn how to refute them. According to Saadiah, the truth taught in the Bible can never be contradicted by the results of scientific or philosophical research.

Thus to Saadiah philosophy and science are mere luxuries, and cannot be considered as handmaids to the Torah. They are not studied on account of their intrinsic value or as helps for the understanding of Holy Writ, but merely for the purpose of procuring proper weapons for theological warfare, or of superadding the conviction that what is known to us from the most trustworthy source is confirmed from other less reliable sources.

The poet and philosopher Solomon ibn Gabirol, who is lost in enthusiasm in contemplating the powers of the human soul, humbly acknowledges that it was his faith that saved him from fall and ruin. Referring to man's faculty of acquiring knowledge, he says in his "Royal Crown" כתר מלכות : "Who can comprehend Thy wisdom in giving to the soul the faculty of acquiring knowledge, on which her existence depends, knowledge being her foundation? She is permanent and immortal in the same measure as her foundation is well established." But, reflecting on human weakness, he expresses his feeling of gratitude to the Creator for His

guidance in the following words: "Thou hast done
yet more for me. Thou hast implanted in my heart
a perfect faith, so that I believe in Thee as the true
God, and in Thy prophets as true prophets; Thou hast
not cast my lot among those that rebel against Thee, or
among those who provoke Thy name, despise Thy Law,
attack Thy servants, and disbelieve Thy prophets."
Knowledge — philosophy and science — is the very
essence, the immortal element of the soul, and yet
without the Word of God man would go astray and
be lost.

The boundaries between faith and reason are more
distinctly set forth in the Commentary on Sefer Ye-
tsirah by Dunash ben Tamim (ed. L. Dukes in *Shire
Shelomoh*, i. p. vi. *seq*.): "All these beings above and
below have been created by God, and it is within the
province of man to explore and to examine all of
them; but he must not pass beyond these boundaries
to investigate into the essence of God; 'for in the city
of his refuge shall he dwell,' and 'if he goeth out of
his place, and the avenger of blood smite him, he hath
no remedy.' Besides, wisdom and science acknowledge that man is unable to comprehend by his own
intellect anything that exists outside the sphere of
created beings."

R. Bachya, son of Joseph hassephardi, who lived
in the eleventh century, treats, in the Introduction
to his " Duties of the Heart," of the three sources
of human knowledge — Holy Writ, Tradition, and
Reason. Bachya is fully convinced that the knowledge derived from the first two sources is complete
and correct. " If you are a man endowed with

knowledge and reason, and are able to demonstrate the principles of your belief and your religious practice, which you have been taught by the Sages in the name of the prophets, it is your duty to do so, and to let reason confirm what Tradition teaches. If you abstain from attempting this investigation, you neglect your duty towards your Creator."

Still more emphatic is Shem-tob ibn Palqera in demanding the right of free inquiry into everything taught by Revelation and Tradition. In a dialogue between the believer and the inquirer (*Hammebhakkesh*) the former is represented as ignorant of everything our mind desires to know; whilst the wise man, who combines belief and confidence in Tradition with the right use of his reason, knows how to satisfy the inquirer, and lays down the rule, " Let the study of the Torah be the foundation, and the study of other things secondary ; believe nothing that is not proved by reason or by God " (*i.e.*, by the word of Revelation).

R. Abraham ben David, in *Emunah ramah:* "Because three out of four scholars (R. Akiba, Ben-azai, Ben-zoma, and Elisha) were unsuccessful in their philo-sophical researches, therefore many turn their backs upon science, and in consequence of this neglect they remain ignorant of the chief principles of our religion." The object of his book is to reconcile religion and science.

R. Judah hallevi, in his " Kuzari," endeavours to convince the Kuzarite king of the truth of the Jewish religion by philosophical arguments, but gives unhesi-tatingly the preference and the higher authority to Divine revelation. He is convinced that reason or

philosophical argument could never refute any principle taught in the Law. He says: "Prophecy is
certainly stronger than logical inference."

R. Abraham ibn Ezra believes that man's intellectual
faculties are insufficient to solve all transcendental problems; thus, *e.g.*, the nature of the spirit of man is
unknown to most, and is only comprehended by him
"whose thoughts are weighed in the balance of reason,
and are established on the four elements of wisdom,
viz., the three R's: reading, writing, and reckoning;
(in Hebrew, the three ס: סְפָר סֵפֶר סִפּוּר) and the Divine
Law." Ibn Ezra recommends the study of science,
united with the belief in Divine revelation. "The
Torah," Ibn Ezra remarks in his Commentary on Ps
xix. 8, "is perfect in itself; it requires no evidence
from without for the truths which it teaches."

Maimonides' "Guide to the Perplexed" is entirely
devoted to the problem how to reconcile Scripture and
reason. Scripture cannot contain anything contrary
to reason; nor can the result of scientific research and
philosophical speculation be conceived as contrary to
reason, which is their very basis. But where any such
contradiction is perceived, *we* are at fault either in our
reasoning or in our interpretation of the Divine Writings. The Incorporeality and Unity of God are doctrines
that have been fully proved, and Scripture cannot teach
anything that is contrary to them. Where we believe
them to be contradicted in the Holy Writings the
contradiction is only apparent, and by assuming an
allegorical use of words and phrases the seeming contradiction is removed.

R. Joseph Albo prefaces his book on the principles

of Judaism as follows : " As the human understanding is incapable of finding out what is true and what is good, there must be a higher Being that assists us in determining what is good and in comprehending what is true. It is therefore necessary, above all, to study and to know the divine Law that guides man in these problems."

R. Eliah del Medigo, in his *Bechinath haddath* (Examination of Religion) says as follows :—

" Let us first see whether or not the study of philosophy is permitted to the followers of our religion ; and, if it be permitted, whether the study is to be considered a duty and a laudable act. The right-minded Jew does not doubt that the Law aims at leading us to humane conduct, good deeds, and true knowledge, the common people according to their capacity, and the more gifted according to their abilities. Certain fundamental truths are therefore set forth in the Law and the Prophets in an authoritative, poetical, or dialectical style ; but the higher order of intellects are encouraged to search for proper proofs. Thus the whole nation is addressed by Isaiah : ' Lift up your eyes on high and see who hath created these,' and the like. Also the chief of the Prophets tells the Israelites : ' Hear, O Israel, the Lord is our God ; the Lord is One.' Those who are more highly endowed than their fellow-men are exhorted, either directly or indirectly, to follow the course which is suitable to them. The direct exhortation to philosophical research is contained in the words : ' *Know* then this day, and take it to thy heart, that the Lord He is God,' &c. ; and indirectly it is contained in the command-

ment to love and to fear God, as has been explained
by R. Moses Maimonides. — The study of science
will certainly be of use to the scholar; it leads
to a knowledge of the created things, and through
these to a knowledge of the Creator. Such study
may even be considered as *necessary* to the Jewish
scholar, though not to the ordinary Jew. The scholar
must, however, not entirely rely on his research, but
on that which is taught in the Law. In this the
scholar and the ordinary man are equal, that both
accept the teaching of the Torah as infallible; only
with this difference, that the scholar can in addition
satisfy his thirst for knowledge and confirm by scientific proof what he has already accepted as true on
the authority of the Bible."

Of modern scholars I only quote Moses Mendelssohn's
theory. He accepts unconditionally the teaching of
the Bible; all its truths are absolute and perfect; no
reasoning whatever can refute them; but difficulties
may sometimes present themselves to us in reconciling the teaching of the Bible with that of our
reason. What have we then to do? The philosopher declares: "If I were to find my reason in
contradiction to the Word of God, I could command reason to be silent; but the arguments, so
long as they have not been refuted, will nevertheless
assert themselves in the innermost recesses of my
heart; the arguments will assume the form of dis-
quieting doubts, which will resolve themselves into
childlike prayers, earnest supplication for enlightenment. I should utter the words of the Psalmist:
'Lord, send me Thy light, Thy truth, that they may

guide me, and bring me to Thy holy mount, to Thy dwelling-place ! ' "

The conception which Moses Mendelssohn had of Jewish belief and its relation to reason we learn from the following passage :—" I recognise no other eternal truths than those which are not only comprehensible to the human mind, but also demonstrable by human powers. This principle by no means brings me into conflict with my own religion ; on the contrary, I consider it an essential element in Judaism, and the characteristic difference between Judaism and Christianity. Judaism has no revealed religion in the sense in which Christianity has. The Jews have a revealed legislation which instructs them in the divinely ordained means by which they may attain the eternal bliss. Laws and rules for conduct in life were revealed to Moses in a supernatural way, but no doctrines, no saving truth, and no general laws of logic. The latter the Eternal reveals to us, as to all men, through nature and through the things themselves ; never through words and letters. The divine book revealed to Moses, though a book of laws, includes an inexhaustible treasure of truths and doctrines. . . . The more we study it the more we wonder at the depth of the knowledge contained in it. But these truths are taught, and not forced upon us as dogmas. Belief does not allow itself to be commanded ; it is based upon conviction. In the Hebrew language, the very word which is generally translated ' faith,' viz., אמונה denotes originally confidence, trust that the promise made will also be fulfilled, and not what we understand by ' religious faith.' "

B

These words of Mendelssohn show how greatly those err who quote his opinions in support of the dictum that Judaism recognises no dogmas.   According to Mendelssohn, Judaism does not consist entirely of laws ; it teaches also certain truths.   We have certain dogmas without which the laws can have no meaning, yet there is no precept, " Thou shalt believe."   Nowhere in our Law, whether written or oral, is *a solemn declaration of our creed* demanded.   In so far Mendelssohn's view is correct ; but when he believes that all the truths we are taught in Scripture can be made evident by logical demonstration he is mistaken.   As to the meaning of אמונה comp. *supra*, p. 4.

THE THIRTEEN PRINCIPLES

OUR CREED.

THE main source of our creed is the Bible, and among the Biblical books, chiefly the Pentateuch (תורה). In these books we find many truths taught by God Himself, or by His inspired messengers, and they form the substance of our creed. It matters little how we arrange them, how we collect them into groups, and subdivide these again, provided we believe in them implicitly. In the Bible they are not arranged systematically; they are intermingled with, and are contained implicitly in, the history and the laws that form the subject-matter of the Scriptures; it is the observance of those laws which constitutes the best evidence of the belief seated in the heart. No declaration or recital of a creed is commanded in the Pentateuch; no tribunal is appointed for inquiring whether the belief of a man is right or wrong; no punishment is inflicted or threatened for want of belief. It became, however, necessary to formulate the truths taught in the Bible, when disputes arose as to their meaning and to their validity. The Mishnah, therefore, declares certain opinions as un-Jewish and contrary to the teaching of the Divine Word. Later on, when controversies

multiplied between the various sections of the Jewish
nation, as well as between Jews and Christians and
Jews and Mohammedans, it was found most important to settle the form and arrangement of our
beliefs.   Moses Maimonides, the great religious philosopher, taught, in his Commentary on the Mishnah,
thirteen principles of faith, which found general
acceptance among the Jews, and are known as the
Thirteen Principles.   They have found their way into
the Prayer-book in two different forms, one in prose
and one in poetry.   Maimonides, in commending them
to the reader, says : " Read them again and again and
study them well, and let not your heart entice you to
believe that you have comprehended their full meaning
after having read them a few times ; you would then
be in a great error, for I have not written down what
occurred to my mind at first thought.   I first thoroughly
studied and examined what I was going to write, compared the various doctrines, the correct ones and the
incorrect ones, and when I arrived at what we ought
to accept as our creed, I was able to prove it by
arguments and reasoning."   The thirteen articles as put
forth by Maimonides, and called by him principles and
foundations of our religion, are the following :—

1. The first principle : The belief in the existence
of the Creator ; that is, the belief that there exists a
Being who requires no other cause for His existence,
but is Himself the cause of all beings.

2. The second principle : The belief in the Unity of
God ; that is, the belief that the Being who is the
cause of everything in existence is One ; not like the
unity of a group or class, composed of a certain

number of individuals, or the unity of one individual consisting of various constituent elements, or the unity of one simple thing which is divisible *ad infinitum*, but as a unity the like of which does not exist.

3. The third principle: The belief in the Incorporeality of God; that is, the belief that this One Creator has neither bodily form nor substance, that He is not a force contained in a body, and that no corporeal quality or action can be attributed to Him.

4. The fourth principle: The belief in the Eternity of God; that is, the belief that God alone is without a beginning, whilst no other being is without a beginning.

5. The fifth principle: The belief that the Creator alone is to be worshipped, and no other being, whether angel, star, or ought else, all these being themselves creatures.

6. The sixth principle: The belief in Prophecy; that is, the belief that there have been men endowed with extraordinary moral and intellectual powers, by which they were enabled to reach a degree and kind of knowledge unattainable to others.

7. The seventh principle: The belief that our teacher Moses was the greatest of all prophets, both those before him and those after him.

8. The eighth principle: The belief in the Divine origin of the Law; the belief that the whole Pentateuch was communicated to Moses by God, both the precepts and the historical accounts contained therein.

9. The ninth principle: The belief in the integrity of the Law; that both the written and the oral Law are of Divine origin, and that nothing may be added to it or taken from it.

10. The tenth principle: The belief that God knows and notices the deeds and thoughts of man.

11. The eleventh principle: The belief that God rewards those who perform the commandments of His Law, and punishes those who transgress them.

12. The twelfth principle: The belief that Messiah will come at some future time, which it is impossible for us to determine; that he will be of the house of David, and will be endowed with extraordinary wisdom and power.

13. The thirteenth principle: The belief in the revival of the dead, or the immortality of the soul.

These thirteen principles (שלשה עשר עקרים) may be divided into three groups, according to their relation to the three principles:— 1. Existence of God. 2. Revelation. 3. Reward and punishment. The first group includes the first five principles, the second the next four, and the third the remaining four. In this order they will now be considered.

1. *Existence of God* מציאות הבורא.

The notion of the existence of God, of an invisible power which exercises its influence in everything that is going on in nature, is widespread, and common to almost the whole human race. It is found among all civilised nations and many uncivilised tribes. The existence of God may be regarded as an innate idea, which we possess from our earliest days. This is the origin of Natural Religion. Thinkers of all ages and nations have attempted to confirm this innate idea by convincing arguments. Prophets and divine poets have frequently directed the attention of those whom they addressed to the marvels of nature in order to inspire them with the idea of an All-wise and All-powerful Creator.

"Lift up your eyes on high, and behold who hath created these? Who is He who bringeth them forth by number? All of them He calleth by name, by the greatness of His might, and for that He is strong in power, not one is lacking" (Isa. xl. 26). "The heavens declare the glory of God, and the firmament sheweth His handywork" (Ps. xix. 2).

The regularity in the rising and setting of the heavenly bodies, which enables us to foretell the exact time and duration of an eclipse of the sun or the moon, is certainly a strong argument for the belief that there is a mighty and wise Creator who fixed the laws in accordance with which these luminaries move.

"Beautiful are the luminaries which our God has created. He has formed them with knowledge, reason, and understanding; He endowed them with power and strength to rule in the midst of the world. Full of splendour and beaming with light, they illumine the whole world; they rejoice when they rise, they are glad when they set, doing in reverence the will of their Master" (Sabbath Morning Service).

A similar regularity we notice when looking on the face of the earth. The various seasons of the year, each with its peculiar aspect and influence, the sequence of day and night at regular intervals, the gradual and systematic development of vegetable and animal life—all point forcibly to the fact that these things do not owe their existence to chance, but to the will of an Almighty and All-wise Creator.

Again, if we consider the structure of a single plant, or of a single animal, we find that every one of the members and parts of which it is composed has its peculiar function or purpose in the economy of the whole plant or the whole animal. Let one of these component parts refuse its function or cease to fulfil its purpose and the whole is disorganised. Certainly there must be a Being who makes the different members of an organism co-operate for the development and advantage of the whole. The idea of purpose which regulates this co-operation cannot have originated in the parts nor in the whole, but in the conception of Him by whose Will these were created.

"The finger of God" is further recognised in the important events of the life of the individual as well as in the history of whole nations. We are frequently reminded of the lesson, "The heart of man deviseth his way, but the Lord directeth his step" (Prov. xvi. 9). "Salvation is the Lord's, and on Thy people it is incumbent to bless Thee" (Ps. iii. 9).

Another argument in support of the belief in the existence of God is taken from the moral consciousness which every human being possesses. This points to the existence of a higher Being, perfect in goodness, as the origin and cause of the moral consciousness in our own heart.

These and similar arguments are employed to strengthen and purify our belief in God. The question, however, arises, Are these arguments alone sufficient to convince us ? Are they strong enough to resist the attacks of scepticism ?

On examining them thoroughly we shall find them of excellent service to the believer. His belief is strengthened against many doubts by which he may be assailed ; and scepticism will be kept at bay by these arguments. But of themselves and unsupported they may not always suffice to establish belief in God ; and if they carry conviction with them for the moment, we are not sure whether fresh arguments of opponents might not again unsettle the mind. Another method was therefore chosen by the Almighty, by which certainty is attained, and a sure guide is given for our moral and religious life. It is *Revelation.* Of this we shall speak later on.

The principal forms of religion or worship that sprang from the natural belief in God are Polytheism, Pantheism, Atheism, Theism, and Deism.

1. The first form of Divine worship of which history and archæology give us information is *Polytheism.* The creating and ruling power of some invisible Being was noticed everywhere. Every manifestation of such influence was ascribed to its peculiar deity, which was worshipped according to the peculiar conception of the deity in the mind of the individual person, family, or nation. This is chiefly the kind of idolatry mentioned in the Bible and combated by the prophets.

A very general object of worship were the stars. Rabbi Jehudah ha-Levi, in Kuzari iv. 1, in trying to explain the origin of this practice, says as follows :——
" The spheres of the sun and the moon do not move in the same way. A separate cause or god was therefore

assumed for each, and people did not think that there was a higher force on which all these causes depended." The ancient monuments and the treasures stored up in our museums show how great was the variety of forms which idolatry took, and to how great an extent people adhered, and still adhere, to this kind of worship. But there have been thinkers and philosophers even among the idolatrous nations who sought a unity in the construction and working of the universe, and early arrived at the idea of a First Cause as the sole source of all that exists.

2. The fact that the influence of the Divine power makes itself perceptible to the observing eye of man everywhere produced another kind of human error: Pantheism (All-God). Modern Pantheism dates from Spinoza; but long before Spinoza, when the secret forces at work in the changes noticed by us in all material objects were recognised as properties inherent in the substance of things, these forces were considered as the sole independent causes of the existing universe, and the combination of these forces, called Nature, was considered to be the First Cause, or God. A modification of this theory is contained in the philosophy of Spinoza. According to this great philosopher's system, the universe in its entirety has the attributes of the Deity: there exists nothing but the Substance (God), its attributes, and the various ways in which these attributes become perceptible to man. Spinoza tried to defend himself from the reproach of describing God as corporeal, but he did not succeed. The attribute of extension or space which God possesses, according to Spinoza, is only conceivable

in relation to corporeal things. The philosophy of Spinoza is in this dilemma : either God is corporeal, or the corporeal world does not exist. Both assumptions are equally absurd. It is true, in one of his letters he complains that he has been misrepresented, as if he believed God to consist of a certain corporeal mass. But we cannot help assuming the existence of a certain corporeal mass, and if this is not God, we must distinguish in our mind God and something that is not God, contrary to the fundamental doctrine of Pantheism. Besides, there are many incongruities and improbabilities involved in this theory. It has no foundation for a moral consciousness. The wicked and the good are alike inseparable from God. They both result with necessity from the attributes of God, and they cannot be otherwise than they actually are. If we, by the consideration that injury done to us by our fellow-man was not done by that person alone, but by a series of predetermined necessary causes, may be induced to conquer hatred against the apparent cause of our injury, we may equally be induced by the same reasoning to consider the kindness and benefits of our friends not worthy of gratitude, believing that they were *compelled* to act in this manner, and could not act otherwise.

3. Pantheism, by teaching All in One and One in All, is opposed to the theory of man's responsibility to a higher Being, denies the existence of God in the ordinary sense of the word, and is, in its relation to true religion, equal to atheism.

In the Bible atheism is stigmatised as the source of all evils. Thus the patriarch Abraham suspected the people of Gerar, that there was " no fear of God" in the place, and was afraid " they might slay him" (Gen. xx. 11); whilst Joseph persuaded his brothers to have confidence in him by the assertion, "I fear God" (*Ib.* xlii. 18). The first instance of an atheist we meet in Pharaoh, king of Egypt, when he defiantly said, " I know not the Lord, neither will I let Israel go" (Exod. v. 2). Another form of atheism is warned against in the words of Moses : " Lest thou sayest in thine heart, My strength and the power of my hand has got for me all this wealth" (Deut. viii. 17); and " Lest they say, Our hand is high, and it is not the Lord that hath done all this" (*Ib.* xxxii. 27). The prophets likewise rebuke the people for want of belief in God. In the Psalms, the crimes and evil designs of oppressors are traced to godlessness. " The wicked says in his heart, There is no God" (Ps. xiv. 1). But this atheism of the Bible is not a theoretical or dogmatic one ; it is not the result of thought, or of deep inquiry into the causes of things, but merely the voice of an evil inclination which tempts man to act contrary to the command of God, and assures him of immunity, under the impression that his actions are not watched by a higher authority. In post-Biblical literature we meet with the phrase, לֵית דִּין וְלֵית דַּיָּן "There is no judgment, and there is no judge," as the basis of atheism.

4. Although the conviction of man's responsibility to a higher authority is the essential element in the belief in God, yet the notion of godlessness was so intimately connected with crime and wickedness, that those who rejected the authority and mastership of the

Deity refused to be called godless or atheists. Many philosophers retained the name " God " (*theos, deus*) for their " First Cause " of the universe, although it is deprived of the chief attributes of God. Thus we have as the principal religious theories resulting from philosophical investigations, Theism and Deism. Literally these two terms denote, Theory of God, or Belief in God ; the one word being derived from the Greek *theos,* the other from the Latin *deus,* both meaning " God."

There is, however, an essential difference between the two theories. Theism and Deism have this in common, that both assume a spiritual power, a divine being, as the cause and source of everything that exists. They differ in this : to Theism this power is immanent in us and the things round us ; Deism considers this power as separate from the things. Revelation or prophecy is altogether denied by the Deists, whilst the Theists would accept it after their own fashion and rationalise it.

All these various systems of religion have this in common, that they attempt to remove from religion everything that cannot be comprehended by human reason. But all attempts to substitute human reason for Divine authority have failed. A limit has been set to human reason, and that cannot be overcome. In every system of religion—the natural and the rational included—there is a mystic element, which may be enveloped in a mist of phrases, but remains unexplained. Whether we call the Creator and Ruler of the universe God, Deus, or Theos, His relation to the universe, and to man in particular, cannot be determined by the laws which determine the natural phenomena in the universe, created by His Will.

What is our conception of the Deity? The fundamental idea, from which all our notions concerning God are derived, and which we have in common with all other believers in God, is that He is the First Cause, the Creator of the universe. This idea expressed in the term הבורא יתברך שמו forms the basis of our creed. It is the Creator that is described in it. Seven of the articles begin, " I believe with a perfect faith that the Creator, blessed be His name," &c.

We do not use the term " First Cause," because it is too narrow; it only expresses part of the truth, not the whole of it. By " First Cause " some understand the cause of the gradual development of the primitive matter into the innumerable variety of things contained in the universe; the development of the original chaos into system and order. It is true that the Creator is the cause of all this; but He is more than this: He is the cause of the primitive matter, and of the original chaos. For He has created the world out of nothing. The first verse of the Bible teaches us creation from nothing (*creatio ex nihilo*): " In the beginning God created the heaven and the earth " (Gen. i. 1); that is, the whole universe. It is true that there were men who explained the meaning of the Hebrew root ברא in a different manner, and desired to assign to it the meaning: cutting out, forming out of a given material. But they certainly misunderstood the spirit of the Scriptures. The eternal coexistence of God and matter would imply a dualism utterly incompatible with the teaching of the Bible. The frequently repeated declaration, " He is our God; there is none besides " (אֵין עוֹד), clearly excludes every form of dualism. Those who assert that the universe could not come from nothing belong to the class of people of whom the Psalmist says, "And they returned and tempted God, and set limits to the Holy One of Israel" (Ps. lxxviii. 41).

If we cannot understand the act of the Creation, it is our own intellect that is limited; and if we were to persuade ourselves that we understand better the eternity of matter, we should deceive ourselves. We cannot conceive matter without form as existing in reality, nor can we have a clear notion of anything infinite. We are human beings, endowed by the will and wisdom of the Creator with limited physical and intellectual faculties, and in things that surpass our powers we cannot do better than follow the guidance of the Divine Word. If we do so we may be sure that we shall be on the right way to truth.

The first principle declared in our creed is this: God is not only the Creator of the heavens and the earth, with all their hosts; He is also the constant ruler of all created beings; He is בּוֹרֵא וּמַנְהִיג. We therefore praise Him in our daily Morning prayer as "Doing wonders; renewing in His goodness the work of the creation every day." When we observe the ordinary phenomena in nature, occurring in accordance with certain fixed laws which have been discovered and described by man, we see in them the greatness of the Creator by whose will these laws are still in force, and by whose will any or all of these laws may one day cease to continue.

It has been asserted that any interruption or change

of these fixed laws would indicate a weakness and want of foresight on the part of the Creator, and a fault in the plan of the Creation. This notion has led people either to deny the truth of the Biblical accounts concerning the miracles wrought by the Almighty, or to admit the correctness of the facts while denying their miraculous character, or to consider the fixed laws of nature, together with their exceptions, as designed in the original plan of the Creation. How short-sighted is man! He cannot even fully comprehend his own short-sightedness! God made him ruler over the works of His hands, and he presumes to be the ruler of God Himself! When we learn from numerous observations and experiments the law that seems to regulate certain recurring phenomena, have we then fathomed the infinite wisdom of God in the Creation? Do we know the reason which led Him to produce certain things according to certain laws, and not otherwise? Have we in discovering a law of nature obtained the power of prescribing the same law to God, and disallowing Him to deviate therefrom? Far be it from us human beings, dust and ashes, to arrogate to ourselves such a right! It may even be one of the objects with which miracles were wrought to teach us that we do not yet know all things, that events may happen which we are unable to foresee, that phenomena may appear which we are unable to explain according to the laws hitherto discovered; in short, that our knowledge and wisdom are limited.

The fact that God has created the universe *ex nihilo* has been expressed by Jewish philosophers as follows:—God is the only Being who demands no cause for His existence; the very idea of God implies exist-once, and cannot be conceived without it. All other beings owe their existence to certain causes, in the absence of which they would not exist. God alone is therefore only active, without ever being passive, only cause without ever being effect, whilst every other being is both active and passive, cause and effect; it has been produced by certain causes, and is in its turn the cause of the existence of other beings. In the first article a phrase expressing this idea has been added: " And He alone is the active cause of *all* things, whether past, present, or future." By the addition of this sentence it was intended to deny the Eternity of matter (קדמות העולם). The reference to past, present, and future is to emphasise the constant action of the Creator, and the dependence of the natural forces on His Will. The first principle has, therefore, the following form :—

" *I firmly believe that the Creator, blessed be His name, is both Creator and Ruler of all created beings, and that He alone is the active cause of* ALL *things, whether past, present, or future.*" [1]

Before passing on to the second principle concerning God let us briefly answer a question that has frequently been asked · What is the relation between the theory of evolution, or in general the results of modern science, and the history of the creation as related in the Bible ? In the Biblical account of the creation the various kinds of plants and animals are described as the result of different and distinct acts of the Creator, whilst according to the theory of Evolution one creative act sufficed, and the great variety of creatures is the result

[1] For the Hebrew see Appendix I.

C

of gradual development according to certain laws inherent in the things created. The Bible tells us of six days of the creation, whilst according to the theory of evolution it must have taken millions of years before the various species could have developed the one from the other. Whilst the Biblical account describes the earth as the centre of the universe, astronomy shows that the earth is one of the most insignificant of the bodies that fill the infinite space of the universe. According to astronomy and geology, the age of the earth numbers millions of years; from the Biblical account we infer that the earth is comparatively young. In the Bible man is described as the aim and end of the whole creation; natural history and the theory of evolution consider man simply as one of the forms resulting from a natural development of the animal world. What shall be our decision in this discrepancy? Shall we shut our eyes to the results of modern science in our firm belief in the truth of the Bible? Or shall we accept the former and abandon the latter?

We should adopt neither of these alternatives. We have great confidence in our reasoning power, and in the results of science based on reason, but we have still greater confidence in the truthfulness of Divine teaching. The conflict is not a modern product; it existed in former times as well. When the Jews first became acquainted with Greek literature and philosophy, faith was shaken in the heart of many a Jew that was led away by the attractive language and the persuasive arguments of the Greek. Such was the case with the Jews in Alexandria, who were almost more Greek than Jewish. Feeling that their faith in their old traditions was beginning to give way, they looked about them for the means of reconciling faith and philosophy. Where the literal sense of Holy Writ was awkward, the allegorical interpretation was substituted for it; but the authority of the Bible was recognised. Later on, in the Middle Ages, when Aristotle, as understood and interpreted in the Arabic schools, was infallible, perplexity again became general, among the educated and learned, as to the course to be pursued in case of a conflict; whether to remain true to the Bible or to join the banner of Aristotle. The most prominent amongst the Jewish theologians who sought the way of reconciliation was Moses Maimonides. This philosopher wrote his famous work, "Guide of the Perplexed," expressly for those scholars who, whilst firmly adhering to the inherited faith, had been trained in the study of philosophy, and were unwilling to abandon either. Maimonides shows the way how to explain Biblical passages implying statements contrary to philosophical teachings, and how to reconcile theology and philosophy. A similar task was undertaken in modern times by Moses Mendelssohn in his "Jerusalem" and "Morgenstunden," in order to show that strict adherence to the Jewish religion is quite compatible with the teaching of philosophy. The various systems of philosophy in Alexandria, in the Mohammedan countries in the Middle Ages, and in Germany in the last century, which threatened to endanger our religion, have lived their time and have gone to their fathers, giving way to new systems and new ideas, whilst the authority of the Word of God has maintained its place. This having been the case in former days, there is no reason why we should not in the present conflict assume, *primâ facie*, that the scientific and philosophical dogmas now in favour, alike with Jews and non-Jews, will have their time, and will ultimately give way to other theories, and the present conflict will then likewise terminate, dying a natural death. This reflection should put us on our guard lest we be persuaded by the plausibility of the modern philosophical and scientific dogmas, and throw aside our religious faith and traditions. We ought to bear in mind that, however correct the conclusions of modern science may appear that can be tested by our senses, theories which are not subject to such tests are in reality nothing but hypotheses to which a greater or lesser degree of probability attaches.

Suppose now—always bearing in mind the imperfect character of our powers of observation—we were to observe that certain plants or species of animals developed by training and circumstances into new species, or to see plants being transformed into animals, or even to notice literally " the foal of a wild ass born a man," what would all this prove ? That the Creator endowed the species of plants and animals with such properties as would enable them to transform into new species, or into any other of the species already in existence ; but it does not follow that the Creator must have adopted the same method in the act of creation. He created as many species as His wisdom determined, although they might all have been able to develop from one single species. Suppose the problem which the Alchymists of the Middle Ages proposed to themselves, viz., to produce an animal being by mere chemical combination, had actually been solved, would any one have believed that all animals had been produced in that way ? Or does the success of artificial hatching of eggs convince any person that all birds have sprung from artificially hatched eggs ? The same argument applies to the geological formation of the earth. We notice changes brought about through natural forces, and mark the amount of change effected in a certain period ; we are then able to calculate what time would be required for such or such a change— provided that only those laws be in force, which we have noticed in our calculation. Is it reasonable or logical to apply to the act of creation the laws which have been brought into force through this very act? " He said, and it was : He commanded, and they were created " (Ps. xxxiii. 9). The word of God produced in a moment what the natural forces established by the Creator would effect by gradual development in millions of years.

It is true that the earth is one of the most insignificant bodies in the universe, and man is a small portion of the creatures on earth, and yet it is neither impossible nor unreasonable to believe that the benefits which man derives from the various parts of the creation, from the sun, the moon, and the stars, were essential elements in the scheme of the All-wise Creator.

Attempts have frequently been made to interpret the Biblical account of the creation in such a manner as to reconcile it with the scientific theories of the time. Thus it has been argued that the period between the creation of "heaven and earth" and the creation of "the light" is not described in the Bible, and may have been millions of millions of years. It has likewise been suggested that the term "day" is to be understood in the sense of "period." It has further been pointed out that the account of the creation of animals indicates a process of development rather than a *creatio ex nihilo;* for it says, "And God said, Let the waters bring forth abundantly living beings," &c. (Gen. i. 20). "Let the earth bring forth living beings," &c. (*Ibid.* 24). These interpretations may be true, and may suffice temporarily to check sceptical ideas that rise in our mind; but without the firm belief in the Word of God, and the consciousness of the insufficiency of human reason thoroughly to understand the plans and ways of God, our faith can never be safe. Supported by this belief we shall always be able to brave the ever-recurring billows of scepticism.

2. The next principle contained in our Creed concerning God is *the Unity of God.*

"I am the Lord thy God, who brought thee out from the land of Egypt, out of the house of bondage: thou shalt have no other gods before me" (Exod. xx. 2—3). This is the first lesson the Israelites were taught when God revealed Himself to them on Mount Sinai. The words, "Hear, O Israel; the Lord is our God, the Lord is One" (Deut. vi. 4), are proclaimed by us thrice every day; we recite them when we rise; keep them in memory during the day, and repeat them in the evening before we go to rest; they form our watchword throughout our life, and with these words upon our lips we end our earthly existence. The Unity of God is the doctrine that distinguishes the Jews from other religious sects, in so far as the Jews were the first nation of Monotheists. From them Monotheism has spread among other peoples, who, however, did not always receive or preserve it in its original purity. We not only proclaim God as One, refusing to recognise as divine any power beside Him, but refrain also from attributing to God anything that might directly or indirectly involve any notion contrary to the Unity of God.

For this reason certain Jewish philosophers considered it unlawful to assign to God any positive attribute. They feared this might lead to dualism, to believe in God and in His attribute as two distinct beings, because attributes are so easily personified and addressed as separate deities. Some theologians even were of opinion that the admission of God's attributes is itself a form of dualism which must be excluded from our faith. Nevertheless, attributes are assigned to God both in the Scriptures and in our Prayers. We must not, however, forget that such attributes do not describe anything inherent in the Divine Being, but only God's relation to man and His actions in such terms as are intelligible to human beings. Most of the attributes are interpreted as being of a negative character, indicating what we must not say of God. When we speak of the Will, Wisdom, and Spirit of God, we do not speak of anything separate from the Divine Being, but of the Divine Being Himself. The Jewish doctrine of the Unity of God does not admit any kind of dualism in the Divine Being, and therefore rejects

the existence of Divine Attributes as distinct from
God Himself.   He is One, simple and indivisible.
Even this property of being One seemed to some
theologians to be contrary to strict unity, and we
are therefore taught that we must not understand
it in the sense of a numerical unit, in which
sense the term is used when applied to created beings.
The second article therefore declares : "The Creator
is One, and there is no Oneness like His in any
way."

The Unity of God is the creed which the Jews have
always proclaimed by word of mouth, to which they
have given expression throughout their literature, and
for which they have willingly sacrificed their lives as
martyrs.   When persecuted by Mohammedans or Christians the Jews were frequently forced to break the Sabbath, to ignore the dietary laws, and to neglect Divine
worship.   They bore all this patiently when under
pressure of persecution, but when they were asked to
renounce the belief in God's Unity they did not doubt
for a moment as to what their duty was ; they adhered
firmly to יחוד השם "the belief in God's Unity," and
sacrificed their lives for קדוש השם "the sanctification
of God's name."

The Jews have been victorious.   In spite of persecution and oppression they have maintained their faith.
The doctrine of the Unity of God, for which they had
to suffer so much in past centuries, is now admitted as
true by most of their former persecutors.

In order to make clear what we mean by unity, and
to express that God could not be conceived as existing
at any time in a double form, we add the words : " And

He alone was, is, and will be our God." The second article runs therefore as follows :—

"*I firmly believe that the Creator, blessed be His name, is One; that there is no Oneness like His, in any way, and that He alone was, is, and will be our God.*"

3. The strict Unity of God, in the sense explained above, implies His *Incorporeality*, which forms the subject of the third article. Corporeality implies substance and form, a dualism which must be rigidly excluded from God. It would not have been necessary to formulate a special article for the exclusion of corporeality from the idea of God but for the fact that many erroneous notions have been entertained on the subject. Besides the fact that the corporeality of God was assumed by certain religious sects, there have been scholars among the Jews who defended the literal sense of anthropomorphic phrases in the Scriptures.

In the Bible anthropomorphic expressions are employed in order to illustrate the different acts of Divine Providence in such a way as to render them more intelligible to us human beings. We consist of body and soul, and we produce an impression or exercise an influence on others by means of our body and by the activity of our bodily organs. How an incorporeal being acts upon the corporeal world we are unable fully to comprehend, much less to describe. If we desire to picture to ourselves or to others the fact that through Divine Providence something has been produced on earth, we must employ the same phrases which we use in describing human acts which effect a similar result. In reality, however, there is no comparison or similarity between God and corporeal beings, between His actions and ours.

When we therefore speak of the house of God we mean the house which we devote to our prayers, in which we feel the omnipresence of the Almighty more than in any other place. The heaven is called the throne of God and the earth His footstool only to express the idea that the majesty of God is far beyond comparison with that of any earthly ruler, and that the house of God built by human hands is not intended to satisfy the requirements of the Supreme Being but those of man. We call Him our Father and He calls us His children, because we love Him as we love our father, and He loves us as a father loves his children. In the same sense the Psalmist (ii. 7) repeats the words of God to him, " Thou art my son ; I have this day begotten thee." Such expressions as these are anthropomorphic.

The Bible frequently exhorts us not to imagine or ascribe to God any form or likeness. Comp. Deut. iv. 15, " Take ye therefore good heed unto yourselves ; for ye saw no manner of form on the day that the Lord spake unto you in Horeb out of the midst of fire." In the same sense the prophet asks in the name of God (Isa. xl. 18), " To whom then will you liken God, or what likeness will you compare unto Him ? " " To whom then will you liken Me, that I should be equal to Him ? saith the Holy One" (*Ibid.* 25).

We declare therefore in the third article :—

" *I firmly believe that the Creator, blessed be His*

name, is not a body, that corporeal relations do not apply to Him, and that there exists nothing that is in any way similar to Him."

4. The next property we declare of God in the Creed is the eternity of God. As He is the cause of everything in existence, and requires no cause for His existence, and as it is impossible to separate the idea of existence from the idea of God, it follows that God is always in existence, and that neither beginning nor end can be fixed to His existence. Maimonides, in expressing his belief in the eternity of God, lays stress only on God being without a beginning, and in this sense he interprets the phrase אֱלֹהֵי קֶדֶם (Deut. xxxiii. 27), "the eternal God" who is without a beginning. That God is without end is equally true, but Maimonides did not desire to introduce this idea into the fourth article as a distinguishing characteristic, as it is not necessary to believe that the universe will once come to an end. If it please the Almighty to give the universe existence for ever, it will continue for ever. Following, however, the example of the prophets, who told us in the name of God, " I am the first, and I am the last," we express this idea in our Creed, and understand it thus: If, by the will of the Almighty, the entire universe should come to an end, God's existence would still continue. Thus the Psalmist says, " Of old hast Thou laid the foundation of the earth ; and the heavens are the work of Thy hands. They shall perish, but Thou shalt endure ; yea, all of them shall wax old like a garment : as a vesture shalt Thou change them, and they shall be changed : but Thou

art the same, and Thy years shall have no end"
(Ps. cii. 26—28).

The fourth article is :—

"*I firmly believe that the Creator, blessed be His
name, was the first, and will be the last.*"

6. After having declared our faith in God as the sole
Ruler of the universe, who is One, incorporeal and
eternal, we proclaim Him as our Supreme Master,
who alone is capable of granting our petitions. All
existing things are under His control; all forces in
nature only work at His will and by His command.
No other being possesses the power and independence
to fulfil our wishes of its own accord, if it were
approached by us with our prayers. It is, therefore,
to Him alone that we can reasonably address our
petitions, and in doing so we have confidence in the
efficacy of our prayers, for " the Lord is nigh to all
those who call upon Him, to all who call upon Him in
truth " (Ps. cxlv. 18).

This article, although expressly directed against
idolatry, and primarily against the worship of "the
angels, the stars, and the spheres," implies our belief
in God as the Omnipotent, who can do everything,
and can help us when we have not any prospect of
relief.

We therefore declare in the fifth article :—

"*I firmly believe that the Creator, blessed be His
name, alone is worthy of being worshipped, and that
no other being is worthy of our worship.*"

The Omnipotence of God is also implied in the first
article, which declares Him the Creator and the Ruler
of the universe. That Maimonides does not directly

make omnipotence, like unity, incorporeality, &c., the subject of a separate article has its good reason, and is not "the result of mere chance." Silly questions were frequently asked ; *e.g.*, how far the omnipotence of God extended, whether it implied the power of making twice two equal to three, or the whole of a magnitude larger than the sum of its parts, and similar logical impossibilities. To avoid misunderstanding, Maimonides did not express our belief in the omnipotence of God in a separate article, but the first and the fifth articles imply it.

We believe of God that He is *immutable* or *unchangeable.* It is, however, not necessary to express this in a separate article. By declaring the Unity of God we proclaim also His Immutability, since unity, in the sense in which we conceive it, is incompatible with any kind of change. Whatever the change might be that we assumed in God, it would destroy the idea of His unity.

There are other qualities which we ascribe to God. We call Him perfect, all-wise, good, kind, merciful, long-suffering, and the like ; in short, whatever we find in our own person good and noble we believe to be present in God in a higher degree, in the most perfect form. But these attributes approach very closely anthropomorphisms, which Maimonides rigidly excludes from the Creed. They express rather the impressions produced in our soul by the different acts of God's Providence, and do not describe God Himself.

Of this class of attributes are the thirteen divine attributes, שלש עשרה מדות (Exod. xxxiv. 6). They describe in thirteen terms the goodness and mercy of God towards man in his various conditions of innocence, guilt, and repentance. These are not distinctly mentioned in our Creed, but when we declare that He is the only Being whom we can address in our prayers, we are certainly conscious and convinced that He, being good, kind, and merciful, listens to our supplications.

2 *Revelation,* תורה מן השמים.

The second group of principles refers to Revelation. The real process of revelation, by what means and in what manner the infinite and incorporeal Being makes His Will known to man, and how the latter becomes conscious and convinced of the fact that a Divine communication has been made to him. remains a mystery to all but those privileged persons who have been actually addressed by the Almighty. " As the blind man who had never possessed the sense of sight is incapable of comprehending the actual process of seeing, so are we, born without that wonderful prophetic eye, without the prophetic faculty of the mind, incapable of comprehending and depicting the process of inspiration that goes on within the mind of the privileged " (Schmiedl, *Studien,* p. 183). God reveals Himself also in nature, in the power and wisdom displayed in its phenomena. He reveals Himself in the history of nations, and especially in the history of Israel. He reveals Himself in the intelligence of man. In all these cases the revelation is made to all alike. Those who have eyes may see, those who have ears may hear, and

recognise, every one according to his capacity, the
presence of the Almighty in the working of the laws of
nature, in the development and fates of nations, and
in the life of every individual person. In all these
cases we can test and prove the revelation by ourselves,
and need not exclusively rely on authority. When,
however, a Divine communication is made to one privileged individual, through whom it is made known to
a whole community, or to mankind, there is no other
means of testing the correctness of the revelation than
the trustworthiness of the privileged individual.

The first lesson or proof given to the Israelites of
the fact that such revelation was not only possible,
but had actually been vouchsafed by the Almighty,
was the revelation on Mount Sinai, the מעמד הר סיני,
which became the foundation of the faith of Israel.
"And the Lord said unto Moses, Lo, I come unto
thee in a thick cloud, that the people may hear
when I speak with thee, and may also believe thee
for ever " (Exod. xix. 9). The trustworthiness of
Moses having thus been tested and established "for
ever," his teaching remained the foundation of the
teaching of all succeeding prophets, and the test of
their truthfulness and genuineness. A prophet who
taught anything opposed to the law of Moses could not
be a true prophet, although he supported his words
by signs and miracles (Deut. xiii. 2, *sqq.*). Besides,
revelation of the Divine Being had taken place before.
God revealed Himself to the first man. Adam heard
the voice of God; he felt the presence of the Almighty, and learnt the amount of evil man brings
upon himself by disobeying the word of God. The

consciousness of the existence of God, and of the fact that He has revealed Himself to man, has been inherited by the descendants of Adam. It has not been preserved in all men in the same strength and purity. The notion of a Divine Being, and of His revelation to man, became in course of time corrupt, and led to the corruption of the human race, with the exception of Noah and his family. "Noah was a righteous man ; perfect he was in his generations : with God did Noah walk" (Gen. vi. 9). The inherited consciousness of God's existence and of His rule over man was strengthened in him by fresh, direct revelation of God. He was told that the wicked would be destroyed by a flood, and that he with his family would be saved. "The righteous man" witnessed the infliction which the wicked brought upon themselves by evil deeds, and also that protection of himself and his family which had been promised and granted by the Almighty. After Noah had left the ark the word of God was again communicated to him, promising that never again would a flood be sent to destroy all living beings—a promise which succeeding generations up to the present have seen fulfilled. In the midst of rain the "sign of covenant," the rainbow, reminds us still of His promise and its fulfilment. Of the descendants of Noah the Semites alone seem to have preserved the belief in God's existence and His revelation to man in its original purity ; and of the Semites it was Abraham who was chosen by Providence to be the founder of a family of faithful believers in God, who formed, as it were, the centre from which the true faith should spread in all directions over the whole face of the earth. Abraham

received Divine communications, and so also his son
Isaac and his grandson Jacob. Even when the children
of Israel were in Egyptian slavery, and when they did
not hearken to Moses " because of anguish of spirit,
and because of cruel bondage," the memory of these
revelations was never entirely extinguished in their
minds ; and when again addressed by Moses and Aaron
" the people believed ; and when they heard that the
Lord had visited the children of Israel, and that He
had seen their affliction, then they bowed their heads
and worshipped " (Exod. iv. 31). Their faith was
strengthened when they witnessed the fulfilment of
the Divine message which was brought to them by
Moses : " And they believed in the Lord, and in Moses
His servant " (*Ibid.* xiv. 31).

The foundation of the belief in the possibility of
Divine revelation having thus been laid, that belief was
further strengthened through the revelation on Mount
Sinai, when every Israelite heard and understood the
words addressed to him by God, " who had brought
them out of Egypt, of the house of bondage ; " they
heard the very words which Moses subsequently told
them in the name of God, and they were convinced
of the truth of the words of Moses. He taught
them that there would be other persons chosen by
God to bring messages from Him to the children of
Israel or to mankind, and at the same time he laid
down the rule by which the truth of such messages
could be tested.

A person favoured by Divine communications was
called a prophet, נביא. That which characterised a
prophet and distinguished him from the ordinary man

D

was the privilege of being chosen by Providence to be מלאך יי "the messenger of God" to man. This notion of the characteristics of a prophet explains the circumstance that, although Daniel was favoured with numerous prophetic visions, the book called after his name was not placed among the Prophets, but among the Hagiographa. It is on account of his addressing his brethren and informing them of the Will of God that a person was called a prophet.[1] By simply receiving a communication, without the direction to impart the knowledge acquired to others, a person may become a man of God, a man in whom there is the spirit of God, but not a prophet.

It is our belief that God would not reveal Himself to any one that is unworthy of such distinction. As a *conditio sine quâ non* it was necessary that the prophets distinguished themselves in every kind of virtue, that they set to their fellow-men an example of purity in thought, loftiness in speech, and nobility in action. As regards general knowledge and experience they were inferior to none of their contemporaries. In the Talmud the saying occurs : אין השכינה שורה על אדם אלא אם כן היה חכם גבור ועשיר "The Divine spirit does not rest on man, unless he is wise, strong, and rich" (Babyl. Talm. Shabbath, 92a). This is certainly a true conception of the character of a prophet, "strong" and "rich" being understood in a figurative sense : "strong" in possessing mastery over his passions, and "rich" in being contented with what he has (Aboth iv. 1). It was a matter of indifference, however, whether the

---

[1] The Hebrew נביא as well as the Greek προφητης "prophet," signifies "speaker" or "preacher."

prophet was strong in body or weak, whether he had many earthly possessions or none at all.

In spite of his distinction from his fellow-men in wisdom, moral strength, and contentedness, the prophet remained a human being; he was, like every other person, exposed to the temptation to sin and liable to error. The sins and errors of prophets are recorded in order to save us from despair when we are conscious of our sinfulness, and to show us the way to repentance. This is illustrated especially in the history of the prophet Jonah. The records of the sins of prophets serve as a warning that we should not consider any man as perfect or deify him.

Although the prophet is assumed to have been wise, surpassing his fellow-men in knowledge and wisdom, it is by no means necessary to believe that he was familiar with all sciences, or that he knew any of the discoveries made in later times. The prophet had frequently to inform his brethren of what would happen in future, to tell them of things which no human eye could foresee. But he had in general no greater knowledge of coming events than other men, except in reference to those events concerning which he had received a message from God for His people or for mankind.

Can a man be trained for the office of a prophet? Was there a school or institution for this purpose? Every one could certainly be trained in the primary conditions of a prophet, in the exercise of all human virtues, and in the acquisition of all available knowledge; and it was the duty and the aim of the prophets to encourage all their brethren to such training by their own example. But the principal element in prophecy

the Divine communication, depended solely on the Will
of God. "The sons of the prophets" are generally
believed to be the pupils of the prophets; they formed
"the schools of the prophets." These schools, however, could not have been schools or colleges in the
ordinary sense of the word. The sons of the prophets
were instructed by the prophets, but not with the
purpose of training them as prophets. It seems
that the sons of the prophets served as agents for
promulgating the inspired messages of their chief.
Most probably they led a simple, pious life, were God-
fearing, and spent their time when meeting together
in music and song, repeating hymns and lessons taught
by their master.

An account of some of the messages and deeds of
the prophets is given in the Biblical books; some
of their speeches also are preserved, in the section
of the Bible called "Latter Prophets," נביאים אחרונים.
The speeches of the prophets were in some cases prepared and written down before they were spoken, in
others delivered *ex tempore* without preparation, and
were written down afterwards from memory, either by
the prophet himself or by one of his hearers, or were
handed down *vivâ voce* from generation to generation
before they were committed to writing.

There is another kind of Divine revelation which
did not find expression in any message to the Israelites or to mankind, but in a certain supernatural
impulse given to the thought or will of a person as
regards his words and actions. Such an impulse is
called inspiration, and the inspired person is moved to
speak or act by the רוח יי "spirit of the Lord."

It was the spirit of the Lord that moved Samson to heroic deeds against the enemies of his people; David likewise felt that Divine impulse when pouring forth his heart before the Lord in his Psalms. He says: "The spirit of the Lord spake in me, and His word was on my tongue" (2 Sam. xxiii. 2). It was the spirit of the Lord that filled the hearts of those who collected and sifted the Holy Writings containing law, history, prophecies, and poetry, and gave them the form in which we possess them now.

We are not quite certain as to the form of the letters in the original copies of the Holy Writings; but from the way in which the Pentateuch is written now in the Synagogue scrolls, we may infer with certainty that the ancient copies of the Torah contained no vowels or accents, and that these have come down to us by oral tradition.

For the multiplication of copies, human copyists had to be employed. It is by no means contrary to our faith in the Bible to assume that, as far as the human work of these copyists is concerned, it must have been subject to the fate of all human work, to error and imperfection. And, in fact, there are many copies of the Bible that abound in mistakes; there are passages in Scripture that vary in the different manuscripts; hence the numerous *variæ lectiones* met with in the critical editions of the Bible. But, on the other hand, it would not be reasonable to assume that the holy literature and the national treasure, very limited in size, should have been neglected by the religious authorities of the time to such an extent that no reliable, correct copy was kept, to be consulted in case of doubt or difference of opinion. This being the case with all Biblical books, it applies with special force to the Torah or Pentateuch, which contains the Divine commandments. The least alteration made by copyists —unknowingly or knowingly—might involve a question of life and death. Must it not have been the duty of the judicial authority to keep a correct authorised copy in a safe place? It is certainly most reasonable to assume that such a copy was kept, and that there were in every generation among the priests or prophets men who had a thorough knowledge of the Law, and could easily detect any interference with the text. As the laws do not form a separate section of the Bible, but are interwoven with a historical account of important events from the Creation to the death of Moses, the entire Pentateuch, composed of both laws and history, was preserved with the same anxiety and watchfulness. That great care was taken in copying the Law we learn from the fact mentioned in the Talmud, that Ezra minutely examined the three scrolls he found in the Temple, and in three passages noticed different readings, of which he adopted the one found in two copies.

The other books of the Bible are of less importance, but the exclusion of error on the part of the copyist, though it has not the same, has yet a high degree of certainty, inasmuch as they too formed part of the holy, national literature. If a mistake should be clearly proved, it would not be contrary to our religious principles to admit it. But we shall find, after thorough study and examination of the impugned passages, that there is in each case far greater doubt as to the correctness of any of the numerous emendations suggested than of the traditional and Massoretic text before us. It may frequently occur that some emendations appear strikingly correct, and yet after due reflection they are found more doubtful than the original. It is therefore our duty thoroughly to examine each proposed emendation, and to hesitate long before admitting the incorrectness of the received text and the correctness of the emendation.

One of the means of preserving the text of the Scriptures in its integrity has been the Massorah. The notes which are found in the margin of Biblical books form part of the Massorah. At first the Massorah was part of the oral tradition; exceptional forms of letters, punctuation, and words were probably taught *vivâ voce*, and learnt by heart, especially by scribes, readers, and teachers. Where a confounding with other and similar forms was apprehended, attention was called to the fact, and by certain notes and rules it was guarded against. The material for the Massorah increased in the course of time, in the same degree as, with the multiplication of copies of the Scriptures, the number of misreadings and misinterpretations increased. Although these notes were arranged and written down at a late period, they helped to preserve the Biblical text in its integrity, and it is therefore stated in the Mishnah (Aboth iii. 13): "Massorah (tradition) is a fence to the Law."

As to the name of the author of each book or section, and the time and place of its composition, we are guided by the headings where such are extant; in the absence of these we are left to the resources of our own judgment or fancy. There is no reason whatever to doubt the correctness of these headings, as the religious and learned authorities of the time were trustworthy men, who would not add a heading where none was handed down to them by tradition. Several books and many psalms are therefore left without a heading; there was no sure tradition about them. How far the heading of a book or section extends, whether it was meant only for the beginning or for the whole of it, is in some cases doubtful, and must be decided by the nature and contents of the book. For instance, the second part of Isaiah, from chap. xl. to the end, has no heading of its own; it is therefore open to discussion whether the heading in the first verse of the first chapter describes only the first thirty-nine or all the sixty-six chapters of the book. It is possible that Psalms, ascribed, according to their heading, to David, consist of two or more parts, of which one only was composed by David. The names of the books do not necessarily imply a reference to the author. The Book of Joshua, *e.g.*, may have received its name from its contents, the history of the Israelites under Joshua being contained in it. The two books of Samuel could not have been written by Samuel, not even the whole of the first book, since the death of Samuel is therein recorded; but they owe their name to the fact that the first book commences with the history of Samuel.

The Books of the Bible, תנ״ך

The collection of books known by these names are ספרי קדש or כתבי קדש "holy books" or "holy writings,' because the authors of these books were holy men their object is a holy one, viz., to train man to holiness, and the contents of the books is holy, free from all blemish and error. The books vary greatly in character, in style, and in purpose, but truthfulness is common to all of them. Whether they narrate events or proclaim God's decrees, or instruct or edify their hearers, what they say is true.

The name *Bible* is derived from the Greek βιβλιον, "book." תנ״ך (pronounced *tenach*) has no meaning in itself, and is a word formed of the initials of תורה נביאים כתובים. Sometimes אנ״ך (the initials of the Chaldee אוריתא נביאין כתיבין) is used instead of תנ״ך. Another name is מקרא "text for reading," as opposed to *vivâ voce* tradition. A passage quoted from the Bible is called קרא or מקרא or כתוב. Christians call the books of the Hebrew Bible the Old Testament as distinguished from the New Testament.

1. תורה *Law.*

The *Torah* or Law is divided into five books, and is therefore called חומש or Pentateuch (Fivefold or Five-book). The names of the five books are: (1) בראשית Genesis (Creation); (2) שמות Exodus (departure, *scil.*, of the Israelites from Egypt); (3) ויקרא Leviticus (on the laws concerning the Levites or priests), also called תורת כהנים "law of the priests;" (4) במדבר Numbers; (5) דברים Deuteronomy, a Greek term denoting "second-law" or "repetition of the law," a translation of the Hebrew משנה תורה.

These names are derived from the beginnings of the books. The Hebrew names are either the first word

of the book, as is the case in the first and the third
books (בראשית and ויקרא), or the first characteristic
word, as is the case in the other three books (שמות the
second word, במדבר the fifth, דברים the second). The
English or Greek names describe the subject-matter of
the first section of the book. This applies also to the
rest of the Biblical writings.

The contents of the five books are as follows :—

The first book (בראשית).—It begins with the important
lesson, the basis of all that is taught in the whole
Bible : that God is the Creator of the whole universe.
Then follows an account of the Creation, the history
of the first man and the first woman, their transition
from the state of innocence and happiness to the
state of sin and toil, their descendants, the beginnings
of industry and civilisation, the deterioration of mankind, the flood, Noah, and the succeeding generations
to Abraham ; the history of the patriarchs Abraham,
Isaac, and Jacob, or Israel ; the immigration of
Jacob with his family into Egypt ; and with the
death of Joseph, the son of Jacob, the book concludes.

The book contains principally history, but mention
is made also of some religious institutions. Reference
is thus made to the institution of marriage (ii. 23–25);
Sabbath (ii. 1–3); the Covenant of Abraham or the
commandment of circumcision (xvii. 1–14); the prohibition of eating flesh cut off from an animal while
alive (ix. 4, אבר מן החי), of murder (ix. 5–6), and of
eating "the sinew that shrank" (xxxii. 33, גיד הנשה).

The second book (שמות).—The history of the family
of Jacob, the Israelites, is continued : their sojourn in

Egypt, the Exodus, the journey to Mount Sinai, the Revelation, the erection of the Tabernacle, and the events in the camp of the Israelites during their stay in the wilderness of Sinai.

The Divine precepts take a more prominent place in this book. Chief among these are the institution of the Jewish Calendar, appointing the month of Abib— Nisan—to be the first month (xii. 2); the Sacrifice of the Passover and the Feast of Unleavened Bread (chap. xii.); the Sabbath (xvi. 22—30); the Decalogue (chap. xx. 1—12); civil legislation (xxi. to xxiii.); the year of release (xxiii. 10, 11); and the שלש רגלים‎ or festivals of pilgrimage to the sanctuary of the Lord; viz., Passover, Pentecost, and Tabernacles (פסח‎, שבועות‎ and סכות‎ xxiii. 14—17).

The third book (ויקרא‎) contains the laws revealed during the stay of the Israelites near Mount Sinai. A few historical incidents are mentioned in illustration of the Law. Leviticus contains the laws concerning the sacrifices (i. to vii.); the initiation of Aaron and his sons as priests (viii. to x.); dietary laws (xi.); laws about cleanness and uncleanness (טהרה וטומאה‎) in man and woman (xii. to xv.); the Day of Atonement (xvi.); prohibition of blood (xvii. 10—14); marriage laws (xviii. and xx. 10—22); laws concerning the holiness of man (xix.); laws concerning the priests (xxi., xxii. 16) and sacrifices (xxii. 17—33); the Festivals of the Lord (xxiii.); the year of release and the year of jubilee, and land-laws connected with these (xxv.); laws concerning the transfer of property to the sanctuary and the priests.

The fourth book records the departure of the Israelites

from Mount Sinai, their journeyings until they came
to the east of the Jordan in the plains of Moab; the
chief incidents during these travels, viz., the consecration of the altar, and the instalment of the Levites
as assistants to the priests in the performance of the
Divine Service; the first appointment of a council of
seventy elders; the punishment of Miriam for slander;
the spies; the rebellion of Korah; death of Miriam;
Moses and Aaron's sin at Meribah, and their punishment; death of Aaron; wars with Sihon and Og; the
blessings of Bileam instead of his intended cursings; the
zeal and distinction of Phineas; war against Midian;
the appointment of Joshua as future leader of Israel.

There is also in the book a list of all the stations
where the Israelites had encamped during their travels
through the Arabian desert (chap. xxxiii.), and a
minute description of the boundaries of the land of
Canaan (chap. xxxiv.).

The following are the principal laws mentioned in
Numbers: the laws concerning Nazirites; concerning
a woman suspected of faithlessness against her husband; the second Passover (פסח שני) for those who could
not fulfil their duty on the 14th of Nisan; the law
of fringes (ציצת); the law of purification of persons
who have become unclean through contact with the
dead body of any person (פרה אדומה chap. xix.); the
law of inheritance (xxvii.); the sacrifices for the festivals (xxviii., xxix.); the laws of vows (xxx.); laws
concerning murder and cities of refuge (xxxv.).

The fifth book (דברים) contains speeches of Moses
which he addressed to the Israelites during the last
year of his life, reminding them of their repeated dis-

obedience to the Divine command, and their want of confidence in Him, and exhorting them to be faithful to God. He frequently emphasises the truth that blessing and happiness can only be obtained through obedience, trouble and curses being the certain result of sin and transgression. Chapter xxviii., called תוכחה "exhortation" or "rebuke" (see also Lev. xxvi.), is especially devoted to this principle. In the song האזינו (chap. xxxii.), which all the people were to learn by heart, Moses rebukes his brethren for their ingratitude to God, and foretells them that, in the remote future, similar conduct will be visited severely, and that after a period of punishment God will show mercy to them, and again restore them to a state of happiness and glory. Before his death he gives a special blessing to each tribe. The book concludes with the death of Moses, the succession of Joshua, and the praise of Moses as the greatest of all prophets.

Many of the commandments are repeated in the course of the exhortations: the Decalogue, the laws concerning the three agricultural and national festivals (שלש רגלים), and such other laws as Moses considered necessary to impress on the heart of the Israelites before he departed from among them. The Israelites being near Jordan, and about to take possession of the promised land, their attention is called to such laws as would then come into practice, *e.g.*, those which refer to the political and judicial arrangements of the country (xvi. to xviii.); and the solemn declaration of allegiance to the Will of God (xxvii.).

The Pentateuch is divided into verses (פסוקים), paragraphs (פסקות), and into sections called סדרות or

" weekly portions." The division into chapters is **of** comparatively modern origin.

2. *The Prophets*

are divided into two groups : Earlier and Latter Prophets (נביאים ראשונים ונביאים אחרונים).

The *Earlier Prophets* do not contain prophecies in the usual meaning of the word. They contain the history of Israel from the accession of Joshua to the leadership of Israel, to the capture of Jerusalem by Nebuchadnezzar, king of Babylon. They are, nevertheless, called " Prophets," for two reasons :—

(1.) The history is written in a prophetic spirit, with the view of illustrating the principle that obedience to the word of God was the cause of Israel's prosperity and success, disobedience the cause of trouble and misery.

(2.) The Earlier Prophets include the history of Deborah, Samuel, Nathan, Ahijah, Elijah, Elisha, and a few anonymous prophets.

No collection of their speeches has been made or preserved in the Scriptures, and they are thus distinguished from the latter prophets, whose prophecies have been collected and form the contents of the " Latter Prophets."

The following books belong to the Earlier Prophets :—

1. *The Book of Joshua* (יהושע), containing the history of the conquest and division of the land of Canaan by the Israelites, from their crossing the Jordan to the death of Joshua.

Among the various ncidents related in the book

the following are noteworthy :—The circumcision of those who had been born during the wandering of Israel in the wilderness; the celebration of the first Passover in the Holy Land; the appearance of "the prince of the host of the Lord" (v. 14), just before the war commenced, in order to remind Joshua that "the place upon which he stood was holy;"[1] the crossing of the Jordan; the taking of Jericho; the disastrous consequences of Achan's sin, as an illustration of the principle that the whole community is made responsible for the crime of the individual till the crime is discovered and punished; the battle at Gibeon, famous through Joshua's exclamation, "Sun, stand thou still upon Gibeon; and thou moon, in the valley of Ajalon !" (x. 12); and the appointment of the cities of refuge.

2. *The Book of Judges* (שׁוֹפְטִים) contains episodes of the history of the Israelites from the death of Joshua to the days of the high-priest Eli. The name "Judge" is identical with that of chief magistrate, or simply chief or leader. The judges were persons chosen by God, and inspired with an extraordinary spirit of courage and bravery, to be the liberators of the country, or part of the country, from the tyranny of oppressors. The virtues that were required in order to qualify them for this mission were patriotism and courage. Some of them may have continued in power after the restoration of peace and order, but on the whole their mission as judges was fulfilled with the cessation of

---

[1] *i.e.*, that the war with the Canaanite tribes was to be carried on as a holy war, in fulfilment of God's command, and not for the purpose of spoil and plunder.

war. They were not the religious teachers of the nation, nor are they set up as examples of piety.

During the period of the judges the tribes of Israel were not united (song of Deborah, Judges v. 15–17). There was no common government, or if there was one, it must have possessed little power and influence. The people became degraded; many worshipped idols and altogether ignored the Divine commandments. But the conscience of the nation was roused when a shocking crime was committed at Gibeah in the tribe of Benjamin, and all Israel united in demanding the punishment of the evil-doers (chaps. xix. to xxi.). The book contains two beautiful poetical passages, the song of Deborah (v.) and the parable of Jotham (ix.).

3. *The two books of Samuel* (שמואל א' וב')—also called the first and second books of Kings—contain the history of Israel during the time of the high-priest Eli, the prophet Samuel, and Saul, the first king of Israel (Book I.); and the reign of David (Book II.).

The following passages are noteworthy:—

ii. 6–7: "The Lord killeth and maketh alive; He bringeth down to the grave and bringeth up. The Lord maketh poor and maketh rich; He bringeth low and lifteth up."

xii. 22: "The Lord will not forsake His people, for His great name's sake; because it hath pleased the Lord to make you His people."

xv. 22–23: "Hath the Lord as great delight in burnt offerings and sacrifices as in obeying the voice of the Lord? Behold, to obey is better than sacrifice, and to hearken than the fat of rams. For rebellion is as the sin of witchcraft, and stubbornness is as iniquity and idolatry; because thou hast rejected the word of the Lord, He hath also rejected thee from being king."

xvi. 7 : "The Lord seeth not as man seeth; for man looketh on the outward appearance, but the Lord looketh on the heart."

xxiv. 14: "Wickedness proceedeth from the wicked."

II., xxiv. 14: "I am in a great strait; let us fall now into the hand of the Lord; for His mercies are great: and let me not fall into the hand of man."

The following poetical passages of the book should also be marked:—

The prayer of Hannah (ii. 1—10); David's lament over Saul's death (II., i. 18—27); Parable of the prophet Nathan (xii. 1—6); Song of thanksgiving by David (xxii.); David's faith in God's justice (xxiii. 1—7).

4. *The first and the second books of Kings* (מלכים א' וב'), also called the third and fourth books of Kings, contain the history of Israel from the death of David to the Babylonian exile. The first book describes the last days of King David, the reign of Solomon, the division of the country into two kingdoms, Judah and Israel, the history of the kingdom of Judah from Rehoboam to Jehoshaphat, and the history of the kingdom of Israel from Jeroboam to Ahab. The second book continues the history of the kingdom of Israel from Ahab to the conquest of Samaria by Shalmanessar, king of Assyria, and that of the kingdom of Judah from Abijam, son of Jehoshaphat, to the conquest of Jerusalem by Nebuchadnezzar, king of Babylon.

I., ii. 2 : "I go the way of all the earth; be thou strong therefore, and show thyself a man."

E

xviii. 2 1 : " How long halt ye between two opinions ? If the Lord be God, follow Him ; but if Baal, then follow him."

II., xiv. 9 : " The thistle that was in Lebanon sent to the cedar that was in Lebanon, saying, Give thy daughter to my son to wife : and there passed by a wild beast that was in Lebanon and trod down the thistle." [1]

Note, besides, prayer of Solomon (I., viii. 1 2–6 1) and message of Isaiah to King Hezekiah (II., xix. 2 1–3 1).

The נביאים אחרונים Latter Prophets, contain the following books :—

1. *Isaiah* (ישעיהו).—Isaiah prophesied chiefly during the Assyrian invasions in Palestine in the reign of Uzziah, Jotham, Ahaz, and Hezekiah, kings of Judah. The book is divided into two main sections, separated from each other by the narrative of Sennacherib's invasion and defeat, Hezekiah's illness and recovery, and the congratulatory message of the Babylonian king to Hezekiah (chaps. xxxvi. to xxxix.).   The first section is divided into five parts with separate headings :—

(1.) Chap. i.—This prophecy was probably repeated by Isaiah many times from the beginning to the end of his prophetic mission.   The Israelites in Jerusalem and Judah are rebuked for their rebellion against God, which has brought a series of misfortunes upon the nation ; God does not accept their sacrifices unless they return to Him and improve their conduct.   They will be punished, but the punishment is only the means

---

[1] King Amaziah of Judah challenged Joash, king of Israel, to fight with him.   Joash considered this challenge as an arrogance to be compared to the arrogance of the thistle in the above fable.

for their purification. When this effect is obtained their redemption will follow.

(2.) Chaps. ii. to v.—The fulfilment of the mission of the Israelites—the Messianic period—is depicted, when the Israelites will be so perfect in the knowledge and the worship of God, that all nations will seek enlightenment and guidance in the house of the God of Jacob. The prophet shows his brethren how they receded from that aim, and, estranging themselves from the Almighty, trusted in things that are powerless. But all these things, grand and high as they may appear, will prove worthless, and the glory of God will in the end be recognised. The prophet illustrates the conduct of the Israelites and their punishment in the beautiful parable of the vineyard (v. 1—7). As special sins are named: greediness, lust, mockery, and injustice. The punishment threatened is the invasion of a cruel conqueror.

(3.) Chap. vi.—On the occasion of the death of King Uzziah, who had presumed to approach God and to offer incense in the Holy of Holies, contrary to the Law, and was punished with leprosy, Isaiah had a vision in which he despairingly contrasted the infinite holiness of the Almighty with his own sinfulness, living as he did among people of unclean lips. He is reassured, and shown that his sin is removed when his words are inflamed by the holy fire taken from the altar of God. He must, nevertheless, not expect a speedy effect from his words to the people ; they will continue in disobedience and bring upon themselves continued punishments, but ultimately, when the leaves have fallen off, the stem will remain—*a seed of holiness.*

(4.) vii. to xii.—The invasion of Judah by Pekah, king of Israel, and Rezin, king of Aram, brings to light the want of faith in God and His word on the part of Ahaz, king of Judah. Isaiah, taking with him his son *Sh'ar-yashub* (" A-remnant-will-return "), a reminder of punishment and of redemption, rebukes Ahaz, and gives him a sign (אות) : " The young woman is with child, and will bear a son, and call his name *Immanuel*" (עמנו אל " God-is-with-us "). Cream and honey shall he eat, when he will know to reject the evil and to choose the good." By this sign Ahaz is informed (1) that at the time of the birth of the child Judah will be freed from the armies of the two kings, and the name Immanuel was to be the expression of thanks for the delivery ; (2) another more serious invasion of the Assyrians will come and devastate the country ; and after their departure the Israelites will not have any corn or bread ; " cream and honey will every one eat that is left in the midst of the land."

The invasion of Syria and Palestine by the Assyrians is also foretold in the very name of Isaiah's own son, Maher-shalal-'hash-baz (" The spoiler hastens to be quick with the spoil "). In spite of such dark prospect the prophet sets forth the testimony and the lesson (תורה, תעודה) : " Hope in the Lord, though He hides His face from the house of Jacob. For often have people in affliction seen great light." " A child[1] has been born unto us, called The Almighty, the

---

[1] The faith of Israel in the Omnipotence of God, who can do wonders for the salvation of His people, is figuratively represented as a child, called " The Almighty, &c., deviseth wonders," &c.

Eternal, the Prince of Peace, devises wonders, for the purpose of increasing the dominion and establishing endless peace upon the throne of David and his kingdom, to order it and support it by judgment and righteousness from now even for ever " (ix. 5, 6). The Assyrian invasion is a punishment for the sins of the Israelites, and its success will continue so long as the Israelites refuse to repent and to return to God. This, however, will ultimately come to pass, and Ashur will then receive the penalty for his insolence and presumptuousness. Israel will in the end be guided by a wise and just ruler, who will spring forth from the roots of Jesse. The Messianic times will then begin, and amidst universal peace all mankind will join in the praises of God.

(5.) xiii. to xxxv.—This group of prophecies was probably delivered during the Assyrian invasion. Isaiah takes a survey of the neighbouring states, their conduct in times of success, and their well-deserved punishment in immediate or the remote future. The prophecies are directed against Babylon, Plesheth, Moab, Damascus, Egypt, Ashdod, Babylon, Dumah, Arab, the Assyrian Shebnah, Tyre, Edom, and Ephraim. Great confusion will ensue, amid which Judah will suffer much, but he will ultimately be delivered through the Divine intervention, and will thus be strengthened in his faith in God. Isaiah rebukes Judah for seeking help from Egypt against Assyria, because such an act indicates want of faith in God. It is only the Almighty that can help in times of distress.

(6.) xxxvi. to xxxix.—The historical chapters which intervene between the two large prophetical sections of the book conclude with an account of Hezekiah's conduct towards the Babylonian ambassadors, and the rebuke he received of Isaiah, who announced to the king that the Babylonians would one day be conquerors of Jerusalem.

(7.) xl. to xlviii.—The prediction of the Babylonian exile is followed by comforting messages and by the good tidings of the promised Restoration. Contrasting the omnipotence of God with the helplessness of earthly powers and idols, the prophet calls for absolute faith in God, who has already appointed the conqueror of Babylon and the liberator of the exiled Jews.

(8.) xlviii. to liv.—It is not only deliverance from exile that the Jews have to hope for, but far greater things. The people of the Lord are to become glorious, and to be the source of salvation to all mankind. They will suffer at the hand of the nations, but the latter will ultimately see what wrong they have done to Israel. Notwithstanding all apparent obstacles, this prophecy will be fulfilled.

(9.) lv. to lx.—The prophet exhorts the people to follow the word of God, to abandon idolatry, and to be sincere in their prayer and repentance; only then might they hope for salvation. God has punished Israel, but the redeemer will come unto Zion.

(10.) lxi. to lxvi.—Encouragement is given especially to the ענוים " the meek," " the broken-hearted ; " the day of vengeance is announced against the haughty and sinners. The prophet prays to God, and God answers him with the promise of the ultimate triumph of the ענוים and יראי יי " the meek and the God-fearing."

2. *Jeremiah* (ירמיה).—Jeremiah prophesied in the thir-

teenth year of Josiah, and continued to prophesy during his reign and that of his successors, and after the fall of Jerusalem, but it is not certain how long he lived after the destruction of the Temple, and where he died. He was the son of Hilkiah, of the priests in Anathoth, in the tribe of Benjamin. He was exposed to cruel persecutions, but these did not deter him from delivering the Divine message with which he was entrusted to the king and to the people. The prophecies of Jeremiah were written down by Baruch, at Jeremiah's dictation (chap. xxxvi.), but the book was seized by King Jehoiakim, and burnt by him. The Book of Jeremiah, in our Bible, is probably the copy made later on by Baruch, and mentioned Jer. xxxvi. 32.

The book is composed of the following parts :—

(1.) Chap. i.—The appointment of Jeremiah as prophet "over the nations and the kingdoms, to pluck up and to break down, and to destroy and to overthrow, to build and to plant" (ver. 10).

(2.) Chaps. ii. to vi.—Jeremiah addresses the inhabitants of Jerusalem. "Israel is a holy portion, belonging to the Lord; whosoever eats of it is guilty, and will be punished." Israel ought therefore to be faithful to God. This they are not, in spite of the benefits bestowed on them; they are exhorted to repentance: in vain. They are therefore threatened with a hostile invasion from the north.

(3.) Chaps. vii. to x.—The prophet addresses the people in the gate of the Temple, exhorting them to true repentance. Without obedience to God the Temple and sacrificial service have no value. The foundation of the Law is, " *You shall be to me a people, and walk in the way which I command you.*" You have not obeyed, and punishment is determined upon. Jeremiah, foreseeing the desolation of the country and the ruin of the nation, laments and weeps, but he is sure that God is עשה חסד משפט וצדקה " one who doth loving-kindness, judgment, and righteousness," and that those nations which indulged in cruelties against the Israelites when under Divine punishment will themselves not escape retribution.

(4.) xi. to xiii.—"The covenant was : Hear my voice, and do what I command you : ye shall be my people, and I will be your God." You have broken this covenant and worshipped idols ; evil must come upon you. This Jeremiah proclaimed in "the cities of Judah and the streets of Jerusalem," and probably also in Anathoth ; whereupon he was threatened with death. Such conduct gave occasion to further prophecies concerning the wickedness of the people and their impending punishment. The fact that Israel has been chosen to be the people of the Lord and has shown himself unworthy of the distinction, is symbolised by a girdle, forming at first an ornament to man, but which when rotten by moisture in the crevices of rocks, is no longer of any use.

(5.) Chaps. xiv. to xvii.—Drought visits Judah ; Jeremiah prays to God for relief from famine. God rejects his petition. The prophet is disappointed, but he is assured that God will protect him from the attacks of the people, if he tries " to bring forth a precious thing from the vile." He tries, but in vain.

(6.) xvii. 19–27.—Exhortation to keep the Sabbath, to abstain from all manner of work, and from carrying burdens out of or into the town.

(7.) xviii.—God changes His decrees according to the deeds of man, as a potter transforms the clay from one vessel to another. Jeremiah is again insulted and threatened, and he prays to God against his persecutors.

(8.) xix. and xx.—In the valley of Hinnom, Jeremiah denounces the idolatry of Israel, and as a symbol of the impending ruin of Israel, he breaks a pot of earthenware. Returning from the valley, he announces the coming evil in the court of the Temple in the presence of the people; he is taken into prison by Pashchur, the chief of the Temple, for one day. When released he repeats the same prophecy, but feels that he has given offence, and in utter despair curses the day of his birth.

(9.) Chaps. xxi. to xxiv.—Nebuchadnezzar attacked Judah, and Zedekiah (later king of Judah) sent to Jeremiah asking him to pray for the safety of the people. But Jeremiah prophesied defeat and disgrace on account of their iniquity. He went even by the command of God to the royal palace, and repeated there the Divine decree against the royal family, Shallum (= Joahaz), Jojakim, and Coniah (= Jehoiachin). There will come, however, one day a righteous offspring of David, who will rule justly and prosperously; He shall be called "The Lord is our salvation." For the present it would be better to submit to the Babylonian rule. They are false prophets who flatter and speak in the name of God of victories over the Babylonians. The false prophets will all be punished—

those who proclaim as their own prophecy the very words they heard from true prophets, those who in different words reproduce messages of the true prophets as their own, and those who invent falsehood. The advisability of submitting to the Babylonian power is also illustrated by the vision of two baskets of figs; good figs representing those who will submit, and bad figs those who prefer war with the Babylonians.

(10.) xxv. to xxvii.—Jeremiah continues, during the reign of Jehoiakim, his prophecies in favour of a peaceful submission to the Babylonians, with the Divine promise of a redemption from the exile and the restoration to their own country and dominion.

(11.) xxviii.—The same prophecy is continued during the reign of Zedekiah. He was opposed by the false prophet Hananiah, to whom Jeremiah foretold that he would be punished and die the same year; this came also to pass.

(12.) xxix. to xxxi.—To the Jews already in Babylon Jeremiah sends a letter of consolation and encourages them in their hopes for the redemption from exile. Of the same tenor were the messages spoken by Jeremiah to all Jews. In days to come a new covenant will be instituted; new in so far as it will not be broken again, the Law remaining permanently written on their heart, "*I shall be their God, and they shall be my nation.*"

(13.) xxxii. and xxxiii.—Jeremiah, kept in prison, bought property from his uncle Hanamel, wrote and signed the document of transfer, and handed it to Baruch. By this he expressed his conviction that the Jews would return from exile and take possession of their land. In addition to this he sent forth from the prison a Messianic prophecy, describing the future greatness of the seed of David, and the restoration of the priests and Levites to the sacrificial service.

(14.) xxxiv. and xxxv.—Jeremiah exhorts the people to keep " the year of release," and held up the family of the Rechabites as patterns of piety, who could not be induced to break their vow of abstinence, though it was voluntarily undertaken.

(15.) xxxvi. to xlv.—Jeremiah continues to prophesy, advising, though fruitlessly, submission to the Babylonian king. Zedekiah made war against Nebuchadnezzar, was defeated, and Jerusalem was taken by the Babylonians. When some Jews wanted to emigrate to Egypt, Jeremiah warned them in the name of God not to do so. He was not listened to; he was even forced to go with them; but he prophesied against them, and foretold their ruin. Baruch, to whom Jeremiah dictated his prophecies, was discontented at being driven from place to place; Jeremiah appeased and encouraged him.

(16.) xlvi. to lii.—Jeremiah prophesies against Egypt, the Philistines, Moab, Ammon, Edom, Damascus, Kedar, Elam, and Babylon. The book concludes with an account of the fall of Jerusalem, similar to that given at the end of the second book of Kings.

3. *Ezekiel* (יחזקאל).—Ezekiel prophesied in exile.

(1.) Chap. i. to vii.—In the fifth year of the exile of Joiachin, Ezekiel, in the vision of the chariot, representing the rule of God over the universe, is appointed a Divine messenger, to warn the people and tell them of the impending danger, that they might not be ignorant of the fate awaiting them, whether they listened or forbore to listen. The message with which he is inspired is represented as a scroll which he swallows. The threatened danger he indicates by symbolic acts, followed by their explanation. The siege of Jerusalem is illustrated by the prophet besieging a brick representing Jerusalem, and the ruin of the nation by cutting and scattering the hair of his head and beard.

(2.) viii. to xi.—In the sixth year, on the sixth day of the fifth month, in the presence of the elders of Judah, Ezekiel is carried in a prophetic vision to Jerusalem, is shown there the sins committed by the Israelites in the very Temple, and the consequent departure of the Divine Presence from the Temple. Israel will suffer for his sins, but will at last repent and improve. God promises, " *I will give them one heart, and I will put a new spirit within you ; and I will take the stony heart out of their flesh, and will give them a heart of flesh ; that they may walk in my statutes, and keep mine ordinances, and do them ; and they shall be my people, and I will be their God* " (xi. 19, 20).

(3.) xii. and xiii.—The prophet indicates the coming captivity by the symbolic act of preparing the things necessary for going into exile. The false prophets and prophetesses, who tell the people to have no dread of any coming exile, will be disappointed and punished. The falsehood of the proverb, " In the length of time every vision faileth," will then be evident.

(4.) xiv. to xix.—Ezekiel describes the sinfulness of Israel, and exhorts them to return to God, or else the threatened calamity will overcome them. He illustrates the approaching calamity by the figure of a cedar-tree and the eagle. Although the fathers have sinned, if the sons abstain from sinning they may prevent the catastrophe ; for the proverb, " The fathers have eaten the sour grapes, and the teeth of the children are set on edge," will prove untrue. If they do not improve, the catastrophe must take place which the prophet depicts in the parables of the lioness caught and of the vine consumed by fire.

(5.) xx.—In the seventh year, the Elders of Israel came to Ezekiel " to inquire of the Lord," לדרש את ה. Ezekiel describes the wickedness of Israel, and the punishment they deserved.

(6.) xxi. to xxiii.—Comparing Jerusalem and Samaria to two sisters, Oholibah and Oholah, he complains that the former, having witnessed the punishment of the latter, has not profited by it.

(7.) xxiv.—On the tenth day of the tenth month in the ninth year Ezekiel prophesies the siege and fall of Jerusalem on the very day on which the siege commenced. The greatness of the calamity, to express which the usual outward signs of grief would be inadequate, is indicated by the Divine command that the prophet on the death of his wife should exhibit no signs of mourning.

(8.) xxv. to xxxii.—Like Isaiah and Jeremiah, he foretells the fate of the neighbouring nations, Ammonites, Moabites, Edomites, Philistines, Tyrians, and Egyptians. The last-named are promised recovery after forty years' desolation of their country.

(9.) xxxiii. and xxxiv.—The prophet describes the duties and responsibilities of watchmen and shepherds, and blames those of his own time as not fulfilling their duties: "But I will save my flock, and they shall no more be a prey; and I will judge between cattle and cattle. *And I will set up one shepherd over them, and he shall feed them, even my servant David: he shall feed them, and he shall be their shepherd. And I the Lord will be their God, and my servant David prince among them*" (xxxiv. 22–24).

(10.) xxxv.—He prophesies against Seir, for their enmity against Israel..

(11.) xxxvi. and xxxvii.—Ezekiel foretells the restoration of Israel in the parable of the dry bones. The union of Israel and Judah is symbolically shown by the union of two staves.

(12.) xxxviii. and xxxix.—Gog, the prince of Rosh, Meshech, and Tubal, will make the last efforts for the destruction of Israel. All his preparations will be in vain. He and his army will fall in the land of Israel. And the Divine promise is given: "*They shall know that I am the Lord their God, in that I caused them to go into captivity among the nations, and have gathered them into their own land, and I will leave none of them any more there: neither will I hide my face any more from them; for I have poured out my spirit upon the house of Israel, saith the Lord God*" (xxxix. 28, 29).

(13.) xl. to xlviii.—In the fourteenth year after the fall of Jerusalem, in the beginning of the year, on the tenth day of the month, Ezekiel is carried in a vision to the land of Israel, and is shown there the rebuilding of the future Temple, and the division of the land among the twelve tribes, the Levites and the priests.

4. *The Twelve Minor Prophets,* הרי עשר—

(1.) *Hosea* (הושע).—Hosea, a contemporary of Isaiah,
prophesied about the sinfulness of the northern kingdom
of the ten tribes, and turns his attention to Judah only
in so far as Judah participated in the sins of Israel,
and their consequences.

(*a.*) Chaps. i. to iii.—In an allegory of a faithless
woman and her three children the sin of the ten tribes
is represented, who faithlessly turned away from the
worship of God in Jerusalem. The consequent three
stages of punishment are represented by the names of
the three children : Jezreel, referring to the catastrophe
of the house of Ahab, ending in the death of Jezebel in
Jezreel ; Lo-ruhama (" Not-pitied "), indicating the fall
of the house of Jehu, from which the mercy of God was
withdrawn after it had been shown in the successes of
King Jeroboam II.; and the third, Lo-ami (" Not-my-
people "), predicting the final dissolution of the kingdom.
But a time of mercy and Divine protection is foretold
by the prophet when he said in the name of God, " I
will betroth thee unto me for ever ; and I will betroth
thee unto me in righteousness and judgment and in
loving-kindness and in mercy ; and I will betroth thee
unto me in faithfulness, and thou shalt know the
Lord ; and I will sow them unto me in the land, and
I will show mercy to Lo-ruhama ; and I will say to
Lo-ami, Thou art my people ; and he shall say, My
God " (ii. 21, 22, 25). This happy time, however,
will only come after a period of trial, represented
in the allegory by the period of trial of a faithless
woman before the husband has again full confidence
in her. " For many days shall the children of Israel
dwell without king, without prince, without sacrifice,

without a statue, and without ephod and teraphim. After that the children of Israel will return and seek the Lord their God, and David their king; and they will anxiously hasten to the Lord and to His goodness in latter days " (iii. 4, 5).

(*b.*) iv. to viii.——Hosea rebukes Ephraim for their sinfulness and obstinacy. When an attempt is made at repentance it is not made in earnest, and is soon abandoned. The sins of Ephraim find imitation in Judah, and therefore the punishment of Ephraim will also affect Judah.

(*c.*) ix. to xiv.——The prophet blames Israel for seeking help in their distress in Egypt or Assyria. He censures their conduct, and contrasts it with the kindness of God in the course of the history of Israel since the time of the patriarchs. Samaria must fall, but Israel need but earnestly return to God, and " he will be like dew to Israel, who will blossom like the lily, and extend his roots like the cedars of Lebanon " (xiv. 6); for " *straight are the ways of the Lord : whilst the righteous walk by them, transgressors stumble by them* " (*Ibid.* 10).

(2.) *Joel* (יואל).——Joel is a contemporary of Isaiah. Locusts have devastated the fields in Judah. Joel exhorts the people to repentance and prayer. His exhortation is acted upon, and relief is promised. At the same time the punishment of the enemies of Israel in the valley of Jehoshaphat is announced. " The day of the Lord, great and wonderful," will be indicated by extraordinary phenomena in heaven and on earth, so clear that all will understand their significance and foresee the coming judgment.

(3.) *Amos* (עָמוֹס).—Amos, a contemporary of the former, prophesied during the reign of Uzziah, king of Judah, and Jeroboam, king of Israel. Amos first mentions in short paragraphs the sinful conduct of the neighbouring states, Damascus, Gaza, Tyre, Edom, Ammon, Moab, and Judah, and the punishment decreed against them, introducing each paragraph with the words, " For three sins of . . . (*scil.*, will I take back the decree of punishment), but for the fourth, I will not take it back." He then dwells on the sins of Israel, laying special stress on the luxuries of the rich, obtained through oppression of the poor, and tells them that, though God has frequently pardoned, He will pardon no more. Amaziah, a priest of Beth-el, warns Amos, and bids him leave the country, but the prophet, nevertheless, continues to proclaim the coming judgment of God, viz., the exile of Israel, adding, however, the comforting prophecy that the time will come when Israel shall be restored to his own land and enjoy lasting happiness.

(4.) *Obadiah* (עֹבַדְיָה).—Obadiah prophesies against the Edomites, and announces the Divine decree against them for their cruel treatment of Judah in times of distress.

(5.) *Jonah* (יוֹנָה).—Jonah, son of Amittai, prophesied success to King Jeroboam II. (2 Kings xiv. 25). He was sent to threaten the inhabitants of Nineveh with the destruction of their city in forty days. Instead of going to Nineveh he set out in a boat for Tarshish ; during a storm he was thrown overboard, swallowed by a fish, and again brought to the shore. He then carried out the Divine mission, the result of which was that the Ninevites repented of their evil deeds and

F

ob;tained a respite. Jonah, disappointed that the threat:
of which he was the bearer was not fulfilled, was rebuked by God, and taught by his own grief at the
destruction of a plant " that had come up in a night "
how wrong it was to wish that God should not show
mercy upon the inhabitants of Nineveh, and to neglect
anything that could lead to their repentance and consequent salvation.

(6.) *Micah* (מיכה).—Micah of Moresha was likewise
a contemporary of Isaiah. He prophesied in Judah.

1. (i.–iii.) He raises his voice especially against the
princes, magistrates, and false prophets, who unite in
oppressing and ruining the people. When Micah tells
them their sins and the coming punishment, they say
to him, " Do not preach ; they do not preach for such
things ; they do not offend " (ii. 6). But the prophet
of the Lord is not deterred from his mission, but continues to denounce their wickedness: " Her chiefs judge
for bribery, and her priests teach for payment, and her
prophets decide for silver ; yet will they lean upon the
Lord, and say, Is not the Lord in our midst ? no evil
shall come upon us. Therefore shall Zion be plowed
into a field, and Jerusalem shall become heaps, and the
mountain of the Temple as the high places of a forest "
(iii. 11, 12).

2. (iv.–v.) Like Isaiah, he depicts the Messianic
period, in which the house of Jacob will be an example
of true faith in God to all nations ; in which Israel
will be restored to his land, under the rule of a descendant of David. But a period of trials and troubles
must precede those happy days, in order to punish Israel,
.and to purify and prepare him for his future greatness.

3. (vi.--vii.) The same principles are taught in the
next part (vi. and vii.) in the form of a controversy
(ריב ליי עם עמו) between the Lord and His people.   The
latter are reminded of the benefits God has bestowed on
them ; and when they ask how they are expected to
show their gratitude, the prophet says, " *O man, He has
told thee what is good ; and what does the Lord require
of thee but to do justice, love kindness, and to walk humbly
with thy God ?* " (vi. 8).

(7.) *Nahum* (נחום).—The fall of Nineveh is predicted.
The power of the mighty Assyrian Empire, hitherto a
terror to Judah and other kingdoms, will come to an
end ; no remedy can save her any more.

(8.) *Habakkuk* (חבקוק).—Habakkuk prophesied at the
time when the Casdim or Chaldeans were about to occupy the place of the Assyrians as conquerors of Syria,
Palestine, and Egypt, and to become the rod in the
hand of God for the punishment of Israel. Habakkuk,
on receiving the mission to announce the Casdim as the
executors of the Divine decree, is at a loss to understand why these wicked and cruel people should be
chosen to chastise those who are far less wicked ; why
the evil-doer should swallow him who is more righteous.   The answer he receives is, " But the just shall
live by his faith."   The evil-doer will in due time
receive his full punishment.   Habakkuk then gives
expression to his implicit faith in the justice of God,
in a hymn which is superscribed, " Prayer (תפלה) of
the prophet Habakkuk on account of errors ; " for
in it he rectifies, as it were, his previous erroneous
opinion.

(9.) *Zephaniah* (צפניה).—He prophesied in the days

of King Josiah.   He proclaims the approach of the
great day of the Lord, on which all those who turned
away from Him will receive their punishment, all the
rich and powerful who say the Lord does neither good
nor evil.   He appeals to the humble in the land
(עַנְוֵי אֶרֶץ) to seek the Lord in prayer, in order to be
saved on "the day of the anger of the Lord."   For the
Philistines, the Phœnicians, Moab, Ammon, and Assyria
will be punished, nor will Jerusalem escape free.   " I
will then turn," he says in the name of God, " a pure
language to the nations, that all of them will call by the
name of God, and serve Him with one accord " (iii. 9).
" In that day shalt thou not be ashamed for all thy
doings wherein thou hast transgressed against me ; for
then I will take away out of the midst of thee them
that rejoice in thy pride, and thou shalt no more be
haughty on my holy mountain.   And I will leave in
thy midst a poor and humble people, and they shall
trust in the name of the Lord.   The remnant of Israel
shall not do iniquity, and they shall not speak falsehood, and a tongue of deceit shall not be found in
their mouth " (iii. 9, 11–13).

(10.) *Haggai* (חַגַּי)—The Israelites, who by the command of Cyrus had discontinued the rebuilding of the
Temple after the foundation had been laid by his permission, were exhorted by Haggai, in the second year
of the reign of Darius, to resume the work.   Guided
by Zerubbabel and Joshua, son of Jehozadak, they
obeyed, and the prophet describes to them the blessing
which they will henceforth enjoy.

(11.) *Zechariah* (זְכַרְיָה) :—

1. (i. to vii.) Zechariah, a contemporary of Haggai,

exhorts the Israelites to listen to the words of the prophets, seeing that the words of former prophets have been fulfilled. The Divine scheme for the restoration of Israel and the rebuilding of the Temple in spite of all obstacles, is shown to the prophet in various visions. In one vision Joshua is appointed high-priest, notwithstanding the aspersions of his adversary (השטן), and *Zerubbabel* or *Zemach*, the political chief of the community. Joshua is exhorted " to walk in the ways of the Lord, to keep the charge entrusted to him, and to guard the House of God and His courts; " and Zerubbabel is reminded that success is not obtained " by might and strength, but by the spirit of the Lord." "Thus the one—Zemach by name— shall sit on his throne and be ruler, and the other— Joshua—shall sit on his throne and be priest, and a counsel of peace shall be between the two " (vi. 13).

2. Chap. viii.—The prophet is asked whether the day of mourning in the fifth month is to be continued. The prophetic answer is as follows : The reason for the mourning was, that your fathers did not listen to the word of God, and were punished for their disobedience. Now, as the time of punishment is over, it is for you to prevent a recurrence of these sad experiences. What you have to do is this : *Speak the truth one to another ; truth and judgment of peace judge in your gates. Let no one plan in his heart the ruin of his neighbour, and do not love to swear falsely.* Let the fasts of the fourth, fifth, seventh, and tenth months be to the house of Judah for rejoicing, joy, and good seasons ; love truth and peace (viii. 16, 17, 19). At the same time the promise is given

that the time will come when nations will seek the Lord in Jerusalem, and say to the Jews, "We will go with you, for God is with you" (viii. 23).

3. (ix.–xi.) The prophet encourages Zion to rejoice in her future mission; her enemies round about will be brought to silence, and her king, meek and humble, "poor and riding on an ass," "will speak peace to the nations, and his rule will extend from sea to sea, and from the river to the ends of the earth" (ix. 9, 10). Judah and Ephraim will unite, and both will enjoy the Divine protection. If this has not yet taken place, it is the fault of the "bad shepherds," *i.e.*, the bad leaders of the people.

4. (xii.–xiv.) The prophet foretells troubles which will come upon Jerusalem when the nations will make the last effort to take that city. They will be defeated, and Judah will be filled on that occasion with "a spirit of grace" (רוח חן ותחנונים), and will pray to God for the safety of his enemy; the very Jews, "whom the enemy desired to pierce," will pray for him, and mourn for his death as a father mourneth for the loss of his only child. Judah will then be free from false prophets and bad shepherds. God will make Himself known to all: "And the Lord will be a King over the whole earth; on that day will the Lord be One and His name One" (xiv. 9). All will come to Jerusalem "to worship the King, the Lord Zebaoth, and to celebrate the feast of Succoth" (*Ibid.* 16), expressing thereby their conviction that God alone is able to afford protection and blessing.

(12.) *Malachi* (מלאכי).—Malachi, the last of the prophets, exhorts the priests to true reverence of the sanctuary, and to conscientious fulfilment of their duties. The distinction of the priest was based on the distinction of his conduct: "The law of truth was in his mouth, and iniquity was not found on his lips; in peace and uprightness he walked with me, and many turned he back from iniquity. For the lips of the priest shall keep knowledge, and instruction shall they seek of his mouth, for he is a messenger of the Lord Zebaoth" (ii. 6, 7). Judah is then rebuked for his faithlessness. Both, the Levites (including the priests) and Judah, will pass through a process of refining; the wicked will be removed, whilst for "those who fear the name of God" the sun of salvation will shine. Those who desire to obtain a place among these latter must "remember the law of Moses, the servant of God, which God commanded him on Horeb for all Israel; statutes and judgments" (iii. 22). Before the great day of the Lord, the day of judgment, the Lord will send "the prophet Elijah, who will cause the hearts of fathers and children to unite in returning to God."

III. *The Hagiographa* (כתובים).—The Hagiographa form the last collection of holy writings, composed by men who, although they were not prophets, were filled with the spirit of the Lord (רוח יי). They include the three larger works: (*a*) תהלים (or תלים) Psalms, משלי Proverbs, and איוב Job; (*b*) the Five Scrolls (חמש מגלות), viz., שיר השירים Song of Songs, רות Ruth, איכה Lamentations, קהלת Ecclesiastes, אסתר Esther; (*c*) the historical books: דניאל Daniel, עזרא Ezra, נחמיא Nehemiah, and דברי הימים the two books of Chronicles.

1. *Psalms* (תהלים).—The Psalms are hymns containing

praises of God's greatness, prayers for His mercy, and
meditations on His wisdom, power, justice, and goodness.   However various the Psalms are in form and
contents, they have this in common, that they all
are based on the purest and sincerest trust in God's
justice and goodness.   "The mighty and proud, זדים
who rely on their own strength and are guided by the
dictates of their own will, cannot succeed for ever;
the poor and humble, ענוים who rely on God's mercy
and are guided by the word of God, will not suffer for
ever." This is the truth which the Psalmist proclaims
in his songs over and over again.   Yet there is a
great variety in the contents of the Psalms.   Some are
simply praises of God's greatness, e.g., viii., xix., xxxii.,
xcii., xcv. to xcix., ciii., civ., &c.   Others are the expression of gratitude, e.g., ix., xviii., xxxiv., lxvi.,
lxviii., &c.   Many are prayers in time of trouble; in
most of these the suppliant feels sure that God will
accept his prayer, and is confident that help will
come.   Such psalms are iii., iv., v., vi., xii., xiii., &c.
To this class belong also all the psalms which refer to
the troubles of David during the reign of Saul, as lii.,
liv., lvi., lix., lxiii., &c.; some of the Asaph-psalms,
lxxiii., lxxvii., lxxix., lxxx.; the penitential psalms,
in which the sinner prays for mercy, as xxv., xxxii.,
xxxviii., li.; and those in which a longing is expressed
for the House of God, e.g., xxvii., xlii., xliii., lxv.,
lxxxiv.   Some psalms are a protest against those who
rely on human force and human cunning instead of
having faith in God, a protest of the ענוים against the
view and creed of the זדים and נאים or גוים e.g., ix. and
x., xi., xiv., xvi., xvii., &c.   Some psalms are of a more

didactic character, showing the way of true happiness
(Ps. i.), depicting a truly pious life (xv., xxiv.), or the excellence of the word of God, as xix., cxix. ; or the use-
lessness of sacrifice without purity of heart (xl., l., li.).

The poetical form of the Psalms, as of Hebrew
poetry in general, is parallelism. The sentences are
formed in such a manner that the psalm can be
arranged in lines divisible into two parts, which are
either two elements of a single idea, or a double
expression of the same idea, or a combination of two
ideas or things opposed to each other, illustrating an
idea by its antithesis. In some of the Psalms the
parallelism is perfect throughout, in others it is partly
abandoned, probably in order not to slavishly subordi-
nate the idea to the form of its expression. The same
is to be noticed as regards other forms of the Psalms.
Some are arranged alphabetically, that is, the successive
verses begin with successive letters of the alphabet ;
but deviations from the plan are met with almost in
all such psalms. There are psalms which are divided
into a certain number of parts or strophes, each part
beginning or ending with the same phrase or verse ;
but almost invariably these phrases or verses undergo
some modification.

The style is naturally poetical, and figurative language is employed throughout. God is a Rock (צוּר), an
habitation (מָעוֹן), a Shepherd (רוֹעֶה), who feeds His flock
with great care and love ; He is an eagle, under
whose wings (כְּנָפָיו, אֶבְרָתוֹ) the weak find protection ; He
rides in the heavens of the heavens of old (רֹכֵב בִּשְׁמֵי
שְׁמֵי קֶדֶם). Man is compared to " grass that withers,"
to a " flower that blossoms in the morning, and in the

evening it is withered and dried up;" the life of man
is but a breath (הבל); a lie (כזב); light in the balance
(במאזנים לעלות); he changes like a garment, like a raiment. The days of a long life are like the days of the
heavens, the sun or the moon (עם שמש, לפני שמש, כימי שמים
or לפני ירח). The mighty are mountains with many peaks
(הרים גבנונים), they have horns like those of the unicorns,
whilst the weak are "a wall bent" (קיר נטוי), "a fence
thrust down" (גדר הדחויה); "they have sunk in deep
mire;" "they have come into fire and into water;"
"the waters have come unto the soul." The meek are
"broken in heart," "crushed in spirit." The wicked
and unjust are like lions and dogs; they have poison
"like the poison of a serpent, like a deaf adder that
stoppeth its ears, that does not listen to the voice
of charmers, to the clever sorcerer." Their words are
smooth like cream and oil, whilst in the heart there are
war, daggers, sharp swords. The threatened one runs
like a hind, escapes like a bird. Those who have no
higher aim than material enjoyments are like "sheep
driven to death;" "man in his dignity, without understanding, is like cattle that perish." Mishaps come
upon man like the waves of the sea. The Divine
judgment visits the wicked like a thunderstorm; it
shakes the earth like an earthquake or volcano. Sinners
receive "the cup of confusion" (כוס התרעלה) at the
hand of God; for "a cup is in the hand of the Lord,
and the wine therein is red; it is full with drink, and
He pours out from it, but its dregs all the wicked of
the earth will suck and drink."

The sinner is punished by his own deed; "he digs
a pit and falls into it;" he feels like a sick person

whose "bones are troubled, and wither;" his purification is the healing of the soul; he is purified with
hyssop; he becomes whiter than snow (li. 9). When
man sins he feels as if he had become a changed creature, as if he had now been born and conceived in sin
(ver. 7); when he repents and improves, God creates
in him a new heart, and renews a firm spirit within
him (ver. 12). The wife of the God-fearing man is
compared to the fruitful vine, his children to young
olive-trees (cxxviii.). The righteous will flourish like
a palm-tree, will grow high like a cedar upon Lebanon
(xcii. 13). Whilst the righteous is like a tree planted
by the brook of water, the wicked are like chaff which
the wind drives away (i. 3, 4). Israel is likened to a
vine brought from Egypt and planted in Palestine
(lxxx. 9). Peacefulness and brotherly love, between
high and low, the mighty and the weak, the rich and
the poor, the wise and the simple, are illustrated by
the fine oil that flows down from the head to the
beard, the beard that descends over the garments, and
the dew of the high Hermon that comes down to the
lower mountains of Zion (cxxx.).

There are some instances of play upon words (lvi. 9),
and of rhymes (cxlv. 11; xxxiv. 6); the latter are
apparently not intentional.

Although we generally speak of the Psalms of
David, only a portion of them was composed by King
David; the headings ascribe also one psalm to Moses,
two to King Solomon, twelve to Asaph, one to Heman,
and one to Ethan; and some have no author mentioned
in the heading. Many have no superscription at all,
and most of these seem to belong to a later period.

The individual psalms have various names. The most general of them is מזמור a poëm, set in music. Of some it is distinctly stated that they were intended to be sung; this is expressed in the heading by the word שיר "song," which either precedes or follows the title מזמור or stands alone without מזמור. The term, שיר "song," is further qualified by חנוכת הבית "of the dedication of the house," ידידות "of love," and המעלות or למעלות "of degrees leading upward," i.e., towards God. Another name occurring in twelve psalms is משכיל "instructive song;" the *maschil* proclaims the lesson that God is King of the universe, and that those are happy who trust in His justice and mercy. A similar meaning attaches to ללמד the word superadded to משכיל in Ps. lx.; lit. "to teach," i.e., that the song be learnt by all, in order that people may strengthen their confidence in God in times of trouble (comp. 2 Sam. i. 18). The meaning of להזכיר which occurs in two psalms (xxxviii. and lxx.), is "for prayer." There is one psalm לתודה (c.), "for thanksgiving;" another "for the Sabbath-day," ליום השבת (xcii.). Four psalms are called תפלה "prayer" (xvii., lxxxvi., xc., cii.); one (cxlv.), תהלה "praise;" one (vii.), שגיון "an error,"[1] referring to the miscalculation of the wicked in preparing weapons against the innocent, which weapons are turned against themselves; and six are superscribed מכתם "a jewel." Such a jewel is the Psalmist's "faith in God," that inspires him with hope and pure joy in the midst of misfortune.

The headings include also instructions for the singers and references to the musical instruments which are to

---

[1] Comp. p. 83.

be used. The most general term is למנצח "to the chief," *scil.*, of the singers or Levites; it refers to the chief of a particular division of the Levites if it is followed by a qualifying phrase, and to the chief of all the Levites if it is not followed by any qualification. The term למנצח describes the psalm as a Temple-song, although this may not have been its original object. Even poems which have been composed by David on certain personal events became—perhaps slightly modified—national songs, and formed part of the public service. The adaptation was easy, because these historical psalms rarely contain any allusion to the particular event mentioned in the superscription.

The term למנצח is qualified by על נגינת "on a stringed instrument," נגינת being the particular instrument of the Levites, of whom this מנצח was the master, The term בנגינות which in several psalms follows the word למנצח is grammatically unconnected with the latter; it means "on stringed instruments," and is the instruction for the מנצח. There were several kinds of such instruments; two kinds are named שמינית and נתית "the *neginath* with eight strings" or "chords," and "the *gittith*" coming from Gath, a town in the land of the Philistines. Other kinds of musical instruments are נחילות (v.), מחלת (liii.), and עלמות (xlvi.); these are hollow flute-like instruments, also called נבלים (1 Chron. xv. 20). In some cases the division of Levites is named instead of the instrument: ידותון "Jeduthun" (xxxix., lxii. and lxxvii.; comp. 1 Chron. xxv. 3); לבני קרח "to the sons of Korah" (xlii. to xlix., and lxxxiv. to lxxxviii.); once the direction occurs לענות (lxxxviii.), "to sing alternately," referring to the two divisions of Levites headed by הימן האזרחי and איתן האזרחי "the Ezrahite Heman," and "the Ezrahite Ethan" (lxxxviii. and lxxxix.).

A few terms are met with in the headings which describe the contents of the psalm in a poetical style. Such are (*a.*) ששנים עדות שושן עדות, עדות and ששנים (lx., lxxx., xlv., and lxix.), "Testimony for the lily or lilies," or "for lilies." The poet calls by this name the flower of the nation, the meek and God-fearing, who are under the special protection of God, and are destined to be crowned in the end with glory and victory. (*b.*) אילת השחר (xxii.), "The strength of the dawn." The phrase refers to the strength given to the sufferer in the darkness of his despair by the awakening of his faith in God, which is compared by the poet to the dawn as the forerunner of daylight. (*c.*) אל תשחת "Do not destroy" (lvii., lviii., lix., and lxxv.). By this heading the author indicates that the psalm is a protest against the self-confidence of the wicked in the success of their wickedness, either with reference to their evil designs against the author himself, or to their plans in general. (*d.*) יונת אלם רחקים "Dove in the force of those far," *scil.*, from God (lvi.). The psalm contains the expression of David's faith in God when he was caught by the Philistines in Gath.

In some of the headings the event is mentioned which prompted the Psalmist to compose the psalm: David's flight from Jerusalem when Absalom rebelled against him (iii.); the slander of the Benjamite Kush (vii.); the death of Labben (ix.); rescue from the hands of Saul and other enemies (xiii.); dedication of the house (xxx.); David's escape from Abimelech, king of the Philistines (xxxiv.); his capture by the Philistines in Gath (lvi.); his stay in the cave of Adullam (lvii., cxlii.); danger of being put to death by the servants of Saul (lix.); war with Aram and Edom (lx.); sojourn in the wilderness of Judah (lxiii.).

The order of the Psalms is not chronological; *e.g.*, chap. iii. refers to the rebellion of Absalom, whilst chap. cxlii. was composed before the death of Saul. The principle which guided the collector in fixing the place of each psalm is not known. But it is certainly not the result of mere chance that the first two psalms speak of the Law of God, and of the punishment of those who rebel against God and against His anointed; and that the last psalm calls upon all to praise God with all their soul: "Let every thing that hath breath praise the Lord, Hallelujah!" Nor is it mere chance that the psalms are divided, like the Law, into five groups or books, each one ending with a doxology. It is possible that the psalms were recited or sung at the public service in a manner corresponding to the reading of the Law and the Prophets.

The first two books contain most of the psalms superscribed לְדָוִד "by David," but there are also some in the other books (one in III., two in IV., fourteen in V.). At the end of the second book (lxxii. 20) the following words are added: "The prayers of David, the son of Jesse, are ended;" *i.e.*, the hope which has just been expressed in the words וְיִמָּלֵא כְבוֹד יי אֶת כָּל הָאָרֶץ "And the whole earth shall be filled with the glory of God," forms the aim and end of all the prayers of David, the son of Jesse. The verse does not mean that the first seventy-two chapters of the Psalms contain all the prayers of David, as there are several psalms of David between chaps. lxxiii. and cl.

The Psalms were composed by David and other authors partly for private use, partly for the public service in the Temple and other places of worship. Of those that were originally for private use some were subsequently adapted for public service, and even those intended from the beginning for public worship were adapted to the different modes of recitation or singing. The Book of Psalms includes, therefore, two recensions of several chapters ; *e.g.*, xiv. and liii. ; xviii. and 2 Sam. xxii. ; lx. 7—14 and cviii. 7—14 ; lvii. 8—12 and cviii. 2—6 ; cv. 1—15 and 1 Chron. xvi. 8—22 ; xcvi. and 1 Chron. xvi. 23—33 ; cxxxv. and cxxxvi.

A considerable portion of our daily prayers consists of psalms. We distinguish the following groups :—
(*a.*) פסוקי דזמרא " Verses of song," Ps. cxlv. to cl. ; to which the following are added on Sabbaths and Festivals : xix., xxxiv., xc., xci., cxxxv., cxxxvi. (called הלל הגדול " the great Hallel "), xxxiii., xcii., and xciii. (*b.*) שיר של יום " Song of the day ;" a different psalm is recited each day of the week after the morning prayer in the following order : xxiv., xlviii., lxxxii., xciv., lxxxi., xciii., xcii. (*c.*) קבלת שבת " Friday evening psalms," xcv. to xcix. (*d.*) Sabbath afternoon psalms : civ., cxx. to cxxxiv. (*e.*) הלל " Praise," cxiii. to cxviii. (*f.*) Penitential psalms after evening prayer on week-days, in the following order : xxv., xxxii., xxxviii., li., lxxxvi.

2. משלי *Proverbs* of Solomon, the son of David, king of Israel. The Book of Proverbs belongs to those Biblical books which are called ספרי חכמה " books of wisdom."

They appeal to the reason of man, and do not support their words by the authority of Revelation, although the authors and those who gave them the final shape were inspired and guided by the רוח ה "the divine spirit." The commandments of God and His ways are referred to as the safest guide for man in all conditions of life. Three books are included in this class: Proverbs, Job, and Ecclesiastes.

"The Proverbs of Solomon" are divided into the following six sections:—(*A.*) Introduction, i. to ix.; (*B.*) Collection of Proverbs: (*a.*) Proverbs of Solomon, x. to xxii. 16; (*b.*) Words of the Wise, xxii. 17 to xxiv. 22; (*c.*) Second group of Words of the Wise, xxv. 34; (*d.*) Proverbs of Solomon collected by the men of Hezekiah, xxv. to xxviii.; (*e.*) Words of Agur-bin-yakeh, xxx.; (*f.*) Words of Lemuel, xxxi.

The fourth section (chaps. xxv. to xxix.) is introduced by the following superscription:—" Also these are the Proverbs of Solomon, which the men of Hezekiah, king of Judah, had removed." The men of Hezekiah seem to have been uncertain whether this section should form part of the book, because of the seeming contradiction between the fourth and fifth verses of the twenty-sixth chapter. The men of the Great Synagogue decided the question in favour of its incorporation in the book, and reconciled the seeming contradiction by their interpretation.

The fifth collection of proverbs is ascribed to *Agur-bin-yakeh,* an allegorical phrase meaning " collection deserving respect." The collection is further called " the burden "—the usual heading of prophecies—in order to give it more weight. Also the rest of the

G

superscription, "The saying of the man *Leïthiel, Leïthiel ve-ucchal,* is of an allegorical character, signifying, "God—*i.e.,* the word of God—is my task, and I shall prevail." The phrase is set forth more clearly in the succeeding verses: human knowledge is insufficient, but "All the word of God is pure; he is a shield to those who trust in him" (xxx. 5). The second half of this collection has the heading *La-alukah,* "For a necklace" (*comp.* i. 9), similar in meaning to the heading מכתם "Jewel," in the Psalms. The form of these proverbs, based on the numbers two, three, and four, is similar to that of the prophecies of Amos (chaps. i. and ii.). The last collection is headed, "Words to Lemuel, the king; the burden wherewith his mother instructed him." The contents of the instruction is, "Be not licentious and intemperate; help the poor and oppressed." The name Lemuel is likewise allegorical, meaning "God-ward." The book concludes with the praises of a virtuous woman.

(*A.*) *Introduction.*—The object of the book is set forth in verses 2 to 7 of the first chapter as follows: "To make man know wisdom and instruction, comprehend words of understanding, and take the instruction of acting wisely, with justice, judgment, and righteousness; to give skill to the simple; to the young knowledge and discretion; that the wise may hear and increase doctrine, and the prudent acquire cleverness to understand proverb and figure, the words of wise men and their allegories. *The beginning of knowledge is the fear of the Lord; wisdom and instruction fools despise.*" This last sentence is the basis of the book. Without fear of the Lord all knowledge and wisdom will prove insufficient for establishing man's true happiness. The Introduction consists of several connected addresses, in which the author persuades the reader to listen to his advice, and keep away from wicked people before it is too late. He exhorts man to entrust himself to the guidance of the Lord, and not to rely on his own understanding. " *Be not wise in thine eyes; fear the Lord, and depart from evil* " (iii. 7). He warns against bad society, against becoming security for debtors, and against idleness. The two ways open to man are allegorically represented by two women, the one wise, the other foolish; the one leading to happiness, the other to ruin; each one inviting man to her house, and displaying in the very act of invitation her full character.

(*B.*) The collections of proverbs begin with the tenth chapter. The proverbs have the form of parallelism, each verse being divided into two parts, mostly containing an anithesis illustrating the difference between the wise and the foolish, the good and the bad, the just and the unjust, the industrious and the idle, the rich and the poor, and the like. Each verse is a proverb by itself, and is independent of the verses which precede and follow. There are only a few passages in which several verses are connected, and these occur in the later collections, *e.g.*, xxii. 22–23, 24–25, 26–27; xxiii. 1–3, 4–5, 6–9, 10–11, 12–13, 20–21, 29–35; xxiv. 3–7, 10–12, 30–34; xxvii. 23–27. The whole of the thirtieth chapter consists of small paragraphs of three or four verses, and the last chapter consists of two continuous parts.

In these collections of proverbs we find advice for

every condition of our life. Our relation to God is
shown; how He loves the good and just :—

> "The way of the wicked is an abomination of the Lord;
> but he loveth him who pursues righteousness"
> (xv. 9).
> "The sacrifice of the wicked is an abomination of the
> Lord, but the prayer of the righteous is his plea-
> sure" (xv. 8).
> "The Lord is far from the wicked, but he heareth the
> prayer of the righteous" (xv. 29).
> "To do justice and judgment is more acceptable to the
> Lord than sacrifice" (xxi. 3).

He protects the poor, the weak, the widow, and the
orphan :—

> "He who oppresseth the poor, blasphemeth his Maker;
> and he who is gracious to the needy, honoureth
> him" (xiv. 31).
> "He who is gracious to the poor, lendeth to the Lord,
> and he will repay him his reward" (xix. 17).
> "Do not rob the poor because he is poor; and do not
> crush the poor in the gate, for the Lord will plead
> their cause, and will take the soul of those who
> rob them" (xxii. 23).
> "The Lord will pull down the house of the proud, and
> will establish the border of the widow" (xv. 25).
> "The rich and the poor meet; the Maker of them all is
> the Lord" (xxii. 2).

He punishes the evil-doer and rewards the righteous :—

> "Do not say, I will repay evil; hope in the Lord, and
> he will help thee" (xx. 22).
> "He who closeth his ear because of the crying of the

poor, he also will call and will not be answered"
(xxi. 13).

" He who keepeth a command, keepeth his soul ; he who
despiseth his ways shall die " (xix. 16).

" When the Lord is pleased with the ways of man, he
will cause even his enemies to make peace with
him " (xvi. 7).

" The Lord will not let the soul of the righteous be
hungry, but the desire of the wicked will he thrust
back " (x. 3).

He knows the heart of man :—

" There is a test for silver, and a refining pot for gold ;
but God trieth the hearts " (xvii. 3).

He directs all events :—

" Man's heart planneth his way, but the Lord directeth
his step " (xvi. 9).

" The horse is prepared for the day of war, but the
victory is the Lord's " (xxi. 31).

His blessing is a true blessing :—

" The blessing of the Lord, it maketh rich, and doth not
increase trouble with it " (x. 22).

His Will alone must be obeyed :—

" There is no wisdom, and no understanding, and no
counsel against the Lord " (xxi. 30).

" Whoso despiseth a word will be punished, but he
who feareth a commandment will be rewarded"
(xiii. 13).

" Without a vision the people cometh into disorder ; but
he who keepeth the Law, happy is he " (xxix. 18).

The fear of the Lord is the basis of a virtuous and happy life :—

> "The fear of the Lord is the beginning of knowledge (i. 7); the fountain of life (xiv. 27); the fear of the Lord adds days, but the years of the wicked will be short " (x. 27).

According as we display wisdom or folly we make others and ourselves happy or unhappy :—

> 'A wise son giveth joy to his father, and a foolish son is the sorrow of his mother " (x. 1).
> "The wisdom of woman buildeth her house, and folly pulleth it down by her hands " (xiv. 1).
> "Eat, my son, honey, for it is good, and honeycomb, which is sweet for thy palate; know that thus is wisdom for thy soul; if thou hast found it, there is a future, and thy hope will not be cut off " (xxiv. 13, 14).
> "The prudent seeth evil, and is hidden; the ignorant pass by, and are punished " (xxvii. 12).
> " As a jewel of gold in a swine's snout, so is a fair woman without discretion " (xi. 22).
> "The simple believeth every word; but the prudent man looketh well to his going " (xiv. 15).

The ways of wisdom and folly are frequently displayed in our words :—

> "In the multitude of words there wanteth not sin, but he who spareth his words acts wisely " (x. 19).
> "A soft answer turneth back wrath, but a harsh word raiseth anger " (xv. 1).
> "Also a fool when silent is considered wise; he who closeth his lips is prudent " (xvii. 28).

" He who keepeth his mouth and his tongue, keepeth his soul from troubles " (xxi. 23).

" By long-suffering the prince is persuaded ; and a soft tongue breaketh a bone " (xxv. 15).

" Answer not a fool like his folly, lest thou be equal to him. Answer a fool according to his folly, lest he be wise in his eyes " (xxvi. 4, 5).

The principal virtues recommended to man are righteousness (צדקה), honesty (אמונה), truthfulness (אמת), meekness (ענוה), industry, thrift, temperance, content-ment, and moderation :—

" Treasures of wickedness are of no profit, but righteous-ness delivereth from death " (x. 2).

" Better a little in the fear of the Lord than a large treasure, and confusion therewith " (xv. 16).

" The righteousness of the upright maketh his way straight, but the wicked falleth by his wickedness " (xi. 5).

" The remembrance of the righteous is for blessing ; but the name of the wicked will rot " (x. 7).

" Guilt is the interpreter of fools, but favour that of the straightforward " (xiv. 9).

" To do justice is joy to the righteous, and a terror to evil-doers " (xxi. 15).

" Like a fountain made turbid and a well that is cor-rupted, is the righteous that yieldeth in the presence of the wicked " (xxv. 26).

" Where a man of honesty is, there is multitude of blessings ; but he who hasteneth to become rich will not be guiltless " (xxviii. 20).

" The lip of truth will be established for ever, but the tongue of falsehood for a moment " (xii. 19).

" A witness of faithfulness is he who does not lie,

but he who uttereth falsehood is a false witness"
(xiv. 5).[1]

"A lip of excellency becometh not a low man; how
much less doth a lip of falsehood a noble man!"
(xvii. 7).

"Pride came, and shame came; but with the meek is
wisdom" (xi. 2).

"Meekness cometh before honour" (xv. 33). "Pride
cometh before the fall, and haughtiness of spirit
before the stumbling" (xvi. 18). "Let another
praise thee, and not thy mouth; a stranger, and
not thy lips" (xxvii. 2).

"He is poor who worketh with a slack hand, but the
hand of the industrious maketh rich" (x. 4).

"Better is he who thinketh little of himself, and is a
slave to himself, than he who thinketh much of
himself and lacketh bread" (xii. 9).

"The hand of the industrious shall rule, but the slack
hand shall be tributary" (xii. 24).

"In all labour there is profit; but when there is only a
word of lips it leads but to want" (xiv. 23).

"Also he who is lazy in his work is a brother to the man
that destroyeth" (xviii. 9).

"I passed by the field of a slothful man, and the vineyard
of a man wanting heart; and behold, thorns have
come up over the whole of it; its surface is covered
with thistles, and its stone-fence is pulled down.
And I beheld, I turned my heart, I saw, I took
instruction: a little of sleep, a little of slumber, a
little of joining the hands to lie down; then thy
poverty cometh like a traveller, and thy want like
an armed man" (xxiv. 30–34).

---

[1] *i.e.*, he who is truthful in ordinary conversation is also a trustworthy witness in a court of justice; those who are accustomed to say
falsehood cannot be trusted in important matters.

" The righteous eateth to the fulness of his soul, but the belly of the wicked shall want " (xiii. 25).

" Wine is a mocker, strong drink roareth, and every one that erreth therein will not be wise " (xx. 1).

" Who hath woe ? who hath sorrow ? who hath contentions ? who hath complaining ? who hath wounds without cause ? who hath redness of eyes ? Those who tarry long at the wine ; those who come to search mixed drink. Do not look upon the wine though it be red, though it send forth its colour through the cup, though it flow smoothly ; in the end it biteth like a serpent and stingeth like an asp ; thine eyes shall see strange things, and thy heart shall speak perverse things ; and thou shalt be like one that lieth in the midst of the sea, and like one that lieth on the top of the mast. They have stricken me, shalt thou say, and I was not sick. They have beaten me ; I felt it not. When shall I awake ? I will seek it yet again " (xxiii. 29–35).

" He who is greedy after gain troubleth his house, but he who hateth gifts shall live " (xv. 27).

" He whose desire is wide stirreth up strife, but he who trusteth in the Lord shall be fattened " (xxviii. 25).

" There are who spend liberally, and there is an increase ; and there are who withhold more than is right, and yet it leads to want " (xi. 24).

" Know well the state of thy flock ; set thy heart to the droves ; for treasure is not for ever, nor a crown for generation and generation. When hay is gone, and grass is spoilt, and the herbs of the field are gathered in, there are lambs for thy clothing, and he-goats are the price of a field : and there will be goats' milk enough for thy food, for the food of thy house, and maintenance for thy maidens " (xxvii. 23–27).

"Lust overcome is sweet to the soul; but to depart from evil is the abomination of fools" (xiii. 19).

"Better is he who is long-suffering than a hero; and he who ruleth his spirit is better than he who conquereth a city" (xvi. 32).

"Like an open town without a wall is the man whose spirit is without restraint" (xxv. 28).

The following proverbs refer to the relation between husband and wife, and between man and his neighbour as friend or enemy, father and child, rich and poor, king and people :—

"He who hath found a wife hath found a good thing, and obtained favour of the Lord" (xviii. 22).

"A virtuous wife is the crown of her husband, but a wicked woman is like rottenness in his bones" (xii. 4).

"House and wealth are the inheritance of fathers, but a wise wife is from the Lord" (xix. 14; chap. xxxi. 10 to end).

"He who revealeth a secret is a slanderer, but he who is faithful in spirit covereth a thing" (xi. 13).

"Hatred stirreth up strifes, but love covereth all sins" (x. 12).

"Better is a meal of herbs where love is, than a stalled ox and hatred therewith" (xv. 17).

"He who covereth transgression seeketh love, but he who repeateth a matter separateth a friend" (xvii. 9).

"Open rebuke is better than secret love" (xxvii. 5).

"He who saith to the wicked, Thou art righteous, him shall the people curse, nations shall abhor him; but to them that rebuke him shall be delight, and a good blessing shall come upon them" (xxiv. 24, 25).

"Faithful are the wounds of a friend, but the kisses of an enemy are like smoke" (xxvii. 6).

"When there is no wood the fire goeth out; so when there is no tale-bearer strife ceaseth" (xxvi. 20).

"A kind man doth good to his soul, and a cruel man troubleth his flesh" (xi. 17).

"Rejoice not when thine enemy falleth, and let not thy heart be glad when he stumbleth, lest the Lord see it and it displease Him, and He turn away His wrath from him" (xxiv. 17, 18).

"The righteous knoweth the feelings of his cattle, but the heart of the wicked is cruel" (xii. 10).

"He who curseth his father and his mother, his lamp shall be put out in obscure darkness" (xx. 20).

"Children's children are the crown of old men, and the glory of children are their fathers" (xvii. 6).

"The eye that mocketh at his father, and despiseth to obey his mother, the ravens of the valley shall pick it out, and the young eagles shall eat it" (xxx. 17).

"Where there is the instruction of the father, there is a wise son; but a mocker will he be who heard no rebuke" (xiii. 1).

"He who spareth his rod hateth his son, and he who loveth him chastiseth him early" (xiii. 24).

"Chastise thy son while there is hope, and let not thy soul turn to his crying" (xix. 18).

"Train the lad in his way, and when he is old he will not depart from it" (xxii. 6).

"Foolishness is bound in the heart of a child, but the rod of correction shall drive it far from him" (xxii. 15).

"Withhold not correction from the child; for if thou beatest him with the rod, he shall not die. Thou shalt beat him with the rod, and shalt deliver his soul from death" (xxiii. 13, 14).

"The benevolent shall be blessed, for he hath given of his bread to the poor" (xxii. 9).

"The liberal soul shall be made fat, and he that stilleth the thirst of others shall also have his thirst stilled " (xi. 25).

" He who despiseth his neighbour sinneth, but whoso is gracious to the poor is happy " (xiv. 24).

" In the multitude of people is the glory of the king; but in the want of people is the destruction of the prince " (xiv. 28).

"The king's wrath is like messengers of death; but a wise man will pacify it " (xvi. 14).

" The heart of a king is in the hand of the Lord like brooks of water; He turneth it whithersoever He liketh " (xxi. 1).

On miscellaneous subjects :—

"There is that maketh himself rich, yet hath nothing; there is that maketh himself poor, yet hath great riches " (xiii. 7).

" The heart knoweth its own bitterness, and a stranger doth not intermeddle with its joy " (xiv. 10).

"If care is in the heart of man, let him still it; if a good thing, let him brighten it up " (xii. 25).

" He is a guide to life who keepeth instruction, but he that refuseth reproof misleadeth " (x. 17).

" Boast not thyself of to-morrow; for thou knowest not what a day may bring forth " (xxvii. 1).

" All the ways of man are clean in his own eyes; but the Lord weigheth the spirits " (xvi. 2).

Job, אִיּוֹב—The Book of Job consists of the following three parts :—

(*a.*) *Introduction* (i. and ii.).—God is figuratively represented as presiding over a council of ministers (בְּנֵי הָאֱלֹהִים " sons of God "), amongst whom also the accuser (הַשָּׂטָן " the hinderer," one who is hostile to the word of God) appears. While God praised the piety of Job, the accuser doubted the purity of his heart, and suggested that if any adversity were to befall Job he would no longer be pious ; Job, exposed to hard trials, remained firm in his faith in God. " Naked came I forth from my mother's womb, and naked shall I return thither ; the Lord hath given, and the Lord hath taken : let the name of the Lord be praised " (i. 21). " Skin for skin," said the accuser, " and everything that man hath, he giveth for his soul ; but stretch now forth thy hand and touch his bone and his flesh : surely he will take leave of thee in thy presence " (ii. 5). The trial was granted. And when Job's wife was surprised that Job was still holding to his integrity, adding " Take leave of God and die," he replied, " Thou speakest like the speaking of one of the wicked women. Are we to accept of God the good, and shall we not accept the evil ? "—" In all this did Job not sin with his lips, and did not find fault with God " (i. 22). His friends came to see him, but felt so distressed that they sat with him for seven days without uttering a word.

(*b.*) *Discussion* between Job and his friends Eliphaz, Bildad, Zophar, and Elihu ; Job asserting his innocence, and consequent inability to see the justice of his afflictions ; his friends contending that he has sinned, and has been justly punished ; Elihu attempts to justify Job's sufferings, on the plea that they are merely a reminder sent by God that Job has sinned, and must seek reconciliation with God, who is All-wise, All-good, and All-powerful ; God addresses Job, and shows him man's inability to comprehend the

Divine power and wisdom in the creation and in the ruling of the universe; whereupon Job repents.

(*e.*) *Conclusion.*—God rebukes the friends of Job, that they have not spoken rightly like His servant Job (xlii. 7), and richly compensates Job for his sufferings and losses.

The book has no heading, and therefore we do not know by whom or when it was written. There is, however, a tradition, mentioned in the Talmud (Baba Bathra, p. 14*b*), that Moses wrote the Book of Job. Even about Job himself it is impossible to ascertain at what time he lived. But the description of his riches and the length of his life leads us to think of the time of the patriarchs. His name is mentioned only in one other book of the Bible. The prophet Ezekiel names him together with Noah and Daniel as a righteous man who would, by his piety, save himself in the time of general calamity, though he would not be able to save his generation (Ezek. xiv. 14). There is also an opinion that Job never existed at all. איוב לא היה ולא נברא אלא משל היה "Job never lived; nor has he had any existence; the story is all only an allegory" (Babyl. Talm. Baba Bathra, 15*a*). This dictum can only refer to the detailed account of the manner in which the misfortune came upon Job, and the poetical discussion of Job and his friends. But it is undeniable that a pious man of the name of Job lived, and escaped from a calamity to which others succumbed; since it is clear that Ezekiel refers to real and not to imaginary personages. Job and his friends were not Israelites. The patriarch lived in the land of Uz in Arabia; the friends came from Teman, Shuah, Naamah, and Buz, in the south, east, west, and north of Uz. Like the Book of **Jonah**, this book conveys the lesson, חסידי אומות העולם יש להם חלק לעולם הבא " The pious of all nations have a portion in the world to come " (Maim., Mishneh-torah I. Hilchoth Teshubah, iii. 5). God rewards the righteous of all nations, punishes those among them who deserve punishment, and pardons the penitent.

The introduction and conclusion are written in prose, but the principal part of the book is poetical, and consequently parallelism is a predominant feature of the book.

The following are a few sentences from the book :—

" Shall we receive good at the hand of God, and shall we not receive evil ? " (ii. 10).

" The small and great are there (in the grave), and the servant is free from his master " (iii. 19).

" Shall mortal man be more just than God ? shall a man be more pure than his Maker ? " (iv. 17).

" Behold, happy is the man whom God correcteth : therefore despise not thou the chastening of the Almighty " (v. 17).

" Is there not an appointed time to man upon earth ? are not his days also like the days of an hireling ? " (vii. 1).

" He is wise in heart, and mighty in strength ; who hath hardened himself against him, and hath prospered ? " (ix. 4).

" Though he slay me, yet will I trust in him " (xiii. 15).

" For I know that my Redeemer liveth, and he will rise in the end over the dust " (xix. 25).

" And when my skin is gone, when worms have destroyed this body, and when my flesh is no more, yet shall I see God " (xix. 26).

" And unto man he said, Behold, the fear of the Lord,

that is wisdom; and to depart from evil, that is understanding" (xxviii. 28).

The following passages are noteworthy, on account of both their lofty thought and their poetical form :—

Eliphaz mildly rebukes Job, exhorting him to repentance (iv.).

Job's charge against the cruelty of his friends (v. 12–30).

Bildad's view of God's justice (viii. 3–13).

Job's conception of God's Omnipotence (ix. 2–12).

Zophar's explanation of God's justice (xi. 2–7, 10–15).

Job's declaration of his faith in God (xiii. 6–16; xix. 23–27; xxiii 3–12).

Job's confession of man's dependence on God's wisdom (xxviii. 1, 2, 12–28).

Job's defence of his innocence (xxxi.).

Elihu's defence of God's justice (xxxiii. 8, 9, 12–30).

Job is shown his ignorance (xxxviii. 3–24); his impotence (xl. 9–14).

Job's contrition (xlii. 2–6).

The three books, Psalms, Proverbs, and Job, are distinguished from the rest of the Bible by their peculiar accents, which are on this account called טעמי א״מת "the accents of the books, תהלים, משלי and איוב."

The Song of Solomon, שיר השירים (lit., The Song of Songs = the most poetical song).—The faithfulness of the beloved to her lover, her resistance to all temptation, and the concentration of all her thoughts on the well-being of her lover, form the theme of the book. The relation between lover and beloved has been interpreted allegorically as representing the relation between God and Israel. The latter remains faithful to his God, throughout all vicissitudes of fortune. " I am for my lover, and my lover is for me," is the centre of this feeling of faith. According to the heading and the tradition, King Solomon is the author of the book.

Ruth, רות—The book contains the history of Ruth, a Moabite woman, who, by her marriage with Boaz, became the founder of the house of David. Elimelech of Beth-lehem in Judah, with his wife Naomi and his two sons, left his country in time of famine in order to stay in the land of Moab. There the two sons marry Moabite women, Orpah and Ruth. Elimelech and the two sons die. Naomi returns to Judah; Orpah, at the request of Naomi, remains in Moab and goes back to her family, but Ruth insists on accompanying Naomi, saying, " Whither thou goest I will go, and where thou lodgest I will lodge ; thy people shall be my people, and thy God my God : where thou diest will I die, and there will I be buried : so the Lord do to me, and more also, if ought but death will part thee and me " (i. 16, 17).

Naomi having lost her property, Ruth was obliged to glean ears of corn in the fields in order to maintain herself and her mother-in-law. She happened to glean in the field of Boaz, a near relative of Elimelech. Boaz having noticed her, and having heard of her conduct toward Naomi, married her; his son was Obed ; the son of the latter was Jesse, the father of David. Thus the virtues of Ruth, modesty, faithfulness, and industry, were rewarded ; this is one of the lessons derived from the book. The principal object of the book, however, is to show the origin of the house of David.

The *Lamentations* of Jeremiah, איכה—The name of

the author is not mentioned in the book, but tradition informs us that the prophet Jeremiah composed these lamentations. The first four chapters are alphabetical; in the third chapter there are three verses for each letter; the fifth chapter is not alphabetical. The cause of the lamentations is the catastrophe of the kingdom of Judah through the victories of Nebuchadnezzar, king of Babylon, although neither Nebuchadnezzar nor Babylon is mentioned in the book.

Ecclesiastes, קהלת—This book contains reflections on the vanity of man's labours and plans; whatever man aims at as the source of his happiness and blessing proves in the end useless and deceptive. Man is disappointed to find everything transient; he discovers just people in misery, and wicked people in apparent comfort; he begins to doubt whether virtue and wisdom are really conducive to true happiness. Thus man, left to himself, is at a loss to find the right way to happiness. The author therefore concludes his reflections with the exhortation: "The end of the word in which everything is heard is, *Fear God, and keep His commandments, for that is the whole of man.* For every deed will God bring to account, together with every hidden thought, whether good or bad" (xii. 13, 14).

Koheleth mentioned in the heading is King Solomon. The philosophical reflections are frequently intermixed with proverb-like lessons and maxims, of which the following are a few examples:—

"For in much wisdom is much grief; and he that increaseth knowledge increaseth sorrow" (i. 18).
"To every thing there is a season, and a time to every purpose under the heaven" (iii. 1).

"The fool foldeth his hands together, and eateth his own flesh" (iv. 5).

"Better is an handful with quietness, than both the hands full with travail and vexation of spirit" (iv. 6).

"Keep thy foot when thou goest to the house of God, and readiness to hear is better than the fools' giving of sacrifice; for they consider not that they do evil" (iv. 17).

"Be not rash with thy mouth, and let not thine heart be hasty to utter any thing before God: for God is in heaven, and thou upon earth; therefore let thy words be few" (v. 1).

"When thou vowest a vow unto God, defer not to pay it; for He hath no pleasure in fools: pay that which thou hast vowed" (v. 3).

"A good name is better than precious ointment; and the day of death better than the day of one's birth" (vii. 1).

"Be not hasty in thy spirit to be angry; for anger resteth in the bosom of fools" (vii. 9).

"Be not righteous over much; neither make thyself over wise: why shouldst thou destroy thyself?" (vii. 16).

"Be not over much wicked, neither be thou foolish: why shouldst thou die before thy time?" (vii. 17).

"There is not a just man upon earth, that doth good, and sinneth not" (vii. 20).

"Let thy garments be always white; and let thy head lack no ointment" (ix. 8).

"A wise man's heart is at his right hand; but a fool's heart at his left" (x. 2).

'He that diggeth a pit shall fall into it; and whoso breaketh an hedge, a serpent shall bite him" (x. 8).

"He that observeth the wind shall not sow; and he that
  regardeth the clouds shall not reap" (xi. 4).

"Remember now thy Creator in the days of thy youth,
  while the evil days come not, nor the years draw
  nigh when thou shalt say, I have no pleasure in
  them" (xii. 1).

"Then shall the dust return to the earth as it was, and the
  spirit shall return to the God who gave it" (xii. 7).

Esther, אסתר—The history of the conception and
frustration of the wicked plans of Haman against
Mordecai and the Jews is described in this book.
Ahasuerus, king of Persia, sent Vashti, his wife,
away, and married Esther, a cousin of Mordecai.
Haman, enraged against the Jews because Mordecai
did not bow before him, planned to kill the Jews on
the thirteenth of Adar; but Esther frustrated Haman's
design; Haman himself and his ten sons were killed;
and the Jews were allowed to take up arms against
those who attacked them. The Jews defended themselves victoriously on the thirteenth of Adar; in
Shushan, the capital, also on the fourteenth. This
deliverance was the cause of the institution of Purim.

The name of the author is not mentioned; the book
was probably written by Mordecai and Esther (comp.
Esther ix. 29).

Daniel, דניאל—The author of this book is not named.
The book is called Daniel because it contains the
history and the visions of Daniel. According to a
tradition mentioned in the Babylonian Talmud (Baba
Bathra, 15*a*), the men of the Great Synagogue wrote
or edited the book probably from trustworthy traditions, partly written, partly oral. The last six

chapters seem to have been written by Daniel himself; he speaks in them of himself in the first person.

The object of the book is to show that God is the Ruler of the Universe. The author, therefore, gives, on the one hand, examples of men of great piety and genuine faith in God—Daniel and his friends; and, on the other hand, examples of men of great wickedness—Nebuchadnezzar and Belshazzar; the former enjoyed glorious victories, the latter received their due punishment. The style is throughout bold and emphatic; the frequent heaping of synonyms is to serve the purpose of emphasis. In the last chapters the author shows that the misdeeds of the wicked and the sufferings of the pious are foreseen by God, and that both the punishment of the former and the redemption of the latter form part of the Divine plan in the government of mankind. We are thus exhorted to remain firm in our faith in time of oppression, and to wait patiently for deliverance, which is sure to come.

Although Daniel belonged to those distinguished men to whom God communicated coming events in visions, he is not classed among the prophets, because he had no Divine message to bring to his fellow-men, and he was not charged to address them in the name of God. Daniel was brought to Babylon, together with other captives, in the third year of Jehoiakim, and remained there during the reigns of Nebuchadnezzar, Belshazzar, Darius the Mede, and the first years of Cyrus the Persian. He distinguished himself by great piety and wisdom, so that in a prophecy of Ezekiel (xiv. 14), in the sixth year of the exile of King Jehoiachin, he is mentioned, together with Noah and Job, as famous for piety, as one of those whom God protects from danger because of their righteousness, although their piety could not save their fellow-men. The same prophet mentions him as a wise man (xxviii. 3).

The book is divided into two parts : (A.) An account written in Chaldee of Daniel's wisdom and piety, with a Hebrew Introduction (i. to vi.). (2.) The visions of Daniel in Chaldee and Hebrew (vii. to xii.). In the introductory chapter the author narrates the principal facts of the training of Daniel in Babylonian wisdom, and his great success at the court of Nebuchadnezzar. Then follows the Chaldee portion, including the following subjects :—

(1.) *Nebuchadnezzar's Dream.*—The king demands that the sages initiated in Babylonian wisdom shall tell him his dream, which he himself has forgotten, and its interpretation. They cannot do it, and many of them are put to death. Daniel arrests the slaughter; for he prays to God, and God reveals to him the king's dream.

When Daniel appeared before the king he began thus : " The secret which the king wants to know, no wise men can tell. But there is a God in heaven, the revealer of secrets, and He has let King Nebuchadnezzar know what will come to pass in the remote future " (ii. 27, 28). The dream was this : He saw a big statue, its head of gold, breast and arms of silver, belly and thighs of brass, legs and feet of iron and clay. A large stone fell upon the legs of the statue, broke them, and the whole statue fell together and was crushed into pieces ; then the stone grew larger, and filled the whole earth. The following was the interpretation of the vision : The statue represented a series of earthly kingdoms; the gold was Nebuchadnezzar, the silver referred to his successors, the brass to the Persian government, the iron to the Greek, and the mixture of iron and clay to the kingdoms that would then follow, all of which would ultimately be overthrown, and the Divine kingdom would then be recognised by all. Daniel was greatly rewarded; he and his friends received high positions in the government of the empire.

(2.) Nebuchadnezzar erected a large statue, and commanded that at certain times all should worship it; disobedience was to be punished with death. Daniel's friends did not bow before it, and were accused before the king. They said to the king, "There is a God whom we worship; he can save us from the burning furnace and from thy hand, O king. And if he does not save us, let it be known to thee, O king, that we shall not worship thy god, and not bow down before the golden image which thou hast set up" (iii. 17, 18).

They were thrown into the furnace, and miraculously saved. Thereupon Nebuchadnezzar sends letters to all the peoples of his empire, testifying to the greatness of God, and narrating what wonderful thing had occurred to him. He had a strange dream, and none but Daniel was able to interpret it; the dream was literally fulfilled according to Daniel's interpretation. The dream, which, after the manner of such phenomena, introduced and mingled together diverse elements, was this: He saw a high tree with many branches and much foliage. Suddenly an angel from heaven came, and ordered the tree to be cut down, but the root to be left for seven seasons, bound with fetters of iron and brass, in the midst of the grass of the field. The heart of man was to be taken from it, and replaced by a heart of beasts. The interpretation was, that the mighty Nebuchadnezzar would be removed from the society of man, and live like a beast with beasts for seven seasons. This happened to him just when he was boasting of his greatness and said, "Is this not great Babylon which I have built for the royal house, in my great power, and to my great glory?" (iv. 27). He was humbled, recognised the dominion of God over the whole universe, and was again, after seven seasons, restored to his former power and dignity. "Praised be God," he exclaimed, "whose deeds are all truth, and whose ways are justice, and who can humble those who walk in pride" (*Ibid.* 34).

(3.) King Belshazzar, in the midst of a banquet, at which the holy vessels of the Temple in Jerusalem were used, perceived a hand writing on the wall opposite him strange signs which none could read. Daniel was called, and read the writing: "*Mene, mene, tekel upharsin,*" and explained it thus: The days of thy government are counted and brought to a close; thou hast been weighed and found wanting; thy kingdom is divided, and given to the Medes and Persians (v. 25–28). That same night King Belshazzar was killed, and the Mede Darius was made king (v. 30–vi. 1).

(4.) King Darius, advised by his officers, who sought to find an opportunity for overthrowing Daniel, issued an order, that within thirty days no god or other being except Darius should be prayed to, and that transgressors against this decree should be punished with death. Daniel prayed to God three times a day at his open window. He was thrown into the lions' den; but God protected him from the mouths of the lions. When he was taken out of the den, his accusers were thrown into it, and the lions immediately devoured them. Thus Darius was forced publicly to recognise the Omnipotence of God.

(5.) A dream of Daniel is related by the author in Daniel's own words, who had written down the dream, and explained the chief points.[1] The following is the dream:—He saw four beasts, viz., a lion, a bear with three ribs in its mouth, a leopard with four wings and four heads, and a fourth beast with iron teeth and ten horns, one of the horns being small, but having " a mouth speaking haughtily." In a court of justice the latter beast was sentenced to death, and the other beasts were to be deprived of their power; but respite was granted to them for a time and a season. The royal power was given to one who approached the judge appearing like a human being, and not like any of the beasts. His rule was to remain for ever. The interpretation of the dream is this: There will be four different kingdoms; out of the fourth ten different kingdoms will be formed. One of these will haughtily presume to oppose the Will of God, and to abolish the festivals and the religion of the holy ones. It will succeed for " a season, seasons, and half a season," and will then be utterly destroyed, whilst the rule of " the holy ones "[2] will in the end be firmly established and continue for ever.

[1] It seems that the author copied the dream as Daniel had written it down, but the interpretation was handed down by tradition.

[2] The Israelites. Comp. Exod. xix. 6.—Part of this vision refers to the time of the Maccabees, part to the Messianic period.

The indefinite character of the vision shows that it was intended to apply to all those oppressors of the Jews who at different times have presumed, or still presume, to be able to abolish the religion of "the holy ones." Whether the oppression lasts a "season of seasons" (or "a season and seasons"), *i.e.*, a very long time, or "half a season," *i.e.*, a very short time, the holy ones are exhorted to remain firm in their faith in God's justice. The truth of this vision is especially illustrated by the failure of the attempts of Antiochus Epiphanes after a temporary success. More definite are the numbers 2300 "evening-mornings" (viii. 14), 1290 days and 1335 days (xii. 11, 12); but the absence of any further description as to the date of the first of these days leaves even to these numbers a certain degree of indetermination. From the context we learn that they are somehow connected with the persecution to which the Jews were subjected by Antiochus Epiphanes. 2300 days (or 6 years 110 days) passed between the decree of the Syrian king enforcing idolatry and the peace with Lysias granting religious liberty; there were 1290 days between the decree forbidding the practice of the holy religion and the enforcement of idolatry in the Temple of Jerusalem, and 1335 days is the period between the latter event and the death of Antiochus.

(B.) The second part contains visions of Daniel as written down by himself.

(1.) In the third year of Belshazzar, Daniel had the following vision :—Being in Susan, in the province of Elam, near the river Ulai, he saw a ram with two unequal horns pushing towards west, north, and south. From the west came a goat with one horn, and overthrew the ram; in the place of the one horn four horns grew up in all directions; there was one small horn which pushed on against the south, the east, and Palestine; it rose even against the host of heaven and the chief of the host, and destroyed his holy place. Daniel heard one holy one saying to another, "This state of things will last till 'evening-morning 2300.'" The angel Gabriel gave him the interpretation of the vision: The ram represented the empire of the Medes and the Persians, the goat that of the Greeks, out of which four kingdoms would be formed; in one of these a wicked king would venture to rise against the Prince of princes, but his power would in the end be destroyed. Daniel was told to keep the vision secret, for it referred to a distant future (viii. 26).

(2.) In the first year of Darius, son of Ahasuerus, of the seed of the Medes, Daniel reflected on the seventy years of exile foretold by Jeremiah, and fervently prayed to God for pardon and the restoration of Jerusalem. At the end of his prayer the angel Gabriel appeared to him, and told him that the hoped-for restoration would not take place before the lapse of seventy weeks of trouble and anxiety. There would elapse seven weeks before the "princely anointed" (משיח נגיד) led the Jews back to Palestine; sixty-two weeks of trouble and anxiety were predicted for the time of the rebuilding of Jerusalem and the Temple; and one week's misery on the arrival of a new prince or governor, who would strengthen the covenant of the enemies and entirely suspend the Divine Service in the Temple for a short time.[1]

(3.) In the third year of Cyrus, king of Persia, Daniel, after three weeks' mourning and fasting, had the following vision on the twenty-fourth day of the first month :—He saw near the river Tigris (Hiddekel) a man of extraordinary appearance, who told him that he came in answer to his prayers ; that for twenty-one days (x. 13) he was opposed by the prince of the kingdom of Persia, and had on his side only one of the princes, Michael. Future events are fore-told : the fall of Persia, the division of the Greek king-dom, the wars between the Northern country (Syria) and the Southern (Egypt), the troubles of the Jews, the ultimate deliverance of the Jews out of danger, and the glorious victory of the teachers " who taught many, and led them to righteousness" (המשכילים ומצדקי הרבים xii. 3). When Daniel asked, " Till when have we to wait for the end of these wondrous things ? " (עד מתי קץ הפלאות Ibid. 6), he was told, " After a season, seasons, and a half (למועד מועדים וחצי Ibid. 7)[2] all these things will come to an end." He further asks, " What then ? " He is told, " The things must remain sealed till the time of the end (עד עת קץ Ibid. 9), when the wise and good (משכילים) will understand them." The vision ends with the words addressed to Daniel : " But thou go toward the end, and thou wilt rest, and rise for thy lot at the end of the days " (xii. 13).

[1] Some are of opinion that the term "weeks" is not to be taken literally, but in the sense of "year," or "a period of seven years." There is, however, no proof for such interpretation. The many attempts to explain the seventy year-weeks have without exception proved a failure.   [2] See p. 121.

Ezra, עזרא—The Book of Ezra relates the first return of the Jews under Zerubbabel from Babylon to Palestine by the permission of King Cyrus (כורש) of Persia, the construction of the altar, the foundation and the building of the Temple by permission of King Darius. It also describes the second settlement of Jews from Babylon in Palestine under Ezra, the Scribe, in the reign of Artaxerxes, and his energy in purifying the community from intermarriages with heathen people. The book is written in Hebrew, with the exception of iv. 8—vii. 27, which includes several documents written in Chaldee by the Persian kings. The author of the book is probably Ezra; he speaks of himself in the first person (vii. 28; viii. 1, &c.); he is also named as the author of the book in the Babylonian Talmud; and lastly, the name of the book is Ezra, although Ezra is only mentioned in the second half of the book. The special merit of Ezra was the promotion of the study of the Law; his name is followed by the title, " A ready scribe of the Law of Moses " (סופר מהיר בתורת ה' vii. 6), and " Scribe of the words of the commandments of the Lord and His statutes for Israel " (ספר דברי מצות ה' וחקיו על ישראל vii. 11); the task he set to himself was " to study the Law of God (לדרוש את תורת ה'), and to practise it, and to teach in Israel Law and judgment " (vii. 10).

Nehemiah, נחמיה—The heading probably indicates the author, " Words of Nehemiah, son of Hachaliah." [1] The book contains the history of Nehemiah's visit to Jerusalem by the permission of King Artaxerxes, and

---

[1] It is, however, possible that דברי, lit. " words," means here " history."

the building of the walls of Jerusalem under Nehemiah's supervision, in spite of the opposition of Sanballat and Tobiah the Ammonite; his example of disinterestedness and of liberality towards the poor, which is followed by the princes and the rich; the reading and expounding of the Law by Ezra; the celebration of the festival of the first of Tishri and of Tabernacles; the renewal of the covenant "to walk in the Law of God, which was given through Moses the servant of God," to keep Sabbath, to abstain from intermarrying with the heathen, and to contribute towards maintaining the Sanctuary; the provision for filling Jerusalem with inhabitants by selecting by lot one-tenth of the general population to dwell in the holy city; the dedication of the walls of Jerusalem; and Nehemiah's energy in enforcing the laws of Sabbath and of marriages. The two books Ezra and Nehemiah are also called by some "two books of Ezra," and by some "the book of Ezra." Nehemiah is written in Hebrew.

The Chronicles, דברי הימים—The two books of Chronicles contain the following three parts: (1) Genealogical tables (I., i.–ix.); (2) the history of the death of King Saul, the history of David and Solomon (I., x.–II., ix.); (3) the history of the kingdom of Judah from Rehoboam till the destruction of Jerusalem by Nebuchadnezzar (II., x.–xxxvi.). Special attention has been given by the author to the arrangements made at various periods for the Temple-service, by King David (I., xxiii. *sqq.*), King Hezekiah (II., xxix.), and King Josiah (II., xxxiv., xxxv.).

The author is not named in the book; according to the tradition it is Ezra. As the genealogical tables give six generations after Zerubbabel (I., iii. 19—24), we may assume that the author wrote about fifty years after Zerubbabel; that is, the last years of Ezra and Nehemiah.

The sources from which the author derived his information were, besides the Biblical books, the following:—The book of the kings of Judah; the book of the kings of Israel, registers probably kept in the Temple archives; the histories of Samuel the Seer, Nathan the prophet, and Gad the Seer; the prophecy of Ahijah of Shilo; the visions of Jedo; the Midrash of the prophet Iddo; the history of Jehu, son of Hanani; the history of Isaiah, son of Amoz, and the history of Hozai.

This is the last book of the series of Holy Writings. Books that were written later, whatever their intrinsic value may be, were not considered holy, and were not received into this collection. There are a number of books known as Apocrypha (גנוזים), lit. "Hidden things" or "put aside," that is, kept separate from the Holy Scriptures. They were not considered as genuine, as they consisted of a mixture of fact and fiction, truth and error. They were, however, not suppressed or forbidden; in the Talmud several quotations from these books are met with. The following are the principal books belonging to the Apocrypha:—

(1.) *The Book of Wisdom*, or the Wisdom of Solomon. Wisdom based on the fear of God, and guided by it, is the source of man's true happiness, and if wisdom and virtue are not rewarded by success in mundane affairs, the reward is sure to come in the future world. This is the quintessence of the lessons taught in this book.

The kings and potentates of the earth are frequently exhorted to be just and kind towards their people, and to remember that they are but human beings, weak and mortal, like the rest of mankind; wisdom alone can raise them to higher perfection and happiness.

"For the very true beginning of her is the desire of discipline, and the care of discipline is love. And love is the keeping of her laws; and the giving heed unto her laws is the assurance of incorruption. And incorruption maketh us near God. Therefore the desire of wisdom bringeth to a kingdom. If your delight be then in thrones and sceptres, O ye kings of the people, honour wisdom, that ye may reign for evermore" (vi. 17–21).

"For regarding not wisdom, they got not only this hurt, that they knew not the things which were good, but also left behind them to the world a memorial of their foolishness, so that in the things wherein they offended they could not so much as be hid. But wisdom delivered from pain those that attended upon her. When the righteous fled from his brother's wrath, she guided him into right paths, shewed him the kingdom of God, and gave him knowledge of holy things that made him rich in his travels, and multiplied the fruit of his labours" (x. 8–10).

(2.) *The Wisdom of Jesus, son of Sirach.*—Proverbs, maxims, and moral lessons collected by Joshua (Jesus), son of Sirach of Jerusalem. After having studied the Law, the Prophets, and the other Holy Writings, he thought it advisable to write a book on knowledge and wisdom for those who seek instruction, in order to lead them to greater obedience to the Law. Joshua's grandson migrated from Palestine to Egypt, and translated the work of his grandfather into Greek for those who could not read the Hebrew original. The translation was made in the thirty-eighth year of King Euergetes II. of Egypt (3888 A.M.).

The contents of the book are similar to those of the Proverbs of Solomon : the author recommends the acquisition of wisdom, patience, faith in God, meekness, obedience of children to parents, charity, cautiousness in the use of the tongue, temperance, honesty, and the like. As models of piety and wisdom the principal heroes in the Bible, from Adam to Joshua, son of Jehozadak, are named, and in addition to these Simon the high priest.

"My son, if thou come to serve the Lord, prepare thy soul for temptation. Set thy heart aright, and constantly endure, and make not haste in time of trouble. Cleave unto him, and depart not away, that thou mayest be increased at thy last end. Whatsoever is brought upon thee take cheerfully, and be patient when thou art changed to a low estate. For gold is tried in the fire, and acceptable men in the furnace of adversity. Believe in him, and he will help thee : order thy way aright, and trust in him " (ii. 1–6).

"But he that giveth his mind to the law of the Most High, and is occupied in the meditation thereof, will seek out the wisdom of the most ancient, and be occupied in prophecies. He will keep the sayings of most renowned men, and where subtle parables are, He will be there also. He will seek out the secrets of grave sentences, and be conversant in dark parables " (xxxix. 1–3).

(3.) *Baruch.*—The book may be divided into two

I

parts.   In the first part Baruch, son of Nerijah, the amanuensis of the prophet Jeremiah, addresses, in Babylon, Jehoiachin, the captive king of Judah, and the other captive Jews; they send money to Jerusalem for sacrifices, with a letter exhorting their brethren to return to God, and comforting them with the prospect of a glorious future.   The second part contains a letter of Jeremiah to his brethren in Jerusalem denouncing idolatry.

The letters are probably not genuine, not being in harmony with the facts related in the books of Jeremiah and Kings.

(4.) *The Book of Tobit.*—Tobit, of the tribe of Naphtali, a good and pious man, was one of those who were carried away into the Assyrian captivity.   One of the charitable acts to which he devoted himself with special zeal was the burying of the dead.   Twice was misfortune brought upon him for practising this deed of piety.   Once he had to flee, and to remain away from his family in misery and want, and a second time something fell into his eyes, and he became blind. In both cases he was saved out of his trouble, and was greatly rewarded for his patience, his faith in God, and his perseverance in the performance of the Divine commandments.   The author of the book is not known.

(5.) *Judith.*—An incident of Jewish history during the Persian rule.   Judith is set forth as an ideal of piety, beauty, courage, and chastity.   Holofernes, a general in the service of Nebuchadnezzar, king of Assyria, conquers many lands, but meets with vigorous resistance in Judea; he besieges Bethulia and endeavours to suppress the Jewish religion.   He falls by the hands of Judith. Thus the stratagem and the courage of the Jewish heroine, combined with the plans of Divine justice, frustrated the wicked plans of the heathen conqueror, and delivered the besieged city.

(6.) Additions to the Books of Daniel and Ezra, containing—

(*a.*) The song of the three men in the furnace (Dan. iii.).

(*b.*) The false charges brought against Susanna, and her deliverance through Daniel.

(*c.*) Bel and the Dragon. Cyrus, the Persian, worshipped these idols, but was convinced by Daniel that they had no claim whatever to man's worship.

(*d.*) The apocryphal Book of Esdras, containing portions of the Books of Chronicles, Ezra, and Nehemiah; only chaps. iii. and iv. being original. In these it is related how Zerubbabel distinguished himself before King Darius in describing Woman and Truth as the mightiest rulers of mankind, and thus obtained permission to return to Palestine and rebuild the Temple. A second apocryphal Book of Esdras is named, in which Ezra is represented as a prophet addressing his brethren in the name of God, and telling them the visions he had.

(7.) *The Books of the Maccabees.*—Three books containing the history of the Maccabees, and various episodes of the wars against the Syrian oppressors, both legendary and historical.

Sixth Principle.—"*I firmly believe that all the words of the Prophets are true.*"

By " the Prophets " the prophets thus designated in

the Bible are to be understood who have proved themselves to be the true messengers of God, and were accepted as such by the people. They either counselled
the people what to do under various circumstances, in
times of peace and in times of war, in times of security
and in times of danger, or they announced the coming
catastrophe as a punishment sent by the Almighty for
disobedience, and foretold future happiness and prosperity in case of improvement and return to God. Those
prophecies that referred to the proximate future have
been verified by subsequent events, and so also will
those prophecies that refer to the remote future and
have not yet been fulfilled.

"A prophet out of thy midst, of thy brethren, like
unto me, will the Lord thy God raise up unto thee;
unto him ye shall hearken" (Deut. xviii. 15). "The
former things, behold, they are come to pass, and new
things do I declare; before they will spring forth, I
shall let you hear" (Isa. xlii. 9). "I have also spoken
unto the prophets, and I have multiplied visions, and
by the ministry of the prophets have I used simili-
tudes" (Hosea xii. 11). "And by a prophet the Lord
brought Israel out of Egypt, and by a prophet was he
preserved" (*Ibid.* 14).

In the sixth article we declare our belief in the
fact that the Almighty has communicated His Will
to human beings, although we are incapable of forming
a clear and definite idea of the manner in which such
communication took place. The selection of the individual for the office of a prophet, as well as of the time,
the place, and the object of the Divine communication,
is dependent solely on the Will of God, whose Wisdom

and Plan no mortals are able to fathom. We know only the fact that Malachi closed the series of Prophets, but are ignorant of the reason why since Malachi no human being has " found a vision from the Lord." Mankind is, however, not altogether deprived of the benefit of prophecy ; the holy book need only be opened, and the message of the prophets is heard once more.

Seventh Principle.—" *I firmly believe that the prophecy of Moses was a direct prophecy, and that Moses was the chief of the prophets, both of those who preceded him and of those who followed him.*"

All that has been said with regard to the sixth article applies to the prophecy of Moses. There is, however, this distinction between the words of Moses and the words of other prophets :—whilst other prophets chiefly addressed their own generation, blaming their brethren for disobedience to the Divine Law, threatening with punishments and comforting with blessings of which experience was to be made in the remote future, Moses addresses all times and generations, communicating to them laws "for all generations," "everlasting statutes," "the things which have been revealed for us and our children for ever." He is therefore proclaimed by the Almighty as the greatest prophet. Whem Miriam and Aaron had spoken against Moses, God rebuked them, saying, " If there be among you a prophet of the Lord, I will make myself known unto him in a vision, I will speak with him in a dream. My servant Moses is not so ; he is faithful in all my house ; with him will I speak mouth to mouth, even manifestly, and not in dark speeches ; and the form of the Lord shall he behold " (Num. xii. 6–8). The

Torah concludes with the praise of Moses, as follows: "And there hath not arisen a prophet since in Israel like unto Moses, whom the Lord knew face to face : in all the signs and the wonders, which the Lord sent him to do in the land of Egypt, to Pharaoh, and to all his servants, and to all his land ; and in all the mighty hand, and in all the great terror, which Moses wrought in the sight of all Israel " (Deut. xxxiv. 10—12)

The phrase "knew God face to face," or "I will speak with him mouth to mouth," and the like, denotes figuratively " the clearest, most direct, and most simple communication," the figure being taken from the way in which men communicate to each other things when they desire to be clearly understood, and to leave no doubt as to the truth and the meaning of the communication.

Eighth Principle.—"I firmly believe that the Law which we possess now is the same which has been given to Moses on Sinai."

The whole Torah, including both history and precepts, is of Divine origin ; nothing is contained in the Torah that was not revealed to Moses by the Almighty, although we do not know in what manner Moses received the information. The history of preceding generations was probably handed down to his time by tradition ; in part it may have been contained in documents then extant, as is likely to have been the case with the various genealogies mentioned in the Pentateuch. But it was by Divine inspiration that Moses knew to distinguish between truth and error, between fiction and reality. The events recorded in the Pentateuch are to demonstrate and to keep constantly before our eyes the fact that there is a higher Power that ordains the fate of men and nations according to their deeds. Everything is described in a simple and objective manner. Although the whole Torah is the work of Moses, the great prophet speaks of himself everywhere in the third person, except in the Book of Deuteronomy, in which he records his addresses to the people in the last year of his life.

The last few verses, which describe the death of Moses, the mourning of the Israelites for the death of their teacher, and his exaltation above all other prophets, have been added to the Torah by Joshua the son of Nun, the leader of the Israelites after the death of Moses. Thus, from that day until the present the Torah, in its integrity, has been in the hands of the children of Israel. It was guarded as the most valuable national treasure, and although there have been not a few generations which were corrupt and idolatrous, Israel has never been entirely bereaved of pious and faithful worshippers of the true God; and when in one generation or period the study and the practice of the Torah were neglected, they were resumed with greater vigour and zeal in the next.

There is a tradition recorded in the Talmud that after the Babylonian exile Ezra, the Scribe, replaced the ancient Hebrew characters in which the Torah had originally been written by the square characters still in use. Nothing, however, was omitted from or added to the contents of the Torah, when the present forms of the letters were introduced by Ezra. In the scrolls of the Law the letters were not provided with vowel-points and accents; the manner in which the words, phrases, and sentences were to be read was a subject of oral teaching. Also many explanations and details of the laws were supplemented by oral teaching ; they were handed down by word of mouth from generation to generation, and only after the destruction of the second Temple were they committed to writing. The latter are, nevertheless, called Oral Law (תורה שבעל פה), as distinguished from the Torah or Written Law (תורה שבכתב), which from the first was committed to writing. Those oral laws which were revealed to Moses on Mount Sinai are called הלכה למשה מסיני "Laws given to Moses on Mount Sinai." There are several passages in the Bible from which it appears that a certain unwritten law must have supplemented the written Law ; *e.g.*, when a man was found in the wilderness gathering sticks on the Sabbath-day, the persons who discovered him brought him to Moses. They must have been taught before, that the gathering of sticks constituted a מלאכה, labour prohibited on the Sabbath-day, although this had not been distinctly stated in the written Sabbath-laws. Had this not been the case the Sabbath-breaker could not have been put to death, since he would have committed the sin in ignorance. The same can be said of the man who cursed the name of God ; he must have known that cursing the name of God was a capital crime ; for he would not have been put to death if the Israelites had not yet been taught that death would be inflicted for such an act. The question which the prophet Haggai (ii. 11) addressed to the priests, and the answers which the priests gave, lead to the conclusion that the details of the laws on uncleanness and cleanness (טומאה וטהרה) must have been known to the priests and the prophets to a greater extent than has been explained in the written Law. Besides, there were many precepts that came at once into force. These must have been fully explained to the people, who were anxious to obey the word of God.

All these explanations and the detailed rules with regard to the written Divine precepts of the Pentateuch, together with laws and institutions established in the course of time by the highest authorities of the nation in obedience to the dictates of the Pentateuch, form the contents of the Oral Law.

The Oral Law or the Tradition has been handed down in two different forms: (*a*) in the form of a running Commentary on the Pentateuch; such Commentaries were called *Midrashim;* (*b*) arranged according to the different subjects, and treated independently of the text of the Torah. This is done in the *Talmud* ("lesson," "tradition").

The principal Midrashim are: *Mechilta* (lit. "measure") on Exodus; *Sifra* ("book") on Leviticus; *Sifre* ("books") on Numbers and Deuteronomy. *Rabboth* on the Pentateuch and the five *Megilloth*. *Yalkut* ("collection") on all the books of the Bible.

The Talmud—which exists in two different recensions, viz., the Jerusalem Talmud and the Babylonian Talmud—consists of two elements, which have to each other the relation of text and commentary, and are called *Mishnah* (משנה "learnt by heart"), and *Gemara* (גמרא lit. "completion," "a thing settled"); the former contains the traditional laws mostly without argumentation; in the latter these laws are further discussed, examined, and finally settled. Following the example of the Pentateuch, the Talmud includes two elements : laws and narratives, or *Halachah* (הלכה) and *Agada* (אגדא) ; the latter, the Agada, contains history, fables, allegory, meditations, prayers, reflections, philosophical and religious discussions, and a large number of moral sayings. The Midrashim likewise include these two elements.

The Mishnah is divided into the following six *orders* or sections (סדרים) : [1]—

1. זרעים " *Seeds.*" Laws referring to agriculture ; preceded by laws on Divine Worship.

2. מועד " *Seasons.*" On Sabbath and Festivals.

3. נשים " *Women.*" Marriage Laws.

4. נזיקן " *Damages.*" Civil and criminal legislation ; the Government.

5. קדשים " *Holy things.*" On Sacrifices.

6. טהרות " *Purity.*" On the distinction between *clean* and *unclean.*

The laws taught in the Talmud are : (1) those which are directly or indirectly derived from the text of the Pentateuch ; they are called " laws derived from the Torah " (מן התורה or מדאוריתא) ; (2) those which trace their origin to the time of Moses, or, in general, to the remote past ; they are called הלכה למשה מסיני " Law given to Moses on Sinai ; " (3) those laws which originated between the period of the Penta-teuch and the close of the Bible ; they are called דברי קבלה ("words of tradition ") ; (4) those which have been introduced in post-Biblical times ; they are laws מדרבנן " laws introduced by our teachers." These are either preventives against breaking any of the

---

[1] The Talmud is also called ש"ס (*Shass*), the initials of ששה סדרים.

Divine precepts, and are then called נֶּדֶרֶת or סְיָג "a fence," or *tekanoth* (תקנות "institutions" or "regulations") made in order to ensure obedience to the Law and improvement of conduct, to remove abuses and prevent error and misunderstanding; (5) *Minhag,* "Custom" (מנהג); religious practices which have not been introduced by any authority or based on a particular Biblical text, but in consequence of long usage have become as sacred as a law established by the proper authority.

These laws, as finally settled, were again codified, in various works, the most important of which are the following two: (1) *Mishneh-torah* (משנה תורה or יד החזקה [1] lit. "Copy of the Law," or "Strong Hand"), by Moses Maimonides (twelfth century) in fourteen books; (2) *Shulchan-aruch* (שלחן ערוך, lit. "Table-arranged"), by Rabbi Joseph Caro (sixteenth century).

Ninth Principle.—"*I firmly believe that this Law will not be changed, and that there will not be any other Law given by the Creator, blessed be His Name.*"

In this article we pronounce our belief in the immutability of the Law. Over and over again the phrase "an everlasting statute" (חקת עולם) occurs in the Pentateuch. It is true that the Hebrew term עולם is used in the Bible in the sense of "a very long time," but in the phrase חקת עולם the word cannot have that meaning. Some indication would have been necessary to inform the people when the laws would cease to be in force. On the contrary, the test of a prophet addressing his brethren in the name of God, as a

---

[1] The word יד is intended to indicate the number 14, the work being divided into 14 books.

Divine messenger, consists in the harmony of his words with the precepts of the Pentateuch. A prophet who, speaking in the name of God, abrogates any of the laws of the Pentateuch is a false prophet. "If there arise in the midst of thee a prophet or a dreamer of dreams, and he give thee a sign or a wonder, and the sign or wonder come to pass whereof he spake unto thee, saying, Let us go after other gods which thou hast not known, and let us serve them : thou shalt not hearken unto the words of that prophet or unto that dreamer of dreams. . . . Ye shall walk after the Lord your God, and fear him, and keep his commandments, and obey his voice, and ye shall serve him, and cleave unto him. And that prophet or that dreamer of dreams shall be put to death; because he hath spoken rebellion against the Lord your God, which brought you out of the land of Egypt, . . . to draw thee aside out of the way which the Lord thy God commanded thee to walk in " (Deut. xiii. 2–6). Moses distinctly says, "The things that are revealed belong unto us and to our children for ever, that we may do all the words of this law " (*Ibid.* xxix. 28).

There is also an express commandment given : " Ye shall not add unto the word which I command you, neither shall you diminish from it, that ye may keep the commandments of the Lord your God which I command you " (*Ibid.* iv. 2). In two ways this law may appear to have been disregarded : there are certain sections of the Law which are at present not in force ; and, on the other hand, there are many apparently new precepts at present in force which have been introduced in the course of time by the religious authori-

ties of the nation. But these are only apparent exceptions; in reality they are entirely in harmony with the
Pentateuch.

As to the first class, there are many of the Divine
commandments the fulfilment of which depends on certain conditions; *e.g.*, the existence of the Tabernacle or
of the Temple and its service, the possession of Palestine
by the Israelites, the independence of the Jewish State.
In the absence of these conditions such laws cannot be
fulfilled. The laws of sacrifices belong to this class.
We are, in reference to these laws, in the same condition as a person who is physically prevented from
doing what he is commanded to do, and what he is
actually longing to do. The Law is not altered; our
circumstances demand a *temporary* suspense of such
laws and not their abrogation.

The second class contains all those precepts which
are known as מצות דרבנן "Rabbinical precepts," תקנות
and מנהגים "Institutions" and "Customs." But these
imply no addition to the Torah; they are merely bye-
laws and regulations as regards the method of carrying
out the laws of the Pentateuch, and are designed to
facilitate or ensure their fulfilment, and to prevent
ourselves from forgetting or disregarding them. Our
teachers, the Rabbis, made it a matter of conscience
to describe their own regulations as דרבנן non-Pen-
tateuchical, and throughout the Oral Law and the
entire Talmudic literature the distinction between
דרבנן and מן התורה is noted and scrupulously upheld.

It is useless to investigate whether it would be in
harmony with the immutability of the Divine Being
to change the laws or any of them, or to grant a new

revelation. Certainly the words " I, the Lord, have not changed " (Mal. iii. 6) have great weight ; so also, " For God is not a son of man that he should change his mind " (Num. xxiii. 19). But the fact that the laws were given by God as " an everlasting statute for all generations " makes all philosophical speculation on that point superfluous. Persons who address us in the name of God as His messengers, and bid us turn away from any of the laws commanded in the Pentateuch, are in our eyes impostors, who, knowingly or unknowingly, give forth their own opinions as Divine inspirations.

3. *Reward and Punishment,* שׂכר וענשׁ.

" Behold I have set before thee this day life and good, and death and evil : in that I command thee this day to love the Lord thy God, to walk in his ways, and to keep his commandments and his statutes and his judgments, that thou mayest live and multiply, and that the Lord thy God may bless thee in the land whither thou passest over Jordan to go in to possess it " (Deut. xxx. 15). "I call heaven and earth to witness against you this day, that I have set before thee life and death, the blessing and the curse : therefore choose life, that thou mayest live, thou and thy seed : to love the Lord thy God, to obey his voice, and to cleave unto him : for that is thy life and the length of thy days " (*Ibid.* xxx. 19, 20).

The doctrine taught in this passage is the alpha and the omega of the sacred literature. The whole history related in the Bible from the Creation to the

Babylonian captivity and the restoration of the Jews
to their land is but one continuous series of illustra-
tions of this doctrine. Obedience to God's word is
followed by His blessings, while disobedience is the
cause of ruin and misery. Thus, in Lamentations the
poet exclaims in the name of his nation, "Just is
the Lord, for I rebelled against his commandment"
(Lam. i. 18). Moses, in his last song exhorting
the people to obedience to the Almighty, begins his
address with a praise of God's justice, saying, "The
Rock, his work is perfect, for all his ways are judgment: a God of faithfulness, and without wrong,
just and right is he" (Deut. xxxii. 4). Even those
who doubted the Divine justice, in respect to the fate
of individual persons or nations, admitted, "Surely I
know that it shall be well with them that fear God,
which fear before him: but it shall not be well with
the wicked, neither shall he prolong his days, which
are as a shadow: because he feareth not before
God" (Eccles. viii. 12, 13). Job, wondering why he
should be subjected to the greatest trials, cannot
help confessing, "Even he will be to me an help, for
there shall not come before him an hypocrite" (Job
xiii. 16). God is therefore called "God of judgment,"
אלהי המשפט (Mal. ii. 17); דין "Judge" (1 Sam. xxiv.
15); צדיק "just," שופט צדיק "just Judge" (Ps. vii. 12);
אל קנא "a jealous God" (Exod. xx. 5); אל נקמות "God
of vengeance" (Ps. xciv. 1); אלהים "God" in the
sense of "Judge." The rejection of this belief by the
wicked is expressed by the phrase אין אלהים "There is
no God." Thus David exclaims, "The fool hath said
in his heart, There is no God; they are corrupt; they

have done abominable things ; there is none that doeth good " (Ps. xiv. 1). In post-Biblical literature we find this unbelief, which is characterised as the source of all corruption and wickedness, expressed by the phrase, לית דין ולית דינא "There is no judgment, and there is no judge" (Targ. Ps. Jonathan, Gen. iv. 8).

There are two different sources from which such unbelief springs forth—limitation of God's powers and limitation of man's capacities. The one of these sources leads to a denial of God's Omniscience, whilst the other deprives man of his freewill. There are some who argue that God is too high to notice the ways and the acts of individual men, and that these must be utterly insignificant in comparison with God's greatness. " They crush thy people, O Lord, and afflict thine heritage. They slay the widow and the stranger, and murder the fatherless. And they say, The Lord shall not see, neither shall the God of Jacob consider " (Ps. xciv. 5–7). "And thou sayest, What doth God know ? Can he judge through the thick darkness ? Thick clouds are a covering to him, that he seeth not ; and he walketh in the sphere of heaven " (Job xxii. 13, 14). The very words which the Psalmist addresses to God with a heart full of gratitude, " What is man that thou art mindful of him, and the son of man that thou visitest him ? " (Ps. viii. 5), are uttered in a rebellious spirit by the unbeliever, who thus " sets limits to the Holy One of Israel " (Ps. lxxviii. 41). But the power of God is not limited, nor is His wisdom or His goodness ; He is not only " the God of heaven," but also " the God of the earth." He who has created everything has certainly a knowledge of everything. "Lift up your eyes on high and see who hath created these things. He who bringeth forth by number their host, calleth all of them by name; not one of them escapeth the knowledge of him who is great in might and strong in power" (Isa. xl. 26). The Psalmist thus replies to those who deny God's Omniscience: "Consider, ye brutish among the people; and ye fools, when will ye be wise? He that planted the ear, shall he not hear; he that formed the eye, shall he not see? He that chastiseth the nations, shall he not correct, even he that teacheth man knowledge? The Lord knoweth the thoughts of man, however vain they be" (Ps. xciv. 8-11). It would indeed be absurd to imagine that the Creator of all things should not take notice of everything that His hands have made. What difference can it make to the Almighty whether He provides for the whole human race or for one individual man? It would be attributing to the Divine Being human weakness and false pride if we assumed that He is too great to take notice of any single creature of His! Rabbi Jochanan said wherever in the Bible we find a description of the greatness of God, there we find His meekness. Thus, *e.g.*, it is said in the Torah: "For the Lord, your God, he is the God of gods and the Lord of lords, the mighty, the great, the strong, and the terrible, who regardeth not persons, nor taketh reward. He doth execute the judgment of the fatherless and widow, and loveth the stranger in giving him food and raiment" (Deut. x. 17, 18).

That man is not insignificant in the eyes of God is clearly expressed in the account of the Creation,

K

where we are taught that man was made by God ruler " over the fish of the sea and over the fowl of the air, and over the cattle, and over all the earth, and over every creeping thing that creepeth upon the earth " (Gen. i. 26). " Man is loved by the Almighty," say our Sages, " because he is created in the image of God; but it was by a love still greater that it was made known to him that he was created in the image of God " (Mishnah Aboth, iii. 18).

One of the chief blessings man received at the hands of his Creator is freewill. Within certain limits man can determine his own actions. When he is about to do a thing, he can reflect on it, examine its nature, investigate into its consequences, and accordingly either do it or refrain from doing it. God said to the Israelites, " I call heaven and earth to witness against you this day, that I have set before thee life and death, the blessing and the curse; and thou shalt choose life " (Deut. xxx. 19). Our freedom, however, is not unlimited. There are various causes that prevent us from remaining firm to our will. If we resolve to do what is beyond our physical condition, we cannot carry it out. Again, if a man chooses to do what would interfere with the will of his fellow-men, he will frequently be compelled to abandon or change his own determination; especially as he is in most cases ignorant of the thoughts and plans of his fellow-men. In a still higher degree this is the case with regard to the designs of the Supreme Being. Hence the great difference between our will and our actual deeds. We have, however, the conviction that בא לטהר מסייעין לו מן השמים בא לטמא פותחין לו " He who wishes to purify himself is helped by Heaven towards his aim, while he who desires to defile himself will find the means thereto " (Babyl. Tal. Shabbath, p. 104).

We admit that there are influences over which man has no control, and which, on the contrary, help to shape his will. No man is so isolated as to be entirely inaccessible to outward influences. Man inherits certain ideas and habits from his parents ; others are forced upon him by his surroundings, especially in his earliest youth ; society and the State compel him to conform to certain notions and laws ; climate and temperature also have no small share in the formation of man's will. But in spite of all these influences man's will is free, and it is by reason of his free-will that he chooses to conform to the rules of society and the laws of the State. Hence it happens that individuals, subject to almost the same influences, still vary greatly in their resolutions. What the one praises is an abhorrence to the other ; what repels the one attracts the other ; what is recommended by the one is denounced by the other.

Although there may be many who profess to believe in predestination or fate, as a matter of fact all nations, ancient and modern, have based their constitutions on the belief in man's responsibility for his actions. Every State has its laws, its system of reward and punishment. A principle so general and so essential for the safety and welfare of society, as well as of each individual, cannot be a mere illusion ; its good effect has been tested and is generally recognised.

In case of criminals and sinners, we make allowance for the possible outward influences under which the offender may have fallen ; we assume the broad principle, אין אדם חוטא אלא אם כן נכנס בו רוח שטות "No one sinneth unless the spirit of folly has entered into him" (Babyl. Talm. Sotah, 3*a*); but no one would go so far as to acquit the sinner altogether from blame. We pity him and try to teach him how to return to the right path, and how to overcome outward evil influences. When David had become aware of the greatness of his sin and sincerely repented, he prayed, "Create in me a clean heart, O God; and renew a right spirit within me. Cast me not away from thy presence; and take not thy holy spirit from me. Restore unto me the joy of thy salvation; and uphold me with a willing spirit. Then will I teach transgressors thy ways; and sinners shall return unto thee" (Ps. li. 10—13). Both elements are here harmoniously united. God's interference is asked for; He helps man to carry out his good resolution; but man has free-will, and the author of the psalm, in seeking the assistance of God, feels nevertheless the weight of his own responsibility.

Tenth Principle.—"*I firmly believe that the Creator, blessed be His name, knoweth all the actions of men and all their thoughts, as it is said, 'He that fashioneth the hearts of them all, He that considereth all their works'* (Ps. xxxiii. 15)."

In the rhymed form of the Creed (יגדל) this article is expressed thus: "He watcheth and knoweth our secret thoughts; He beholdeth the end of a thing in its beginning." Here the author proclaims not only the Omniscience of God, but also His foresight; His knowledge is not limited, like the knowledge of mortal beings, by space and time. The entire past and future lies unrolled before His eyes, and nothing is hidden from

Him. Although we may form a faint idea of the knowledge of God by considering that faculty of man that enables him, within a limited space of time, to look backward and forward, and to unroll before him the past and the future, as if the events that have happened and those that will come to pass were going on in the present moment, yet the true nature of God's knowledge no man can conceive. " God considereth all the deeds of man," without depriving him of his free-will; he may in this respect be compared to a person who observes and notices the actions and the conduct of his fellow-men, without interfering with them. It is the Will of God that man should have free-will and should be responsible for his actions; and His foresight does not necessarily include predetermination. In some cases the fate of nations or of individual men is predetermined; we may even say that the ultimate fate or development of mankind is part of the design of the Creation. But as the actual design in the Creation is concealed from man's searching eye, so is also the extent of the predetermination a mystery to him. To solve this problem is beyond the intellectual powers of short-sighted mortals; it is one of " the hidden things that belong to the Lord our God."

David, in Ps. cxxxix. 1—12, describes the Omniscience and the Omnipresence of God in the following way: " O Lord, thou hast searched me, and known me. Thou knowest my down-sitting and mine up-rising; thou understandest my thoughts afar off. Thou searchest out my path and my lying down, and art acquainted with all my ways. For there is not a word in my tongue, but lo, O Lord, thou knowest it altogether.

Thou hast beset me behind and before, and laid thine hand upon me. Such knowledge is too wonderful for me; it is high, I cannot attain unto it. Whither shall I go from thy spirit? or whither shall I flee from thy presence? If I ascend up into heaven, thou art there; if I make my bed in the grave, behold, thou art there. If I take the wings of the morning, and dwell in the uttermost parts of the sea: even there shall thy hand lead me, and thy right hand shall hold me. If I say, Surely the darkness shall cover me, and the light about me shall be night; even the darkness hideth not from thee; but the night shineth as the day; the darkness and the light are both alike to thee."

Our belief in God's Omniscience is beautifully expressed in the Musaph prayer of New-year: "Thou rememberest the work of bygone times, and thinkest of all the imaginations of former days; all hidden things are revealed before thee; also all the multitude of hidden things which are from the beginning. For there is no forgetting before the throne of thy glory, and nothing is concealed from thine eye. Thou rememberest every deed, and no thought is hidden from thee. Everything is revealed and known before thee, O Lord our God, who beholdest and seest to the end of all generations."

Eleventh Principle.—"*I firmly believe that the Creator, blessed be He, rewards those who keep His commandments, and punishes those who transgress His commandments.*"

The immediate reward and punishment for our conduct we receive in the pleasure and happiness we experience in doing something good, and in the grief and remorse we ought to feel on learning that we have displeased the Almighty by our conduct. As a rule, every good act leads to further good acts, and every sin to further sins ; and our Sages say therefore : " The reward of a good act (מצוה) is another good act, and the punishment for a transgression is another transgression."

But when we speak of the principle of Retribution, we generally mean such reward and punishment as is given in addition to the feeling of happiness or unhappiness inseparable from our actions.

This principle of retribution has been proclaimed in the grand Revelation made to all Israel on Mount Sinai, in the Decalogue which has been accepted by all civilised nations as the basis of religion : " I the Lord thy God am a jealous God, visiting the iniquity of the fathers upon the children, upon the third and upon the fourth generation of them that hate me ; and showing mercy unto thousands of them that love me and keep my commandments" (Exod. xx. 5, 6). We understand the doctrine of retribution only in its general outlines ; we are convinced of the truth of the Divine words, " There is no peace to the wicked " (Isa. lvii. 21); but how the law is applied in every single case is known to God alone. It is presumptuous on the part of short-sighted man to criticise God's judgments, and to find injustice in the seeming prosperity of the wicked and the seeming misery of the righteous. What man is able to estimate the merits of his neighbour fully and correctly ? " For the Lord seeth not as man seeth ; for man looketh on the outward appearance, but the Lord looketh on the heart " (1 Sam. xvi. 7).

This our inability of rightly estimating the merits of our neighbour's actions, is illustrated by the Biblical narrative of Cain and Abel. Both brought sacrifices to the Lord; and we cannot discover any difference in their actions, and yet the sacrifice of Cain was rejected by God and that of Abel was accepted. Some important element there must therefore be in man's deeds which is hidden from his neighbour's eye, but is known to the Almighty. The inability of man to penetrate into the secret of God's rule is also illustrated by the prophet Habakkuk. He asked, " Wherefore lookest thou upon them that deal treacherously, and holdest thy peace when the wicked swalloweth up the man that is more righteous than he; and makest men as the fishes of the sea, as the creeping things that have no ruler over them ? " Whereupon he receives the Divine answer: " Write the vision, and make it plain upon tables, that he may run that readeth it. . . . Behold, there is crookedness in the eyes of him whose soul is not straight; but the just will live by his faith " (Hab. i. 13, 14, and ii. 2, 4).

One of the Psalmists (Asaph; Ps. lxxiii. 2 *seq.*) confesses that this problem had greatly troubled him and endangered his faith. He says: " As for me, my feet were almost gone; my steps had well nigh slipped. For I was envious of the arrogant, when I saw the prosperity of the wicked. For there are no bands in their death; but their strength is firm. They are not in trouble as other men; neither are they plagued like other men. . . . Therefore his people return hither: and waters of a full cup are wrung out by them. And they say, How doth God know ? and is there knowledge in the Most High? Behold, these are the wicked, and being alway at ease, they increase in riches. Surely in vain have I cleansed my heart, and washed my hands in innocency; for all the day long have I been plagued, and chastened every morning. If I had said, I will speak thus; behold, I had dealt treacherously with the generation of thy children. When I think how I might know this, it is trouble in mine eyes: until I come into the sanctuary of God; then shall I consider their latter end." The temporary success and seeming prosperity of the wicked does not shake the firm belief of the singer in the justice of God; his communion with God, his coming into the sanctuaries of God, is a blessing which the soul of the pious yearns for, and in comparison with which all the wealth and power of the wicked is but a deceitful shadow.

The Book of Job illustrates the vanity of man's attempts to lift the veil that conceals the plan of God's decrees. The reader is informed beforehand why Job is afflicted with pains and troubles. But Job and his friends have not been informed. Job desires to know what act of his has brought upon him that terrible calamity, if it is to be endured as a punishment; he protests his innocence, and criticises the justice of the Almighty. The three friends declare with certainty that Job's sufferings are a punishment for sins committed, and are angry that Job does not accept their view.

God appears, rebukes Job for his presumption, but declares that the view expressed by his friends, insinuating sinful conduct to Job, was wrong, and that Job,

who contended that he did not know the cause of the
suffering, spoke more rightly than his friends. For Job
had not been afflicted because of his sins, and this was
shown to the friends of Job by the compensation which
God gave Job for all that he had lost and suffered.

Koheleth likewise shows the futility of man's endeavour to find independently of Divine revelation the
aim and object of man's life on earth, or the share his
free-will has in the performance of his actions and the
determination of his fate. Man is lost in a labyrinth
of problems, out of which he can extricate himself only
by faith in God and His guidance. The result to which
the investigations of Koheleth led him is expressed
thus : " Fear God, keep his commandments ; for this is
the whole of man's duty. For every action God will
bring to judgment together with all hidden thoughts,
whether good or evil " (Eccles. xii. 13).

The acts of Divine justice recorded in the sacred
literature serve as a warning to the evil and an encouragement to the good. They are all of a material
character, as only in this shape can they be perceived
by man. But by no means do they exhaust all the
ways of God. The Divine retribution so frequently
referred to in the Law points mostly to the good or
evil consequences which the conduct of the Israelites
will bring upon the whole community or state, because
the whole community is benefited by the virtues and
injured by the misconduct of each of the members
composing it ; it is the duty of the authorities, by
watchfulness and by well-defined punishments, to prevent the spread of disobedience to the Divine Law.
What other rewards or punishments await the indi-

vidual in this life or after death we do not know. But
there are, especially in the Psalms, numerous indications that the pious sufferer was sure that everlasting
happiness would more than compensate for the absence of material and transient success in this life.
The following passages may serve as an illustration :—

" Many sorrows shall be to the wicked, but he that
trusteth in the Lord, mercy shall compass him about "
(Ps. xxxii. 10).

" How precious is thy loving-kindness, O God! and
the children of men take refuge under the shadow of
thy wings. They shall be abundantly satisfied with
the fatness of thy house ; and thou shalt make them
drink of the river of thy pleasures. For with thee is
the fountain of life : in thy light shall we see light "
(xxxvi. 8—10).

" For evil-doers shall be cut off : but those that
wait upon the Lord, they shall inherit the land "
(xxxvii. 9).

" For the Lord loveth judgment, and forsaketh not
his saints ; they are preserved for ever : but the seed
of the wicked shall be cut off " (*Ibid.* 28).

" Mark the perfect man ; and behold the upright :
for the latter end of that man is peace. As for transgressors, they shall be destroyed together ; the latter
end of the wicked shall be cut off " (*Ibid.* 37, 38).

In these and similar passages the pious and enthusi-
astic singer has in his mind something more durable
and permanent than this short life, or otherwise the
conflict between his hopes and the reality would have
shaken his faith.

Twelfth Principle.—" *I firmly believe in the coming of*

Messiah; and although he may tarry, I daily hope for his coming."

When Abraham was chosen by God to be the founder of a nation proclaiming the Unity of God, when he was commanded to separate from his relatives and friends and to travel a stranger in a foreign land, the blessing promised to him was not to be enjoyed by him in the present, but by his descendants in remote future: " All the families of the earth shall be blessed in thee " (Gen. xii. 3). The same promise was repeated when Abraham stood the trial, and was ready to bring any sacrifice in obedience to the Will of the Supreme Being : " All the nations of the earth shall bless themselves in thee " (*Ibid.* xxii. 18). The conviction that the seed of Abraham have the distinction and the mission to become a source of a blessing to all mankind was transmitted from generation to generation ; from Abraham through Isaac to Jacob or Israel, whose descendants, the Israelites, guarded the inherited charge, as their peculiar treasure. Before receiving the Decalogue on Mount Sinai, the Israelites were reminded of this their mission in the words, " And ye shall be unto me a kingdom of priests and a holy nation " (Exod. xix. 6). It was not by force of arms or by persuasion that they were to influence the whole earth, but by setting an example of noble, pure, and holy conduct. A special spot was selected for them where they should, in seclusion from the rest of the world, be trained in the true worship of God and in the practice of virtue. Zion and Jerusalem became in course of time the religious centre from which " instruction came forth and the word of the Lord." The Israelites became negligent in their mission and faithless to their holy charge. Instead of leading other nations to the true worship of God, they allowed themselves to be misled by them to idolatry; instead of living a pure life of justice and righteousness, they yielded to luxury and lust, and committed acts of injustice and oppression. They were punished. Troubles followed troubles; they lost their independence and their religious centre. The men of God, the prophets, from Moses to the last of the prophets, Malachi, foretold the catastrophe, but at the same time added words of comfort and encouragement, pointing to a distant future, when " her appointed time of trouble will be complete, and her guilt atoned for ; " when Israel will be restored to his land, and under the guidance of Messiah, " the Anointed of the Lord," he will be filled with the fear of the Lord and an earnest desire to do that which is just and right. Moses, in one of his last addresses to Israel, said, " And it shall come to pass, when all these things have come upon thee, the blessing and the curse, which I have set before thee ; and thou shalt call them to mind among all the nations whither the Lord thy God hath driven thee, and shalt return unto the Lord thy God, and shalt obey his voice, according to all that I command thee this day, thou and thy children, with all thine heart, and with all thy soul ; that the Lord thy God will return thy captivity, and have compassion on thee, and will return, and gather thee from all the peoples whither the Lord thy God hath scattered thee. If any of thy outcasts be in the uttermost parts of heaven, from thence will the Lord thy God gather thee, and from thence will he fetch thee," &c. (Deut. xxx. 1-3).

The glorious times of Messiah are described by Isaiah in the following words: "And it shall come to pass in the end of days, that the mountain of the Lord's house shall be established in the top of the mountains, and shall be exalted above the hills, and all nations shall flow unto it. And many peoples shall go and say, Come ye, and let us go up to the mountain of the Lord, to the house of the God of Jacob, and he will teach us of his ways, and we will walk in his paths, for out of Zion shall go forth the Law, and the word of the Lord from Jerusalem. And he shall judge among the nations, and shall reprove many peoples; and they shall beat their swords into plough-shares, and their spears into pruning-hooks: nation shall not lift up sword against nation, neither shall they learn war any more" (Isa. ii. 2—4). The same has been prophesied in almost identical words by Micah (iv. 1—4), a contemporary of Isaiah. The peace of the Messianic period is figuratively described by Isaiah in the following verses: "And the wolf shall dwell with the lamb, and the leopard shall lie down with the kid; and the calf, and the young lion, and the fatling together; and a little child shall lead them. And the cow and the bear shall feed: their young ones shall lie down together, and the lion shall eat straw like the ox. And the sucking child shall play on the hole of the asp, and the weaned child shall put his hand on the basilisk's den. They shall not hurt nor destroy in all my holy mountain; for the earth shall be full of the knowledge of the Lord, as the waters cover the sea" (Isa. xi. 6—9). In the days of Messiah all people will unite in the proclamation of the Unity of God and in

His worship: "And the Lord shall be King over all the earth: in that day shall the Lord be one, and his name one" (Zech. xiv. 9). "Then will I turn to the peoples a pure language, that they may all call upon the name of the Lord, to serve him with one consent" (Zeph. iii. 9).

The distinction given to Israel and to his land will again appear in all its glory. Israel is punished, deprived of independence, even despised and ill-treated at times; but with all this he is loved by God, and not rejected by Him for ever. Isaiah prophesies as follows: "Remember these things, O Jacob and Israel, for thou art my servant: I have formed thee; thou art my servant; O Israel, thou shalt not be forgotten of me" (Isa. xliv. 21). "For the mountains shall depart, and the hills be removed; but my kindness shall not depart from thee, neither shall my covenant of peace be removed, saith the Lord that hath mercy on thee" (*Ibid.* liv. 10). Comp. lix. 20, 21; lx. 19–21; lxvi. 22; Jer. xxxiii. 25, 26; Hos. ii. 21, 22.

Those who during the years of Israel's punishment have despised and ill-treated him will repent of their conduct when they witness his wonderful redemption. Their repentance is beautifully depicted by Isaiah in the passage beginning, "Behold, my servant will be successful" (lii. 13). Israel, the servant of God, patiently bears insults and persecution, faithfully waiting for the fulfilment of the Divine promise. Israel's oppressors will then, on seeing how God loves him, confess their wrong and own that Israel has innocently suffered at their hands. With the redemption of Israel is connected the restoration of the throne of David. " A branch of the house of David " will be at the head of the nation, upon whom " the spirit of the Lord will rest, the spirit of wisdom and understanding, the spirit of counsel and might, the spirit of knowledge, and of the fear of the Lord " (Isa. xi. 2). Thus Jeremiah prophesies : " Behold, the days come, saith the Lord, that I will raise unto David a righteous branch, and he shall reign as king, and deal wisely, and shall execute judgment and justice in the land. In his days Judah shall be saved, and Israel shall dwell safely : and this is his name, whereby he shall be called, The Lord is our righteousness " (xxiii. 5, 6). All the attributes of Messiah are those of a human being in his highest possible perfection. No superhuman qualities are ascribed to him ; all his glory, all his success, is dependent on the Will of God. He is an ideal man, and an ideal king, but not more ; if miracles are to be wrought, it is not Messiah who will perform them, but God, who will act wondrously for Messiah and Israel. The advent of Messiah is not expected to change the nature of man, much less the course of the world around us. The only change we expect is, that the Unity of God will be acknowledged universally, and that justice and righteousness will flourish over all the earth. Those who believe in a superhuman nature of Messiah are guilty of idolatry. Our Sages express this principle in the words, אין בין העולם הזה לימות המשיח אלא שעבוד מלכיות בלבד, " There is no other difference between the present time and the days of Messiah but the restoration of Israel's independence."

An opinion is mentioned in the Talmud in the name

of a Rabbi Hillel—not the great Hillel, the Babylonian —that " there is no Messiah for the Israelites, because they have already enjoyed the blessings of Messiah in the reign of Hezekiah " (Babyl. Talm. Sanhedrin, 98*b*). This can only refer to the miraculous defeat of the enemy, and the direct benefits derived therefrom by the Israelites. But the Rabbi by no means rejects our belief that Messiah will come, and with him the universal worship of the One God, the universal practice of virtue in all its forms, and universal peace and prosperity.[1] Hillel, however, found no support for his view; on the contrary, his error is at once shown to him, that he forgot the prophets who prophesied after Hezekiah.

There are some theologians who assume the Messianic period to be the most perfect state of civilisation, but do not believe in the restoration of the kingdom of David, the rebuilding of the Temple, or the repossession of Palestine by the Jews. They altogether reject the national hope of the Jews. These theologians either misinterpret or wholly ignore the teaching of the Bible, and the Divine promises made through the men of God.

The hopes with which our religion inspires us can never lead us to intrigues, political combinations, insurrection, or warfare for the purpose of regaining Palestine and appointing a Jewish Government. On the contrary, our religion teaches us to seek the welfare of those nations in whose midst we live, and to conscien-

---

[1] According to Rashi, Rabbi Hillel meant to say that the Jews would not be redeemed by any Messiah, but by God Himself. Comp. Hagadah for Seder-evening, " And I will pass through the land of Egypt ; I myself, and not an angel."

L

off offoff offoffoffoffoffoff

tiously take part in the work for their national progress and prosperity, whilst patiently waiting for the miraculous fulfilment of the prophecies. Even if a band of adventurers were to succeed in reconquering Palestine for the Jews by means of arms, or reacquiring the Holy Land by purchasing it from the present owners, we should not see in such an event the consummation of our hopes.

Does the advent of Messiah and the rebuilding of the Temple in Jerusalem imply the restoration of the Sacrificial Service? The last of the prophets, Malachi, declares that "then the offering of Judah and Jerusalem shall be pleasant unto the Lord, as in the days of old, and as in ancient years" (Mal. iii. 4). In the same spirit all the prophets spoke, and when in some cases prophets denounce sacrifices, it is only the sacrifices of the wicked that they denounce. Sacrifices must be preceded by purification of the heart, and by the earnest resolve to obey the word of God, otherwise they constitute an increase of sin. When we express our longing for the rebuilding of the Temple and the restoration of the Temple-Service—the return of the priests to their service, and the Levites to their song and music—it is solely our desire for the opportunity of serving God according to His Will and command, and is not a feeling that should be modified by fashion or taste. It is because of our sins that we have been deprived of our Temple; the rebuilding of the Temple and the restoration of the Sacrificial Service will be the result of our own purification, and the consequent Divine pardon.

When will this take place? We do not know, and

are content to bear in mind that the time of our redemption is one of the " hidden things which are the Lord our God's ; " " If it tarries," says Habakkuk, " wait for it, for it will surely come, and not later than the time fixed " (ii. 3). Certain numbers of days and weeks are mentioned in Daniel,[1] but it is not stated how these are to be counted ; to which period they are intended to apply ; whether to the time of the restoration under Zerubbabel, to the period of the Maccabees, to the destruction of the second Temple, or to the future and final redemption. It is also possible that these numbers have some symbolic signification. In reference to these mysterious numbers Daniel says (xii. 8–10) : " And I heard, but I understood not ; then said I, O my lord, what shall be the issue of these things ? And he said, Go thy way, Daniel ; for the words are shut up and sealed till the time of the end. Many shall purify themselves and make themselves white, and be refined ; but the wicked shall do wickedly, and none of the wicked shall understand ; but they that be wise shall understand." These words of Daniel are a warning to all those who are inclined to compute by means of the numbers given in Daniel the exact year of Messiah. Many have disregarded the warning and have fallen into gross error. It is the duty of the pious Israelite to have faith in God's wisdom, goodness, and power : " The righteous shall live in his faith " (Hab. ii. 4).

Thirteenth Principle.—" *I firmly believe that there will take place a revival of the dead at a time which*

---

[1] Comp. *supra*, p. 122.

will please the Creator, blessed be His name and exalted His memorial for ever and ever."

As imperfect as is our conception of a creation from nothing, so imperfect is our notion of the resurrection of the dead. We only perceive the dissolution of the body into its elements, which enter into new combinations and form new bodies; and it is almost impossible for us to imagine a reconstruction of the original body out of its own elements. There is no doubt that the Almighty produces fresh life from death—we need only observe the action of Nature in the world around us to convince ourselves that God is מחיה המתים "that he gives life to things dead." But how this will be done in reference to our own selves, whether we shall enjoy the same life, whether our future life will be an improved edition of the present one, whether *all* will be restored to life, or whether the new life after death will be enjoyed by the soul alone, or by body and soul jointly: these and similar questions transcend the bounds of human knowledge. We know nothing but the bare fact that God can restore to life that which is dead, and that a resurrection will take place. But all further description of this event rests on man's imaginative powers. The fact itself is stated by Daniel (xii. 2): "And many of them that sleep in the dust of the earth shall awake, some to everlasting life, and some to shame and everlasting contempt;" it is indicated in the Pentateuch in the words, "I shall kill and I shall make alive; I have wounded and I shall heal" (Deut. xxxii. 39). According to Maimonides, the author of the Thirteen Principles, the doctrine of the resurrection of the dead is identical with that of the immortality

of the soul, calling the life of the soul after separation
from the body, resurrection; the verse quoted from
Daniel is accordingly interpreted in a figurative sense.
The belief in תחית המתים " the resurrection of the dead,"
emphatically enjoined in the Talmud, was thus restricted by Maimonides to the separate life of man's
soul after his death, because the immortality of the
soul appeared to him more rational and more acceptable to thinking man. This may be the case, but we,
human beings, a combination of soul and body, are, in
reality, as unable to conceive the separate existence of
our soul as we are to comprehend the resurrection of
our body. We are taught that there exists for us a
life beyond the present one. But any attempt to
describe that life must be considered merely as an
act of imagination rather than of knowledge. It is
probably for this reason that no distinct ordinance in
the Pentateuch sanctioned the belief in future life, or
in the immortality of the soul. The belief, nevertheless, existed among the Israelites, and found expression
in several passages of the Bible. Foremost among
these is the following verse of Koheleth (xii. 7):
" And the dust shall return to the earth as it was,
and the spirit shall return unto God who gave it."
David also gives frequent expression to this belief in
his Psalms. In the Seventeenth Psalm, *e.g.*, he speaks
with contempt of the wealth and the success of the
wicked, and says of himself: " As for me, I shall see
thy face in righteousness; I shall be satisfied, when
I awake, with beholding thy likeness " (Ps. xvii. 15).
Similarly he says in Ps. xvi. 8—11 : " I have set the
Lord always before me ; because he is at my right

hand, I shall not be moved. Therefore my heart is glad and my glory rejoiceth : my flesh also shall dwell in safety. For thou wilt not leave my soul to death, neither wilt thou suffer thine holy one to see corruption. Thou wilt show me the path of life ; in thy presence is fulness of joy, in thy right hand there are pleasures for evermore." In the Book of Proverbs (xii. 28) we read : " In the path of righteousness there is life, and a smoothed way where there is no death." These and similar verses show that the belief in the immortality of the soul was firmly established among the Israelites, and found frequent expression in the words of the men of God.

The belief in the Resurrection assists us in our endeavour of reconciling the apparent contradictions between the justice of God and our own experience. The latter comprises only the transient pleasures of the wicked and the sufferings of the just in this short life, and cannot be compared with the pleasure of the good and the suffering of the bad in the future, eternal life. Another benefit derived from this belief consists in its raising us above the ordinary sphere of earthly gains and losses ; it turns our minds to higher aims ; it purifies our heart and elevates it.

Opponents of this belief quote some passages from Job in support of their view ; *e.g.* : " Before I go whence I shall not return, even to the land of darkness and of the shadow of death " (x. 21). " As the cloud is consumed and vanishes away, so he that goeth down to the grave shall come up no more " (vii. 9). These and similar words were uttered by Job when he suffered great pain, and wished, as many would wish under similar circumstances, to be relieved by death from his momentary troubles, unconcerned as to what might happen in distant future. Besides, Job is not an Israelite; he is described as a man just and upright, but need not have had the same convictions and beliefs as the Israelites. How little the above verses represent the exact view of Job may be learnt from the fact that he gives also expression to the opposite belief: " If a man dieth, will he live again ? All the days of my appointed time will I wait, till my relief cometh " (xiv. 14). " And when my skin is gone, when worms have destroyed this body, and when my flesh is no more, yet shall I see God " (xix. 26).

NOTES.

————

On page 19 *sqq.*

The Number of the Principles of our Creed.—The contents of
our Creed has its source in the Bible ; there the Principles are
taught, some directly, others indirectly ; but they are neither
formulated nor enumerated.   The most ancient declaration of
faith is contained in the verse : " Hear, O Israel, the Lord is
our God ; the Lord is One " (Deut. vi. 4).   There is even a
tradition (Midrash Rabboth **Gen. ch.** xcviii.) that these words
were first uttered by the sons of Jacob, when their father,
in the last hour of his life, wished to know whether all his
children were faithful to the inherited religion.   We repeat
these words twice a day, in the morning and in the evening ;
with these words on their lips the martyrs of our nation
suffered death ; these words are the last which the pious
Israelite utters before " his spirit returneth to him who hath
given it."   When the Israelites took possession of Palestine,
at the solemn assembly between the mountains of Gerizim
and Ebal, they were not commanded to recite or sign a series
of articles of faith, but to declare their determination to obey
the Will of God as expressed in the Torah.   This was also
done by our forefathers when standing round Sinai.   They
declared, " All that the Lord hath said, will we do and
hear " (Exod. xxiv. 7).   When Elijah on Mount Carmel
had demonstrated the perverseness of the Baal-worship, the

Israelites declared, " The Lord, he is God." Jonah describes
himself thus : "I am a Hebrew ; and I fear the Lord, the
God of the heavens, who hath made the sea and the dry
land " (Jonah i. 9).—Also, after the Restoration in the days
of Zerubbabel, Ezra, and Nehemiah, the Jews were exhorted
to act according to the words of the Torah, and they renewed
their covenant with God in this respect, but nothing is
known of a declaration of belief, of reciting or signing articles
of faith.—The struggle with the Samaritans produced special
legislation with regard to certain religious observances, but
there was no need for the formulation of a creed. But care
has been taken that the principles of our faith should find
expression in our daily prayers. Thus the sections which
precede and follow the *Shema* contain an indirect declaration
of the three fundamental principles of our religion, the
Existence of the Creator, Revelation, and Divine Justice.
The first section, called ברכת יוצר praises God as the sole
source of everything, of light and darkness, of good and evil.
In the second section (ברכת אהבה) we acknowledge in gratitude the benefits of Revelation ; and in the third (ברכת גאולה)
we thank God for the redemption of our forefathers from
Egypt, by inflicting punishment on our oppressors. Although much stress is laid on faith (אמונה), and he who was
found wanting in faith was stigmatised as כופר or כופר בעיקר
unbeliever or infidel, yet no creed was officially formulated.
Even the discussions between the Sadducees and Pharisees,
which concerned also the principles of faith, brought only
about certain changes in the prayer—such as the substitution
of מן העולם ועד העולם for עד עולם in the responses of the
congregation during the public service, in order to establish
the belief in the existence of another world and another life
beyond the grave.

The necessity of formulating the principles of faith arose
when the contact and intercourse with other religious com-

munities gave frequent occasion to discussions on these and similar subjects. Without some fixed basis, it was feared, disorder and confusion would disturb the peace in the camp of Israel.

Thus Saadiah says in *Emunoth Ve-deoth :* "I have seen men drowned, as it were, in the sea of doubts, covered by the waves of error, and there was no diver to bring them up from the depth, nor any swimmer to take hold of them and draw them out. As I possessed enough of what God taught me to support them, and had the power for upholding them granted to me, I considered it my duty to assist and guide my fellow-men according to the best of my abilities." In ten chapters Saadiah discusses the various theological problems, and defends the following articles of faith : Existence of God ; His Unity ; Revelation ; Free-will ; Immortality of the Soul ; Resurrection of the Dead ; Final Redemption of Israel ; Reward and Punishment. Although these principles do not seem to have been shaped into the form of a solemn declaration or embodied in the prayer, they are treated as themes familiar to the reader, and as elements essential in the Jewish faith (אשר אנחנו מחויבים להאמין).

Rabbi Abraham ben David (Rabad, רא״בד), in his *Hae-munah haramah* ("The Lofty Faith"), seems to assume three principles : Existence of God, Prophecy, and Reward and Punishment, which to defend from the attacks of the unbeliever, he considers as the first duty of the Jewish scholar (התורני) ; but he does not follow this decision in his book. He comprises all religious truths which he has to demonstrate under six heads (עיקרים). The first of them he calls "Root of the faith ;" it expresses the conviction that all things in the universe owe their existence to a "First Cause"—God. Next comes "Unity of God," which is followed by "Attributes of God," "The intermediate causes of natural changes," "Prophecy"—or האמונה האחרונה, "the subsequent belief," *i.e.*, the belief which follows the belief in God—and "Divine Providence."

Rabbi Jehudah ha-levi explains to the Kuzarite king his faith as follows : "We believe in the God of our forefathers, who brought the Israelites forth from Egypt by signs and miracles, sustained them in the wilderness with manna, divided for them the sea and Jordan, gave them the Law through Moses, exhorted them through His prophets to obey His commandments : in short, we believe all that is written in the Torah" (Kuzari, i. 8). He then explains philosophically "the root of the faith" in the following ten propositions : (1) The universe is finite ; (2) it had a beginning ; (3) the time of the beginning had to be determined by the Divine Being ; (4) God is without a beginning ; (5) God is eternal (*i.e.*, without an end) ; (6) incorporeal ; (7) omniscient ; (8) all-wise, all-powerful, living ; (9) free in His actions ; (10) without change. To these must be added the belief in prophecy, in the truth of the prophecies, and in man's free-will, which he fully discusses in the course of the book.

Rabbenu Bachya, in his "Duties of the Hearts" (חובות הלבבות), considers also faith as one of these duties, and expresses it in the most simple form, "Belief in God and in His Law." He does not, however, devote a special chapter to faith. The first chapter treats of the distinctively Jewish creed of God's Unity, but less as a duty of belief than as a duty of research and study for the purpose of philosophically establishing that God is One. The author states only briefly in the prefatory notes to the first chapter, that it is our duty to believe in the Existence, Providence, and Unity of God, as commanded in the verse, "Hear, O Israel, the Lord is our God, the Lord is One."

Maimonides comprehended our belief in thirteen articles, known as the Thirteen Principles of our Creed. He insists on the fact that these articles are not the product of chance; they are the result of long study and deep research. Every one of them is essential, and he who rejects any of them is an infidel (כופר), and puts himself by such rejection outside the Jewish community (יוצא מכלל ישראל).

Rabbi Joseph Albo criticised Maimonides' thirteen articles of faith (עיקרים). Whilst recognising all of them as true, he would make a difference between fundamental principles (עיקרים) and secondary beliefs (שרשים). The former are all those dogmas by which Judaism falls and stands, without which Jewish faith cannot be imagined; the latter are those principles which are actually true, but Judaism can be conceived without them. To the former he counts, *e.g.*, the belief in the existence of God, to the latter the belief that to Him alone prayer is to be offered. For Judaism cannot be conceived without the belief in God's existence, but could be conceived without the belief that only God is to be prayed to. Albo further finds fault with Maimonides for not having embodied in the Creed the belief in man's free-will, in the truth of the Biblical account of the miracles, in the *Creatio ex nihilo*, and the like. To these objections Maimonides would reply, that the articles enumerated by him were all actually fundamental, the question whether Judaism could be imagined without this or that principle being of no importance whatever; and that the dogmas named by Albo as omitted, were implied in the Thirteen Principles. According to Albo there are three fundamental principles (עיקרים): Existence of God, Revelation, and Reward and Punishment. The first includes four articles (שרשים): Unity of God, His Incorporeality, Eternity, and Perfection; the second implies three: God's Omniscience, Divine inspiration, and Divine messengers (prophets); the third only one: Providence. Albo's criticisms on Maimonides have passed away without effect. The Principles of Faith as formulated by Maimonides have found their way into the daily Prayer-book in prose and poetry, and have since formed an essential element in every text-book of Jewish religion. Modern theologians erroneously quote Albo in favour of rejecting some of the articles, because he speaks of three fundamental principles; but they forget that Albo never rejects any of the thirteen principles; he only insists on making a difference between those which are more and those which are less fundamental.

On the First Principle, pp. 22 sqq.

Maimonides does not mention the term Creator except in the beginning of each paragraph as a substitute for "God." He employs the philosophical term "First Cause" in defining the existence of God. In the sixty-ninth chapter of the first book of "The Guide" we find the explanation thereof. He says: "The philosophers, as you know, call God the First Cause (עִלָּה and סִבָּה); but those who are known by the name Mutakallemim (Mohammedan theologians) are very much opposed to the use of that name, and prefer to call Him 'Maker' (פּוֹעֵל), believing that there is a great difference whether we use the one term or the other. They argue thus: Those who say that God is the Cause, implicitly assume the coexistence of the Cause with that which was produced by that Cause, and believe that the universe is eternal, and that it is inseparable from God. Those, however, who say that God is the Maker do not assume the coexistence of the maker with his work; for the maker can exist anterior to his work; we cannot even imagine how a maker can be in action unless he existed before his own work. This is an argument advanced by persons who do not distinguish between the potential and the actual. For there is no difference whether we say 'cause' or 'maker;' 'cause' as a mere potentiality precedes its effect; and 'cause' as actuality coexists with its effect. The same is the case with 'maker;' so long as the work is not done, he is a maker potentially, and exists before his work; he is an actual maker when the work is done, and then he coexists with his work."

"The reason why the philosophers called God 'the Cause' and did not call Him 'the Maker' is not to be sought in their belief that the universe is eternal, but in other principles, which I will briefly explain to you. Everything owes its origin to the following four causes: the substance, the form, the *agens*, the final cause. The philosophers believe —and I do not differ from them—that God is the *agens*, the form, and the final cause of everything; in order to express this, they call God 'the Cause' of all things. Every one of these three causes leads, through a chain of causes, to God as the First Cause." Maimonides further points out in this chapter that the choice of the term by no means decides the question whether the universe has had a beginning or not.

Maimonides has been severely criticised by his successors for the absence of the belief in "Creation from nothing" from the Creed. In "The Guide" Maimonides distinctly states that the arguments for "Creation from nothing" and the arguments against it are equi-balanced, and that for this reason he follows the literal interpretation of the Scripture as regards Creation. Were the arguments in favour of the eternity of the universe stronger, he would not have found any difficulty in interpreting Scripture accordingly. Such being the view of our great philosopher, he could not make the belief in Creation part of the Creed, or declare that all who denied the Creation from nothing were unbelievers.

However strange this argumentation of Maimonides may appear, and however arbitrary his treatment of Scriptural teaching, his view is not without justification. It seems strange that, in spite of all his reverence for the Bible, he should have entrusted himself entirely to the guidance of his own reason, and forced, as it were, the Bible by peculiar interpretations to follow his reasoning. In truth, however, the method of Maimonides is neither strange nor arbitrary. There is no doubt that figurative language is extensively used in the Scriptures, especially in the poetical and the prophetical books. Whether a certain expression or phrase was to be understood in its literal meaning or in a figurative sense must be learnt from the context; in some cases—as, *e.g.*, in the exhortation, " Ye shall circumcise the foreskin of your heart " (Deut. x. 16)—the figurative sense is accepted by all, whilst in other cases opinions are divided. Our decision in favour of the one interpretation or the other is based on our conviction that the Bible contains nothing but truth. When we discover a contradiction between a Biblical statement and the dictates of our reason, we are sure that we have erred either in the right understanding of the words of the Bible or in our reasoning. On finding the mistake in our reasoning we abandon what we have hitherto considered as fully established; but so long as we are unable to discover where our reasoning is faulty, we either suspend our judgment for the present and consider the question as one of the problems which we have not yet been able to solve satisfactorily, or, whenever possible, we attempt to reconcile by figurative interpretation the teaching of the Bible with the results of our research. Maimonides is therefore justified in saying that so long as reason does not decide against the teaching of the Bible in its literal sense he would adhere to the latter, and only if reason were to decide against the *Creatio ex nihilo,* he would follow reason and interpret Scripture accordingly.

It cannot be denied that Maimonides travelled here on rather slippery ground, and set a dangerous example when he admitted that he would interpret Scripture according to his preconceived view of the world's beginning. But, on the other hand, it must be owned that many passages of the Bible admit of a figurative interpretation, and the reader must follow his own reason and discretion in deciding in each particular case which of the two interpretations is the correct one. Maimonides has not made excessive use of this license.

Saadiah in his *Emunoth Ve-deoth* devotes the first chapter to the problem of the Creation. It is headed חדוש "Creation," and examines thirteen different opinions as to the origin of the universe. In the conclusion of this chapter he makes the following remarks: "Perhaps some one might ask in what manner something was produced from nothing. To this we reply as follows: If we were able to understand this, we should not have ascribed the creative act to God alone. But we declare God as the only Creator, because we can form no idea as to the manner in which something is created from nothing. Those who desire us to show them how to do this, desire, in fact, that we should make them and ourselves creators. We only conceive in our mind the fact of the Creation, but cannot form an idea or image of the process itself. . . . There may be some who think little of the universe, and wonder that this should be the result of all the power and wisdom of God. We reply that He created as much as, according to His knowledge, would be within the range of man's observation and perception, and would be sufficient to teach man the existence of God. . . How can we conceive the idea that the universe counts only 4633 years? But the universe has been created, as we believe, and must have had a beginning at a certain time. Suppose we had been living in the year 100; we should then not have been surprised: why should we be surprised now?" The question as to the purpose for which the uni-

M

verse was created, Saadiah makes three attempts to answer. Maimonides, however, in "The Guide," more correctly, shows that the question is unanswerable and superfluous. For, whatever purpose we assume, we must always further inquire what is the purpose of this purpose, and so on *ad infinitum*, till we arrive at the answer, it was the Will of God. If the prophet declares that God "hath not created it in vain, but hath formed it for dwelling," he likewise says implicitly it was *the Will of God* that the earth should be for a dwelling.

The question, however, arises whether the Biblical account of the Creation harmonises in all its parts with the results of scientific research. To prove the existence of harmony between the two discordant elements has been since days of old the task which theologians proposed to themselves; philosophic culture forced them to accept the doctrines of a certain school of thought as established truths, whilst religious feeling would not allow them to abandon the teaching of the inspired writers. But the search after this harmony was superfluous, and the harmony found was illusory. For, whilst the teaching of the Bible remains unchanged, the systems of philosophy and science, like everything human, have no claim to permanency; each system has its season; it begins to shine, and rises higher and higher; and when it has reached the zenith, it begins steadily to decline till it disappears beneath the horizon of science. So long as Aristotle and Ptolemy were dominant, theologians exerted themselves to show that the account contained in the first chapter of Genesis fully harmonises with Aristotle and Ptolemy. When these princes were dethroned, and their places were occupied by others, the old harmony was gone, and a new method had to be invented. Maimonides has clearly pointed out how the conflict between reason and faith, where it existed, could best be brought to a conclusion.

Such of the laws of nature as have been established by human acumen and human observation have been discovered in the phenomena of existing nature; but the phenomenon of creation has never been observed in nature from which we could learn the laws of creation.

In the seventeenth chapter of the Second Book of " The Guide" Maimonides says as follows: " Everything produced comes into existence from non-existence; even when the substance of a thing has been in existence, and has only changed its form, the thing itself which has gone through the process of genesis and development, after having arrived at its final state, has properties different from those which it possessed at the commencement of the transition from potentiality to reality or before that time. . . . It is quite impossible to infer from the qualities which a thing possesses after having passed through all the stages of its development what its condition was at the moment when this process commenced; nor does the condition of a thing at that moment show what its previous condition had been. If you make this mistake, and attempt to prove the nature of a thing in potential existence by its properties when actually existing, you will fall into great confusion; you will reject evident truth and admit false opinions. . . . If philosophers would consider this well, and reflect on it, they would find that it represents exactly the dispute between Aristotle and ourselves. We, the followers of Moses, our teacher, and of Abraham, our father, believe that the universe has been produced from nothing, and has developed in a certain manner, and that it has been created in a certain order. The Aristotelians oppose us, and found their objections on the properties which the things in the universe possess when in actual existence and fully developed. We admit the existence of these properties, but hold that these properties themselves have come into existence from absolute non-existence. The arguments of our opponents are thus refuted; they have demonstrative force only against those who hold that the nature of things as at present in existence proves the Creation. But this is not my opinion."

This reasoning holds good with regard to the modern theory of Evolution. We may be able to discover numerous facts in evidence of this theory, we may well conceive the idea of a protoplasm developing into a whole system of worlds, and yet our belief in the truth of the Biblical account of the Creation is not shaken in the least. The laws of Evolution are *the result* of the creative act of the Almighty, and not its *causes;* they include nothing that could disprove the correctness of the theory of *Creatio ex nihilo.*

Rabbi S. R. Hirsch, in his " Commentary on Genesis " (i.) says : "The word בראשית 'in the beginning,' teaches that nothing preceded the act of Creation ; that there was a *Creatio ex nihilo.* This truth forms the foundation of the faith which the Divine Law is intended to establish in our hearts. The opposite theory is the doctrine of the eternity of the substance, a theory which leaves to the Creator nothing but the function of giving form to the substance that has existed already from eternity, and which has been the basis of the heathen belief up to the present day. . . . The first word of the Torah dispels the darkness of this false belief; and the words, 'The opening of thy word giveth light' (Ps. cxix. 130), have in the Midrash correctly been applied to the word בראשית. Everything, the matter and the form of all beings, is the result of the free will of the Creator, who continues to rule matter and form, and to determine both the natural forces and the laws of their action. For it is His free will that created matter, endowed it with certain forces, and fixed the laws by which the forces impress the different forms on it."

The idea of development and evolution is not entirely excluded from the account of the Creation. Not in one moment or in one day was the universe produced, but in six days by successive creations of a systematic order. In Mishnah Aboth (v. 1) this is expressed in the following way : " By ten words (מאמרות) the universe was created, although this could have been done by one word." Commentators have variously attempted to explain this fact, and to show that the order observed in the Creation was determined by the nature of the things themselves. Thus Ibn Ezra believes that the successive creations were the results of the continued action of light and heat.[1] But it is by no means necessary to reconcile the Biblical account with every theory that happens to be considered by some scholar or school as the right one. There may be found in nature and in the working of the natural laws some facts analogous to certain acts of the creation ; but a perfect equality of two such incongruent things as the creation from nothing and development of created beings is impossible. By forcing the text of the Bible into such harmony we deprive the account of its poetry and beauty, and weaken the force of its teaching.

Science teaches that millions of millions of years must have elapsed before the earth received its present form ; that it took millions of years before the light of certain stars could reach the earth. In all these calculations one important factor is ignored, viz., that for every development something must be given, which is subject to the process of developing ; to determine in what condition that something was, when it passed from the passive state of creation to the active state of developing, is a problem for the solution of which there is no analogy in nature. He who could create a germ endowed with all the natural forces required for

[1] See Essays on the Writings of Ibn Ezra, by M. Friedländer, p. 7 note 1.

development and differentiation into the great variety of forms which we perceive at present, must certainly have been able to create the things actually endowed with these forms. Thus, also, the various strata of the earth, whatever forms they contain, cannot with certainty be described as the results of development; they may just as well have come directly from the hand of the Creator.

Maimonides (The Guide, xxx.) says in reference to this question: "You should also know the dictum of our Sages —'All the beings of the work in the beginning (מעשה בראשית) were created in their full height, their fully developed reason, and endowed with the best of properties.' Note this, for it involves an important principle.—The work of the Creation went on for six days; every day brought to light a new force, a new result of a creative action, but on the seventh day 'God declared[1] the work which He had done as finished,' as endowed with the properties and forces required for their further development" (The Guide, I. lxvii.).

Science has proved, it is maintained, that the earth does not form the centre of the universe, and that man does not form the principal object in nature, in opposition to the teaching of the Scriptures that the earth is the centre round which the whole universe revolves, and that man on earth is the lord of the creation. Whatever view the authors of the Biblical books held as regards the systems of the universe, whether they placed the earth in the centre or not, whether all the stars and systems of stars existed, in their opinion, only for the sake of the earth or for the benefit of man, their object was to address man, to instruct him, and to teach him the omnipotence, wisdom, and goodness of God. For

---

[1] The Piel of a verb has frequently this meaning, *e.g.*, קדש "to be holy;" Pi., "to declare as holy;" טהר "to be pure;" Pi., "to declare as pure;" so כלה "to be at an end;" Pi., "to declare as being finished."

this reason the account of the Creation is given in such a manner that man should be able to reproduce in his mind the work of each day of the Creation, to view it from his standpoint, and to recognise the benefits each day's work bestowed on him. The fact that other beings are benefited at the same time, and that the benefit they derive is likewise part of the Creator's design, is by no means denied by those who believe that the well-being of man was included in the design of the Creator. It is part of our duty of gratitude to ascribe the benefits we enjoy to their Author. The prophets and the inspired singers knew well the place which weak and mortal man occupies in the universe; but they did not ignore the dignity and importance with which the Creator endowed him in spite of all his weakness and apparent insignificance. "*What is man,*" exclaims the Psalmist, "*that thou art mindful of him? and the son of man, that thou visitest him? And yet thou hast made him a little lower than angels, and hast crowned him with glory and honour*" (Ps. viii. 5, 6).

On the Fifth Principle, p. 44.

The principle that no other being but God is worthy of being addressed in prayer implies the belief that God can fulfil our petitions. We believe in the efficacy of prayer. It is true that when we communicate our wishes to the Most Holy, our just Lord and our loving Father, we are *eo ipso* reminded to examine our desires, whether they contain anything unholy, anything unjust or ignoble. Prayer to God has therefore the salutary effect of purifying, refining, and ennobling our heart. It banishes evil thoughts, and thus saves us much pain and sorrow. This effect may have been designed by the Creator, and it may be for this purpose that He has endowed us with a natural impulse to pray, and has taught us to pray in His Holy Word. But this cannot be the direct object of prayer. The immediate effect sought to be obtained by this act is the fulfilment of our wishes. Every such fulfilment implies a miracle, a deviation from the regular course of nature. We are not in the habit of praying for things which we expect as the sure result of the natural laws; we may praise and admire nature in its workings, but we shall never ask nature for the fulfilment of our desires. Only those things which we believe to be dependent solely on the free decision of the Supreme Being can form the substance of our petitions; and since we believe that everything, the regular working of the natural laws not excepted, depends on the Will of God, we include in the objects of prayer whatever concerns the well-being of individual man and society at large.

There have been thinkers that formed such an idea of God that they were compelled to deny Him every direct influence on human affairs. Some thought it incompatible with the notion of God's Unity and Immutability that He should be moved by man's prayer to do something which otherwise He would not have done. Again, others believe that the laws of nature—whether given by God or not— are so permanent that they never change under any circumstances. Prayer has therefore been explained to be of a purely subjective character, and to effect only the above-mentioned improvement of man's heart. But could we really pray to God to grant us the one thing or the other if we were convinced that He cannot grant us anything, but must allow nature to take its course? Can a prayer offered in such a frame of mind be called a "prayer without lips of deceit"? In opposition to such theories our teachers purposely introduced into the daily prayer here and there a reminder of the true theory in words like the following: המחדש בטובו בכל יום תמיד מעשה בראשית "Who repeateth anew every day regularly the work of the Creation." He is constantly מחיה, בורא חשך, יוצר אור

המחים; He constantly "formeth light," "createth darkness," "giveth life to the dead," &c. ; they have expressed our gratitude to God על נסיך שבכל יום עמנו ועל נפלאתיך וטובתיך שבכל עת "for His miracles which in our behalf He performs every day, and for His wonders and kindnesses shown at all times."

"This idea of God's real and active rule in the universe is the basis of prayer. It is not only the belief in the truth of the Biblical account of miracles that enables us to pray to our Father, but the conviction that wonders and miracles are constantly wrought by Him. In the Talmud and in the Midrash man's earning his daily bread (פרנסה) is declared to be a miracle by no means inferior to the miracles wrought for the deliverance of the Israelites from Egypt.—'Is need greatest, is God nearest,' is a well-known saying, the truth of which many have experienced in the course of their life. Those who have been dangerously ill, and after having found that man, with all his science and resources, was incapable of affording relief, gradually recover their former health; those who have shared with others a common danger, and while their companions, under exactly the same circumstances, perished, were themselves saved; those who, having exhausted every means conceivable to them of obtaining a livelihood, at length find a new path of subsistence opened to them: all these have experienced the Divine help and His nearness in their distress; they have learnt to recognise the miraculous power of Providence. But it is not only in such extraordinary events that the finger of God is seen; to him who has eyes to see they appear daily and hourly. We are exposed to many dangers, the existence of which we frequently only learn when we are safe; we escape them by a miracle."[1]

The Immutability of God and of His decrees is frequently

---

[1] *Die Religions-Philosophie der Juden*, by S. Hirsch, p. 445 *ff.*

insisted upon in Scripture. "I, the Lord, I change not" (Mal. iii. 6). "God is not a man, that he should lie; neither the son of man, that he should repent" (Num. xxiii. 19). "The Strength of Israel will not lie nor repent; for he is not a man, that he should repent" (1 Sam. xv. 29). "And he hath established them for ever and ever: he hath made a decree, and it shall not pass away" (Ps. cxlviii. 6). —This immutability, however, does not interfere with the free-will of man and its consequences. The teaching of the Bible is beautifully expressed in the well-known sentence: תשובה תפלה וצדקה מעבירין את רע הגזרה "Repentance, prayer, and good deeds remove the evil of the divine decree" (Musaf of Rosh ha-shanah); whatever a man has forfeited by evil deeds, he may recover by prayer and improved conduct. This lesson is taught in the Bible on every page, and is illustrated by the history of Israel. For this reason the prophets were sent to the people of Israel to exhort them, and to show them how they could, by means of repentance, ward off the impending catastrophe. To non-Israelites the same mercy was extended, as is shown by the history of the mission of the prophet Jonah.—Mishnah Aboth (iv. 13) therefore declares, "Repentance and good deeds are like a shield against punishment," תשובה ומעשים טובים כתרים בפני הפרענות.

The seeming incongruity of the two principles, God's immutability and man's hope for mercy and pardon from God, has to some extent occupied the attention of our ancient teachers. "If our condition for a whole year is determined in advance, what is the good of our daily prayers and our supplication for God's help in times of trouble?" Such is the question asked in the Babylonian Talmud, Rosh ha-shanah (16a), and the answer is given, יפה צעקה קודם נזרה ואחר נזרה "Prayer is of good effect both before the decree and afterwards." It is always in the power and in the will of the Almighty to accede to our petitions and to fulfil our wishes. The question has since been repeated frequently, but no better solution has as yet been supplied.

Abraham, who was the first teacher of monotheism, has also been made by tradition the father of prayer. In the Biblical account he is the first who uttered a prayer; a prayer in the true sense of the word, not for himself, but for his fellow - men. The words of Cain, נדול עוני מנשא "My punishment is greater than I can bear," have not the character of prayer, nor can the "calling by the name of God" in the age of Enosh be considered with certainty as an expression of prayer. Tradition relates, therefore, that before Abraham there was no one that called God by the name אדון "Lord." Abraham was the first who recognised God as Lord of man, in whose hand his fate lies,—the condition *sine quâ non* of prayer. From Abraham onwards prayer remained the chief refuge in danger, and the best solace and relief in time of trouble.

Whilst, however, insisting on the belief in the efficacy of prayer, our Sages teach us that it would be wrong to expect that every petition uttered before God must be granted. We pray to the Almighty, being convinced that it is in His power to grant what we pray for; but we must trust in the wisdom and mercy of God, that the rejection of our petition is also for our good. " He is near to all those who call on him, to all those that call on him in truth," who continue to trust in Him and His goodness even when their wishes are not fulfilled. It would be almost equal to superstition to believe that any words, however earnest and devout, uttered by us will infallibly have the desired effect. The Mishnah (Aboth ii. 13) therefore teaches : אל תעש תפלתך קבע אלא רחמים ותחנונים " Do not make thy prayer a fixed claim or demand, which must be fulfilled, but a supplication for mercy, which may or may not be granted."

The belief that the prayer will undoubtedly be fulfilled is denounced in the Talmud as עיון תפלה "Looking out with certainty for the effect of the prayer."[1] Since the principal object of prayer is the granting of our petitions, prayer will be superfluous when no wants will any longer be felt, לעתיד לבוא התפלות בטלות "In future prayers will be discontinued;" only תפלת תודה אינה בטלה לעולם "The prayer of thanksgiving will never be discontinued." "In the enjoyment of the purest blessings our feelings of gratitude will never die out" (Yalkut on Ps. lvi.).

Rabbi Joseph Albo, in the book *Ikkarim*, says (IV. xvi.): "Although Prayer is not one of the principles of our Torah, it is intimately connected with the belief in Providence, and every one who believes in Providence ought to believe in the efficacy of prayer. For he who does not pray to God in time of trouble either does not believe in Divine Providence, or if he does believe, he doubts whether God is able to supply his wants; in both cases man is an unbeliever. It is also possible that a person who believes in Divine Providence and in God's Omnipotence doubts whether he deserves that his prayer should be granted—a feeling of humility which ought indeed to fill the heart of every person—but this idea must not prevent him altogether from praying to God concerning his wants. If he does not pray from this reason, he may believe in God's justice, but he does not believe in His mercy and kindness. It is also contrary to the teaching of the Bible. 'Not relying on our righteousness do we offer our supplication before you, but on your great mercy!' For the benefits bestowed by God on His creatures are acts of love, not of recompense. . . . Man receives benefits, whether he is entitled to them or not, because prayer gives him a qualification which he does not possess by nature, and enables

---

[1] The phrase עיון תפלה is also used in the sense of "devotion during prayer."

him to receive such good things as could not be obtained from any other being or through any other means. . . .

"There are some who doubt the efficacy of prayer; they argue thus: We must assume that a certain good thing has been either decreed or not decreed in favour of a certain person: if it has been decided, prayer is not wanted; and if it has not been decided, how can prayer effect a change in the Will of God, who is unchangeable? Neither righteousness in action, nor prayer, is of any avail in procuring any good thing that has not been ordained, or in escaping any evil that has been decreed. This is also the argument of Job in chap. xxi. But the answer to these arguments is this: Whatever may have been decreed, certain conditions must be fulfilled before the decree is executed. If a good harvest is decreed to a certain person, he must plough and sow before he can secure such a harvest; if punishment is decreed against him, the punishment is not inflicted in the absence of continued and repeated sinning. The history of King Ahab shows that the evil decreed against any sinner takes no effect if the sinner repents and is turned into another man. The change that takes place· in man himself is the direct effect of prayer and righteousness; it prepares and qualifies him for receiving benefits and protection from evil. Our Sages say therefore: Prayer has its good effect both before and after the Divine decree. The Immutability of God is not less consistent with Efficacy of Prayer than it is with His knowledge of things which are possible, and may happen or may not happen. God and His knowledge being unchangeable, everything must be certain and nothing merely possible. And yet we are convinced of the existence of these things, and believe at the same time in the Immutability of God's knowledge. In the same manner we are convinced of the Efficacy of Prayer w **ithout** doubting the Immutability of God's Will."

On Revelation, p. 46.

The term נביא "prophet" only expressed the prophet's
function of addressing his fellow-men when inspired and
impelled by the Spirit of the Lord. The verb "to prophesy" is therefore in Hebrew expressed by the *nifal* or
passive. In so far as the Word of God has been revealed to
him he is called ראה, חוזה and צפה "Seer," איש אלהים "Man
of God," איש הרוח "The inspired." In the time of Samuel
the title ראה was generally given to the prophet instead of
נביא (1 Sam. ix. 9), as his advice was also sought by
many who believed him to be able to foresee coming events
and to know everything. As, however, the word נביא only
describes the prophet as addressing his fellow-men, it is
used both of the true and the false prophets, and also of
teachers and preachers generally. The Targum on the Prophets (Jer. xxix. 15; Isa. xxix. 10) renders, therefore,
the term נביא in some instances: מלפין "teachers," ספריא
"scholars."

The enthusiasm manifested by the prophet in his mode of
address, or in his endurance of insult and ill-treatment, made
him sometimes appear in the eyes of the public as though
he were struck with madness, so that scoffers used נביא and
משגע "mad," as synonyms (Jer. xxix. 26), and מתנבא is
both one who acts as a prophet and one who imitates the
appearance of a prophet (1 Sam. xviii. 10).

The false prophets are divided by Jeremiah into three
classes: there were those who were guilty of a direct plagiar-
ism, preaching the Divine messages of the true prophets and
describing them as their own inspiration. There were others
who plagiarised and reproduced true prophecies in a form
and style of their own, and others again who altogether
invented dreams and visions. The principal test for dis-

tinguishing between the true and the false prophets was the purity of moral and religious conduct. In matters wholly indifferent as regards morality and religion the prophet was believed after having established his trustworthiness in some way or other, and his advice was acted upon. The prophet himself could easily detect the fraud of a false prophet ; for what he was commanded by God to do, another prophet could not, speaking in the name of the same God, order not to be done. The prophet, therefore, who deceitfully induced "the man of God" to return to Beth-el by the very way which the word of God had forbidden him to go again (1 Kings xiii. 18), could not have been a true prophet, although he was subsequently entrusted with a Divine message for "the man of God." Bileam was likewise for a certain purpose made the bearer of God's words, although he was by no means a good man. In either case the sinful intention of the false prophet was stigmatised as contrary to the Will of the Most High, and both had, as it were, to own the wickedness of their intention or the wrong of their actions.

The subject-matter of the prophecy is called "the vision," "the word of God," or "the burden of the word of God." In the days of Jeremiah the term "burden of the Lord" seems to have been used contemptuously of the prophetic utterances in the sense of "trouble" and "strife" (comp. Deut. i. 12), and the prophet was ironically asked by the people, "What is the burden of the Lord?" Jeremiah exhorts them to say, "What hath the Lord answered thee?" or "What hath the Lord spoken?" "But the burden of the Lord shall ye remember no more ; for the burden shall be the man's to whom His word is brought" (Jer. xxiii. 36).

On the Sixth Principle, p. 131.

Saadiah in *Emunoth ve-deoth* iii. says : " Some men believe that we have no need of prophets, our reason being able to distinguish between good and evil. But if this were the case, God would not have sent messengers to us, because He does not do a thing that is purposeless. I considered the question thoroughly, and found that the mission of the prophets was necessary, not only for the promulgation of categorical commands, but also for that of rational precepts. Thus the duty of thanksgiving to God for His goodness is dictated by our own reason, but the Divine messengers had to fix the time and the form of thanksgiving. Again, adultery is rejected by our reason as a crime ; but the Divine teaching determines the conditions of the bond that unites man and wife. . . .

" As a test of the prophet's truthfulness and trustworthiness a sign is given, which consists of an act implying a deviation from the ordinary laws of nature (comp. Exod. iii. and iv.). The Israelites are therefore frequently reminded of 'the great wonders which their eyes saw' (Deut. vii. 19). Those who believed after the sign was given were 'the righteous,' whilst those who did not believe 'went astray.' . . .

" The object of 'the wonders' was to produce belief in the prophecies ; except for such a purpose as this, the regular course of Nature is not disturbed, so that man can make his plans and arrange his affairs on the basis of the continuance of the laws of Nature. The messengers sent by God were not angels, but men like ourselves, in order that the force of the sign may be more apparent ; for, seeing that beings like ourselves perform things which we cannot perform, we conclude that a higher Being has endowed them with extraordinary power for a special purpose. If, however, angels had been chosen for the task of prophets, we should not have considered their performance as signs; but, not knowing the nature of angels, we should have thought that such acts were within the regular and natural powers of angels. Prophets, like other human beings, cannot dispense with the regular functions of the organs of their body; they are subject to the different conditions of health; to poverty, ill-treatment on the part of their fellow-men, and to ignorance about future events, except those communicated to them by Divine inspiration. —I found it necessary to state this here, because there are people who believe that the prophet does not die like ordinary people; others deny him the sensation of hunger and thirst; others again think that he does not suffer from violence and wrong directed against him, and some even believe that nothing is hidden from him. These 'do not know the thoughts of the Lord, and do not understand His counsel.'

" It is, further, my conviction that the prophets were satisfied, by some extraordinary supernatural phenomena, that they were addressed by the Almighty. (Comp. Exod. xxxiii. 9 and Ps. xcix. 7 : 'In a pillar of cloud he speaketh to them.')

" As to the relation of the Egyptian Magicians to Moses, we are informed that ten miracles were wrought by Moses and only three by the Magicians. Even these three were only mentioned in order to show the difference between Moses and the Magicians. Moses acted openly, the Magicians secretly ; the effect of Moses' doing was felt throughout the whole country, that of the Magicians only in a limited space. . . .

" Some one might ask, ' How could Jonah have been chosen for his mission ? Wisdom would forbid us to appoint for an important mission a messenger that is disobedient.' But I have examined the Book of Jonah, and have not found any statement as regards the disobedience of Jonah. On the contrary, I assume that he, like all prophets, brought the Divine message to the Ninevites. We frequently find in the

N

Pentateuch, 'Speak to the children of Israel and tell them,' and we assume that Moses told the Israelites, although this is not distinctly mentioned. The reason why Jonah fled is this: the first message which he actually brought to the inhabitants of Nineveh contained simply a summons to repentance. He feared that he would be again sent to threaten with punishment if they did not return; and if they returned and the threatened catastrophe did not occur, they might in course of time begin to doubt the veracity of his words. He therefore left the land, which was distinguished as the land of prophecy (Jonah iv. 2)."

Rabbi Jehudah ha-levi, in the book *Cuzari* (V. xii.), describes prophecy as an extraordinary gift granted by the Almighty to such human beings as are qualified for it by the highest degree of intellectual development, moral conduct, and an earnest desire for communion with God. Such qualification is found only in a few privileged individuals—"the heart of mankind" (לב האדם)—who, as it were, possess it as an inheritance transmitted from generation to generation, but it can only be possessed or acquired under certain favourable conditions, *e.g.*, that the prophet live in Palestine, the land of prophecy, or have his attention directed to Palestine (I. xcv.).

It was, however, necessary that mankind should derive a benefit from the revelations made to the prophets. All had to learn that it was possible for a human being to receive a direct communication from God. This lesson was given when the Israelites stood round Mount Sinai, and suddenly became prophets. For, although the Israelites believed in the Divine mission of Moses after he had done many wonderful deeds, there remained yet a doubt in their minds whether God could speak to man, and whether the Torah did not originate in the plans and schemes of human beings, which by the help and assistance of God developed to perfection; for it seemed strange to them to ascribe speech, which is corporeal, to a spiritual being. It is this doubt which God intended to remove from their hearts; they were therefore commanded to sanctify themselves inwardly and outwardly, whereby they were prepared for the condition of prophets and for hearing the words of God which were to be directly addressed to them. After a preparation of three days they received the Decalogue, not from any prophet or other person, but from God Himself. But they felt their weakness and their inability to witness such a great sight again. They were convinced that the Torah was communicated by God to Moses, and was not the result of human invention; that prophecy does not consist in the union of the soul of man with the active intellect, in his attaining to great wisdom, or in his mistaking his own words for the words of God. Such erroneous opinions were refuted by the revelation on Mount Sinai.—But, objects the king of the Cuzarites, to believe that God spoke to the Israelites and wrote the Decalogue on the tables of stone amounts to believing in a corporeification of the Deity.—To which objection the following reply is given:—"Far be it from us to think that the Torah contains anything contrary to reason. The Decalogue commences with the commandment to believe in God, and prohibits in the second commandment the representation of God in any corporeal form. How could we, who deny corporeality even to some of His creatures, attribute any corporeal property to the Supreme Being? For it is not the tongue, heart, or brain of Moses that speaks to us, instructs and guides us, but his soul which is rational, incorporeal, and not subject to the relations of space; we ascribe to the soul attributes of angels, of spiritual beings. How much more is this the case with God! We have, therefore, no reason for rejecting the Biblical account of the revelation on Mount Sinai; but we admit that we do not know how the idea became corporeal and was turned into audible speech, what new thing was then created or what things then in existence were annihilated. He is Almighty, and when we say that He created the tablets and covered them with His writing, it was done, like the creation of the heavens, by His word ; that is, it was His Will that His thought should become corporeal to a certain extent and assume the form of tables, and that a certain writing be inscribed on them. Just as the division of the sea and the formation of a broad path between the walls of water was done directly by His Will, without using instruments or employing intermediate causes, so the air that reached the ear of the prophet assumed such a form that sounds were perceived expressing the idea which God desired to communicate to the prophet or to the people" (I., lxxxvii.— lxxxix.). In describing the different meanings of the names of God, *Elohim* and the *Tetragrammaton*,[1] the author says : "The nature of *Elohim* can be perceived by reason, which teaches us that there exists a being who governs the universe. The opinions at which people arrive vary according to the different modes of reasoning which they employ ; the opinions of the philosophers have the greatest probability. But the idea contained in the *Tetragrammaton* cannot be found by reasoning, but is perceived intuitively by that prophetic vision during which man is almost separated from his fellow-men, transformed into an angel, and filled with another spirit ; . . . previous doubts concerning God disappear, he smiles at the arguments by which men generally arrive at the idea of a deity and unity ; he then worships God in love, and would rather sacrifice his life than abandon the worship of God " (IV., xv.).

---

[1] *I.e.*, the name of God consisting of four letters (י, ה, ו and ה). The correct pronunciation of the word not being known, *adonai,* "Lord," is substituted for it.

Abraham Ibn Ezra explains the words "And the Lord spake to Moses" as referring to true speech and not to speech with the mouth, which is merely a representation of the other. "God spake to Moses" as man speaketh to his neighbour; that is to say, directly and not through a messenger (On Exod. xxxiii. 11).—In commenting on the Nineteenth Psalm he says: "The first part shows how the intelligent man can find in nature evidence for the existence and power of the Deity; but there is a far better and more trustworthy witness: the Law, &c., called by David 'perfect,' because no other evidence is required in support of the Divine utterances contained in the Holy Writings" (On Ps. xix. 8).—Ibn Ezra is so firm in his belief in the truth of the Divine Writings that he sets aside the contrary opinions of men as absurd. "We believe in the words of our God and abandon the vain opinions of the sons of man" (On Gen. vii. 19). — Whatever message they brought from God was true, and its realisation could be relied upon provided that the conditions were fulfilled, which were either expressed or implied. In other things, however, which were not contained in the Divine message they were not infallible (On Exod. iv. 20). The prophets were trained for the office. The sons of the prophets (or "the disciples") led a contemplative life of seclusion, in the hope of receiving inspiration, every one according to his faculty (On Exod. iii. 15). The first step in this preparation was "the training in the fear of the Lord," which leads man to heed the negative precepts of the Law. Then follows "the worship of God," which includes the observance of all positive precepts (Yesod Mora, vii.).

Maimonides (Mishneh torah, I.; Yesode ha-torah, vii. 1): —"One of the principles of our faith is to believe that God inspires men. The inspiration can only take place in men who distinguish themselves by great wisdom and moral strength; who are never overcome by any passion, but, on the contrary, overcome all passions; who possess wide and profound knowledge. If those who are endowed with these various gifts, and, being physically perfect, enter the garden of speculation, are absorbed in these great and difficult problems, have the mind to understand and to comprehend, sanctify themselves more and more, abandon the ways of the common people that walk in the deep darkness of the time, and zealously train themselves in freeing their mind from useless things, the vanities and tricks of the time, in order always to keep the mind free for reflecting on higher things, on the most holy and pure forms, on the whole work of the Divine Wisdom from the first sphere to the centre of the earth, and to comprehend thereby the greatness of God: then they will at once be inspired with the holy spirit, their soul will then be in the society of angels, they will become other beings, they will feel that they are not the same as before, that they are above other men, even above the wise. Thus it is said of Saul, 'And thou wilt prophesy with them, and be turned into another man'" (1 Sam. x. 6).

The same opinion is expressed by Maimonides in his " Commentary on the Mishnah" (Sanhedrin, xi. 1), and in "The Guide" (III., xxxii.). In the latter (*l. c.*) the various views on prophecy are fully discussed, and the difference between the view of Maimonides and that of the "philosophers" is given more distinctly. According to the philosophers, the highest physical, moral, and intellectual development is the sole means for the acquisition of the prophetic faculty. Maimonides demands in addition to this the Divine Will; he reserves, as it were, for the Supreme Being a kind of veto, and believes that the prophetic faculty may, by Divine interference, *i.e.*, by a miracle, be withheld from a person in spite of all preparation and fitness. He compares this interference to the sudden paralysis and equally sudden recovery

of the hand of King Jeroboam (1 Kings xiii. 4). Although
the physical conditions for the motion of the hand were
present, the motion could not take place, because it was the
Will of God that the hand should at that particular time not
be able to perform its natural functions.

The question naturally suggests itself, Why, then, is the
number of prophets so exceedingly small? Why are there
no prophets amongst the large host of philosophers whose
intellectual faculties have been most highly developed, and
who apparently live in a sphere of ideals far above earthly
and ordinary passions? Maimonides denies the fact that the
conditions are fulfilled; he believes that the life of the philosophers is on the whole not so pure as would qualify them
for the office of prophecy (II., xxxvi.).

But Bileam, Laban, and Abimelech enjoyed the privilege
of Divine communication, although they had not attained to
the highest degree of moral sanctity. Maimonides says in
reference to the dreams of Abimelech and Laban (*ibid.*, chap.
xli.) : "The sentence, 'And Elohim (an angel) came to a
certain person in the dream of the night,' does not indicate
a prophecy, and the person to whom Elohim appeared is not
a prophet; the phrase only informs us that the attention
of the person was called by God to a certain thing, and at
the same time that this happened at night. For just as
God may cause a person to move in order to save or kill
another, so He may cause, according to His Will, certain
things to rise in man's mind in a dream by night. We
have no doubt that the Syrian Laban was a wicked man
and an idolater. Abimelech, though himself a virtuous
man, is told by Abraham, 'I said, Surely there is no fear
of God in this place' (Gen. xx. 11). And yet of both
it is said that Elohim appeared to them in a dream.
Note and consider the distinction between the phrases
'Elohim came' and 'Elohim said;' between 'in a *dream*

by night' and 'in a *vision* by night.' In reference to Jacob it is said, 'And an angel said to Israel in visions by night' (Gen. xlvi. 2), whilst in reference to Abimelech and Laban it is said, 'Elohim came to Abimelech (or to Laban) in the dream by night' (*Ibid.* xx. 3 and xxxi. 24). Onkelos therefore renders this phrase : 'A word came from the Lord,' and not 'God revealed himself.'"

Bileam is, according to Maimonides, in some respect like Laban and Abimelech; what God told him in a dream by night was not a prophecy. In other respects he is described by this philosopher as a person endowed with רוח הקדש "the holy spirit ;" *i.e.*, he felt that some influence had come upon him, and that he had received a new power which encouraged him to speak for a certain object (The Guide, xlv.). Maimonides adds that at that time Bileam was still a virtuous man.—This view of the position which Bileam occupies in the class of inspired men is different from the place assigned to him in the Midrash, where the following passage occurs : "'There arose no prophet again in Israel like Moses;' that is to say, in Israel none arose, but among other nations there was a prophet as great as Moses, namely, Bileam" (Sifre, Deut. xxxiv. 10). Whatever may be the meaning of these words—whether they are meant as a satire or not—they seem to indicate that Bileam possessed a high degree of prophetic faculty. But comparing the deeds of Bileam with those of Moses, we find that the latter guided the Israelites and led them to good deeds and to a virtuous life, whilst Bileam misled those who followed his guidance to sin and vice.

The view of Maimonides, that man after due preparation and training may still be debarred from the rank of prophet, is severely criticised by the Commentators of the Guide. They maintain that God, after having invited and encouraged man to approach Him, would not then thwart

the very hope He had implanted. According to their opinion, God's hand is extended to all; every one may acquire
the prophetic faculty, and those who have not acquired it
have not been duly qualified for it. (Comp. the Comm. of
Ephodi, Narboni a. o. on "The Guide," II., xxxii.).

Albo (Ikkarim, III., vii. *sqq.*) likewise admits that it is
impossible to imagine a prophet who has not attained a high
degree of moral and intellectual perfection. But he does
not consider the prophetic faculty as a natural development
of man's intellectual faculties. It is solely and directly due
to Divine inspiration (שפע אלהי), by means of which man
acquires a knowledge of things which are otherwise beyond
the limits of human intellect. Of what nature the inspiration is, how it gives certitude to the prophet, and by what
psychical process it is accomplished, only the prophet himself can fully comprehend. Albo, like Maimonides, assumes
different degrees of inspiration from the inspiration (רוח
ה') which moved Samson to heroic deeds and David to
sacred songs, to the prophetic communion of Moses with
God "face to face." The clearness of the prophet's utterances varies according to the different degrees of his prophetic
faculty, although all are equally true.

On the Seventh Principle, p. 133.

The words שנבואת משה רבנו ע״ה היתה אמתית have been
wrongly translated "that the prophecy of Moses was true,"
because this is contained in the sixth principle, which applies equally to Moses and to all other prophets. The term
אמתית does here not denote "true," but "real," "perfect," or
"direct;" and the difference between the Divine inspiration
of Moses and that of other prophets is expressed in the
above phrase, in accordance with the distinction made in the
Pentateuch (Num. xii. 8). It has been considered neces-

sary to formulate this distinction between Moses and other
prophets in a separate article, because it is of great importance in the proof of the Immutability of the Law.

Maimonides in "The Guide" (chap. xxxv.) and Mishneh
torah (I., Hilchoth Yesode ha-torah vii. 6) fully describes the
difference between Moses and other prophets. He enumerates
four points :—(1.) Other prophets received the Divine message in a vision or a dream, whilst Moses received it in a state
of complete consciousness, being awake, and apprehending
the words like those spoken by a man to his fellow-men.
(2.) Other prophets received the message in images, which
they had first to interpret before communicating it to their fellow-men ; Moses was addressed by God in clear words and not
in figurative speech. (3.) Other prophets were overcome by
the sight, and were in a state of fear and trembling ; Moses experienced nothing of this kind. (4.) Moses was sure to receive a
Divine reply whenever he sought it ; not so the other prophets.

Maimonides comes thus to the conclusion that the term
"prophet" when applied to Moses cannot have the same
meaning as it has when applied to other Divine messengers ;
and the prophecy of Moses differs from that of other prophets
not only in degree, but in kind. There are, however, other
theologians who hold that the prophecy of Moses is of the
same kind as that of other prophets, and excels the rest
only by a higher degree of prophetic faculty. (Comp. Albo
Ikkarim, III., xvii.)

On the Eighth Principle, p. 134.

The integrity and authenticity of the Pentateuch has
been subjected to all kinds of tests by critics of every
age. The Massoretic remarks, to which allusions are found
in the Talmud, seem to include the result of critical examination of the text of the Bible. Thus we read in the

treatise Aboth di-Rabbi Nathan (chap. xxxiv.) : " There are ten passages in the Pentateuch which are provided with points on the top of the letters, namely, Gen. xvi. 5 ; xviii. 9 ; xix. 33 ; xxxiii. 4 ; xxxvii. 12 ; Num. iii. 39 ; ix. 10 xxi. 30 ; xxix. 15 ; Deut. xxix. 28. What is the meaning of these points ? Ezra—who is supposed to have added them—said, 'If Elijah should come and show me that the reading was wrong, I should tell him that for that reason I marked them with points ; and if he should say that I wrote correctly, I should remove the points.' " In the treatise So-ferim (vi. 4) the following passage occurs :—" Rabbi Simeon ben Lakish said, Three copies of the Pentateuch were found in the hall of the Temple ; they are called *Sefer meonah*, *Sefer zatute*, and *Sefer hee*. In the one מעון was written instead of מעונה (Deut. xxxiii. 27), in the other זאטוטי (Exod. xxiv. 5) instead of נערי, and in the third eleven times היא instead of הוא. The reading that was found only in one of the three copies was rejected, and that of the other two pre-ferred. The received text has therefore מעונה, נערי, and היא."

These instances which tradition has preserved, are evi-dence of the great care and conscientiousness with which Ezra the Scribe and other men transcribed and multiplied copies of the Pentateuch. We learn further from these instances that the text was never altered, even where the sense did not seem quite clear ; and where the reading had been changed in some cases, the Massoretic notes show the way how to read the word whilst the text was retained in its original form. This is the cause of the *Keri* and *Kethib*, " How the word is read " and " How it is written." In the Talmud a certain number of passages are described as *tikkun soferim*, " The style of the scribes ; " others as *ittur soferim*, " Elegance of the scribes." Commentators have interpreted these terms as indicating alterations of the text ; but the instances quoted for illustration do not contain any trace of such a process. An instance of *tikkun soferim* is,

"And Abraham stood yet before the Lord" (Gen. xviii. **22**). These words were believed to continue the account of the Divine vision introduced by the words, "And God appeared to Abraham" (*ibid.* xviii. 1), and interrupted by the narrative of the visit of the three angels. The reader might have expected, "And God stood yet before Abraham." The method of expressing the same in the above form for the sake of euphemism is called *tikkun soferim.* From the instances of *ittur soferim* quoted in the Talm. Nedarim 37*b*, we infer that the occasional omission of the copulative *vav* was designated by that name. (Comp. Gen. xviii. 5, אחר).

In Midrashic interpretations of the Bible we frequently meet with the phrase אל תקרי, "Do not read," seemingly implying an emendation of the Biblical text. It is, however, certain that the authors of such interpretations did not for a moment entertain the idea that the passage in question was corrupt and required correction. What was meant by the above phrase is this : A Jewish audience was supposed to be familiar with the text of the Bible, and it was therefore believed that the lessons which the teacher or preacher desired to impart would better reach the heart of the listener, and be more easily retained in his memory, if it were expressed in the words of some Biblical passage. If a passage could, by a slight alteration, be made to serve this purpose, such alteration was adopted and introduced with the words אל תקרי, "Do not read, . . . but . . ."

There are also some instances in the Talmud and the Midrashim of Biblical quotations not in harmony with the received text. This discrepancy is either due to the fact that preachers and expounders quoted from memory, and may have erroneously confounded two similar passages, or it is due to the carelessness of the copyists. Indications of a Biblical text at variance with the received text are found in the ancient Versions. But, with the exception of the Chaldee Version of the Pentateuch by Onkelos, and that of the Prophets by Jonathan, we have no authorised Version, and it is uncertain how many of the discrepancies have their origin in a corrupt text in the hands of the translator, and how many of them are due to the error of the translator in misreading or mistranslating the correct text before him. By no means are these facts sufficient ground for doubting the correctness of the received text, however plausible the suggested emendations may appear.

Samaritans and Mohammedans have accused the Jews of having altered the text of the Bible; but they have not proved the charge. (See Emunah-ramah, 5th Principle, chap. ii.)

Modern critics have impugned the authenticity of most of the Biblical books. We will discuss their opinions concerning three of these books, and these are the most important ones concerning which Tradition speaks most decidedly, viz., the Pentateuch, the Prophecies of Isaiah, and the Book of Daniel.

The existence of the Pentateuch at the time when the other Biblical books were written is clear from the frequent references to the history and the laws contained in it. Such are, *e.g.* : " Only be thou strong and very courageous, that thou mayest observe to do according to all the law which Moses, my servant, commanded thee," &c. " This book of the law shall not depart out of thy mouth," &c. (Jos. i. 7, 8). " As Moses, the servant of the Lord, commanded the children of Israel, as it is written in the book of the law of Moses," &c. " And he wrote there upon the stones a copy of the law of Moses which he wrote in the presence of the children of Israel. And afterward he read all the words of the law, the blessing and cursings, according to all that is written in the book of the law " (*Ibid.* viii. 31, 32, 34). " Keep the charge of the Lord thy God, to walk in his ways, to keep his statutes and his commandments, and his judgments, and his testimonies, as it is written in the law of Moses," &c. (1 Kings

ii. 3). "But the children of the murderers he slew not: according unto that which is written in the book of the law of Moses," &c. (2 Kings xiv. 6). "Keep the passover unto the Lord your God, as it is written in the book of the covenant" (*Ibid.* xxiii. 21). "Remember the law of Moses, my servant, which I commanded unto him in Horeb for all Israel, statutes and judgments" (Mal. iii. 16).

The authors of the other books of the Bible show famili arity with the words, the phrases, and the contents of the Pentateuch. Thus Psalm civ. is based on the first chapter of Genesis; the flood is mentioned in Ps. xxix. and in the prophecies of Isaiah (liv. 9); the history of the Patriarchs and of the Israelites in Egypt and in the wilderness in Ps. cvi., lxxviii.; the history of Jacob is alluded to in Hosea xii.; the destruction of Sodom and Gomorrah in Isa. i. 9, Amos iv. 11.

Of the laws contained in the Pentateuch many are men- tioned or alluded to in the books of the Prophets and the Hagiographa; the feast of Passover (Jos. iv.), Tabernacles (Zech. xiv. 16–20, Ezra iii. 4, Neh. viii. 14–18); the first day[1] of the seventh month (New-year) is mentioned as a "holy day" (Neh. viii. 10). The dietary laws are referred to by Isaiah (lxvi. 17); the laws of cleanness and uncleanness form the text of a prophecy of Haggai (ii. 10 *sqq.*). Such phrases as "Uncircumcised in heart" (Jer. ix. 25) and "Thou wilt purify me with hyssop and I shall be clean" (Ps. li. 9) show familiarity with the laws of the Pentateuch. Sabbath and sacrifices are frequently mentioned. Critics, however, assert that certain laws seem to have been unknown or out of practice in the period of the Judges and the Kings. There is, *e.g.*, a perfect silence as to the celebration of "the Day of Blowing the *shofar*" and "the Day of Atonement," even where such

[1] The "second day" (Neh. viii. 13), as a day of devotion and medi- tation on the Word of God, is probably the Day of Atonement.

mention is suggested by the context, as Kings viii. 65, 66, and Nehemiah viii. But the inspired historians preferred to describe the celebration of those festivals that had been neglected, or those that were also of national and political importance by concentrating the mass of the people in the capital ; such festivals were Passover and Tabernacles. The Day of Blowing the *shofar* and the Day of Atonement were set aside for quiet, private devotion and meditation, the additional service in the Temple being in the hands of the priests, and the observation of these days as holy days in accordance with the Law was a matter of course, and was not considered by the authors as a memorable event that required special notice. One of the prophecies of Isaiah (chap. lviii.) seems to have reference to the Day of Atonement.

That in the days of the Judges, when "every man did what was right in his eyes," and during the reign of wicked kings many laws were ignored or broken is not at all surprising. When the sacrifices offered up by Samuel and Solomon are adduced as a proof that the Law, which only allows priests to sacrifice, was not known in those days, the argument is based on a misinterpretation of the Biblical text. When laymen brought sacrifices, the priests performed the service for them ; the principal thing to be mentioned was in whose name or in whose presence the sacrifice was brought ; it was unnecessary to state that the priests had to sprinkle the blood and to burn certain portions upon the altar ; no one doubted it.

Another argument against the authenticity of the Pentateuch has been based on the fact related in the second book of Kings (xxii. 8 *sqq.*) : " And Hilkiah the high priest said unto Shaphan the scribe, I have found a book of the law in the house of the Lord. And Shaphan the scribe showed the king, saying, Hilkiah the priest hath delivered me a book. And Shaphan read it before the king. And it came to pass when the king had heard the words of the book of the law, that he rent his clothes." It is maintained by some scholars that the book, which seems to have been an unknown thing to those who found it and to the king, had only just then been written. This is not what is directly stated in the Bible. Hilkiah speaks of *the Law* התורה, the well-known Torah; he would not have said so if the Torah had not been in existence before. Furthermore, the king on hearing the words of the book rent his garments, and sent to inquire of the Lord concerning the words of this book; for "great is the wrath of the Lord that is kindled against us because *our fathers have not hearkened unto the words of this book.*" These words of the king clearly show that the king was convinced of the divine character of the book, and also of its existence in the time of his forefathers. The fact that King Josiah accuses "the fathers" suggests the following explanation of the event :—During the reign of the wicked King Manasseh the reading of the Law was interrupted; the book itself was hidden lest it should be destroyed by the idolatrous priests; now that it was found again, the king was reminded that the Torah had been neglected in the interval through the sin of the preceding generation. Whether there was another copy of the Law in the Temple, whether the one found by Hilkiah was complete, or contained only a portion of the Law, perhaps Deuteronomy, chap. xxvii. and chap. xxviii., which are in the Pentateuch called "the words of this covenant" and also "the words of the curse," titles which occur also in reference to the above copy in the books of Kings and Chronicles; to these and similar questions the Biblical account gives no decided answer. Only so much is certain that the book found was not new or unknown to those who found it, and the king recognised it as the book of the Torah.

Far from finding in the other books of the Bible any evidence—whether positive or negative—of the later origin ot the Torah, we feel convinced that their contents pre-suppose not only the existence of the Torah, but also the authors' familiarity with it. Without the Torah the other books are unintelligible. There is nothing in the Pentateuch that betrays a post-Mosaic origin. If the Pentateuch had been written in the period of the Kings, the author would have mentioned Jerusalem as the appointed place for the Sanctuary; in the rebukes (תוכחה), in addition to idolatry, the social corruption pointed out by the prophets would have been mentioned; the restrictive law concerning the marriage of heiresses would have been superfluous, as it only applied to the first generation that entered Palestine.

The phrase עבר הירדן has been quoted as a proof that the author of the Pentateuch must have lived in Palestine, or else he could not have called the east banks of the Jordan "the other side of Jordan;" but this translation is wrong. The phrase only means the banks of Jordan.

In the Talmud the Pentateuch in its entirety is ascribed to Moses. "Moses wrote his book and the book of Bileam" (Babyl. Talm. Baba Bathra, 14*b*). The book of Bileam is the section of Numbers which contains the parables of Bileam (from xxii. 2 to xxiv.).

There is, however, a difference of opinion with regard to the last eight verses of the Pentateuch. According to Rabbi Jehudah (or Rabbi Nehemiah) Joshua wrote this passage. Rabbi Shimeon objected: "Is it possible that the Torah was incomplete when Moses was told, 'Take this book of the law?' (Deut. xxxi. 26).[1] God dictated the last eight verses of the Pentateuch to Moses, and the latter wrote them with tears."

With this exception, no doubt was entertained by any

---

[1] It is here assumed that the Torah was not intended to be written in a chronological order, and that this commandment was given after the Blessing of Moses was written.

O

of the Rabbis as to the integrity of the Torah. Various, however, were the opinions as to the method followed by Moses in writing down the events and the laws. Rabbi Jochanan, following the opinion of Rabbi Banaah, held that the Torah was written by Moses piecewise at different times, just as the events happened or as each law was revealed to him. Rabbi Shimeon ben Lakish said "it was given at one time in its entirety" (Babyl. Talm. Gittin 60a).

Passages of the Torah which seemed to contradict each other, or to be contradicted by statements found in other books of the Bible, were thoroughly discussed and explained. The belief in the integrity and divinity of the Torah was so strong that those who rejected either of these beliefs were considered as unworthy of the blessings of the future world (Babyl. Talm. Sanhedrin 99a).

With the rise of Karaism Bible criticism received new encouragement, as in the warfare between Karaism and Rabbinism, or Scripturalists and Traditionalists, it furnished both sides with sharp weapons. Some, however, of the commentators went further, and gave utterance to all sorts of heterodox views. Thus a certain Yitzchaki of Spain was of opinion that Gen. xxxvi. 31–43 was a later addition, on account of the phrase, "These were the kings who ruled over Edom before a king ruled over Israel." The critics forgot that this passage is intended to point out the advance which Esau's descendants had made, when the prophecy, "And kings shall come forth out of thee" (xxxv. 11) had not yet been fulfilled in the case of the Israelites.

Of the Commentators of the Middle Ages, Ibn Ezra is generally singled out as an advanced scholar who held certain passages of the Pentateuch as later additions. Ibn Ezra was far from such views, and he sharply rebuked those who entertained them. Thus he says of Yitzchaki, the author of the above criticism, "Every one who will hear this will laugh at him, and his book deserves to be burnt." With equal vigour he criticises a grammarian who pointed out certain passages as grammatically incorrect, and also another scholar who in his interpretations of the Bible did not take sufficient notice of the traditional accents. The error concerning Ibn Ezra has its origin in his habit of adding the phrase, "The words have some deeper sense" (יש לו סוד), whenever the literal interpretation does not quite satisfy him, or when the object of the author in adding a seemingly superfluous sentence is not clear to him; as, for instance, in the four passages referred to in the Commentary on Deuteronomy i. 2, namely, "The Canaanite was then in the land" (Gen. xii. 6), "On the mount of the Lord will it appear" (*Ibid.* xxii. 14), the repetition of the sacrifices of the twelve princes (Num. vii.), and the stations enumerated in Numbers (chap. xxxiii.), in addition to the detailed geographical description of Deut. i. 1 *sqq.* The meaning of this remark has been misunderstood by the early expounders of Ibn Ezra's Commentary, and since then the mistake has been repeated by most of the critics of the Bible. Spinoza, in his theological treatise, quotes Ibn Ezra, with the usual misinterpretation, in support of his view concerning the Torah.

Modern critics have attempted to analyse the Pentateuch, and to assign to it several authors, revisers, and editors. But there is little harmony among the critics; the one considers as the latest addition what the other holds to be the oldest portions of the book. Numerous emendations are made by every one of them in order to establish his special theory. The fundamental principle of most of them is that the section in which the name *Elohim* is prevalent could not have been written by the author of another section in which the *Tetragrammaton* is employed. But the two names, though denoting the same Being, are not identical in meaning: the one signifies the Almighty, who is the Ruler of the universe, the Master and Judge of all beings; the other is the name of the Merciful Father, who reveals Himself to man, interferes in his behalf, and has especially revealed His Providence and Kindness to the Israelites.

A careful study of the Hebrew Bible will show that it is not the author, or the age of the author, but the contents of the passage that determined which of the Divine names was to be used. The same author repeats the same account with some variation, according to the lesson which he intends to convey to the reader. The proofs which are based on the differences discovered in two accounts of apparently the same event, or on seeming contradictions or anachronisms, are so indifferently supported that they are not able to conquer the fortress of Faith and Tradition. The difficulties pointed out by the critics vanish before patient study and the earnest longing for instruction and comfort offered by the Bible.

The Book of Isaiah has likewise been subjected to the analytical test of the critic, and it is generally believed that the prophecies contained in the book have not all been written by the same author or in the same age. The book is divided into two large sections; the second section, from chap. xl. to chap. lxvi., is thought to have been composed shortly before the return of the Jews from Babylon. Although it is possible that anonymous prophecies were added to a book, the reasons which induced critics to make such a division are untenable. The first reason is the difference in style; but we must take account of the difference in the contents of the two sections. The prophecies in the first section have mostly a threatening tendency with regard to imminent punishment, whilst in the second section Israel is to be encouraged in his faith in the Almighty and in his hopes for a better future. It is but natural that the style should not be the same in both sections.

Another reason for ascribing the second section to a later prophet is the fact that Koresh (Cyrus), king of Persia, is mentioned by name, and the fall of Babylon and the consequent
deliverance of the Jews are described as well-known facts of
the past. This and similar arguments are based on a misunderstanding of the character of the prophecies. The critics
ignore the essential difference between the writings of inspired
messengers of God and those of ordinary men. They deny to
the man of God the power of foreseeing and foretelling coming
events of which his fellow-men could not have any knowledge. By such arguments the critics set limits to the power
and wisdom of God, and employ the same measure for both
that which is Divine and that which is human. A Divine
prophet has, by the Will of the Almighty, the future unrolled
before him ; he sees the catastrophe which is to come centuries later, and perceives its effect and its end. Even when
he reviews the present state of affairs and takes the immediate
future into consideration, his eyes frequently behold scenes
and events of "the end of the days" (באחרית הימים), which
he points out as the goal of our hopes and aspirations. When
he warns, advises, or encourages his brethren with regard to
their present wants, the virtues and the happiness of the Messianic age are not rarely introduced. Earlier events, though
still future in time, appear then in the light of accomplished
facts, and in their description the past tense is used instead
of the future. Thus it happened that the prophet Isaiah,
who flourished during the reign of King Hezekiah, could take
his standpoint on the return of the Jews from Babylonia,
look back at the exile as a thing of the past, and reveal to his
brethren further troubles, the succeeding final redemption,
and the ultimate triumph of the faithful and God-fearing
over the faithless and wicked.

It is true that it is an unusual thing for a prophet to
name a king who is to rule centuries after the death of the

prophet, unless the name is a common noun, and has by
its meaning some bearing on the prophecy. The name
Cyrus fulfils, perhaps, this condition; according to Ktesias,
it signifies "sun," an appropriate name to be given to the
king who is destined to be the deliverer of a captive people.
King Cyrus may have assumed this name when he became
convinced of the mission entrusted to him by Providence.

The authenticity of the Book of Daniel has likewise been
impugned, and its advocates are, it must be admitted, at present very few. The narratives which the book contains are
considered as improbable or even impossible, and its visions
as prophecies *ex facto*. It was written, according to these
critics, in the period of the Maccabees, and the name of
Daniel was chosen in order to give more weight to the contents of the book, Daniel being known as a man famous for
his piety among his fellow-exiles. Against this we have the
distinct evidence in the book, in which the author is described
as the same Daniel that lived during the Babylonian exile;
Jewish tradition knew of no other author of the book than
Daniel. Although the Book of Daniel was not placed amongst
the books of the Prophets, because he was not charged with
any mission to his fellow-men, the visions described in
Daniel were nevertheless, in Jewish literature, considered as
true and genuine prophecy. The narratives have the distinct object to teach that piety and firmness in obedience to
the word of God can conquer the rage of the most powerful
tyrants; this tendency on the part of the author is especially
noticed in the manner in which every circumstance bearing
on this lesson is depicted. This, however, does not detract
the least from the truth and genuineness of the facts which,
by the plan of Providence, seem to have taken place for
this very purpose. The demand of the king that the magicians should tell him his dream, which he himself had forgotten, and that failing to do so they should be put to death;

the decree commanding his subjects to worship the idol and to pray to him, and other foolish royal acts, almost incredible to us, are strange indeed, but would appear less strange if all the records of the acts of Eastern tyrants had been preserved. It has been contended that the history of the Syrian wars with Egypt, and the suffering of the Jews through the Syrian invasion, is given in such detail as could only be done by a contemporary. But apart from the fact that a careful study of the visions of Daniel will convince us that we have here only a faint outline of the Syrian wars and not a detailed description, it must not be forgotten that the author only reproduces what was shown to him by the Omniscient concerning the most important event in the history of the nation—the preservation of the holy religion through the firmness and the courage of a few faithful servants of God. The fulfilment of the portion of the vision which referred to the period of the Maccabees is a guarantee for the fulfilment of the prophecies yet unrealised.

In like manner have the authenticity and the integrity of other Biblical books been rejected; the method and the arguments are the same; they are based on a misunderstanding of the true essence of prophecy and inspiration, and originate in a want of belief in the Omniscience and Omnipotence of the Divine Being.

On the Ninth Principle, p. 139.

In the Pentateuch there is not the slightest indication that the laws revealed on Sinai might be superseded by a future Revelation. On the contrary, we meet repeatedly with the phrases, חקת עולם, "an everlasting statute," לדרות עולם, "for everlasting generations," and similar expressions, which clearly show the intention of Him who gave the laws that these should last for ever. The Israelites were told that

Prophets would be sent to them, and that they must listen
to the Prophets and obey them, but at the same time they
were commanded to put to death a prophet who would
attempt "to turn them aside from the way which the Lord
commanded them to walk therein" (Deut. xiii. 6). Besides,
the Prophets never speak of a new Revelation, which would
supersede the Torah. When Jeremiah prophesies about a *new
covenant*, the context teaches the reader what is meant by the
"new covenant." He speaks of the future and final restoration of Israel as follows: "Behold, days will come, saith the
Lord, when I shall make a new covenant with the house of
Israel and with the house of Judah. Not like the covenant
which I made with their fathers on the day when I took hold
of their hand to bring them out of the land of Egypt, because they broke my covenant, and I rejected them, saith the
Lord. But this is the covenant which I shall make with the
house of Israel after those days, saith the Lord, when I set
my Law among them and write it upon their heart : both I
shall be to them a God, and they shall be to me a people"
(Jer. xxxi. 31–33). The Law is not to be altered, but it
will dwell more firmly in the heart of Israel ; the deliverance
from Egypt was soon forgotten, but the future deliverance
will plant the fear and love of God—here called the Law of
God—in the hearts of the people in such a manner that it
will take a deep root and will not be plucked out of it again.
There occur, however, in Talmud and Midrash sayings
which seem to imply a future alteration of the Law ; *e.g.*,
"In future all prayers will cease except that of thanksgiving ; in future all sacrifices will cease except that of thanks-
offerir " (Midrash on Ps. c.). In these sayings their authors
simply intended to emphasise the duty of thanksgiving ; even
in the state of physical and moral perfection, when there
will be a perfect absence of trouble and fear and a perfect
immunity of sin, so that there will be nothing to be prayed

for, nothing to be atoned for through sacrifice, the duty
of offering prayers and sacrifices of thanksgiving will still
remain in full force. Another saying of this kind is: "If
all festivals were to cease, Purim will never be forgotten"
(Piyyut for Sabbath Zachor); that is, even if other festivals
should be neglected, Purim is so much liked that it will
never be forgotten by the Jews. In Talmud Jerus. Megillah
(i. 7) we read: "The reading from the Prophets and the
Hagiographa may at some future time be discontinued, but
the reading of the Pentateuch will never be abolished."
The idea expressed by this dictum is, that the warnings or
consolations or prayers may become superfluous by the
changed condition of the future, but the laws and statutes
of the Pentateuch will always remain in force.

In sayings of this kind the time to which they are
meant to apply is not defined. "The future" (לעתיד לבא)
may mean the time of Messiah, or else the time of the
Resurrection, or what we are used to call "the future life."
As in the above quotation, the authors aimed at inculcating
some moral lesson for the present state of things, and not at
describing the results of philosophical speculation with regard
to remote times. A new revelation, or the abrogation of the
Law or part of it, is nowhere mentioned.

On the contrary, it is emphasised in the Talmud that the
Torah has been given to Israel in its entirety, and nothing
has been reserved for a second revelation. "The Law is not
any longer in heaven," it is entirely in the hands of man.
The only authority recognised in the interpretation of the
Law was that based on knowledge, tradition, and common
sense. Authority claimed for this purpose on the ground
of supernatural privilege, prophecy, *bath-kol* or miracle, was
not recognised (Babyl. Talm. Baba Metsia, 59*b*).

Maimonides (Mishneh torah, Hilchoth Yesode ha-torah
ix.) says on this principle as follows:—"It has been distinctly stated in the Torah that its precepts remain in

force for ever without change, diminution, or addition. Comp. 'The word which I command you that you must keep to do, thou shalt not add ought unto it nor take ought away from it' (Deut. xiii. 1); 'That which has been revealed for us and for our children for ever is to do all the words of this Law' (*Ibid.* xxix. 28). Hence it follows that we are bound for ever to do according to the words of the Torah. It is further said, 'An everlasting statute for all your generations' (Exod. xii. 14, 17, *et passim*); 'It is not in heaven'[1] (Deut. xxx. 12). Hence we see that a prophet cannot reveal any new law. If, therefore, any man, whether an Israelite or a non-Israelite, should rise, perform signs and miracles, and say that the Lord sent him to add one precept or to abolish one of the Divine precepts, or to interpret a precept in a way different from what has been handed down to us from Moses, or assert that the precepts which were given to the Israelites had only temporary force and were not permanent laws : such a man is a false prophet, because he contradicts the prophecy of Moses. The mission of the Prophets after Moses is to exhort the people to obey the Law of Moses, and not to make a new religion."—Comp. " The Guide," II. xxxix. ; and Saadiah, *Emunoth ve-deoth*, III. chap. vii. to x.

Rabbi Jehudah ha-Levi, in the book *Cuzari*, seems to have a different view. He likewise believes in the permanent character of the Torah, but he modifies his view in accordance with his interpretation of the words, " And thou shalt do according to the word which they—viz., the priests and the judge that shall be in those days—will tell thee from that place which the Lord shall choose ; and thou shalt observe to do according to all that they will teach thee " (Deut. xvii. 9, 10). According to his view, these words

---

[1] Maimonides accepts for this verse the Midrashic explanation : nothing of the Torah has remained in heaven for later revelations.

imply that from time to time prophets or inspired men, or the highest authority of the nation, whilst the *Shechinah* was still filling the Temple, issued laws and orders, which had legal force, and all were bound to obey them. But since the destruction of the Temple there has not been any man or any court that had the authority to make new permanent laws. According to Maimonides, however, there were no additions made to the Torah; the Rabbinical laws are either temporary regulations or served as a means of ensuring the strict observance of the Torah.

Albo, in criticising the principles of faith as laid down by Maimonides, objects also to the Ninth Principle, and contends that it is not fundamental, since the belief in the Divine origin of the Law does not necessarily imply the belief in its eternity. But although the possibility of a second revelation superseding the first is admitted in principle or theory, it does not follow that such revelation has in reality been made. If any person asserts that he is sent by God to repeal the old laws or to alter them, he must prove his Divine mission before he can be believed. We are fully convinced of the Divine mission of Moses, and our conviction of the Divine mission of the new prophet must at least be equally strong. The Divine character of the mission of Moses was revealed to the Israelites by God Himself; and only such direct revelation could satisfy us as to the trustworthiness of the new prophet (Ikkarim III. xix.).

R. Abraham ben David, in his book *Emunah-ramah*, finds in various passages of the Bible indications that the Torah was to remain in force permanently. Thus Isaiah and Zechariah, speaking of the remote future, refer respectively to the celebration of Sabbath and New-moon, and to the celebration of Sukkoth. Again, in refuting the claims of Christians on behalf of Jesus, and of Mohammedans on behalf of Mohammed, to a Divine mission to substitute a new covenant for the old one, Rabbi Abraham argues thus : " The divinity of the old covenant, or the Torah, has been admitted by both Jesus and Mohammed ; we need not prove it. But the Divine authority asserted by them for its abrogation or change is not admitted by us ; it must be proved ; and since no proof has been given, it must be rejected " (Fifth Principle, chap. ii.).

On the Tenth Principle, p. 148.

It is noteworthy that this principle is exceptionally supported by a Biblical verse. The same may be noticed in the book *Cuzari* (V. xviii.), in the enumeration of the principles of faith according to the methods of Mohammedan Theologians (*Medabberim*); the principle of God's Omniscience is supported by a Biblical verse, only with this difference, that in the *Cuzari* it is not exactly the principle of God's Omniscience, but its proof derived from the Creation, that is supported by a quotation from Ps. xciv. The reason of the anomaly is this : Some of the opponents of this principle contend that it would be derogatory to the greatness of God if He were to take notice of the doings of each individual being. To this the reply is given : The Psalmist, who was far from saying anything derogatory of God, declared that God knows the deeds and the thoughts of each individual.

The problem how to reconcile God's Prescience and Omniscience with man's Free-will has of course engaged the attention of all Jewish theologians and philosophers, and, though in different ways and words, they all assume that God's knowledge of a thing is by no means the *cause* of its existence. (See *Cuzari*, V. xx. ; " Guide," III. xx. ; Saadiah, *Emunoth*, II. chap. ix.)

Perhaps a reconciliation is not necessary at all, there being no conflict. We should not call it a defect in God if His Omniscience were restricted to things knowable ; a prescience of things to be determined by man's free-will is contradictory in itself, and illogical, and to say that God would not be omniscient if He did not know them, is as absurd as to say that God would not be omnipotent if He could not make twice two to be three.

On the Eleventh Principle, p. 150.

The subject of this creed has been the main thought of the lesson preached by the prophets, of the hymns sung by the psalmists, and of the narratives written by the sacred chroniclers, as has been illustrated above (p. 155) by Biblical quotations. To these may be added (1.) the song *haazinu*, the professed object of which was to remind the Israelites of God's Justice whenever evil should befall them. The words which form the basis of the song, viz., "The Rock, perfect is his work," &c. (Deut. xxxii. 4), are also at present recited at funeral rites, as צדוק הדין, an expression of our firm belief in God's Justice. (2.) The prophet who laments over the fall of Jerusalem declares : "Out of the mouth of the Most High do not come forth the evil things and the good (*i.e.,* man causes them by his evil or good deeds, which are the result of his own free will and not of the Will of God). Why should man complain (of what has befallen him), being master over his sins ?" (Lam. iii. 38, 39).

In the Talmud the doctrine of God's Justice is expressed thus : "Thy employer is trustworthy, that he will pay thee the reward of thy deeds" (Aboth ii. 21). "The shop is open, and the merchant gives on credit, and all who like may come and borrow ; but the collectors go constantly about, and exact payment whether the debtor is willing to pay or not, for they have something to rely upon, and the judgment is a just judgment ; and everything is prepared for a banquet" (Aboth iii. 20). "God does not withhold ought of the desert of any creature" (Pesachim, 118*a*).

It is, however, emphatically declared in the **Talmud that** the reward of good deeds is given to the righteous in the future life, עולם הבא, " The reward for obedience to the Divine commandments is not to be expected in this world " (Kiddushin, 39*b*). " The Law says with reference to the Divine precepts, ' Which I command thee *this day* to do them ;' hence we infer that their performance is to take place *this day, i.e.*, in this life, but their reward will be received in the future life " (Abodah-zarah, 3*a*).

" Rabbi Elazar ha-kappar used to say, ' Those that have been born will die ; those that have died will come to life again ; those that have come to life again will be judged.' He said so in order that he himself might bear in mind, and tell others, and that it might become generally known, that God, who has formed and created man's heart and understands all his doings, is the Judge, the Witness, and the Prosecutor ; He before whom there is no wrong, no forgetfulness, no partiality, and no bribery, will one day judge. Let thy imagination not persuade thee that the grave is a refuge for thee. For without thy consent hast thou been born, and without thy consent wilt thou die, and without thy consent thou art brought to life again to account for thy deeds before the King of kings, blessed be He " (Aboth iv. 22).

The immediate enjoyment of the reward is, however, not excluded. We read in the Law, " Do this and thy days will be long ; " and the Mishnah teaches, " These are the good acts, the fruit of which man enjoys in this life, whilst the full reward awaits him in the world to come : honouring father and mother, the practice of charity, peace-making between man and man, and above all the study of the Law " (Mishnah, Peah. i. 1).

The faithful Israelite is not discouraged at the sight of the successes of the wicked ; on the contrary, he believes : " If to those who break the Divine laws such kindness is shown

by God, what must be His goodness to those who obey Him ! "
(Midrash Yalkut on Isaiah viii. 1). As regards the troubles
of the good, our Sages teach that the good will receive their
reward " in proportion to their suffering." Yet pious men
do not seek trouble and pain merely for the prospect of
future compensation ; on the contrary, they avail themselves
of every possible means to secure relief, and would even
renounce in their agony all compensation in the future world,
in order to secure release from pain in the present (Babyl.
Talm. Berachoth, 5*a*).

As the life of Adam and Eve in the garden of Eden was
free from care and trouble, and such a life was the ideal of
human hopes and wishes, the Garden-Eden, עֵדֶן גַּן (lit., " the
garden of pleasure "), became the symbol of man's happiness in its perfection, such as will fall to the share of the
good and the righteous. On the other hand, the valley of
Hinnom, near Jerusalem, was a place of horror and dis-
gust ; a place where at one time children were burnt to
Moloch, and where later the refuse of the city was cast.
Dwelling in the valley of Hinnom (גֵּיהִנּוֹם) became the symbol of the punishment to be inflicted on the wicked. Gan-
eden or Paradise, and Gehinnom or Hell, are thus mere
figures to express our idea of the existence of a future retribution, and must not be taken literally as names of certain
places.

The detailed descriptions of Paradise and hell as given
in books both profane and religious are nothing but the
offspring of man's imagination.

The question has been asked, How long shall the punishment of the wicked last ? Will it be eternal ? and if so, is it
compatible with God's goodness ? This and similar questions
do not concern us in the least. Our task is to do what the
Lord has commanded us to do, and to trust, as regards the
future, in Him, who knows best to combine goodness and

justice. We must here bear in mind that "God's thoughts are not ours."

Equally ignorant are we as to the cause of the suffering and of the death of each individual; but of this we are certain, if death is punishment, that every one dies for his own sin. This theory is so frequently repeated in the Bible that it is surprising how the theory of Vicarious Death and Vicarious Atonement could be considered as harmonising with the teaching of the Bible. We are taught that God visits the iniquity of the fathers upon the children, upon the third and upon the fourth generation; but at the same time we are told that the children are only punished if they repeat the sins of their fathers, and even then only for their own sins (comp. p. 251). It has been asserted that Isaiah in chap. liii. assumes the principle of vicarious atonement. That this is not the case we can easily see if we turn from the Anglican Version to the original Hebrew, and translate it literally and in accordance with the context. Isaiah, in describing the future glory of the servant of the Lord (= Israel). tells us what those people who oppress Israel will then feel, and how they will give expression to their feeling of shame and regret, saying, "Surely he hath borne griefs caused by us, and carried sorrows caused by us : yet we did esteem him stricken, smitten of God, and afflicted. But he was wounded through our transgressions, bruised through our iniquities" (comp. Family Bible, Anglican Version, revised by M. Friedländer). Sin-offerings were brought, but not as a vicarious atonement, although the sinner might well have felt that he himself deserved the treatment endured by the sacrifice. The sin-offering could not have been a vicarious atonement, as it was not offered when the sin was committed knowingly. Maimonides explains the various laws concerning sin-offering as based on the principle that the sacrifices serve as the means of reminding us more vividly of our sins, and of their evil consequences (The Guide, III. xlvi. ; comp. Mic. vi. 6–8).

On the Twelfth Principle, p. 155.

A belief in Messiah, although not directly taught, is assumed in the Mishnah as existing ; and the days of Messiah (ימות המשיח) are spoken of as an event that admits of no doubt (comp. Mishnah Berachoth, i. 5). That this belief was in reality taught by the religious heads of the Jewish community is clearly shown by the introduction into the *Amidah* of a prayer [1] for the speedy appearance of Messiah.

The belief in the coming of Messiah in some future time has been, like the belief in the Unity of God, the source of vexatious disputations between Jews and non-Jews. Mohammedans and Christians tried by all means in their power to convince the Jews that the Anointed whose advent was prophesied by the Prophets had already appeared, the former pointing to Mohammed, the latter to Jesus, as the person realising those predictions. The Biblical passages adduced as evidence prove nothing of the kind. *E.g.*, the three names, Sinai, Seir, and Paran, in Deut. xxxiii. 2, were interpreted by Mohammedans to refer to three revelations through Moses, Jesus, and Mohammed ; and Mohammed being mentioned last, his revelation was to be the final one. It is not necessary to contradict such reasoning; one need only read the text in order to see the absurdity of the argument. Christians quoted passages from Isaiah which had no reference whatever to Messiah in evidence of the Messianity of Jesus. Children born in the days of Isaiah (vii. 14 ; viii. 18), whose names had reference to good or evil events of the time, were wrongly interpreted as referring to the birth of Jesus ; the sufferings and final relief of the

---

[1] את צמח דוד עבדך.

servant of the Lord, that is, Israel (chaps. lii. and liii.), were applied to Jesus; the Psalmist who sings of victories which God will grant to David (cx.) is made to declare the divinity of Jesus.

Commentators and philosophers have taken notice of these arguments and refuted them. Of the many works on these topics a few may be named: "Nitsachon" (נצחון), by Lippman Mühlhausen (1400), "Strengthening of Faith" (חזוק אמונה), by Isaak ben Abraham Treki (1594), "Vindiciæ Judæorum," by Manasseh ben Israel (1650).

In refuting arguments brought by Christians and Mohammedans against Jews and Judaism, and rejecting the Messianic claims of Jesus and Mohammed, Jews are ready to acknowledge the good work done by the religions founded by these men, Christians and Mohammedans, in combating idolatry and spreading civilisation. Maimonides says as follows:—"The King Messiah will in some future time come, restore the kingdom of David to its former power, build the Temple, bring together the scattered of Israel, and all the ancient laws will again be in force: sacrifices will be offered, and years of release and Jubilees will be kept as prescribed in the Law. Whoever does not believe in him, or does not hope for his coming, shows a want of faith not only in the Prophets, but also in the Law; for the Law testifies concerning him in the words: 'And the Lord thy God will again bring back thy captivity, show mercy to thee, and again gather thee, &c. If thy outcasts be at the end of the heavens, thence will the Lord gather thee,' &c., 'and the Lord will bring thee,' &c. (Deut. xxx. 3–5), &c.

"You must not imagine that Messiah must prove his Messianity by signs and miracles, doing something unexpected, bringing the dead to life, or similar things, &c. The principal thing is this: the statutes and precepts of our Torah remain for ever, and nothing can be added to them nor ought taken from them. If, therefore, a descendant of David earnestly studies the Law, observes, like David his father, what the Law, both the written and the oral, enjoins, causes all Israelites to act similarly, exhorts those who are lax in the performance of the commandments, and fights the wars of the Lord : he may possibly be Messiah. If he succeeds, builds the Temple in its place, and gathers the outcasts of Israel, he is certainly Messiah ; and if he does not succeed, or is killed in war, it is certain that he is not the Messiah promised in the Law ; he is like all the noble and good kings of the House of David who have died ; and the Almighty only caused him to rise in order to try us thereby, as it is said, ' And of the wise some will stumble, and through them the people will be tested, purified, and made white, till the time of the end comes ; for there is yet a vision for an appointed time ' (Dan. xi. 35). Also Jesus, the Nazarene, who imagined that he would be Messiah, and was killed through the court of law, is alluded to in the Book of Daniel, as it is said, ' And the sons of the transgressors among thy people will rise, in order to establish a vision, and will stumble ' (*ibid.* xi. 14). Can there be a greater stumbling than this ? All the prophets said that Messiah will be a redeemer and a saviour to the Israelites, will bring together their outcasts, and will strengthen their obedience to the Divine precepts, but he (Jesus) caused destruction by the sword to Israel, the dispersion of those left, and their humiliation ; he changed the Law, and misled many people to worship a being beside God. But the thoughts of the Creator of the universe cannot be understood by any human being, for the ways of men are not His ways, nor their thoughts His thoughts ; for all the events connected with Jesus and with Mohammed, that rose after him, served only to pave the way for the King Messiah, who will reform all mankind and lead them to the unanimous service of God, as it is said, ' For then will I turn to the peoples a pure language, that all may call by the name of God, and serve him unanimously' (Zeph. iii. 9). How can this be done? Almost all people have through them — Jesus and Mohammed — become acquainted with the idea of Messiah, with the words of the Torah and the Divine precepts. Through them the knowledge of the Bible spread even unto the remotest islands and unto many nations 'uncircumcised' in heart and uncircumcised in flesh. They seek to justify their disobedience to the precepts of the Torah; some of them say that these precepts are Divine, but are not in force at present, and were never intended to be permanent laws; others maintain that they must not be taken literally, as they are mere symbols, the meaning of which has already been explained by Messiah. But when the true King Messiah will rise, he will prosper, be high and exalted; all will then at once know that it was falsehood what their fathers have inherited, and that their prophets and their teachers have misled them.

"Do not imagine that in the days of Messiah the course of Nature will be altered in any way, or that any new creation will take place. When Isaiah said, 'The wolf will dwell with the lamb, and the leopard will lie down with the kid,' he merely employed allegorical and figurative speech; and he meant to say that the Israelite will dwell in safety together with his enemy, who has been as cruel to him as wolves and leopards, &c.; all will join the true religion; they will not rob, nor commit any violence, &c., and in the days of Messiah the meaning of the allegories will be clearly known.

"Our Sages said that there will be no other difference between the present time and the days of Messiah but the independence of the people of Israel.

"It appears from the literal meaning of the prophecies that the Messianic period will be preceded by the war of Gog and

Magog, and that before the war a prophet will appear to guide the Israelites, and to direct their hearts to repentance. Comp. ' Behold, I will send you Elijah,' [1] &c. (Mal. iii. 23). Elijah will not come to declare unclean that which is clean, or clean that which is unclean ; nor to disqualify persons who are believed to be qualified for joining the congregation of the Lord, or to qualify persons who are believed to be disqualified ; but he will come to establish peace on earth, as it is said, ' He shall turn the heart of the fathers to the children ' [2] (*Ibid.* 24).

" Some of our Sages believe that Elijah will come before Messiah, but of all these and similar things no man knows how they will come to pass ; they are unexplained in the Prophets, and our Sages have no tradition about them ; they only adopt what they believe to be the meaning of the Biblical passages which refer to this subject. Hence the difference of opinion. At all events, the order and the detail of these events do not form an essential portion of our creed ; we must not take too much notice of Agadoth and Midrashim speaking on these and similar themes. We must not attribute great importance to them, for they do not lead to the fear or the love of God. We must also abstain from calculating the time of the coming of Messiah, &c. All we have to do is to believe in the coming of Messiah, to wait and hope.

" It is not because they desired to have dominion over all lands and nations, and be honoured by all people, or because they desired to have plenty to eat and drink, and other pleasures, that the wise men and the prophets longed for the Messianic days, but because they would then be at leisure to study the Law and its teaching without being

---

[1] He is probably called Elijah on account of the zeal which he will display in bringing men back to the service of God.

[2] Mishnah Eduyoth viii. 7.

interrupted by any oppressor, and would thus make themselves worthy of the life in the world to come (עולם הבא).

"There will not be in those days any famine, war, jealousy, or quarrel, because the good things will be in plenty, and even luxuries will be found everywhere; all will only busy themselves with trying to know the Lord. Therefore the Israelites will be great sages, knowing things which are at present hidden; they will obtain a knowledge of their Creator as far as is possible by human understanding; 'For the earth is full with the knowledge of the Lord as the waters that cover the sea'" (Maim., Mishneh-torah xiv.; Hilchoth Melachim xi.–xii.).

The war of Gog and Magog against the Holy Land referred to by Maimonides is described by the prophet Ezekiel (chaps. xxxviii., xxxix.) as preceding the complete restoration of Israel. Saadiah has a different view of this war. The punishment of Israel in exile is to come to an end at a fixed time, or as soon as the Israelites by earnest and thorough repentance show themselves worthy of Divine grace. In that case no war of Gog and Magog will be waged against them. But if the Israelites should allow the approach of the time fixed for the redemption without having given signs of repentance and improvement, great troubles will be brought upon them, which will forcibly remind them of the necessity of returning to God; they will come together under a leader, Messiah ben Joseph, under whose leadership they will fight against their enemies, but will be beaten, and Messiah ben Joseph himself will be killed. Then Messiah ben David will appear, and with him the period of glory, of permanent peace and prosperity, and of the worship of the One God by all nations. The idea of a double Messiah, a warlike and a peaceful, an unsuccessful and a successful, is not expressed in any of the prophecies in the Bible, and seems to be of a later origin. Maimonides is silent about Messiah ben Joseph; so also Albo in *Ikkarim*, and Rabbi Jehudah ha-levi in the book *Cuzari*. Albo discusses the question about Messiah in chap. xlii. of the fourth section of *Ikkarim*. He refutes the opinion of those who maintain that the Messianic prophecies refer to the reign of Hezekiah or to the restoration of Israel under Zerubbabel and Ezra. The condition of the Israelites in the reign of Hezekiah did not resemble the state of prosperity and glory and universal peace as depicted in the Messianic prophecies; the fulfilment of these prophecies is still hoped for, and our hope is founded on our belief in the truthfulness of the Word of God. (Comp. Saadiah, Em. ve-deoth, VIII. iii.).

On the *Thirteenth Principle*, p. 16

The belief in the Resurrection of the Dead has been formulated in the Mishnah (Sanhedrin x. 1) as an essential creed: "He who says that the belief in the Resurrection of the Dead is not implied in the Law has no portion in the world to come." There is no doubt that the Almighty has the power to give fresh life to the body in which life has been extinct. We set no limits to the Omnipotence of God. But it is different if we ask whether it is the Will of God to give new life to the dust and ashes of the dead, and to restore the soul to the dead body in which it has dwelt before. Maimonides substitutes the Immortality of the Soul for the Resurrection of the Dead, and has been vehemently attacked by those who had a different opinion. He defended his view in an essay called מאמר תחיית המתים, "On the Resurrection of the Dead," in which he attempts to prove that the Agadoth and Midrashim in depicting the future life employed figurative language, but in reality meant only a spiritual life, without any material enjoyment.

Saadiah defends the literal interpretation of " Resurrection

of the Dead" (*Emunoth ve-deoth*, VII.), and believes that
the event will take place at the time of the final redemption
(גאולה אחרונה).   Rabbi Jehudah ha-levi, in *Cuzari*, though
mentioning this principle, seems to understand it as identical
with the Immortality of the Soul.   The king, who was at
first surprised at the scarcity of references to the future life in
our prayers, confessed his complete satisfaction, after having
heard the exposition of our prayers by the Jewish scholar.
"I see," he says, "that I was in error; those who pray to
have the Divine light vouchsafed to them during lifetime,
who long to see it with their own eyes, and to attain to the
degree of prophecy, they certainly seek something better even
than the future life, and they who attain it may be sure that
they will also enjoy the blessing of the future life; for if
the soul of a man, troubled by the wants of the body, is
nevertheless cleaving to the Divine glory, how much more
may this be the case after the soul has left this body!"
{III. 20)

II.

OUR DUTIES.

INTRODUCTION.

THE king, in Rabbi Jehudah ha-levi's Cuzari, anxious to lead a good and religious life, was told by an angel who appeared to him in a dream that his heart was good, but his deeds were not acceptable. The purity and goodness of our heart certainly ennobles our deeds and gives them the stamp of sincerity and holiness, though they may not be marked by absolute perfection. But an inner voice, our conscience, does not allow us to be content with the goodness of the heart; we feel the necessity of seeking also perfection of words and deeds. We wish not only our heart but also our entire self to be good, so that our inner life and outer life, our feeling and thinking, our speaking and doing, may combine into one harmonious whole, which comes as near perfection as possible.

It has been shown above that one of the principles of faith which we confess is our belief in the Divine origin of the Torah, and in the obligatory character of its precepts. When we pray to God to make us understand the Torah we are not content with the mere knowledge of the words of the Law; we also seek God's assistance to enable us "to obey, to observe, and to

perform " all that He has commanded us. Man's nature
is not the same in all individuals; one person finds
special delight in the performance of this duty, another in the performance of that. Every one likes to
devote his energies to that work for which he considers
himself best qualified, and which promises to yield the
best fruit. But this individual liking or aptitude must
not mislead us into thinking that the Law is divided
into important and unimportant precepts. So far as
they represent the Will of the Almighty they are all
alike, and equally demand our attention and our obedience. Thus the קבלת עול מלכות שמים,[1] our unconditional
submission to the Will of the Almighty as our King, is
followed in our Service by קבלת עול מצות,[1] the acknowledg-
ment of the binding force of His precepts.

There are persons who question the wisdom and
usefulness of the precepts; they call it legalism, and
are opposed to the tendency of subjecting every act of
ours to the control of the Law. They argue that legalism
tends to weaken our regard for the Law, and trains
hypocrites rather than true servants of the Lord. It
is a bold assertion, but one that rests on imagination
and prejudice. Is it possible that such a constant reminder of God's presence as the Divine precepts supply
should not have a beneficent influence over us, by making us feel encouraged by His presence when we are
engaged in a good cause, and discouraged when we are
about to do wrong? If persons are found who are

---

[1] Lit., "The accepting of the yoke of the heaven's dominion;" "The
accepting of the yoke of the precepts." The expression "yoke" is
here by no means derogatory. It simply indicates the duty which in
the one case "the dominion of heaven," and in the other case "the
Divine precepts," impose upon us.

devout worshippers at one time and criminals at another, it only shows human weakness in the moment of trial in spite of good resolves and genuine devotion ; and were it not for the effect of such devotion, the number of crimes would probably be far greater.

A truly pious man will never imagine that he may freely transgress one set of the precepts, if he strictly obeys another set ; that he may, *e.g.*, wrong his neighbour, and compensate for his sins by regular attendance at the place of worship, or by a strict observance of the dietary laws, or the laws of Sabbath and Festivals; or that he may freely break the latter, if only he is honest, just, and charitable. The precepts have all the same Divine origin ; the all-wise and all-kind God, who has commanded us to walk in the way of justice and righteousness, has also ordained the Sabbath, given the dietary laws, and established the sacrificial service. He who selects some of the precepts and rejects the rest substitutes his own authority for that of the Almighty, and places his own wisdom above the wisdom of Him who gave us the Law.

" Be as zealous in the performance of an unimportant precept as of an important one," is one of the maxims taught in the " Sayings of the Fathers." A difference between precept and precept is here admitted, but only in so far as they seem to us more or less important, with regard to the good which their observance produces or the evil which is caused by their neglect. In case of a conflict of two duties we give the preference to that which seems to us more important. In times of religious persecution the question frequently arose how far resistance was necessary, and how far religious practice might yield to physical force. The rule has been laid down, that when our life is threatened we may transgress any precept; but we must not allow ourselves, under any circumstances, to be forced to idolatry, murder, or adultery (עבודה זרה גלוי עריות ושפיכות דמים); we must prefer death to committing any of these sins. But in times of trouble and persecution the spirit of resistance is as a rule too strong to be kept within the strict lines of demarcation, and life is willingly and heroically sacrificed for any religious duty. This is not surprising, for every religious act which is chosen by the enemy as a test to prove the faithfulness or the faithlessness of the persecuted sect to its own religion, receives thereby the stamp of great importance.

Similar questions are also asked in times of peace, when some of our brethren reject the authority of the Oral Law, while others refuse even to recognise the authority of the Written Law, when some set aside the Divine precepts out of convenience, and others from principle, and still others from ignorance; when some limit their Judaism to the nominal membership of the Jewish race, and others to a negation of other creeds. Are all these Jews? Whatever the answer to this question may be from a practical, political, social, and communal point of view, the fact is that they are Jews. They may have forfeited certain privileges, they may be disqualified for certain religious offices, they may be dangerous to the religious peace of our family or community: they are notwithstanding Jews, and are bound to live in accordance with the Law which the Almighty has given to the Jews and for the Jews. Our Sages say: אף על פי שחטא ישראל הוא, "Although a man may have sinned, he is an Israelite still." No theologian, Rabbi, or teacher, or Beth-din, or Sanhedrin, has the power of granting ab-solution, or telling those who break or reject any portion of the Divine precepts that they are not doing wrong. No human being has the authority to abrogate laws re-vealed by God. Why then, some may ask, do prophets and moralists, the Rabbis of the Talmud not excluded, single out ethical principles for special recommendation to their fellow-men, generally observing silence about the rest of the Divine commands ? The answer is simple. The ethical principles and the Divine commandments embodying them are different in kind from the rest of the commandments. The latter are distinct, well de-fined, and the punishment for their transgression is fixed; they are unchangeable, and not capable of expansion.

The dietary laws, *e.g.*, are exactly the same now as they were in the days of Moses. So also the laws concerning Sabbath. What was then prohibited by the Sabbath is prohibited still. The ethical principles, however, are capable of development, and the moral standard rises with the progress of civilisation. Hence the constant dissatisfaction of prophets, preachers, and teachers with the moral principles of their followers. They have a higher standard of morality, and strive to raise the moral consciousness of their generations to their own height.

It is, therefore, no wonder that the prophet Isaiah exhorts his brethren : " Wash you, make you clean ; put away the evil of your doings from before mine eyes ; cease to do evil : learn to do well : seek judg-ment, relieve the oppressed, judge the fatherless, plead for the widow " (i. 16, 17). " He that walketh righteously, and speaketh uprightly; he that despiseth the gain of oppressions, that shaketh his hands from holding of bribes, that stoppeth his ears from hearing of blood, and shutteth his eyes from looking upon evil, he shall dwell on high," &c. (*Ibid.* xxxiii. 15, 16). In the same sense the virtuous man is described by all prophets; also in Ps. xv. and Ps. xxiv.

R. Akiba says: "'Thou shalt love thy neighbour as thyself' (Lev. xix. 18) is an important principle in the Torah," but at the same time he shows what importance he ascribes to all other principles and precepts of the Law by most carefully examining the details of every one of them alike. The great Hillel told the Gentile who desired to become a Jew: "'Do not to thy neighbour what is hateful to you;' this is our whole religion;" but that he did not ignore the remainder of the Torah, or consider it as not essential, is proved by the additional words: "The rest is its explanation; go and learn" (*Babyl. Talmud, Sabbath,* 31*a*). Hillel only gave the proselyte a lesson which would lead him to obey all the words of the Almighty.

Rabbi Simlai (Yalkut on Micah vi. 8) said: "Six hundred and thirteen commandments were given to Moses on Mount Sinai; David reduced them to eleven (Ps. xv.); Isaiah reduced them to six (xxxiii. 16, 17); Micah (vi. 8) to three; then Isaiah reduced them again to two (lvi. 1); and Habakkuk to one—Faith (ii. 4)." This Rabbi does certainly not mean to say that Isaiah cancelled some of the eleven virtues mentioned by David, or that Habakkuk only demanded Faith, and did not consider it essential that man should be righteous, truthful, &c. Rabbi Simlai intended only

to point out that by training ourselves in the practice
of certain virtues, the fulfilment of all Divine precepts
will be greatly facilitated.

All the commandments of the holy Torah are equally
Divine. Laws concerning justice and humanity, and
laws concerning Sabbath and Holydays, are equally introduced by the declaration, " And the Lord spake unto
Moses, saying." The commandments, " Thou shalt love
thy neighbour as thyself," and " A garment of diverse
kinds, of linen and wool, shall not come upon thee,"
stand side by side in the same paragraph. The
equality of all the precepts as the expression of the
Will of the Almighty is clearly set forth in the Law,
in the frequent exhortations that the Israelites should
obey all the precepts, whatever their nature may be,
whether they be of the class of " statutes " or of "judgments," or of any other class of Divine commands.
(Comp. Exod. xv. 25, 26; Lev. xxvi. 15, 43; Num. xv.
39, 40; Deut. iv. 1, 5, 8, &c.)

As to the various terms employed in the Pentateuch
to designate the Divine precepts: words (דברים), commandments (מצוות), statutes (חקים), judgments (משפטים),
and laws (תורות), they may be considered as synonyms signifying similar things. But even synonyms
are as a rule distinguished from each other by a
certain variation in their meaning, especially when the
terms occur in one and the same sentence. A definition of these terms is not given in the Pentateuch or
in the Bible; from the context, however, in which
they occur the following distinction may be drawn :—

חק or חקה, " statute," is applied to those laws which
are absolute and do not depend on certain conditions,

whilst *mishpat*, "judgment," is a law the performance
of which varies according to circumstances.   Thus the
Paschal sacrifice is called *chukkah*, and must absolutely
be performed, whilst the civil laws concerning slaves,
damages, &c., are *mishpatim*, because cases of slavery
or damages need not occur, and the respective precepts
are then not carried into effect.   In a similar manner
Jewish theologians divide the Divine precepts into
מצות שמעיות and מצות שכליות precepts which our duty
of obedience to God makes us perform, and precepts
which, without distinct Divine command, our own
reason would impel us to do.—The other terms, *mitsvah*, " commandment," and *mishmereth*, " charge," are
used in a general sense, the former in reference to the
Giver of the law, and the latter in reference to those
to whom it is addressed.

The division of the precepts into שמעיות and שכליות
is a vague one, and the line of demarcation will be
moved farther to the one side or the other, according
to the judgment exercised by the interpreter.   Of
greater importance is the division into positive and
negative precepts, commandments, and prohibitions,
מצות עשה and מצות לא תעשה.   The prohibitions are of
two kinds: such as admit of amends being made
for their transgression and such as do not admit:
שיש בה קום עשה, and שאין בה קום עשה.

The number of the commandments is, according to
Rabbi Simlai, 613 (תרי"ג), and in some editions of the
Pentateuch the number of each commandment has
been noted in the margin.   Rabbi Moses ben Maimon,
in the introduction to his *Mishneh-torah*, enumerates
the 613 *mitsvoth*.   They are also contained in liturgical

compositions, called אזהרות "exhortations," or "precepts," such as are met with in the Machzor for the Feast of Weeks.

Maimonides, in "The Guide" as well as in Mishneh-torah, treats of the precepts of the Torah under the following fourteen heads: (1) Fundamental principles of our faith;[1] (2) Divine worship; (3) Sabbath and festivals; (4) Marriages; (5) Forbidden food and forbidden relations of the sexes; (6) Vows; (7) Agriculture; (8) The Temple and the regular sacrificial service; (9) Occasional sacrifices; (10) Cleanness and uncleanness; (11) Compensation for damages; (12) Transfer of property; (13) Contracts; (14) Administration of the law.

Another theologian, Rabbenu Jakob, divided the code of laws into four sections: (1) Divine worship, Sabbath, festivals, and fasts; (2) Things forbidden and things permitted in satisfying our bodily desires; (3) Marriages; (4) Civil laws.

The latter work was recast by Rabbi Joseph Caro,

---

[1] Hebrew titles of books are often fanciful names, which more or less distinctly imply either the nature or contents of the books, or the name of their authors. The Hebrew names for the fourteen books of Mishneh-torah are as follows: (1) מדע "Knowledge;" (2) אהבה "Love;" (3) זמנים "Seasons;" (4) נשים "Women;" (5) קדושה "Sanctification;" (6) הפלאה "Distinction;" (7) זרעים "Seeds;" (8) עבודה "Service;" (9) קרבנות "Sacrifices;" (10) טהרה "Purity;" (11) נזיקין "Damages;" (12) קנין "Acquisition;" (13) משפטים "Disputes;" (14) שופטים "Judges." Rabbenu Jakob calls his work ארבעה טורים "Four Rows," a name borrowed from Exod. xxviii. 17. The names of the four parts are: ארח חיים "Path of Life" (Ps. xvi. 11); יורה דעה "Teacher of knowledge" (Isa. xxviii. 9); אבן העזר "Stone of Help" (1 Sam. vii. 12, and Gen. ii. 18), and חשן משפט "Breastplate of Judgment" (Exod. xxviii. 15).

Q

and in the new form, with the new title *Shulchan Aruch*, it has become the standard work of Jewish law and life, and its authority has been recognised and upheld by Jews in the East and the West. Annotations (הגהות) were added by Rabbi Moses Isserles, but his opinion, when differing from that of Rabbi Joseph Caro, was only accepted by the Polish and German Congregations, not by the Sephardim.

Rabbi Joseph Caro, Rabbenu Jakob, and Maimonides appear, in their respective codes, not as legislators but as compilers. The Torah and the Talmud were the sources from which they all drew their laws. But laws, *minhagim* or customs, and institutions (תקנות) of a post-Talmudic date were not neglected. Questions arising in the course of time, through new and changed conditions of life, are, as a rule, discussed and decided in notes and commentaries on the *Shulchan Aruch*. There are also numerous special works on such occasional questions; they are called " Responsa " (תשובות " Answers," or שאלות ותשובות " Questions and Answers "), and the importance attributed to them varies according to the reputation of the respective authors.

What is the object of the Divine laws? This is a question that naturally rises in the minds of those to whom they are addressed. But the question has been anticipated by Him " who knoweth the thoughts of the sons of man," and the answer is found in clear and distinct words in the fountain of living waters, the Torah, that never fails to satisfy our thirst for truth: " Thou shalt keep his statutes and his commandments which I command thee this day, *that it may be*

well with thee and thy children after thee" (Deut. **iv.**
40). "And now, O Israel, what doth the Lord **thy**
God require of thee, but to fear the Lord thy God, **to**
walk in all his ways and to love him, and to serve
the Lord thy God with all thy heart and with all **thy**
soul: to keep the commandments of the Lord and **his**
statutes which I command thee this day, for thy good "
(*ibid.* x. 12, 13). It is for our benefit, for our well-
being, that the laws were revealed to us; they serve
to make us good and happy; they train us in the
mastery over our appetites and desires, in the practice
of charity and justice, and in the conception of noble,
pure, and lofty ideas, and bring us nearer and nearer
in perfection the Being in whose image and likeness
we have been created.

What share each individual precept has in the
attainment of this end we cannot state with certainty,
because in the Torah the reason and purpose of each
precept is, with very few exceptions, withheld from us.
In many cases our reflection on the nature of a special
law, or on the context in which it occurs in the Pentateuch, leads to a discovery of some reason for it. But,
whatever reason we may thus discover, we must not
lose sight of the fact that it is we who have found it,
we whose knowledge is imperfect, and that we or
others might in future discover a better reason. If
we, *e.g.*, find that certain dietary laws serve to train us
in temperance, and see that the virtue of temperance
is frequently recommended in the Bible, we may well
obey these dietary laws, and strive to be temperate in
every respect in accordance with the spirit we detect in
them. It would, however, be a gross error if, believing

the training in temperance to be their only object, we assumed that we could neglect them, and attain the same object by substituting our own insufficient knowledge and imperfect reason for the Will and Wisdom of the most perfect Being.   Moralists, our teachers and preachers of ancient and modern times, have found in these precepts an inexhaustible treasure of lessons exhorting to virtue and warning against vice, and the great variety of inferences thus drawn from the same source proves the error of those who imagine that their own exposition is the only right one.   Whatever reason we assign to a religious precept, and whatever wholesome lesson we derive from it, our first duty towards the commandment, and towards Him who commanded it, is strict and unconditional obedience.

Maimonides, who may be considered as the representative of the school which seeks to establish a rational explanation for all precepts, admits that the reason we may assign to any of the commandments cannot affect their validity and immutability, and we are bound to obey them, although the supposed reason may be of a local or temporary character.   According to Maimonides, the object of the Law is to promote the well-being of our body and the well-being of our soul ; and every commandment has therefore some bearing upon one of the following three things : the regulation of our opinions, the removal of sin, or the teaching of good morals.   He does not except the " statutes " from this rule, but confesses that in a few cases he is unable to show clearly the relation of the commandment to any of these objects.   He also restricts the principle of rational interpretation to the main element in each commandment, and does not apply it to its details; the latter, as a rule, do not demand an explanation. He says:—

"The general object of the Law is twofold: the well-being of the soul and the well-being of the body" (Guide, iii. 27). "I am prepared to tell you my explanations of all these commandments (the so-called *chukkim* or "statutes"), and to assign for them a true reason supported by proof, with the exception of some minor rules and of a few commandments. I will show that all these and similar laws must have some bearing upon one of the following three things, viz., the regulation of our opinions or the improvement of our social relations, which implies two things: the removal of wrong-doing and the teaching of good morals" (*ibid.* xxviii.). "The repeated assertion of our Sages that there are reasons for all commandments, and the tradition that Solomon knew them, refer to the general purpose of the commandments, and not to the object of every detail. This being the case, I find it convenient to divide the six hundred and thirteen precepts into classes; each class to include many precepts of the same kind. I will first explain the reason of each class of precepts, and show their common object, and then I shall discuss the individual commandments and expound their reasons. Only very few will be left unexplained, the reason for which I have been unable to trace unto this day. I have also been able to comprehend in some cases even the object of many of the conditions and details of the laws as far as it can be discovered" (*ibid.* xxvi.).

"It is also important to note that the Law does not take into account exceptional circumstances; it is not based on conditions which rarely occur." "We must therefore not be surprised when we find that the object of the Law does not fully appear in every individual case." " From this consideration it follows that the Law cannot, like medicine, vary according to the different conditions of persons and times. Whilst the cure of a person depends on his particular constitution at the particular time, the Divine guidance contained in the Law must be certain and general, although it may be effective in some cases and ineffective in others. If the Law depended on the varying conditions of man, it would be imperfect in its totality, each precept being left indefinite. For this reason, it would not be right to make the fundamental principles of the Law dependent on a certain time or a certain place. On the contrary, the statutes and the judgments must be definite, unconditional, and general, in accordance with the Divine words : ' As for the congregation, one ordinance shall be for you and for the stranger ' (Num. xv. 15). They are intended, as has been stated before, for all persons and for all times " (*ibid.* xxxiv.).

In the present treatise our religious duties will be expounded under the following seven heads :—

1. Exposition of the Decalogue.
2. General ethical principles—
    (*a.*) Duties towards God.
    (*b.*)   ,,   ,,   our fellow-men.
    (*c.*)   ,,   ,,   ourselves.
3. Outward reminders of God's Presence.
4. Sabbath, Festivals, and Fasts.
5. Divine Worship.
6. Dietary Laws.
7. Jewish

I. *The Ten Commandments.* עשרת הדברות

The " Ten Words " are distinguished from all other lessons of the Torah both on account of their intrinsic value and on account of the extraordinary manner in which they have been revealed by the Almighty on Mount Sinai. They form the contents of " the covenant which God made with us " (Deut. v. 3).

But it must not be forgotten that they are not the only Divine commandments. When, therefore, Moses repeated them before his brethren in the plain of Moab, he prefaced it by the exhortation: " Hear, O Israel, *the statutes and the judgments* which I speak unto you to-day, and learn them and keep them to do them " (*ibid.* 1); and after he had finished reciting them he reminded the Israelites how they received the Ten Commandments from the midst of the fire, and how they prayed that further commandments should be given to them through Moses; adding that the Almighty, in compliance with their petition, said to him: " Stand thou here with me, and I will tell thee the whole commandment, both the statutes and the judgments which thou shalt teach them " (*ibid.* 28).

" And God spake all these words, saying : "

First Commandment.

" *I am the Lord thy God, who brought thee out of the land of Egypt, out of the house of bondage.*"
The Israelites who now stood round Mount Sinai

and heard the voice of God saying, "I am the Lord
thy God," were the same who a very short time before
had been slaves in Egypt; they were delivered from
slavery, and saw their cruel taskmasters perish in the
waves of the Red Sea. Pharaoh, the king of the
Egyptians, and his people had believed that they were
the masters of the Israelites, and that they could do
with them as they pleased. And Pharaoh said, "Who
is the Lord, that I should listen to his voice? I know
not the Lord, nor will I let Israel go." It has now been
shown that Pharaoh and his people were not the true
masters; that there was a higher Being that ruled
over all men, over kings and their peoples. After the
Israelites had crossed the Red Sea, they sang with
Moses: "This is my God, and I will praise him, the
God of my father, and I will exalt him." They all
felt that their liberty was not obtained by human
strength and skill; that there must be a higher Being
who is All-powerful, All-wise, and All-good; and that
it was He who freed them, and punished the wicked
Egyptians by whom they had been kept in slavery.
What the Israelites at first felt in their hearts they
were now, when standing round Sinai, taught by God
Himself, in plain, clear, and intelligible words: "I am
the Lord thy God, who brought thee out of the land
of Egypt, out of the house of bondage."

This is the first commandment; it is only one
commandment, but it contains several important
lessons:—

1. God has shown great kindness to our nation;
we Jews must therefore more than other people show
ourselves grateful to Him, love Him as our Deliverer

and Benefactor, and do willingly all that He commands us to do.

2. When we are in trouble we must trust in God, pray to Him, and hope that He will help us when our fellow-men cannot do so. When they give us up as lost we need not despair; for the Almighty can help where human wisdom and power are insufficient.

3. The wicked may for a time succeed in doing wrong, whilst the good and just suffer; but this does not last for ever. There is a Master above all of us, who in due time punishes the wicked and saves the good.

Second Commandment.

" *Thou shalt have no other gods before me. Thou shalt not make unto thee a graven image, nor the form of anything that is in heaven above, or that is in the earth beneath, or that is in the water under the earth. Thou shalt not bow down thyself unto them, nor serve them, for I, the Lord thy God, am a jealous God, visiting the iniquity of the fathers upon the children upon the third and upon the fourth generation of them that hate me; and showing loving-kindness to the thousandth generation of them that love me and keep my commandments.*"

There are no other gods in existence; it is impossible for us to have other gods. There is only one God, as we repeatedly declare, "Hear, O Israel, the Lord is our God, the Lord is one." The commandment is nevertheless not superfluous. There have been whole nations, and there are still people, who, in their ignorance and folly, attribute Divine power to things that have no Divine power, and who give the name of god to things that are not gods. Such people are called heathens, idolaters, or idol-worshippers. The second commandment forbids us to do any such thing.

It was the custom in some countries to worship the king, either during his lifetime or after his death, as a Divine being; it is still the custom in some countries to pray to departed saints. All this our holy religion forbids us to do. We must respect our king, we must honour the memory and the name of good men, but only as human beings, not as gods; we may not deify them. As to our prophets, our great men, the Patriarchs, the kings, their names are a pride unto us, their memory a blessing, זכרונם לברכה—they are honoured by us as human, mortal beings: they are not worshipped. When we visit the graves of those near and dear to us, and honour their memory by reflecting on their virtues, when we revere those holy men who have devoted their lives to the service of God, or the martyrs who have sacrificed their lives for the sanctification of the Name of God (קדוש השם), we do not endow them with Divine attributes, and do not offer up any prayer to them.

The second commandment, in forbidding all kinds of idolatry, includes the following prohibitions :—

(1.) The worship of sun, moon, stars, animals, human beings, or any part of Nature, as endowed with Divine power.

(2.) The worship of images representing things that exist in reality or in man's imagination.

(3.) The worship of angels as Divine beings. They

are only messengers of God, and we must not pray to them.

(4.) The belief in evil spirits, demons, devils, and the like, and the fear of them.

(5.) The belief in charms, witchcraft, fortune-telling, and similar superstitions.

The words, " *For I, the Lord thy God, am a jealous God,*" are to be understood in a figurative sense ; we cannot say of God that He is jealous, in the literal sense of the word. It is only because we call a person jealous who is anxious that no one else shall enjoy the same right or privilege as he enjoys, that we imply the term " jealous " figuratively to God, because He does not concede Divine worship and service to any other being. He demands of His worshippers that they serve Him alone and none besides.

Those who break this commandment " hate God," and will surely receive their punishment. He " visits the iniquity of the fathers upon the children upon the third and upon the fourth generation." The bad example set by a man frequently corrupts his children, grandchildren, and great-grandchildren. In that case they will all receive their punishment, and there is no excuse for them, that they were misled by the bad example of their father or their forefathers. A bad example must not be followed, even if it be set by those whom we love dearly.

The good example of a man should always be followed, and his good deeds bear good fruit and are the source of blessing even long after his death. For to those that love God and keep His commandments God " showeth mercy even to the thousandth generation."

Third Commandment.

" *Thou shalt not take the name of the Lord thy God in vain ; for the Lord will not hold him guiltless that taketh his name in vain.*"

We pronounce the name of God when we read the Bible, when we pray, when we take an oath, or when we speak of God's wisdom, power, and goodness. We take the name of God in vain when we read the Bible without attention, or pray without devotion, or take an oath without necessity or contrary to truth. When we utter the name of God we must bear in mind that it is the name of the most Holy and most Perfect Being that we are pronouncing; that it is a privilege to us to be allowed and to be able to pronounce it.

The more we meditate on the greatness and holiness of God, the more careful should we be " not to utter the name of God in vain." We should guard ourselves from falling into the bad habit of uttering it thoughtlessly to no purpose whatever. Many people are heard to exclaim every minute, " O God," or similar phrases. To them the sacredness of the name is entirely lost, and they are no longer reminded by it of the holiness of Him who is designated by that name. Still greater is the thoughtlessness of those who swear by God without any necessity. In swearing by God we call upon God to bear witness that our words are true. But such a testimony is only required when our statement is not believed. If we swear before we know whether we are believed or not, we indicate that, according to our estimate of ourselves, we are not trustworthy, and it has often been observed as a fact that those who swear most are least to be believed. The worst of all forms of swearing is to swear falsely, that is, to swear that something is the case without knowing that it is true, or knowing that it is not true. This is a terrible crime, and is called " the profanation of God's name," חלול השם.

There is still another kind of חלול השם " profanation of God's name : " if we Jews who are called by His name, the people of the Lord, or children of the Lord, bring contempt upon God's people by disgraceful conduct, we profane the name of God. We sanctify it by noble and generous deeds ; by leading a pure and blameless life we cause a קדוש השם " sanctification of the name of God."

The third commandment forbids us—

(1.) To utter the name of God unnecessarily in our common conversation.

(2.) To read the Bible carelessly, or to pray without attention and devotion.

(3.) To swear otherwise than when required by the law to do so, as, *e.g.*, in courts of law.

(4.) To swear when we are not fully convinced of the truth of our declaration.

The additional sentence, " for he will not hold him guiltless who taketh his name in vain," is to remind us that it is against God the Omniscient that we sin in breaking this commandment. God knows our innermost thoughts, whether we think of what we utter or not ; whether we are convinced of what we declare on oath or not. He will punish us if we break His commandments, although we may be able to conceal our sins from men and escape condemnation by a human tribunal.

Fourth Commandment.

"*Remember the Sabbath day to keep it holy. Six days shalt thou labour and do all thy work. But the seventh day is a Sabbath unto the Lord thy God: in it thou shalt not do any work, thou, nor thy son, nor thy daughter, thy manservant, nor thy maidservant, nor thy cattle, nor thy stranger that is within thy gates. For in six days the Lord made heaven and earth, the sea, and all that is therein, and rested the seventh day; wherefore the Lord blessed the Sabbath day, and hallowed it.*"

The Sabbath day, that is, the day of rest, is to be kept holy. In two ways it should differ from other days; it is to be *a day of rest* and also *a holy day.* We keep it as a day of rest by not doing on it any kind of work; we keep it as a holy day by devoting the greater part of it, since we are free from our ordinary occupation, to prayer and to reading the Bible.

We are thankful to God for having commanded us to keep the Sabbath, and give expression to our feeling of gratitude in our prayers, especially at the beginning and the end of the Sabbath; thus, on Friday evening, before the meal, we praise God for sanctifying the Sabbath by a prayer called *Kiddush,* "sanctification," and on Sabbath evening, after the close of the Sabbath, we recite the *Habdalah,* in which God is praised for the distinction made between Sabbath and the six week-days.

The Israelites were told to remember *the* Sabbath day; that is, the well-known day of rest, the same day which was instituted as a day of rest in connection with the manna. On five days they collected one omer of the manna, on the sixth day two omers for each person; on the seventh day no manna was collected nor was any found, and the Israelites were commanded to bake and to cook on the sixth day not only for the sixth day, but also for the seventh, on which day baking and cooking was not to be done. *This same seventh day* we are told in the fourth commandment *to remember* to keep holy, that we should not forget it, or choose another day instead of it. It is the same seventh day on which God rested after the six days of the Creation, and which "he blessed and sanctified."

It is to be a day of rest not only for ourselves; we must not have work done for us by our children, or by our servants, or by strangers; even our cattle must rest. After six days of work we enjoy the blessing of one day's rest, and are rendered more fit to work another six days. The harder we work on six days, the more welcome is the rest of the seventh day to us. When Moses repeated the commandments, he laid special stress on the rest of the servants, reminding the Israelites that they themselves had once been slaves, and must therefore recognise the necessity of granting a day of rest to their servants.

It is not to be a day of mere idleness. Complete idleness leads to evil thoughts and evil deeds. Whilst our body rests our mind should be occupied with holy thoughts; we should commune with God, reflect on His works, learn from them the power, wisdom, and goodness of God, study the Word of God, listen to the instruction of our teachers and preachers, and altogether try to raise ourselves into a loftier sphere.

On the day of rest we reflect on the works of God, on the work of Creation which He completed in six days, and thus by keeping the Sabbath we testify to our belief in God as the Creator of the Universe. On this account it is that the Creation is referred to in this commandment as the reason why rest was enjoined for the seventh day. "For in six days," &c.

"Therefore the Lord blessed the Sabbath day;" the rest on the seventh day is a blessing to those who have worked hard during the preceding six days; it is a blessing to those who spend the Sabbath in a proper manner. "And he hallowed it" by giving man an opportunity to sanctify himself by more frequent communion with the Most Holy.

The fourth commandment tells us—

(1.) To remember to keep the same day as Sabbath which has been set apart as such from the beginning.

(2.) To abstain on that day from all kind of work.

(3.) To devote part of the day to our sanctification.

Fifth Commandment.

"*Honour thy father and thy mother: that thy days may be long upon the land which the Lord thy God giveth thee.*"

The strongest desire that animates a father and a mother is to see their children good and happy.

From the first day of their existence children are guarded by the watchful eyes of their parents that no evil may befall them. How delighted are father and mother when they notice the progress of their child in health and strength, in heart and soul! What an amount of trouble and anxiety parents undergo when they see their child suffering! No sacrifice is too great for them so long as it ensures the child's well-being. It is painful to them to be compelled to deny their child anything, or to rebuke or to punish it. To this they are impelled only by the anxiety for the welfare of the child. The mutual affection between parent and child is one which nature has implanted. Without it the home would be the dwelling of misery and misfortune; with it comfort and happiness flourish therein. The loving parents have pleasure in whatever they do for the benefit of the child, and the affectionate child is delighted with the goodness of its parents.

"*Honour thy father and thy mother,*" says the Almighty to us. How does a child honour father and mother? In the eyes of the child father and mother must be the king and the queen of the house, however small that may be. Every word that comes from their mouth, every desire that they express, must be regarded as of the greatest importance, and be well remembered by the child. When the king or the queen speaks, all present stand and listen respectfully; their words are read by every one with the greatest interest. So it must be with the words of our parents. Whenever they tell us to do or not to do a thing, obedience is a blessing to us; disobedience is the chief cause of all misery and trouble. We feel pleasure and honour in

R

being able to do something that gratifies our parents, and we like to give them at times some material token of our affection. The best present we can give them is a good heart, sincere love that prompts us to avoid everything that would grieve them, and to do everything we can to give them pleasure and to make them happy.

This is one of the few laws the reward of which is distinctly stated, " That thy days may be long upon the land, which the Lord thy God giveth thee." We can easily understand the good effect of keeping the fifth commandment. Pleasure and contentment contribute a good deal to the health and well-being of man, whilst anger, trouble, and dissatisfaction produce ill-health and weakness. The mutual affection between parent and child is therefore the cause that the days of both the parents and the children are prolonged, and the harmony and happiness of the house firmly established. The blessing attending children's obedience and love towards their parents does not end here. The whole State consists of small homes and families, and the greater the well-being of the individual homes, the greater is the well-being of the whole country. Thus the child by acting in accordance with this Divine commandment contributes its share towards the prosperity of the whole country.

When our parents are not present, we should, out of love towards them, obey those who take their place, as, *e.g.*, our elder brothers or sisters, our guardians, and our teachers, since all these only do what the parents would themselves like to do were the opportunity granted them.

We are bound to honour our parents not only so

long as we are under their care and live in their house, but also when we have left our parents' home, and have become independent. Even when they have become old, weak, and poor, and we support them, we must not forget the natural relation between parent and child, and the honour due to parents from their children must still be shown to them. When they have departed from this life, and we are no longer able to show our feeling of love and respect in the usual way, we must honour their name and memory, and hold in respect the wishes and commands which they expressed when still alive. Death is no bar to true love and sincere affection.

Thus we obey the fifth commandment—

(1.) By listening respectfully to the words of our parents and obeying what they say.

(2.) By doing that which pleases them, and avoiding that which would displease them.

(3.) By supporting them when they are weak and poor by all our best exertion and with genuine pleasure.

(4.) By honouring their name and memory after their death.

(5.) By being obedient to our elder brothers or sisters, to our guardians, and to our teachers.

Sixth Commandment.

" *Thou shalt not murder.*"

Murder is a most terrible thing; we shudder at the sound of the word, even at the mere idea of it. We wonder how it is possible that a person should be so wicked, so cruel, and so unnatural as to take the life of another human being! One who can do such a thing must have lost all human feeling, and is rather a brute than a being created in the image of God. But, unfortunately, there have been and there are such wicked people. We read in the Bible that a dispute arose between the two sons of Adam, and the one, Cain, slew the other, Abel. He repented it, but he could not restore to his brother the life which he had taken. The severest punishment is therefore inflicted on those who have committed this crime.

This commandment and those which follow it have their root in the principle, " *Love thy fellow-man as thyself*," applied to the life (sixth commandment), the home (seventh commandment), the property (eighth commandment), and the honour of our fellow-man (ninth commandment). We wish to enjoy life as long as possible ; it must therefore be our desire to see our fellow-man enjoy the longest possible life. But we must not rest satisfied with the mere desire. An earnest desire is followed by acts dictated by it. We must try our utmost, even as we do with regard to ourselves, to preserve the life of our fellow-man. We have, *e.g.*, seen before how by obeying the fifth commandment we lengthen not only our own life, but also that of our parents, whilst by breaking this law we shorten their life as well as our own.

By supporting the poor and nursing the sick we may be the means of increasing a human life by many days or even years, whilst by neglecting the duty of charity we neglect to save the life of our fellow-man when it is in our power to do so.—Another instance of criminal neglect it would be if a person saw another in actual danger of life, and did not try everything in his power to save him.

Without having directly broken the sixth commandment, without having taken the life of our neighbour by violence, we may still be guilty of having shortened his life and caused his untimely death. Talebearers and slanderers, *e.g.*, often undermine the peace and happiness of an individual, and even of a whole family, and sow the seed of misery and ruin where well-being and prosperity seemed well established.

The sixth commandment enjoins that we should respect the life of our fellow-man, and forbids us therefore—

(1.) To take it by violent means.

(2.) To do anything by which the peace and well-being of our fellow-man might be undermined.

(3.) To neglect anything in our power to save our neighbour from direct or indirect danger of life.

Seventh Commandment.

" *Thou shalt not commit adultery.*"

The institution of marriage is of very ancient date. When Eve had been formed out of the rib of Adam, and was brought to him, he exclaimed, " She is bone of my bones and flesh of my flesh," and the account of the first marriage concludes thus : " Therefore man shall leave his father and his mother and cleave unto his wife, and they shall be one flesh " (Gen. ii. 24). Every married couple, husband and wife, bind themselves by a solemn promise to be true and faithful to each other, to remain throughout life united in love and affection, and to establish a home founded on purity and sanctity. Adultery is the breaking of this promise. That love and affection which unites man and wife cannot be shared by a third person without involving a breach of the seventh commandment.

Jewish homes have always been distinguished by sanctity and purity. In order to retain this distinction it is necessary that we should be trained in this virtue from our childhood. Our language must be pure and holy; unclean and indecent expressions must never be uttered in our homes, either by the old or by the young. The purer our speech is, the more sanctified will our heart be. Bad society often corrupts the heart of the young through bad example in words and conduct. It is therefore essential that immoral persons should not come in contact with our children; that everything that is contrary to the virtue of modesty (צניעות) should be rigorously excluded from Jewish homes.

The seventh commandment forbids:—

(1.) Faithlessness of a man to his wife, or a woman to her husband.

(2.) The use of improper and indecent language.

(3.) Immodest conduct.

(4.) Associating with immoral persons.

Eighth Commandment.

" *Thou shalt not steal.*"

We do not like that any one should take a part of our property without our knowledge or consent. An old saying of the Rabbis teaches: " Let the property of thy neighbour be as dear in thy eyes as thine own" (Aboth ii. 12); that is to say, as you do not wish a diminution or destruction of what is yours, so you must not cause a diminution or destruction of what belongs to your neighbour.

By secretly taking anything for ourselves that does not belong to us, we steal, and break the eighth commandment.

This commandment has also a wider sense, and forbids every illegal acquisition of property, whether it be directly by theft or robbery, or by cheating, by embezzlement or forgery. Property acquired by any of these or similar means may be considered as stolen property, and is by no means a blessing to him who possesses it. Even if human justice does not reach the evil-doer, he is watched by an All-seeing Eye, and will in due time receive his full punishment.

This commandment prohibits:—

(1.) Theft and robbery.

(2.) All kinds of fraud and dishonesty,

Ninth Commandment.

"*Thou shalt not bear false witness against thy neighbour.*"

It gives us pain to hear that others speak ill of us. "Let the honour of thy neighbour be as dear to thee as thine own" (Aboth ii. 10). We must therefore not speak ill of our neighbour. But it is not only the speaking ill of others that this commandment forbids; we must not say of our fellow-man anything that is not true. If we are called as a witness in a court of justice, we must be most careful that every word we utter be perfectly true. We must weigh our words well and guard ourselves against stating as facts things about which we are not quite certain. If we are careless we may become false witnesses, and may even be guilty of perjury.

The consequences of false evidence are of a very grave nature; it misleads the judge, perverts justice, ruins innocent people; and the false witness himself—whether he sinned with intention or by carelessness—will not escape punishment.

God declared through the mouth of the prophet Zechariah (v. 4): "I will bring forth the curse, saith the Lord of hosts, and it shall enter into the house of the thief and into the house of him that sweareth falsely by my name; and it shall remain in the midst of his house, and shall consume it, with the timber thereof and the stones thereof."

In order to guard ourselves against the possibility of such a crime, we must train ourselves in speaking the exact truth in everything, however trifling it may appear to us. Even in their play children must be careful in what they utter. Idle talk, gossip, frequently leads us to speak of our neighbours what is not in harmony with facts. Though we may believe it to be harmless and to have no evil consequence, it has in reality very pernicious results; for we get into the habit of being careless about our words, and of ignoring the line that parts truth from falsehood, and when we have then to speak on more important things, or even in a court of justice, we may prove ourselves equally careless. There is a proverb (Prov. xix. 5):

"A faithful witness is he who doth not lie, but he who uttereth lies will be a false witness;" *i.e.*, the conduct of a witness with regard to truth in ordinary and less important utterances is a test of his trustworthiness in more important matters.

The ninth commandment—

(1.) Forbids us to give false evidence; and

(2.) To utter an untruth of any kind whatever.

(3.) It commands us to be careful in our utterances.

Tenth Commandment.

" *Thou shalt not covet thy neighbour's house; thou shalt not covet thy neighbour's wife, nor his man-servant, nor his maid-servant, nor his ox, nor his ass, nor any thing that is thy neighbour's.*

The coveting which the tenth commandment forbids is the root from which the crimes forbidden in the four preceding commandments spring. Coveting is a desire to possess what we cannot get in an honest and legal manner. An instance of such coveting is the desire of Ahab to possess the vineyard of Naboth. It must have been more than an ordinary desire, for it led him to most wicked acts (1 Kings xxi.).

It is not every desire that is prohibited. If we see a thing that pleases us, we begin to feel a desire for its possession. Our reason must then step in and tell us whether we can obtain it in an honest way or not. In the latter case we must conquer our desire and suppress it, lest it obtain the mastery over us.

We must work and try to make progress. We cannot be blamed if we are not quite content with our present condition, and wish to improve it. Without such a desire all industry and progress would disappear. But we must consider that the improvement of our material condition, the increase of our property, is not the whole mission of man. We must not forget that we have a higher mission : to improve our heart and our moral conduct, and to make ourselves worthy of being called "the children of God." The increase of our property must not impede the progress of the purity and goodness of our heart.

The tenth commandment—

(1.) Forbids us to covet that which does not belong to us; and

(2.) Commands us to suppress any such desire when it rises in our heart.

NOTE 1.—There is another way of enumerating the Ten Commandments, namely, to combine the first and the second into one, and to divide the tenth into two. The Masoretic text seems to point in this direction; for there is no pause between the first and the second commandments, while there is one in the middle of the tenth. The inference from the Masoretic text, however, is not quite certain. It is possible that the first two commandments were joined closely together in order to separate more pointedly those commandments in which God speaks of Himself in the first person from those in which He speaks of Himself in the third person; or, to use the words of the Midrash, to separate the first two, which the Israelites heard directly from God, from the rest, which they heard through Moses. The last commandment was, on account of its great importance, given in two different forms. In the first the general term "house" is employed; in the second the various elements constituting the "house" are enumerated instead. The two forms of the commandment are separated by the

sign of a pause, because each of them is complete in itself
Tradition supports our division of the Decalogue. "I
am" (אנכי) and "Thou shalt not have" (לֹא יהיה לְךָ) are
mentioned in Talmud and Midrash, also in Targum, as two
distinct commandments. According to Philo (On the Ten
Comm.) and Josephus (Antiq. III. v. 5), the verse, "Thou
shalt have . . . before me" belongs to the first commandment.

The text of the Decalogue, as repeated by Moses in the
plain of Moab (Deut. v. 6–8), differs from the original
(Exod. xx. 2–14). One of the differences, the first word of
the fourth commandment—זכור, "Remember," in Exodus,
and שמור, "Observe," in Deuteronomy — is pointed out
in Midrash and Talmud, and also in the hymn for the
Eve of Sabbath, beginning, "Come, my friend" (לכה דודי).
Tradition explains the first expression as referring to affir
mative commandments, and the second to prohibitions; it
further teaches that "both expressions were spoken by God
simultaneously;" that is to say, the fourth commandment
in Deuteronomy, though different in form, does not imply
anything that has not been revealed by God on Mount
Sinai. The same applies to all points of difference.

Why did Moses introduce the alterations? Ibn Ezra,
in his Commentary on the Decalogue, is of opinion that the
question need not be asked, or answered if asked, because in
the repetition of a Divine message the original words may
be changed so long as the sense remains intact. But the
addition of the phrase, "as the Lord thy God commandeth
thee" in two cases, and the reference to the deliverance
from Egyptian servitude, substituted (in Deut.) in the fourth
commandment for the reference to the Creation (in Exod.),
lead us to think that the changes were not introduced un-
intentionally or without any purpose. The repeated Decalogue is a portion of an address in which Moses exhorted
a new generation in the plains of Moab to obey the Divine
Law. It is, therefore, not unlikely that he made additions

and alterations for the sake of emphasis, where he noticed
a certain laxity among those whom he addressed. Having
come in contact with heathen nations and observed their
rites in connection with their sacred days, the Israelites may
have been inclined to imitate them; they were therefore exhorted to sanctify the Sabbath in the way God commanded;
hence also the more emphatic "Observe," שָׁמוֹר.—A similar
reason may have caused the addition of the same phrase, "as
the Lord, &c.," to the fifth commandment. The participation
of a portion of the Israelites in the licentious feasts of the
Moabites and Midianites disturbed the peace of their homes
and loosened the sacred family tie. Moses therefore points
to the Divine origin of the law commanding obedience to
parents, and also emphasises the blessings which it will yield
by adding the words, "and in order that it may be well with
thee."—The change of circumstances has also caused another
alteration in the fourth commandment. During the forty
years which the Israelites were compelled to spend in the
wilderness, they almost forgot the condition of their former
servitude; the new generation did not know it at all, and
they grudged their slaves the one day of rest in the week.
They were therefore reminded of their servitude in Egypt,
and were asked to remember it in order that they might,
out of gratitude to the Almighty, keep the Sabbath as He
commanded them.

Another indication that changed circumstances caused
the alterations is noticed in the tenth commandment.
Having arrived at the border of Palestine, the Israelites
were about to take possession of houses and fields, and two
and a half tribes were already in possession of landed property. The term "house" (בַּיִת), which at first denoted "the
home" or "the household," including the wife, was now in
the minds of the people chiefly "a permanent building."
"The wife," the centre and the chief element in the home,
was therefore substituted for "the house" in the first part of

the commandment, and *vice versâ*, "the house" for "the wife" in the second part, where appropriately "nor his field" has been added.—The substitution of "Thou shalt not desire" (לא תתאוה) for the original "Thou shalt not covet" (לא תחמוד) may have been intended to teach the Israelites that all kinds and degrees of desire were forbidden, and to remind them of the consequences of desire which they had experienced at "the graves of the desire" (קברות התאוה Num. xi.). —One more important alteration is to be noticed, the conjunctive "and" (ו) before the seventh and the following commandments, which served to create in the minds of the hearers the idea that the crimes forbidden in the second part of the Decalogue are to some extent connected, and that he who broke one of these commandments was likely to break the others also. We are thus bidden to be on our guard, and to take good care that none of them be violated by us.

Note 2.—Ibn Ezra, in his Commentary on Exodus xx. 9, says: "Rabbi Jehudah ha-levi asked me why it is said in the Decalogue, 'who brought thee out of the land of Egypt, out of the house of bondage,' and not 'who created heaven and earth.' My answer was as follows: Know that those who believe in God have not all the same kind of faith. Some believe because they were told of His existence by others; those who believe in God because the holy Torah teaches this belief possess a higher degree of faith. If an unbeliever argues with either of these, they are not able to refute his argument. Those, however, who study sciences— Astronomy, Botany, Zoology, and Anthropology—learn to understand the works and the ways of God, and from these the Creator Himself. The words 'I am the Lord thy God' can only be understood by the wise and intelligent of all nations. For they all see that God has made heaven and earth. But there is this difference: the Israelites believe that the Creation has taken place five thousand years ago: non-Israelites assume that God has been continually creating from eternity. Now, God wrought signs and wonders in Egypt by which He delivered the Israelites out of Egypt, and thus showed them His Divine justice and goodness. In reference *to these miracles* it is said, ' *Thou hast been shown to know that the Lord is God;*' all Israelites, wise and simple, equally witnessed His miracles. The beginning of the Decalogue, therefore, ' I am the Lord thy God,' is well understood by the wise; but for the rest of the nation the words 'who brought thee out,' &c., have been added, in order that all without exception should understand it."

NOTE 3.—Don Isaac Abarbanel, in his Commentary on Exodus xx., says: "The Ten Commandments are distinguished from the other Divine precepts in three things: they were directly communicated by God to the Israelites, not through a prophet; they were revealed to a whole nation at once; and they were written on the two tables of stone by the finger of God. Such distinction necessarily indicates a greater intrinsic value of the Ten Commandments. My opinion is therefore that they are laws of a general character, and principles including all the 613 precepts which the Holy One, blessed be He, gave to His people. *E.g.*, love and worship of God, sanctification of His Name, submission to His judgment, fear of God, reverence of His sanctuary, and other duties towards God; Passover, Tabernacles, Tefillin, Mezuzah, and such other precepts as are ' a memorial of the departure from Egypt;' the separation of the first-born, tithes, &c.—all these duties are implied in the first commandment. Also Rabbi Levi ben Gershon and the Gaon Saadiah assume that all the 613 precepts are implicitly contained in the Decalogue. Although all precepts involving practice (מצוות מעשיות) are implied in the Decalogue, and even allusions to each one of the thirteen principles of faith may be discovered in it, there is no precept concerning our faith. It has already been proved by Rabbi Chisdai that by the Divine commands we are either told *to do* a certain thing, or told *not to do* a certain thing; but what we have *to believe* or *not to believe* the Almighty *taught* us through signs, wonders, and revelation. The words 'I am the Lord thy God, who brought thee out of the land of Egypt, out of the house of bondage,' teach a certain truth, a principle from which many of the 613 precepts may be derived, but which is in itself no commandment.—The Decalogue (עשרת הדברים) must therefore not be understood as designating ten commandments, but 'ten words' or 'ten paragraphs' indicated in the Hebrew text by the pauses, or spaces left between two paragraphs.

"The 'ten words' were written on two tables, five on each. The first five, containing positive and negative precepts, with the announcement of reward and punishment, were exclusively addressed to the Israelites. The latter five are simple prohibitions without any mention of punishment; because they were addressed to man as man, and include only such laws as are also suggested to him by human reason, without direct revelation."

Rabbi R. S. Hirsch, in his Commentary on Exodus xx., says in reference to the first commandment: "As this verse is not understood as a mere declaration, but as a commandment (מצוה), it does not say 'I am thy God,' but 'I, the Lord, *shall be* thy God,' and thus contains as the foundation of all our duties towards God an exhortation to acknowledge the sovereignty of God, קבלת עול מלכות שמים.

"The so-called 'belief in the existence of God,' as ancient and modern theologians generally express this idea, differs widely from that which underlies this fundamental doctrine of Judaism. The truth which affords me the foundation of a Jewish life is not the belief that there is a God, or that there is only one God, but the conviction that this One, Only, and true God is *my* God; that He has created and formed me, has placed me here, and given me certain duties; that He constantly makes and forms me, preserves, protects,

directs, and guides me ; not the belief that I, an accidental
product of the Universe whose First Cause He was millions
of years ago, am through a chain of thousands of inter-
vening beings related to Him, but the belief that every
moment of my existence is a direct personal gift from the
Almighty and All-good, and that every moment of my life
ought to be spent in His service ; not the knowledge that
there is a God, but the recognition of God as my God, as
the sole Cause of my fate, and my sole Guide in all that
I do, gives me the foundation for my religious life.   The
response to the exhortation, 'I shall be thy God,' is 'Thou
art my God.'"

NOTE 4.—The importance attached to the Decalogue may
be gathered from the various attempts made, on the one
hand, to classify the Divine laws according to the Ten Commandments, showing that the latter contain all the 613
precepts ; and, on the other hand, to find in such important
passages as the *Shema* and Leviticus xix. a parallel for each
of the Ten Commandments.   (Jerus. Talm. Ber., chap. i. ;
Rabboth, Vayyikra *ad locum.*)

II. *General Moral Principles.*

The Ten Commandments, flowing as it were from
the one source, "I am the Lord thy God," branch
off in all directions, and penetrate all man's relations,
guide him in his conduct towards God, towards his
fellow-men and towards himself, and teach him how to
rule his thought, his speech, and his actions.   When
the Almighty proclaims to us, "I am the Lord thy
God," we willingly respond, "Thou art my God."   But
this declaration involves also duties on our part, the
fulfilment of which is the natural consequ nce and
the verification of our response.   If our words, "Thou

art my God," come from our hearts, and are not empty sounds, uttered merely by the lips, we must be conscious of the duties they impose on us. These are :—

A. Duties towards God, as our Master, Creator, and Father.

B. Duties towards our fellow-men, as children of one God.

C. Duties towards ourselves, as the object of God's Providence.

A. Duties towards God.

(a.) *Duties of the Heart*

1. *Fear of God.* יראת השם—The true knowledge of God, of His Wisdom and Greatness, as visible in His works, leads us to fear God; that is, to fear doing anything that might displease Him and make us unworthy of His love. It is not a fear that terrifies us and drives us away from His presence; on the contrary, it draws us nearer to Him, and causes us to try to become more and more worthy of His love.

" And now, O Israel, what doth the Lord thy God require of thee but to fear the Lord thy God ? " (Deut. x. 12).

" It thou wilt not observe to do all the words of this law that are written in this book, that thou mayest fear this name which is to be honoured and revered, the Lord thy God; then the Lord will make thy plagues wonderful" (Deut. xxviii. 58).

" The fear of the Lord is the beginning of knowledge " (Prov. i. 7).

S

" The beginning of wisdom is the fear of the Lord " (Ps. cxi. 10).

" The fear of the Lord is to hate evil " (Prov. viii. 13).

" The fear of the Lord prolongeth days " (Prov. x. 27).

" Fear God, and keep his commandments; for this is the whole duty of man " (Eccles. xii. 13).

" He who possesses learning but is without fear of God, resembles a treasurer who has the key for the inner door, but not for the outer one " (Babyl. Talm. Sabb. 31*b*).

" Everything is in the hand of God except the fear of God " (Babyl. Talm. Ber. 33*b*).[1]

2. *Love of God.* אהבת השם—The true fear of God is associated with the love of God. The latter means the constant longing for communion with Him, feeling happy and joyful when with Him, but unhappy and miserable when without Him. Love of God creates in us an anxiety to do everything in our power that might please the Almighty. He who is filled with love of God is חסיד, pious; he does not rest content with doing what he is commanded, but *anxiously seeks the opportunity* of fulfilling a Divine command; he is רודף אחר המצות, " eager in the pursuit of Mitsvoth." The fear of God is the beginning of knowledge, but love of God is the aim and end of all our religious thinking and striving.

" Thou shalt love the Lord thy God with all thine heart, and with all thy soul, and with all thy might " (Deut. vi. 5).

---

[1] *I.e.*, if a person has no fear of God, he is himself the sole cause of its absence, and he alone is responsible for it.

"The Lord preserveth all those who love him (Ps. cxlv. 20).

"Thou wilt show me the path of life. In thy presence is fulness of joy; in thy right hand there are pleasures for evermore" (Ps. xvi. 11).

"As the hart panteth after the water brooks, so panteth my soul after thee, O God" (Ps. xlii. 2).

"Blessed are they who dwell in thy house: they will be still praising thee" (Ps. lxxxiv. 5).

"The desire of our soul is to thy name, and to the remembrance of thee" (Isa. xxvi. 8).

"I will rejoice in the Lord; I will joy in the God of my salvation" (Hab. iii. 18).

3. *Gratitude towards God.*——All that we possess, the very breath we breathe, is a present received at the hands of the Almighty. Whatever success we desire to achieve, whatever undertaking we desire to accomplish, we must ourselves first strive for it to the utmost of our power, and this done, we may hope for the Divine blessing. When we have attained what we sought, we are warned against believing that "our power and the strength of our hand hath gotten us this wealth." We are to "remember the Lord our God, for it is he that giveth us power to get wealth" (Deut. viii. 17–18).

"For all things come of thee, and of thine own hand have we given thee" (1 Chron. xxix. 14).

"Whoso offereth the sacrifice of thanksgiving glorifieth me" (Ps. l. 23).

"Though all sacrifices should cease, the sacrifice of thanksgiving will never cease" (Vayyikra Rabba ix.).

4. *Reverence for His Name.*——The more we fear and love God, the deeper and the more intense is our feeling

of reverence for everything which is connected in our thoughts with the name of the Almighty. Whenever we enter a place dedicated to His worship, or open the Book that bears His name, or celebrate the days set apart as " seasons of the Lord," this feeling of reverence overcomes us, and finds expression in our conduct. The reverence for the name of God impels us also to respect ministers and teachers who spend their life in spreading the knowledge of God and His Will.

" How awful is this place! this is none other but the house of God " (Gen. xxviii. 17).

" I will come into thy house in the multitude of thy mercy : and in thy fear will I worship toward thy holy temple " (Ps. v. 8).

" When I will publish the name of the Lord, ascribe ye greatness unto our God " (Deut. xxxii. 3).

5. *Obedience to the Will of God.*—Whatever the Almighty, whom we love and fear, bids us do, we not only do, but find pleasure in doing.

" To obey is better than sacrifice, and to hearken than the fat of rams. For rebellion is as the sin of witchcraft, and stubbornness is as iniquity and idolatry " (1 Sam. xv. 22, 23).

" But this thing commanded I them, saying, Obey my voice, and I will be your God, and ye shall be my people " (Jer. vii. 23).

" Thy statutes have been my song in the house of my pilgrimage " (Ps. cxix. 54).

" Thy testimonies have I taken as an heritage for ever : for they are the rejoicing of my heart " (Ps. cxix. 111).

" Sacrifice and offering thou didst not desire ; mine

ears hast thou opened ; burnt offering and sin offering hast thou not required. Then said I, Lo, I come with the volume of the book written for me : I delight to do thy will, O my God: yea, thy law is written within my heart " (Ps. xl. 7–9).

6. *Faith and Confidence in God.*—God is All-kind, All-wise, and All-powerful. The Lord is good to all, and His mercy is over all His creatures : He wills that which is good for us. Being All-wise, He knows best what is good for us, and by what means it can be attained ; being All-powerful, He can always carry His Will into effect. He is, therefore, the only Being to whom we can safely entrust ourselves every-where and always. In His words and commands, exhortations and warnings, we have the best and surest guide through life. Our confidence in God causes us to turn to Him for help in time of need, and for comfort in time of sorrow.

" Into his hand I commend my spirit, when I sleep and when I wake ; and with my spirit my body also : the Lord is for me, and I shall not fear " (Daily Prayers, Morning Service).

" Blessed is the man that trusteth in the Lord, and whose hope the Lord is " (Jer. xvii. 7).

" Trust in the Lord, and do good " (Ps. xxxvii. 3).

" Wait on the Lord : be of good courage, and he shall strengthen thine heart ; and wait on the Lord " (Ps. xxvii. 14).

" The Lord is my shepherd, I shall not want " (Ps. xxiii. 1).

7. *Resignation to the Will of God.*—Trusting in God's goodness, we are contented with the lot which

He determined for us. When we are prosperous we hope for His protection, lest we become corrupted and unworthy of His goodness; when we fail, faith in God will keep us from despair and encourage us to fresh attempts; when misfortune befalls us which it is impossible for us to remedy, we resign ourselves unto His Will, and say, "The Lord gave, and the Lord hath taken away! blessed be the Name of the Lord!"

"My flesh and my heart failed; but God is the strength of my heart and my portion for ever" (Ps. lxxiii. 26).

"I am in a great strait: let us fall now into the hand of the Lord; for his mercy is great" (2 Sam. xxiv. 14).

"We are bound to bless God in evil even as we bless Him in good fortune. It is written: 'And thou shalt love the Lord, thy God, with all thine heart, and with all thy soul, and with all thy might' (Deut. vi. 5); love Him *with all thy soul or life—i.e.*, even though for His sake thou risk thy life; *and with all thy wealth*—that is, whatever measure He metes out to thee, acknowledge with exceeding gratitude"[1] (Mishnah Berachoth ix. 5).

(b.) *Duties towards God: In Speech.*

The feelings of fear and love of God, of reverence, obedience, faith, gratitude, and resignation, must also

---

[1] The words of the Mishnah are בכל מדה ומדה שהוא מודד לך הוי מודה לו מאד The meanings of three roots are combined in this interpretation of the words בכל מאדך viz., מאד "exceedingly," מודד "measuring," and מודה "thanking." The three words are similar in sound.

find adequate expression in our speech. God, the Omniscient, knows our thoughts and sentiments, and there would be no necessity for giving them an outward expression, if we only intended thereby to make them known to the Almighty. But as in our relations to our fellow-men—*e.g.*, to our parents or to our children—we frequently, in obedience to an irresistible impulse, communicate to them in words what we think and what we feel, even when convinced that we only tell them things well known to them already, so we address the Almighty, who is everywhere near unto us, and listens to our speech, although our wishes are known to Him before we utter them, and our innermost feelings are open before Him before we express them in words. We are aware that there is an immeasurable difference between the Divine Being and earthly creatures like ourselves. We know that He is not subject to human weaknesses, and that the audible sound of words cannot move Him more than the thoughts and feelings that prompt the words to come forth. And yet the mere communion of our heart with our Creator does not satisfy us; we feel ourselves impelled by some inner force to give it an outward expression. Besides, there is a constant interaction between our thoughts and our spoken words. Thoughts and feelings that remain unspoken, are seldom permanent: we soon cease to be conscious of them ourselves, and they often disappear without leaving any trace behind them, whilst sentiments and ideas expressed in spoken words become strengthened and take a deeper and firmer root in our hearts. The relationship between our lips and our heart is therefore of mutual benefit to both : the words uttered with the lips receive their value and importance from the heart, and the emotions of the heart derive strength and support from the lips.

I. *Prayer.*—All our feelings and sentiments towards the Almighty, our love and fear, faith and confidence, gratitude and resignation, find in Divine worship their due expression. When our soul is full of the love of God, and yearns for His presence, we call upon Him in hymns and songs of praise, and He is " nigh to all them who call upon him, to all that call upon him in truth " (Ps. cxlv. 18).

" I will sing unto the Lord as long as I live ; I will sing praise to my God while I have any being. Let my meditation be sweet unto him : I will rejoice in the Lord " (Ps. civ. 33, 34).

" Praise ye the Lord : for it is good to sing praises unto our God ; for it is pleasant, and praise is comely " (Ps. cxlvii. 1).

" I will bless the Lord at all times : his praise shall continually be in my mouth " (Ps. xxxiv. 2).

" O Lord, open my lips ; and my mouth shall show forth thy praise " (Ps. li. 17).

Our desire to please Him whom we love sincerely, our longing for an opportunity to do what is good in His eyes, ought not to remain hidden and silent. The sooner and the more frequently we give expression to these wishes in audible words, the sooner do they become realised, and the sooner are the promptings of our heart followed by deeds.

" With my lips have I declared all the judgments of thy mouth " (Ps. cxix. 13).

" How sweet are thy words unto my palate ! yea, sweeter to my mouth than honey " (Ps. cxix. 103).

" Let my tongue sing of thy word ; for all thy commandments are righteousness " (Ps. cxix. 172).

We fear lest we offend and displease Him by our words or acts ; we recall to our mind the holiness of a God " who has no pleasure in wickedness, and with whom evil shall not sojourn " (Ps. v. 5) ; we not only meditate on the Holy One, but speak and sing of Him. Our meditation finds expression in songs on the holiness of God, and these songs again supply fresh material for meditation ; we thus hope to fence and guard our heart against the intrusion of anything unworthy of the presence of the Most Holy.

" Who shall ascend the hill of the Lord ? and who shall stand in his holy place ? He that hath clean hands and a pure heart " (Ps. xxiv. 3, 4).

" I will wash mine hands in innocency ; so will I compass thine altar " (Ps. xxvi. 6).

Our weakness and helplessness in many conditions of life fill us with trouble and care. When we enjoy good health, we fear a change might take place ; in possession of wealth, we are in anxiety : it might be taken from us. The pleasures of home and family we know to be but temporary : how soon may sorrow visit us there ! From all these fears and anxieties we seek and find refuge in Him, who is " a stronghold to the weak, a stronghold in times of trouble " (Ps. ix. 10). We tell Him confidently all the troubles and cares of our heart, as we would do to a friend who is always willing and ready to help us. We have faith in God, and therefore we approach **Him** with our petitions; and when we have poured forth our heart before the All-merciful we feel more at ease, and our faith and confidence have gained in strength.

"He shall call upon me, and I will answer him: I will be with him in trouble; I will deliver him and honour him" (Ps. xci. 15).

"When they have cried unto the Lord in their trouble, he will save them out of their distresses" (Ps. cvii. 6).

"Because he hath inclined his ear unto me, therefore will I call upon him as long as I live. When I find trouble and sorrow, then will I call upon the name of the Lord. When I take the cup of salvation, then will I call upon the name of the Lord" (Ps. cxvi. 2, 4, 13).

"What sufferings may be called chastisements of love? Such as do not prevent us from prayer" (Babyl. Talm. Ber. 5a).

"Even when the edge of the sword touches already a man's neck, even then he must not abandon his faith in praying to God" (Babyl. Talm. Ber. 10a).

"'I was asleep, but my heart was awake;' I have no sacrifices, but I have 'Shema' and 'Prayer'" (Shir ha-shirim Rabba on v. 2).

"'Hope in the Lord,' and pray again" (Rabboth, Deuter., chap. ii.).

Our Rabbis teach, "Prayer is good for man both before his fate has been decreed and after it has been decreed" (Babyl. Talm. Rosh-hashshanah, p. 16a). But at the same time we are warned against impatiently expecting and demanding an immediate effect from the words uttered by our lips, however devoutly they may have been spoken. Such expectation—denounced in

the Talmud as עִיוּן תִפְלָה [1]—would indicate our confidence
in the wisdom of our petition, whilst confidence in the
wisdom and goodness of God would suggest that "the
Lord will do what is good in his eyes."

We give expression to our feelings of *gratitude*
towards our benefactor by acknowledging the fact, that
whatever we enjoy, we are enabled to enjoy through
His kindness. The various blessings formulated by
our Sages serve a double purpose: first, they facilitate the expression of our feelings; secondly, they
remind us of the presence of the Almighty, and of
His goodness in providing for us and all His creatures. From the time we awake in the morning till
the evening when we lie down to sleep, there is not a
moment that does not bring to our knowledge some
Divine act of kindness towards us. In the morning
we perceive the benefit of light, in the evening we
have reason to welcome the blessing of repose it
brings with it, while the interval between the two
periods constantly reveals to him who does not wilfully
shut his eyes the hand of Him "who is good, and
whose loving-kindness endureth for ever."

"I will give thanks to thee, for thou hast answered
me, and art become my salvation" (Ps. cxviii. 21).

"I will sacrifice unto thee with the voice of thanksgiving" (Jon. ii. 10).

"Though all prayers were to be discontinued,

---

[1] The term עִיוּן תִפְלָה (lit., "reflecting on prayer") has two meanings: (1) reflecting on the prayer while uttering it; devotion; in
German, *Andacht*; (2) reflecting on the prayer after having uttered
it, while we are waiting for the sure fulfilment of the wishes expressed
in it.

prayers of thanksgiving will never be discontinued" (Vayyikra Rabba, chap. ix.).

When things happen which are not pleasant to us, which give us pain and sorrow, we ought to consider that the plans of God are different from our plans, and His ways from our ways, and what He wills is better for us than our own wishes. With resignation, without murmuring, we ought to utter words of praise and thanks to the Almighty.

"The Lord gave, and the Lord hath taken away; blessed be the name of the Lord" (Job i. 21).

"Learn to say, 'Whatever the Almighty does, is done for our good'" (Babyl. Talm. Ber. 60b).

Public Service.—Man has a natural desire to communicate his sentiments to his fellow-men, and finds a certain pleasure or relief in knowing that others share in his joys and sorrows. The same is the case with regard to his sentiments towards the Most High. If, yearning for communion with God, we fervently appeal to Him in solitude, where we are undisturbed by the intrusion of any other person, it will not be long before we shall feel ourselves in the very presence of Him who is " nigh to all those who call upon him in truth." Standing before the Almighty, the Creator and Master of the whole Universe as well as of ourselves, we should like all nature to join in His praises, and we summon the inhabitants of the heavens above, His angels and hosts, sun, moon, and all the stars of light; and the dwellers on earth below, inanimate and animate, irrational and rational, kings with their peoples, to come and to praise the name of God (Ps. cxlviii.). Such moments of solitary devotion are very precious, and are by no means to be despised. But they are not frequent, and not always successful. Public worship has this advantage, that the object of our meeting, the holiness of the place, and the union in a worship with our fellow-men combine to create, maintain, or intensify our devotion. Although each one has his individual wants, joys, and sorrows, there are many wants, joys, and sorrows which we have all in common, and concerning which we may in common give expression to our feelings in prayer, praise, and thanksgiving.

"Bless ye the Lord in congregations" (Ps. lxviii. 27).

"If ten pray together, the presence of God is with them" (Babyl. Talm. Ber. 6a).

"'But as for me, my prayer is unto thee, O Lord, in an acceptable time' (Ps. lxix. 14): which is the acceptable time? The time of public worship" (Babyl. Talm. Ber. 8a).

2. *Study of the Law* (תלמוד תורה).—Another way of employing speech in the service of the Lord is the reading and the study of the Word of God: the Holy Scriptures and their Commentaries. Our love and reverence of God ought to induce us frequently to consult the book which contains His commandments, and which He has given us as a guide and companion. Even if we derived no further benefit than the consciousness of having spent some time in reading His Word revealed to us by the mouth of the Prophets, the time thus spent would not be wasted. But we derive a further advantage. It is impossible to imagine that our devoting a certain time, however short it may be, to the reading of the words of the Most Holy should have no purifying influence upon us, provided

we approach the book before us with due reverence, and with the intention to be guided by its teachings.

Joshua, when placed at the head of the nation, is exhorted by the Almighty as follows: "This book of the law shall not depart out of thy mouth; but thou shalt meditate therein day and night, that thou mayest observe to do according to all that is written therein" (Joshua i. 8).

"As for me, this is my covenant with them, saith the Lord: my spirit that is upon thee, and my words which I have put in thy mouth, shall not depart out of thy mouth, nor out of the mouth of thy seed, nor out of the mouth of thy seed's seed, saith the Lord, from henceforth and for ever."

3. *Teaching.*—The gift of speech is of service also in communicating our thoughts, feelings, and convictions to our fellow-men. They who are able to read the Word of God and to understand it, ought to read and expound it to those who are less favoured; they who feel the presence of God, and comprehend His holiness, goodness, and unity, ought to direct the hearts of their brethren to God, His words and works. It is a special duty and privilege of the Jew to proclaim and teach the Existence and the Unity of God—יחוד הבורא

"And thou shalt teach them diligently unto thy children, and shalt talk of them when thou sittest in thine house, and when thou walkest by the way, and when thou liest down and when thou risest up" (Deut. vi. 7).

"Happy are we! how goodly is our portion, and how pleasant is our lot, and how beautiful our heritage! Happy are we who early and late, morning and evening, twice every day, declare, ' Hear, O Israel, the Lord is our God, the Lord is One ' ! " (Daily Prayers, Morning Service).

4. *Reverence of the Name of God.*—The mention of the name of God ought to make us most careful about that which we utter in connection with it. If a person makes a promise or statement on oath carelessly or with levity, he shows that he has no reverence of the name of God; no fear of God. It is only through such irreverence that a person is capable of breaking the third commandment. Blasphemy, a sin treated in the Bible as a capital crime, has likewise its source in want of due reverence of God's name. In order to preserve and strengthen that reverence we must avoid pronouncing the Divine name too frequently. Hence arose the custom of substituting such words as השם "the Name," המקום "the Omnipresent," for the names of God, and employing in ordinary writing letters like ה or ד or ״ instead of any of the Divine names. In writing single letters instead of the full names we also intend to guard ourselves against causing irreverence towards the name of God; as our writing is frequently destroyed or liable to be thrown among the refuse. This precaution, dictated by a feeling of reverence for God and His name, serves at the same time to strengthen that feeling.[1]

From the same reason, the word which is exclusively

---

[1] In the whole Book of Esther the name of God does not occur even once. It is not mere chance ; there are several passages where the mention of the Divine Being is expected, and it is believed that the omission is due to the fear of a subsequent desecration of the book in the hands of the Persians.

used as a name of God, the Tetragrammaton,[1] was rarely pronounced, and in reading the Bible the word *Adonai,* " My Lord," is substituted wherever it occurs. It was only pronounced in the Temple by the High-priest on the Day of Atonement, in the Confession of Sins, and in the Prayer for Forgiveness; and by the ordinary priests when they blessed the people in accordance with the Divine precepts (Num. vi. 24–26). Since the destruction of the Temple the Tetragrammaton has not been pronounced, and thus it has come about that the right pronunciation of the word is at present unknown.

5. The consciousness that we frequently address the Almighty with our lips, and read His Holy Word, ought to make us strive for the utmost purity and holiness in our speech. When the prophet Isaiah, in a Divine vision, perceived the majesty of the Most High, and heard the sound of His ministering angels proclaiming His holiness, a sense of his own failings forced even from this chosen messenger of God the confession, " Woe is me! for I am undone; because I am a man, unclean in lips, and I dwell in the midst of a people unclean in lips, for mine eyes have seen the King, the Lord of hosts " (Isa. vi. 5).

Duties towards God: In our Actions.

Rabbi Jose teaches, " Let *all thy deeds* be in the service of heaven," כל מעשיך יהיו לשם שמים (Sayings of the Fathers, ii. 12).

The feeling of love and fear of God which fills our

I.e., the word consisting of four letters, *yod, hé, vav* and *hé.*

heart and soul, and to which we frequently give expression in words, must also be visible in our actions. Our whole life must be devoted to His service, and ought to be one continuous worship of God. Every act of ours must aim at the sanctification of His name. He has revealed unto us His Will, and shown us the way in which we should walk; unconditional submission to His guidance and strict obedience to His command should distinguish the people of the Lord. True love of God and faith in His goodness make us "bold as a leopard, light as an eagle, swift as a stag, and strong as a lion to carry out the will of our Father in heaven" (Sayings of the Fathers, v. 20). For what could be the value of our professions of love for God, if we refused to listen attentively to His voice, to walk in the way He has prepared for us, or to observe His statutes? From this point of view we may consider all our duties as duties towards God, since their fulfilment implies obedience to His Will. But there are certain duties which chiefly or exclusively concern our relations to God. Such duties are: the observance of Sabbath and Festivals, providing reminders of God's Presence, establishing and supporting Public Worship, sanctifying God's Name (קדוש השם), and imitating His ways. Of these duties, the first three will be fully treated in special sections.

The sanctification of God's Name is a duty incumbent on all mankind, but it is incumbent on us Jews in a higher degree, for we are called the people of the Lord, the chosen people, a holy nation, and a kingdom of priests. We sanctify the name of God by remaining faithful to Him and to His Word, resisting every kind

T

of force or temptation to turn us away from our faith, making sacrifices for our holy religion, and conducting ourselves in such a manner that our fellow-men may become convinced that the tree of our Law bears good and holy fruit. Every action that brings disgrace upon us as Israelites, and causes our neighbours to despise "the people of the Lord, who profess to be the guardians of the revealed Torah," is חלול השם "Profanation of the Name of God." "And ye shall not profane my holy name, but I will be hallowed among the children of Israel" (Lev. xxii. 32).

"Profanation of the name of God is a greater sin even than idolatry" (Babyl. Talm. Sanhedrin 106a).

Imitating the Ways of God.—We know that God is perfect, and that all His ways are perfect; we are conscious also of our weakness and of the impossibility of ever becoming perfect. But this conviction must not deter us from seeking perfection as far as our nature permits it, or from setting before us the ways of God as an example for us to follow, as the aim which should direct the course of our life, the balance in which to weigh our actions, and the test by which to determine their value.

"Ye shall be holy; for I, the Lord your God, am holy" (Lev. xix. 2).

"I set the Lord always before me" (Ps. xvi. 8).

"'Ye shall walk after the Lord your God' (Deut. xiii. 5). Is it possible for man to walk after the Lord? Has it not been said, 'The Lord thy God is a consuming fire'? (*ibid.* iv. 24). The meaning of the verse, however, is this: Follow the ways of God: He clothes the naked, as we are told, 'And the Lord God

made coats of skin for Adam and his wife' (Gen. iii.
21); do the same. He visits the sick, as is indicated
in the words, 'And God appeared to him in the plain
of Mamre' (*ibid.* xviii. 1); you must also visit the
sick. He comforts the mourners, as appears from the
passage, 'And it came to pass after the death of Abraham, that God blessed his son Isaak' (*ibid.* xxv. 11);
do the same, and comfort mourners," &c. (Babyl. Talm.
Sotah 14*a*).

It may happen that we are sometimes disposed to
exclude a fellow-man from our brotherly love. It
would be against human nature to love those who have
hurt or wronged us. But, on the other hand, we are
taught that we must keep our heart free from feelings
of revenge and hatred. If an offence has been committed against us by our brother, the Law directs us
as follows: " Thou shalt not hate thy brother in thine
heart; thou shalt surely reprove thy neighbour, and
not bear sin against him. Thou shalt not revenge, and
thou shalt not keep a grudge against the children of
thy people, but love thy fellow-man like thyself: I am
the Lord " (Lev. xix. 17, 18). The traditional interpretation illustrates revenge and grudge in the following way: If your neighbour, after having been unkind
to you, is in need of your assistance, and you refuse it
on the ground of his want of kindness towards you,
you are guilty of revenge; if you grant him his request,
but at the same time remind him of his unkind conduct, you are guilty of " bearing a grudge against
your neighbour." (Sifra, *ad locum.*)

B.—*Duties towards our Fellow-creatures.*

(a.) *Duties towards our Fellow-men in General.*

"Have we not all one father? hath not one God created us?" (Mal. ii. 10). "Thou shalt love thy fellow-man as thyself" (Lev. xix. 18). These are the sentiments which, according to the Will of God, ought to guide us in our relation to our fellow-men. When, therefore, a Gentile came to Hillel and asked him to explain to him in one moment the duties which Judaism enjoins on its adherents, he replied, "What is displeasing to thee, that do thou not to others. This is the text of the Law; all the rest is commentary; go and learn" (Babyl. Talm. Shabbath 31*a*). In a different form this idea has been expressed by Rabbi Akiba and by Ben-Azai, who respectively quoted as a fundamental principle of the Law, "Love thy neighbour as thyself," and "This is the book of the generations of man; in the day that God created man, he made him in the likeness of God" (Yalkut on Gen. v. 1).

From this principle we derive the following general maxims with regard to our neighbour's (1) life and health, (2) property, (3) honour, and (4) well-being :—

1. *Life and Health of our Fellow-man.*—Life is a precious treasure which the Almighty has given us; if it is once taken from us, no man is able to restore it. Among the first lessons revealed to man in Scripture is the value of the life of a human being, created by God in His own likeness, and when the first murder had been committed, God said to the murderer, "What hast thou done? the voice of thy brother's blood is heard that crieth unto me from the

ground" (Gen. **iv.** 1C). The first commandment in
the second section of the Decalogue is directed against
this crime : "Thou shalt not murder." The significance of these words, the general lessons implied in
this commandment, and the extent to which a person,
though not an actual murderer, may become guilty
of having broken this commandment, have already
been explained in the chapter on the Ten Commandments (p. 261). It has been shown how the sixth
commandment forbade—

(1.) The taking of the life of a fellow-man by violent
means.

(2.) The doing of anything by which the health,
the peace, and the well-being of our fellow-man is
undermined.

(3.) The omission of any act in our power to save
our fellow-man from direct or indirect danger of life.

2. *The Property of our Neighbour.*—The eighth commandment in its wider sense comprehends all our
relations to our neighbour's property. It prohibits, as
has been shown above (p. 263), the appropriation of
anything that belongs to our neighbour—

(1.) By theft and robbery, or

(2.) By any kind of fraud and dishonesty.

Our Sages teach : "Let the property of thy fellow-
man be as dear to thee as thine own" (Aboth ii. 12);
i.e., you do not like to see your own property damaged,
diminished, or destroyed; so it would be wrong if
you were to cause loss and ruin to your fellow-man,
whether you did it directly or indirectly.[1] Let every

---

[1] *E.g*, by giving bad advice and transgressing the law, "Thou shalt
not put a stumbling block before the blind" (Lev. xix. 14).

one enjoy the labour of his hands; partake of the gifts of the earth and the Divine blessings as much as his physical and mental powers enable him to do in a righteous manner.

It is not only direct illegal appropriation of our neighbour's goods that is condemned as theft or robbery; it is equally wicked to buy things which one knows to have been stolen by others.[1] He who does it is worse than the thief; for, whilst the latter injures only the person whom he robs, the former encourages and corrupts the thief, hardens his heart, helps to silence the voice of his conscience, and thus obstructs the way to repentance and improvement.

There are transactions which are legal and do not involve any breach of the law, and which are yet condemned by the principles of morality as base and disgraceful. Such are all transactions in which a person takes advantage of the ignorance or embarrassment of his neighbour for the purpose of increasing his own property. Usurers frequently belong to this low and heartless class of society. The worst thing, however, they do is, that they plan the ruin of others; in many cases they bring about disaster by inducing young and inexperienced persons to borrow money and to spend it in luxuries, or increase the embarrassment of the distressed by charging exorbitant interest and imposing cruel conditions, which make it impossible for those who have once fallen into the hands of usurers to free themselves from their bondage.

---

[1] Comp. the saying, לא עכברא גנבא אלא חורא גנבא "Not the mouse is the thief, but the hole."

It makes no difference whatever whether the victim be a Jew or a non-Jew; the transaction is equally condemnable, and the usurer equally wicked. This statement would be superfluous, were it not for the misunderstanding that exists both among some of our co-religionists and among non-Jews with regard to the principle it involves. Great stress is laid in the Pentateuch on the prohibition of taking interest for advances of money or articles of food. " And if thy brother be waxen poor and fallen in decay with thee, then thou shalt relieve him : yea, though he be a stranger or a sojourner, that he may live with thee. Take thou no interest of him, or increase : but fear thy God, that thy brother may live with thee. Thou shalt not give him thy money upon usury, nor lend him thy victuals for increase. I am the Lord your God," &c. (Lev. xxv. 35–38 ; comp. Exod. xxii. 24). —It is one of the characteristics of the pious who is worthy to " abide in the tabernacle of God," that " he putteth not out his money to usury " (Ps. xv. 5).

The strict prohibition to take interest on advances of money or goods served a twofold purpose. In the first place, the surplus money of the wealthy was to be employed in disinterested charity. Secondly, labour and activity, both physical and mental, were to be the sources of income and wealth for the individual as well as for the whole nation ; money without labour was not to bear any fruit or produce any increase.

An exception from this law was made for the bene-fit of the stranger. The inhabitants of a town or a country who lived in the midst of their relatives, friends, and countrymen could, as a rule, be trusted to return the loan in due time. If they were not known themselves, they could find persons who would recognise them or even offer themselves as security for them. It was different with the stranger (הנכרי) "who came from a far land" (Deut. xxix. 21); he was not known; he was, as a rule, without friends; he had none to offer security for him.[1] When in need, therefore, he would be unlikely to obtain a loan, if the lender were not permitted in such cases to take interest as compensation for risking the capital itself. The same reason explains also a second exception made in the law with regard to a stranger when a debtor. The payment of old debts is, as a rule, a great hardship to the insolvent, especially at a time when the benefit derived from the loan has already been forgotten. It was therefore ordained that every seven years a remission of all debts should take place. The debtor that lived in the country could easily be urged or forced to pay his debts, and the creditor could safely expect that he would receive his money before the year of release began. This was not the case with the stranger, who might with impunity keep out of sight for some time before the beginning of the seventh year: a circumstance that increased the uncertainty of the repayment, and would have rendered it almost impossible for a stranger to enjoy the benefit of a loan in times of temporary embarrassment, but for the exception made in his case from the law commanding the remission of all debts in the seventh year.

---

[1] Those who become security for a stranger are blamed (Prov. vi. 1 *seq.*) as acting rashly, and foolishly endangering their peace and welfare.

We see here a difference made in our duties towards our fellow-men between an Israelite and a stranger, but solely for the benefit of " the stranger." At present, when the original relation between the Israelite and the stranger has ceased, the spirit of charity and justice towards the stranger (נכרי) or non-Jew, which is the basis of this law, must continue to regulate our intercourse with our neighbours, and if the non-Jew would recognise the prohibition of taking interest as equally binding upon him as upon the Jew, the latter would not be allowed to take any kind of interest from a non-Jew. At all events, if any of our co-religionists take this law as a pretext for imposing upon their non-Jewish fellow-men, and injuring and ruining them by exorbitant usury, they pervert alike the letter and the spirit of the Divine command ; they do not act in a Jewish spirit, and instead of being members of a holy nation or the people of the Lord, they are guilty of חלול השם, the profanation of the name of God, and do not deserve to be honoured by the name of Jews.

Denunciations are sometimes levelled against the Jews, on account of the misdeeds of some individuals, as cruel usurers. Those non-Jews who would take the trouble of thoroughly studying Jews and Judaism would soon discover the error and the baselessness of such denunciations. Judaism has never sanctioned usury, but, on the contrary, always condemned it.[1]

With regard to the property of our neighbour our Sages expressed the following maxim :—

" There are four characters among men : he who

[1] See p. 294.

says, 'What is mine is mine and what is thine is thine,' his is a neutral character; some say this is a character like that of Sodom; he who says, 'What is mine is thine and what is thine is mine' is a boor; he who says 'What is mine is thine and what is thine is thine' is a saint; he who says 'What is thine is mine and what is mine is mine' is a wicked man" (Aboth v. 10).

We are not only commanded to abstain from injuring our neighbour with regard to his property, but we are exhorted to protect it as far as lies in our power. "If thou meetest the ox of thine enemy or his ass going astray, bring it back to him" (Exod. xxiii. 4). "Thou shalt not see thy brother's ox or his sheep go astray, and hide thyself from them: thou shalt surely bring them again unto thy brother" (Deut. xxii. 1). "Thou shalt not see thy brother's ass or his ox fallen down by the way, and hide thyself from them: thou shalt surely help him to lift them up again" (*ibid.* ver. 4).

3. *The Honour of our Fellow-man.*—"Let the honour of thy fellow-man be as dear to thee as thy own" (Aboth ii. 10). We are very sensitive about our own honour; and many of us—nay, all right-minded persons—are more anxious for the good name acquired through integrity of character than for the safety of their property. We must be equally sensitive about the honour of our fellow-man, and take good care lest we damage his repute by falsehood, slander, or spreading evil reports in apparently innocent gossip. An evil tongue (לשׁן הרע) is a serious failing from which few are exempt; even if a person is not guilty of the sin of evil speech, he does not entirely escape "the dust

of the evil tongue" (Babyl. Talm. B. Bathra 165*a*). Calumny, it is said, kills three—the slanderer himself, him who listens, and the person spoken of. We therefore add to the *Amidah* the words: " My God, guard my tongue from evil, and my lips from speaking guile ; " and in one of the Psalms we read : " Who is the man that desireth life, and loveth days, that he may see good ? Keep thy tongue from evil and thy lips from speaking guile " (Ps. xxxiv. 13, 14).

Our Sages are very severe against those who attack the honour of their fellow-men. In one passage it is said : " Whoever causes by offensive words the face of his fellow-man to turn pale is almost guilty of shedding blood " (Babyl. Talm. B. Metsia 58*b*). Another passage runs thus : " Rather let a man throw himself into a furnace than publicly offend his fellow-man" (*ibid.* 59*a*).

The Law does not only forbid the utterance of evil reports, but also the encouragement given to the tale-bearer by listening to his stories. " Thou shalt not take up a false report " (Exod. xxiii. 1). In the Book of Proverbs the evil consequences of listening to slander are thus depicted : " If a ruler hearkeneth to falsehood, all his servants are wicked " (Prov. xxix. 12). " He who giveth heed to wicked lips causeth evil-doing ; he who giveth ear to a mischievous tongue feedeth lies " (*ibid.* xvii. 4).

When we hear evil reports about our neighbour, we should try to defend him ; when we are convinced that he has done wrong, we must rebuke him, lead him back to the right way, and not utterly reject him ; we may still find some redeeming feature in his character that makes it worth our while to save him.

Thus Joshua, the son of Perachjah, teaches us:
" Judge every man favourably " (Aboth i. 6); that
is, if you are uncertain as to a man's faults, let him
have the benefit of the doubt.   When we criticise our
neighbour's character—and idle gossip frequently leads
to this practice—we are too often inclined to dwell
upon his weak points—his vices—and to pass over
his merits in silence ; but we ought to consider how
little we should like to see the same treatment applied
to ourselves.   Another fault of ours is to judge the
doings of other people without fully understanding
all the circumstances and the causes that led to such
actions.   Hillel said, " Do not judge thy neighbour
until thou hast come into his place ; " that is, do not
pass judgment upon your neighbour before you are
able to place yourself in his position, and to say with
certainty what you would have done under the same
circumstances.   The Law forbids us to use divers
weights and divers measures in our business transactions, lest we damage the property of our neighbour ;
equally unlawful is the use of one kind of weights and
measures for weighing our own words and deeds, and
another kind for weighing the words and the deeds
of others, to the injury of our fellow-man's name and
repute.   Contrary to the usage of courts of justice,
our neighbour's words and deeds are generally re-
ported by us, interpreted, tried and condemned in his
absence, when he is unable to defend himself, to show
his innocence, or to prove the falsehood of the report,
the error of the interpretation, and the injustice of the
trial and the condemnation.

The perversity of such conduct is evident, especially

in the case of the departed. The prohibition, "Thou shalt not curse the deaf" (Lev. xix. 14) has been interpreted to apply to all kinds of slander about those absent or dead. Our respect for the memory of the dead is expressed in the Latin maxim, "*De mortuis nil nisi bonum;*" or in the Hebrew, אחרי מות קדשים אמור [1] "After their death say of them 'saints.'" Similar maxims are the following : " We must not refute the lion after his death ;" מיתה מכפרת "Death atones for all offences."

4. *The Well-being of our Fellow-man.*—The duties expounded in the above are of a negative character. The commandment, "Love thy neighbour as thyself" implies also certain positive duties, which are comprehended in the terms, צדקה and גמלות חסד "charity."

The literal meaning of the term *tsedakah* is "righteousness," but it occurs also frequently in the sense of "charity ;" and we may infer from this that charity was to the Hebrew a mere act of righteousness. In the Book of Daniel and in post-Biblical Hebrew *tsedakah* is "alms," and distinguished from *gemilluth-chesed,* "charity." The former is given to the poor ; the latter to poor and rich alike : *tsedakah,* consisting of money or things that can be purchased for money, is a duty chiefly incumbent on the wealthier class ; *gemilluth-chesed,* consisting of personal acts of kindness, is a virtue that can be acquired and practised by every one, whether he be poor or rich ; and whilst *tsedakah* can only be given to those that live, *gemilluth-chesed* can be shown even to the departed.

---

[1] The Hebrew is composed of the names of the three consecutive Sidras, Lev. xvi.–xxiv.

When Jacob asked his son for a burial in the cave
of Machpelah, he relied on his son's חסד ואמת, "Kindness and truth ; " and the Midrash adds the remark,
" Kindness shown to the dead is an act of true love,
as there can be no prospect of gratitude or repayment."

The principal kinds of גמלות חסד are the following :—

(1.) בקור חולים Visiting the sick.[1] The object of the
visit ought to be to cheer up the sufferer by pleasant
conversation, to assist him by good advice, to render
him any service that is wanted, to inspire him with
hope, and to strengthen his faith in God by the comforting words of Scripture and by prayer.

(2.) הלוית המת " Accompanying the dead " to his last
resting-place, and doing everything that our love and
regard for the departed requires. Almost every Jewish
community includes an association whose members
undertake to perform personally, as far as possible,
these acts of love. Such a society is generally called
חברת גמלות חסדים " Association for practising loving-
kindness towards our fellow-men," or חברא קדישא " Holy
Association ; " that is, an association for a holy object.

(3.) נחום אבלים Comforting the mourners, who find
relief in the conviction that their fellow-men have
sympathy with them.

(4.) הבאת שלום בין אדם לחברו " Peace-making."—War,
whether carried on between nations, or between parties,
or between one individual and another, is equally
detestable ; and all those who by their exertion and
intercession contribute to a diminution of warfare are

[1] Lit., inquiring, scil., what the condition of the patient is, and what
is needed for his recovery.

engaged in praiseworthy work. The principal prayers in our Liturgy conclude with a petition for peace, and we look forward for the state of uninterrupted peace, the Messianic time, as the most perfect condition of mankind. Forbearance, a kind word, a judicious counsel, frequently averts the great evil of strife and enmity.—Peace, harmony, and friendship are best promoted by—

(5.) Judging favourably the deeds and words of our fellow-men. It is not an easy task to correctly estimate the motives which guide our neighbour in his actions, and in doing so we err frequently; but it is better to err by over-estimating them; since this produces far less harm than going astray in the other direction and speaking ill of others without any justifiable cause. Conduct like this leads to peace and happiness within and without. "Speaking peace to all his seed" is the climax of the virtues praised in Mordecai, the Jew (Esther x. 3).

Charity (*tsedakah*) in its narrower sense, as a duty towards the poor, includes—

(1.) Alms-giving to the poor for the purpose of alleviating temporary suffering.

(2.) Providing for the comfort of the aged and sick, widows and orphans.

(3.) Assisting the stranger. The Law lays special stress on this branch of charity, and reminds us that we all have once been strangers in the land of Egypt. Even in the various countries of which we have become citizens, our forefathers, three or four generations back, were strangers; and, besides, we are told by the Almighty, "Ye are strangers and sojourners with me" (Lev. xxv. 23). This kind of charity is known by the name הכנסת אורחים

(4.) Support given to the poor towards obtaining a livelihood, by procuring occupation for them, teaching them a trade and giving them a start in it.

(5.) Providing for the religious and secular education of the children of the poor.

(6.) Raising their intellectual, social, and moral condition by personal intercourse with them, and by kind words of advice, comfort, and encouragement.

(7.) Helping those who have gone astray and have fallen into vice or crime to return to the path of virtue, industry, and righteousness.

There are generally associations formed for the various branches of *gemilluth-chesed,* the number of which grows, especially in large towns, with the increase of misery. It is our duty to support such institutions, as combined action is in most cases more practical and productive of good result. But the existence of public institutions, and our support given to them, by no means exempt us from assisting individually those who apply to us for help. We must be judicious in our charitable acts, lest we nurse poverty and promote imposture. But, on the other hand, we must not be over cautious, and must not unduly suspect every applicant for assistance as guilty of idleness or other vices, lest by refusal or hesitation to help we become guilty of neglect, when by prompt action we might save from utter ruin a person or a whole family well worthy of our sympathy. In this regard we are warned by King Solomon: "Withhold not good from them to whom it is due, when it is in the power of thine hand to do it. Say not unto thy neighbour, Go, and come again, and to-morrow I will give; when thou hast it by thee" (Prov. iii. 27, 28).

(b.) *Special Duties towards our Fellow-men.*

1. *Children towards their Parents.*—"*Honour thy father and thy mother*" is one of the Ten Words which God spoke to the Israelites on Mount Sinai. The child honours his parents by considering them as his superiors, as endowed with authority over him, and entitled by experience to be his guides and instructors; by listening respectfully when they speak to him, and by speaking with reverence when he speaks of or to them.

The love of parents towards their child should find an echo in the heart of the latter.

The child's love of his parents finds expression in willing, cheerful obedience; in the endeavour to do everything that pleases them, in the sacrifice made for the purpose of giving them pleasure, in the assistance given them when, through age, sickness, or misfortune, they are in need of aid.

The parents' duty towards the child is to do everything that true love demands, for his physical, moral, and intellectual well-being.

With regard to the child's duty towards his parents the following verses from Proverbs may be noticed:—

"The eye that mocketh at his father, and despiseth to obey his mother, the ravens of the valley shall pick it out, and the young eagles shall eat it" (xxx. 17).

U

" Whoso robbeth his father or his mother, and saith,
It is no transgression, the same is the companion of a
destroyer " (xxviii. 24).

" Whoso curseth his father or his mother, his lamp
shall be put out in obscure darkness " (xx. 20).

" He that wasteth his father and chaseth away his
mother is a son that causeth shame, and bringeth reproach " (xix. 26).

" The glory of children are their fathers " (xvii. 6).

2. All other special duties towards our fellow-men
may be divided into (i.) Duties towards our equals;
(ii.) Duties towards our superiors and towards our
inferiors.

(i.) *Duties towards our Equals.*

(1.) A bond of friendship frequently exists between
equals.

Friends have certain duties to fulfil towards each
other. It is expected that friends should have faith
in their mutual friendship. " As in water face answereth to face, so in the heart man answereth to
man " (Prov. xxvii. 19). As the water reflects the
face of him who looks into it, so the heart of man
reflects the friendship and faithfulness of him who has
penetrated into it. Our estimation of our friend's
feeling toward us is the measure of the genuineness
and value of our own friendship towards him.

Disinterestedness is an essential condition of genuine
friendship. Every service we render to our friend
must be prompted by the desire to be of use to him.

and not to advance our own interest. If any other motive enters our mind, if we speculate on his gratitude, and think that our kindness must eventually be returned with interest, we have no knowledge or feeling of friendship. Thus our Sages declare, " Friendship dictated by a selfish motive comes to an end together with the speculation; but friendship which is not based on any selfish motive comes never to an end. An instance of the first kind is the friendship between Amnon and Tamar (2 Sam. xiii.); of the second kind, the friendship between David and Jonathan (1 Sam. xviii.)" (Aboth v. 16).

Friends bound to each other by genuine and sincere love find great pleasure in the fulfilment of the duties involved in friendship. They do not hesitate to bring sacrifices for each other's well-being; they evince heartfelt sympathy for each other in good and evil fortune.

All the duties of charity—*gemilluth chesed*—which we owe to our fellow-men in general, apply with increased force when our fellow-man is also our friend. One of these duties demands our special attention, because it is frequently neglected through human weakness: truthfulness and openness. Flattery, objectionable as it is in every case, is most detestable between friends. We must encourage our friends by kind words, and acknowledge their merits, but we must not spoil them by undue flattery. If, on the other hand, we discover errors or vices in our friend, it is our duty to communicate to him openly our opinion, and to do all that is in our power to bring him back to the path of righteousness and truth.

" Thou shalt surely rebuke thy friend, and not suffer sin upon him " (Lev. xix. 17).

Friendship is mostly formed without premeditation, and without any aim ; we are friends, we do not know how and why ; some similarity in our character, in our talents, in our views, in our successes and failures, or in our fortunes and misfortunes, draws us together, and we become friends before we are aware of the fact. But as far as we have control over our feelings we ought to be careful not to plunge into friendship without knowing something of the character and the tendencies of those with whom we are to associate ourselves in such close relationship. In Proverbs we are told, "Make no friendships with an angry man, and with a furious man thou shalt not go " (xxii. 24). Bensira (vi. 6) exhorts us, " If thou wouldst get a friend, prove him first, and be not hasty to credit him." Our Sages say, " It is easy to make an enemy ; it is difficult to make a friend " (Yalkut on Deut. vi. 16).

The acquisition of a true friend is by no means an easy task. But it is a task that cannot be dispensed with. Persons who enjoy a life spent in loneliness uncheered by friendship are exceptions to the rule; such a life is miserable, and the climax of all the evils complained of by Heman the Ezrahite (Ps. lxxxviii. 19) is : " Lover and friend hast thou put far from me, and darkness is mine acquaintance." Job in his great sufferings longs for " the love which is shown to the unhappy by his friend " (Job vi. 14).

Friendship being one of our most valuable possessions, it must be well guarded and cultivated, lest it be lost or weakened. " Thine own friend and thy father's friend, forsake not" (Prov. xxvii. 10). "Let thy foot be seldom in thy friend's house, lest he be weary of thee, and so hate thee" (*ibid.* xxv. 17).

True friendship can be extended only to a few; but those who are not our friends need not be our enemies. They are all our fellow-men, and our conduct towards them is to be guided by the principle, "Love thy fellow-man as thyself." We are distinctly commanded, "Thou shalt not hate thy brother in thine heart" (Lev. xix. 18), "brother" having here the same meaning as fellow-man. Enmity, like friendship, comes frequently unawares; we dislike or even hate a person without knowing why. But it is our duty, as soon as such an ill-feeling has stolen into our heart, to search for its origin; and this being done, we shall generally feel ashamed of having allowed our heart to be invaded by such an unworthy intruder. We must keep away from evil-doers, and not associate with wicked people; but this is a very different thing from hating our neighbour. The pious wish, "May sinners cease to exist, and the wicked be no more" (Ps. civ. 35), is explained in the Talmud in the words of Beruria, daughter of Rabbi Meir, as follows: "May sins cease to exist, and the wicked will be no more." We often conceive just indignation at the misdeeds of our neighbours, and cannot well separate the doer from the deed. But we ought in such cases of indignation to examine ourselves, whether the source of our indignation is pure, or has its root in selfishness. Such an analysis of our motives would soon purify our heart of all ill-feeling.

In our conduct towards those whom we consider our

enemies, or who consider us their enemies, we must show forbearance and a desire to offer or to seek forgiveness, according as we are the doers or the sufferers of wrong. Self-love and self-esteem, if not kept within due limits, easily produce feelings of revenge. Without entirely suppressing human nature, we are bound to control our feelings, and to let love of our fellow-men in all conditions occupy the first place in our heart. We are taught by our Sages, " He who is forbearing, receives also pardon for his sins " (Babyl. Talm. Yoma 23*a*) ; " Be of the persecuted, and not of the persecutors " (*ibid.* Baba Kama 93*a*) ; " To those who being offended do not offend, being insulted do not insult, the verse applies : ' And they who love him shall be as the sun when he goeth forth in his might ' " (Judges v. 31 ; Babyl. Talm. Shabbath 88*b*).

(2.) *Man and wife* are united by the holy bond of marriage. They owe to each other love, faithfulness, confidence, and untiring endeavour to make each other happy. The neglect of these duties turns a happy home into an abode of misery and wretchedness.[1] The last of the prophets, Malachi, rebuking such neglect, says : " The Lord hath been witness between thee and the wife of thy youth, against whom thou hast dealt treacherously, yet is she thy companion and the wife of thy covenant."

(3.) As *citizens* of a State we must take our proper share in all work for the welfare of the State. When the State is in danger we must evince patriotism, and must not withdraw ourselves from those duties which, under

---

[1] Comp. *supra*, p. 261.

such circumstances, devolve upon every citizen. All
our means, our physical and intellectual faculties, must
be at the disposal of the country in which we live as
citizens. Thus Jeremiah exhorts his brethren in Babylonia: "Build ye houses and dwell in them; and plant
gardens, and eat the fruit of them; . . . and seek
the peace of the city whither I have caused you to be
carried away captives, and pray unto the Lord for it:
for in the peace thereof shall you have peace" (Jer.
xxix. 5, 7). Similarly we are taught, "Pray for the
welfare of the government" (Aboth iii. 2).[1]

An important dictum of Samuel, a Rabbi famous
for his decisions in questions of civil law, is accepted
in the Talmud as law: "The law of the State is binding upon us," דינא דמלכותא דינא (Babyl. Talm. Baba
Kamma 113*a*). It is, according to the teaching of
the Talmud, incumbent upon us, as citizens of the
State, to obey the laws of the country. There is no
difference between Jews and their fellow-citizens with
regard to the duty of loyalty. It is only in case of
an attempt to force us aside from our religion that
we are not only justified in resisting and disobeying
laws framed with this intention, but we are commanded
to do so. But in the absence of such intention, we
must fulfil all those duties which devolve upon all
citizens alike—such as military service in countries
that have general conscription—although such obedience may carry with it a breach of some of the laws
of our religion. On the contrary, evasion and deser-

---

[1] The prayer for the head of the State, beginning הנתן תשועה
למלכים has its origin in this sense of loyalty towards the State in
which we live.

tion of all national obligations is a serious offence against our holy Law.

(4.) *As members of the same religious community,* we must unite in working for the well-being of the whole body. " Do not separate thyself from the congregation " (Aboth ii. 4) is a principle taught by the great Hillel. A Jew who violates this principle, and keeps aloof from his brethren, unwilling to take his share of the communal burdens, is guilty of a serious dereliction of duty, and is set forth in the Talmud as an example of most disgraceful conduct. " When your brethren are in trouble, do not say, ' I have my home, my food and drink ; I am safe.' If you ever were to think so, the words of the prophet would apply to you : ' Surely this iniquity shall not be purged from you till you die." " He who does not join the community in times of danger and trouble will never enjoy the Divine blessing " (Babyl. Talm. Taanith, p. 11*a*) ; " He who separates from the ways of the community has no portion of the world to come," הפורש מדרכי צבור אין לו חלק לעולם הבא (Maim., Mishneh-torah, Hilchoth Teshubah iii. 6).

(5.) *As to members of another community,* we have to show due regard for their religious convictions, and not to wound their feelings in respect of anything they hold sacred. Respect for the religious feelings of our fellow-men will increase their regard for our own religion, and evoke in them the same consideration for our religious feelings. All our duties towards our fellow-men are equally binding upon us whether in relation to members of other faiths or of our own.

(6.) *Employers and employed, sellers and buyers,* must act towards each other with the strictest honesty. In cases of dispute a friendly explanation or discussion is more likely to promote the interest of both parties than mutual animosity. Each party must bear in mind that prosperity depends on the co-operation of the other party, and not on its ruin.

NOTE.—We meet in the Talmud and works based on the Talmud with dicta which seem at first sight to exclude Gentiles (עכו״ם, נכרי or גוי) from our duty of love towards our fellow-men. This, however, was never intended. Sayings of this kind originated in days of warfare between the oppressor and the oppressed, and were an outburst of feelings of pain and anger, caused by an enemy who was not restrained from tyranny and cruelty by any sense of justice and humanity. But this state of affairs has ceased, and such sayings have since entirely lost their force and meaning, and are practically forgotten. Some of these passages have been removed from the Talmudical works by hostile censors ; but having led, and being still likely to lead, to errors or misunderstanding, less on the part of Jews than of non-Jewish readers, they ought to be eliminated in future editions of any of these works by Jewish censors, especially as the notices on the first page of the books, that the terms גוי, עכו״ם or נכרי do not apply to our non-Jewish neighbours at the present day, appear to have proved ineffectual against calumny and persecution.

(ii.) *Duties to our Superiors and Inferiors.*

Although we are all equally children of one God, and before the Most High all our petty differences disappear, His infinite wisdom willed it that there should be a certain degree of inequality among His creatures ; that some men should be wise, others simple ; some talented, others less skilful ; some strong, others weak ; some high, others low ; some imperious, others submissive; some rulers, others subjects; some fit to guide, and others only fit to be guided. This inequality is the source of certain special duties between man and man. " Be submissive to your superior, agreeable to your inferior, and cheerful to every one " (Aboth iii. 12).

(1.) The teacher who patiently strives to benefit his pupils by his instruction and counsel has a just claim on their respect. It is in the interest of the pupils themselves to regard their teacher as a friend, to have confidence in him, and faith in his superiority. It is themselves they benefit most if they lighten the labours of their teacher by due attention and obedience, and themselves they injure most, if by want of proper respect they render his task difficult and disagreeable.

On the other hand, it is the duty of the teacher to try to win the respect and the affection of the pupils by conscientiousness in his work, by patience and forbearance, by kindness and justice, by genuine interest in the progress and welfare of those entrusted to his care, and, above all, by a pure, good, and noble life.——The pupils owe much to their teachers, but the latter also owe something to their disciples. " Much have I learnt from my teachers, more from my fellow-students, most from my pupils," is a well-known Talmudical saying (Babyl. Talm. Taanith 7a). Of the priest, who in ancient time used to be the principal teacher, the prophet Malachi says: " The priest's lips shall keep knowledge, and they shall seek the law at his mouth; for he is the messenger of the Lord of hosts " (Mal. ii. 7). Rabbi Jochanan, in commenting on these words, said, " If the teacher is like the messenger of the Lord, *i.e.*, leads a pure life in the service of the Lord, then people shall seek instruction at his mouth ; if not, they cannot be instructed by him in the Law " (Yalkut *ad locum*).—" Let the honour of thy disciple be as dear to thee as thy own, and the honour of thy colleague as dear as the fear of thy teacher, and the fear of thy teacher as dear as the fear of Heaven " (Aboth iv. 15).—" He who has been taught something by his neighbour, whether it be a chapter, a law, a verse, a phrase, or a letter, owes him respect.   Thus David, who only learnt two things from Ahitophel, called him ' teacher, chief, and friend ' " (*ibid.* vi. 3).

Reverence is shown by a pupil to his teacher, not only by outward signs of respect, but also by refraining from opposing him, his teaching, or his decisions (Maimonides I. Hilchoth Talmud torah v. 1).   A pupil who altogether relinquishes the teaching of his master is to the latter a source of intense grief.—Among the outward signs of regard for the teacher we find the ancient custom or rule to pay a visit to the teacher on the three festivals : Passover, Feast of Weeks, and Tabernacles (*ibid.* v. 7).

(2.) *Master and Servant.*—The relation between master and servant is legally regulated by the same rules as that between employer and employed.   Strict honesty in the fulfilment of the duties undertaken by either party is the basis of a good understanding between master and servant.   The former must not exact from the latter more than was agreed upon, and the latter must not fail to perform all that he has undertaken to do. The relation between master and servant can be made more pleasant on both sides, if they are sensible enough to recognise their mutual obligations. On the part of the master, it is necessary that he should consider his servant as a human being like himself, who has a right to expect due reward for faithful service. A treatment of the servant from this point of view inspires him with a feeling of regard and attachment for his master, which finds expression in good and honest service. The servant will feel comfortable in his work, and be convinced that to be a servant is no degradation.—"Thou shalt not defraud an hired servant that is poor and needy, whether he be of thy brethren or of thy strangers that are in the land within thy gates" (Deut. xxiv. 14).

(3.) *Rich and Poor.*—"The rich and poor meet together: the Lord is the maker of them all" (Prov. xxii. 2). Those who are fortunate enough to possess more than is wanted for the necessities of life, are expected to spend part of the surplus in relieving those who possess less than they require for their maintenance. Sympathy towards the poor and needy is the duty of the rich; gratitude towards the generous and benevolent is the duty of the poor. But the rich must by no means make their gifts dependent on the signs of gratitude on the part of the poor; they must even avoid eliciting expressions of thanks, as these lead too often to flattery, hypocrisy, and servility. The rich find ample reward for their benevolence in the joyous feeling that Providence has chosen them as the means of diminishing the sufferings, the troubles, and the cares of some of their fellow-men

(4.) The following have a just claim on our respect :—

Learned Men (תלמידי חכמים), who, even if not directly our teachers, in many ways benefit us by their learning. "It is a great sin to despise or to hate the wise: Jerusalem has chiefly been destroyed as a punishment for the contempt shown for the learned; as it is said (2 Chron. xxxvi. 16), 'They mocked the messengers of God, and despised his words, and misused his prophets, until the wrath of the Lord arose against his people till there was no remedy'" (Maimonides, *l. c.* vi. 11). "He who despises *talmide-chachamim*," says Rab, "has no remedy for his disease" (Babyl. Talm. Shabbath, 119*b*), and belongs to those who forfeit their portion in the world to come (אין להם חלק לעולם הבא, *ibid.,* Sanhedrin 90).

The Aged.—"Thou shalt rise up before the hoary head, and honour the face of the old man, and fear thy God" (Lev. xix. 32). The Bible illustrates, in the history of Rehoboam (1 Kings xii.), the evil consequences of the contempt shown by this king to the words of the old men.—"With the ancient is wisdom, and in length of days understanding" (Job xii. 12). "The building of the young is destruction; the destruction of the old is building" (B. T. Megillah 31*b*).[1]

Great men who have accomplished great works in the interest of mankind, and have thus merited the gratitude of all.

The great men of our nation, their works and the institutions founded by them at various periods of our

---

[1] *I.e.,* When the old and experienced counsel to pull down a house, the pulling down is essential to its rebuilding; whilst the counsel of young and inexperienced men to build may imply destructive elements.

history. "Do not despise thy mother, though she
hath become old" (Prov. xxiii. 22). The feeling of
piety and reverence towards our Sages and Teachers of
former generations, and towards institutions of ancient
times that have come down to us, is an essential element
in our inner religion (חובת הלבבות).

The magistrates, judges, and statesmen, who devote
their time, their talents, and their energy to promoting
the well-being of the State.

The Head of the State.—"Fear the Lord, O my son, and
the king, and do not mix with rioters" (Prov. xxiv. 21).

(c.) *Kindness to Animals.*

"Be fruitful, and multiply, and replenish the earth,
and subdue it : and have dominion over the fish of
the sea, and over the fowl of the air, and over every
living thing that moveth upon the earth" (Gen. i. 28
and ix. 2, &c.; comp. Ps. viii. 7, &c.). Thus spake the
Creator to the first man. He gave him a right to
make use of the animals for his benefit; and man
makes the animals work for him ; they serve him as
food, provide him with clothing and other necessary
or useful things. In return for all these services the
animals ought to be treated with kindness and consideration. It is a necessity to force certain beasts to
work for us, and to kill certain animals for various
purposes. But in doing so we must not cause more
pain than is absolutely necessary. It is a disgraceful
act to give pain to animals merely for sport, and to
enjoy their agony. Bullfights and similar spectacles
are barbarous, and tend to corrupt and brutalise

the heart of man. The more we abstain from cruelty to animals, the more noble and loving is our conduct likely to be to one another. "A righteous man regardeth the feelings of his beast, but the heart of the wicked is cruel" (Prov. xii. 10).

The following are instances of kindness to animals enjoined in the Pentateuch:—

"Ye shall not kill an animal and its young on one day" (Lev. xxii. 28).

"If a bird's nest happen to be before thee on the way upon the earth or upon a tree, with young ones or eggs, thou shalt not take the mother with the young. Let the mother go away; then thou mayest take the young ones, in order that it may be well with thee, and thy days be long" (Deut. xxii. 6, 7).

"Thou shalt not muzzle the ox when he treadeth out the corn" (*ibid.* xxv. 4).

In the Talmud we have the following saying in the name of Rab:—"We must not begin our meal before having given food to our cattle; for it is said, 'And I will give you grass in thy field for thy cattle,' and after that 'thou shalt eat and be full'" (Deut. xi. 15; Babyl. Talm. 40*a*).

C.—*Duties to Ourselves.*

Our duties to ourselves are to a great extent included in our duties towards God and towards our fellow-men, because these likewise tend to promote our own well-being.

The fundamental principle of our duties towards

ourselves is to make the best use of the gifts which the kindness of God has bestowed upon us.

1. *Life and health* are precious gifts received by us at the hands of Divine Providence. We must therefore guard them as valuable treasures, and must not endanger them without absolute necessity. On the contrary, as much as lies in our power, we must improve our health and preserve our life. Food and bodily enjoyment, however pleasant for the moment, must be let alone if they are injurious to health. If we find ourselves inclined to exceed the right measure in the enjoyment of a thing, it is advisable to turn, for a while at least, to the other extreme and avoid that enjoyment altogether. Thus persons that are easily misled to excess in drink should become total abstainers from drink. But in ordinary cases the golden mean is preferable, especially for us Jews who are trained by the Dietary Laws, and by other precepts, to have control over our appetites. We are not commanded to be ascetics and to lead a gloomy, miserable life. On the contrary, we are frequently told in the Pentateuch, " And ye shall rejoice before the Lord your God." The Psalmist exhorts us to " serve the Lord with gladness ; to come before his presence with singing " (Ps. c. 2). " He who doeth good to his own soul is a man of love ; and he who troubleth his own flesh is a cruel man " (Prov. xi. 17) ; *i.e.*, he who does good to himself is of a cheerful disposition, and is likely to do good to others ; but he who deprives himself of enjoyments is often also cruel to his fellow-creatures. The Nazirite had to bring a sin-offering after the expiration of the period of his

vow. "What sin has he committed?" was asked. The answer is given in the Talmud by Samuel: "Because he deprived himself of wine;" and the Rabbi further infers from this, that it is prohibited to impose a voluntary fast upon oneself. Rabbi Eleazar, however, thinks that the vow of a Nazirite is a praiseworthy act, and his view found many followers, especially in the Middle Ages. Abraham Ibn Ezra, *e.g.*, explains that the sin of the Nazirite consists in not prolonging the state of Naziritism. But, however different their opinions may be theoretically, all agree that no voluntary fast should be undertaken, if it endangers the health of the faster, changes cheerfulness into sadness, and disables him from doing necessary or useful work.

2. *Wealth*, if acquired in an honest manner, by hard work, is conducive to our well-being. But in our search for wealth we must bear in mind that it is not an end in itself, but serves only as a means of securing our well-being. Koheleth tells us, what experience endorses, that there are "riches kept for the owners thereof to their hurt" (Eccles. v. 12). It is true we must struggle for the means of our existence. But in the struggle for wealth we must not entirely suppress the claims of our moral and intellectual wants, and if we were to suppress them, we should only work for our own ruin. "Two things have I required of thee; deny me them not before I die: Remove far from me vanity and lies; give me neither poverty nor riches; feed me with food convenient for me: lest I be full, and deny thee, and say, Who is the Lord? or lest I be poor, and steal,

X

and take the name of my God in vain " (Prov. xxx.
7–9). To this golden mean we should adhere. It is
our duty to seek an honest livelihood, but we are told,
" Labour not to be rich : cease from thine own wisdom "
(Prov. xxiii. 4). One of the various duties of parents
towards their children is to take good care that they
learn a trade, and " he who does not teach his son
a trade," say our Sages, " is as guilty as if he
directly taught him to rob " (Babyl. Talm. Kiddushin, p. 29a).

There is an erroneous opinion abroad, that commerce
is more congenial to Judaism than handicraft. In our
Law no trace of such preference is noticeable ; on the
contrary, agriculture was the principal occupation of
the Israelites. " When thou eatest the labour of thine
hands, happy art thou, and it is well with thee " (Ps.
cxxviii. 2). " Love work, and hate lordship " is a well-
known lesson of the sayings of the Fathers (Aboth i.
10). Bible and post-Biblical literature equally teach
us the lesson that our comfort and happiness do not
depend on the amount of wealth we have amassed, but
on the degree of contentment our heart has acquired.
" Sweet is the sleep of the labourer, whether he eat
little or much : but the abundance of the rich will not
suffer him to sleep " (Eccles. v. 11).

Industry is one of the sources of human happiness ;
but the blessing of industry is easily lost, if it is not
combined with thrift and temperance. In days of
prosperity we must bear in mind that days of misfortune may come ; we must, so far as we can, provide for
them, so that we may be able to hold out " till the storm
has passed." Temperance is inseparable from thrift

and industry. Intemperance not only consumes the products of thrift and industry, but in course of time destroys these very sources of our prosperity. Even with regard to Sabbath, in honour of which some degree of comfort and even of luxury may be indulged in, the principle is laid down : " Treat thy Sabbath like an ordinary day, if additional expense is likely to make thee dependent on charity " (Babyl. Talm. Shabbath 118*a*).

3. *Knowledge.*—God has made man " a little lower than the angels, and has crowned him with glory and honour " (Ps. viii. 6) ; He has endowed him with the faculty of acquiring knowledge : " There is a spirit in man, and an inspiration of the Almighty, that gives him understanding " (Job xxxii. 8). It is our duty to cultivate this faculty, to nurse it with all possible care, that it may grow. produce beautiful blossoms, and bear goodly fruit. The training must begin very early, at an age in which we are entirely dependent on the assistance and guidance of others. Parents, to whom the Almighty has entrusted the care of their children, are therefore commanded to provide for their education ; and as parents are not always capable of doing this, the duty devolves on the community or on the State. Every civilised country has its schools, colleges, and seminaries for the development of the intellectual and moral faculties of its inhabitants, and as these institutions increase in number and efficiency, the prosperity of the nation grows in like proportion. But the success of these educational institutions, however well provided they may be with an excellent teaching staff and the best appliances, depends on the regular and punctual attendance of the children, their atten-

tion, and their industry. It is the duty of parents to see, as far as it is in their power, that these conditions be fulfilled. Among the various branches of knowledge we seek to acquire, there is one branch of paramount importance, the absence of which would make all other knowledge valueless: it is—

4. *Moral and Religious Training.*—"The fear of the Lord is the beginning of knowledge; fools despise wisdom and correction" (חכמה ומוסר Prov. i. 7). The author of the Book of Proverbs teaches that knowledge must be combined with יראת השם "fear of God;" and that it is a perverse idea to separate wisdom (חכמה) from moral training (מוסר), and to seek knowlege (דעת) without the fear of the Lord (יראת ה'). Our Sages teach us that our training should include both fear of God and wisdom. "If there is no wisdom, there is no fear of God; and in the absence of the latter there is no wisdom" (Aboth iii. 17). Fear of the Lord, however, and fear of sin must have precedence. "Rabbi Chanina, son of Dosa, says: "If a man's wisdom is preceded by fear of sin, his wisdom is well established; if the fear of sin is preceded by wisdom, his wisdom is not well established" (*ibid.* 9).

The result of our training must be the acquisition of good manners and noble principles. Avoid extremes, and hold to the golden mean, is an excellent rule that leads us safely through the various conditions of life and wards off many troubles and dangers. The following examples may serve as an illustration of this rule: Do not ignore your own self; let self-love and self-respect influence your conduct; but these must not be allowed to develop into selfishness and arrogance. Look after your own interests, but do not consider them as the supreme rulers of your actions. Be self-reliant, and keep equally far from self-conceit and self-distrust. Haughtiness and self-contempt are extremes to be avoided : be modest. When wronged or insulted by your neighbour, be neither callous nor over-sensitive ; ignore insult and wrong in most cases, forgive them readily in others, and resent them only when forced to do so. In disputes and discussions be neither weak nor obstinate : be firm. Be neither passionate nor indifferent : be calm. Do not trust every one, lest your credulity mislead you ; do not suspect every one, lest you become misanthropic : be discreet. Do not seek danger, nor fear it ; but be prepared to meet it with courage. Be temperate in eating and drinking, and avoid both excess and needless privation. In spending your earnings show neither niggardliness nor recklessness : be economical. Work, but not in such a manner as to ruin your health. As to your future, be neither too sanguine in your hopes, nor despondent : do your duty, and trust in God.

There are, however, exceptions from this rule ; for in certain cases there is only the choice between two extremes. Such is *Truthfulness.* It is our duty to approach nearer and nearer the extreme of this virtue, and to consider the least deviation from it as vice. From our earliest youth we should train ourselves in the practice of this virtue. Every word that we desire to utter should be well examined before it passes our lips. We must be on our guard that nothing should escape our lips that is not in harmony with what we

feel or think. In small matters as well as in important
things truthfulness must be the principle which guides
us in our utterances. "The lips of truth shall be
established for ever, but for a moment only the tongue
of falsehood" (Prov. xii. 19). "Keep thee far from
a word of falsehood" (Exod. xxiii. 7). "Falsehood,"
say our Sages, "has no legs to stand upon; whilst
'truth' is declared to be the seal of the Holy One,
Blessed be He" (אמת חותמו של הקב"ה).

Our moral and religious training is based on the
Word of God, on the Torah, and the study of the
Torah, תלמוד תורה, is an essential element in Jewish
education. The term *Torah* is to be understood in no
narrow sense, but as including the written and the oral
Law, all the books of the Holy Writings, and such
works as have from time to time been composed for
the purpose of facilitating and promoting the study
of the Torah. The importance of this duty has been
recognised from ancient times, and Jewish congregations, before building a synagogue, made provision for
the religious education of the young and for the study
of the Law, by establishing schools and colleges (בית ספר
or בי רב and בית המדרש).

Talmud-torah is one of those duties to which no
measure was fixed (אשר אין להם שיעור Mishnah Peah
i. 1). Whenever we can find time and leisure, we
ought to turn to the Word of God, every one according
to his capacity and his opportunities. The readings
from the Torah, both the written and the oral, which
form part of our Service, have been introduced for the
purpose of facilitating for the general public the fulfilment of the duty of Talmud-torah.

The study of the Law and the regular and punctual attendance at the Beth-hammidrash belong to those religious acts which "bear fruit here on earth and procure bliss in the future life" (*ibid.*). Our Sages exhort us in various sayings to devote ourselves earnestly to the study of the Torah. The object of this study is, in the first instance, to enable us to live in accordance with His Commandments; secondly, to purify our thoughts by turning them from common, ordinary things to higher and loftier subjects; for while we are reading the Divine messages and reflecting on them, we move in a purer atmosphere and must be inspired with holy and noble thoughts.

The book which is expected to produce these results must be approached "with awe, with meekness, with cheerfulness, and with purity" (Aboth vi. 6). Our intention must be to be instructed and guided by what we read. We must not presume to criticise the Divine decrees therein recorded. If we meet with passages that strike us as strange or objectionable, we may be sure that we have not yet comprehended the true sense of the Divine words. Modesty must cause us rather to assume shortcomings on our part than to find fault with the Holy Writings. "Turn it over, and read it again and again; for all is in it, and behold everything through it; and even when old and weak, cleave to it, and do not move away from it; for there is no better guide for thee than this one" (Aboth v. 22). There is one great advantage in the study of the Torah; it constantly supplies us with one of the best means of promoting our moral training, viz., with good company.

The society in which we move and the persons

with whom we associate are an important factor in the formation of our character. Bad companions corrupt us, and lead us to ruin; good companions improve our moral conduct by their example and not rarely by their words. " If one joins mockers, he will be a mocker; if he joins the lowly, he will show grace " (Prov. iii. 34). " Keep away from a bad neighbour; do not associate with the wicked, and do not believe thyself safe from evil " (Aboth i. 7). In our daily prayers we ask God for His assistance in our endeavour to act according to this principle.

The aim and end of all our moral training must be to keep our mind pure from evil thoughts, to make our heart the seat of noble and lofty desires; to accustom our tongue to the utterance of that which is good and true, and to lead a pure, honourable, and godly life. If we succeed, we establish our well-being during our life on earth, and secure Divine blessing for our soul in the future world.

III. SIGNS AS OUTWARD REMINDERS OF GOD'S PRESENCE.

The voice that comes from within, from our own heart and conscience, is the best reminder of God's Presence and Will. But it does not always sound with sufficient force to make itself heard, and we, weak mortals, have the weakness of forgetting even most important duties, unless we are reminded of them from time to time. The Divine Law has therefore set up signs as outward reminders. Such are the commandments of ציצת " fringe," תפלין " ornaments," and מזוזה " door-post symbol."

ציצת "*Fringe*" or "*Tassel.*"

"Thou shalt make thee fringes upon the four corners of thy vesture, wherewith thou coverest thyself" (Deut. xxii. 12). The object of this commandment is described as follows:—"It shall be unto you for a fringe, that ye may look upon it, and remember all the commandments of the Lord, and do them, and that ye seek not after your own heart and your own eyes, after which ye use to go astray: that ye may remember and do all my commandments, and be holy unto your God" (Num. xv. 39, 40).

In obedience to this commandment, we have two kinds of four-cornered garments provided with "fringes." The one is small, and is worn under the upper garments the whole day; it is called *arba' kanfoth,* "four corners," or *talith katan,* "small scarf." The other and larger one is worn over the garments during the Morning Service.[1] It is called simply *talith,* "scarf," or *talith gadol,* "large scarf."

The form of the blessing which accompanies the performance of this *mitsvah* varies according as it refers to the small *talith* or to the large one. In the former case the blessing concludes with על מצות ציצת "concerning the commandment of *tsitsith;*" in the latter with להתעטף בציצת, "to wrap ourselves with a garment provided with *tsitsith.*" [2]

---

[1] There are some exceptions to this rule :—The Reader wears the *talith* during every Service; in some congregations mourners wear it when they recite *kaddish.* On the Day of Atonement the whole congregation wear the *talith* during all the Services. On the Fast of Ab the *talith* is put on before the Afternoon Service instead of during the Morning Service.

[2] There are two forms of the blessing which accompanies the per-

The *tsitsith*, which is appended to each of the four corners, consists of four long threads drawn through a small hole about an inch from the corner; the two parts of the threads are bound together by a double knot; the largest thread—called *shammash*, "the servant"—is then wound seven, eight, eleven, and thirteen times round the other seven halves of the four threads, and after each set of windings a double knot is made.— If one of the four *tsitsith* is not in order, *e.g.*, two of the threads being torn off, the *talith* is called *pasui*, "disqualified" for the *mitsvah*, and must not be worn till that *tsitsith* is replaced by a new one.

There is, however, an important element in this Divine commandment, which is now altogether neglected, viz., "And they shall put upon the fringe of the corner a thread of תכלת purple blue wool" (Num. xv. 38). Tradition determined the exact shade of the purple blue indicated by the term תכלת; in the Talmud (Menachoth 42*b*) the various ways of its preparation are given. But the colour seems to have been rare, and we are warned against using imitations of *techeleth*. Regulations were also made provid-

formance of a Divine precept: the precept is expressed (1) by a noun which is preceded by the preposition על "concerning;" (2) by the infinitive of a verb preceded by the preposition ל "to," *e.g.*, "concerning the commandment of *tsitsith*," and "to wrap ourselves with a garment provided with *tsitsith*." The latter form is used (1) when the blessing is recited before the performance of the *mitsvah* has commenced; (2) when he who performs the *mitsvah* is personally commanded to perform it. In all other cases the first form is used. Hence על מצות ציצת, because we are, as a rule, not in a fit state for prayer when we put it on, and therefore recite the blessing later on; על מקרא מגלה; because he who reads might just as well be one of the listeners. We say להניח תפלין at the commencement of the *mitsvah;* על מצות תפלין before the second part. (See Babyl. Talm. Pesachim, p. 7.)

ing for the case when *techeleth* could not be obtained. The natural white colour was then substituted, and no other colour was allowed. After the conclusion of the Talmud doubts seem to have arisen as regards the exact shade of the purple blue demanded by the Divine precept in the term תכלת, and thus the use of the thread of purple blue wool gradually ceased to form part of the *tsitsith.* The exact time when it ceased cannot be fixed.

תפלין [1] " *Ornaments.*"

Four times the Law repeats the commandment concerning the *tefillin :* " And thou shalt bind them " —the words of God—" for a sign upon thy hand, and they shall be for a frontlet between thine eyes " (Deut. vi. 8 and xi. 18); " And it shall be unto thee for a sign upon thy hand, and for a memorial between thine eyes, in order that the Law of the Lord be in thy mouth " (Exod. xiii. 9); " And it shall be for a sign upon thy hand, and for a frontlet between thine eyes " (*ibid.* 16).

The object of this commandment is to direct our thoughts to God and His goodness, and to remind us of the important lessons taught in the following four paragraphs, in which the commandment of *tefillin* is mentioned :—

(1.) The first paragraph (קדש Exod. xiii. 1—10) teaches

[1] The term תפלין reminds us of הפלה " prayer," and denotes things used during prayer. Originally it had probably the more general signification : ornament or head-ornament ; in the Chaldee Version it is the translation of טוטפות, which denotes " head-ornament." (Comp. Mishnah Shabbath vi. 1.)

that we must, in various ways, express our belief in God as the King and Ruler of the universe. Two laws are contained in this paragraph which are to serve this object—the sanctification of the first-born to the service of the Lord, and the celebration of the Feast of Unleavened Cakes.

(2.) The second paragraph (והיה כי יביאך Exod. xiii. 11—16) reminds us of the wonderful way in which God delivered our forefathers from Egyptian bondage. Remembering this deliverance, we are strengthened in our faith in God in days of trouble, for His ways are not ours, and when *we* do not see any prospect of relief God may be preparing help for us.

(3.) The third paragraph (שמע Deut. vi. 4—9) proclaims the Unity of God, and teaches us to love God and obey Him out of love.

(4.) The fourth paragraph (והיה אם שמע Deut. xi. 13—20) teaches that Providence deals with men according to their merits, according as each deserves reward or punishment.

Tradition has handed down to us the way in which this precept is to be carried out. The four abovementioned paragraphs are written twice on parchment, once on one piece, and once on four pieces, each piece containing one paragraph. The two sets are put into two leather cases (בית), one of which is divided into four compartments, for the four separate slips of parchment, and marked outside by the letter *shin*.[1] Through

---

[1] Two sides of the *bayith* have the *shin* impressed on them, the right and the left ; but in different forms, on the right the letter has three strokes (ש), on the left it has four strokes (שׁ), in order to ensure the right order of the four paragraphs (פרשיות) which the *bayith* contains from right to left.

a loop attached to each *bayith* a leather strap (רְצוּעָה) is passed, the two parts of which are tied together [1] in such a manner as to hold the *bayith* on the arm or on the head. On the arm the case is placed that contains the four paragraphs written on one piece, on the head that which contains them written on four pieces. The former is called *tefillah shel yad*, "tefillin of the hand;" the latter *tefillah shel rosh*, "the tefillin of the head."

The *tefillin* are put on in the following way :—(1.) *Tefillah shel rosh*. The case is placed in front, just over the forehead in the middle, and the knot of the straps (קֶשֶׁר) on the back of the head over the middle of the neck ; the remainder of the two straps hang down in front, one on each side. (2.) *Tefillah shel yad*. The case containing the parchment is placed on the inner side of the left upper arm, near the elbow ; the knot is kept near it, and the strap is twisted seven times round the arm and three times round the middle finger ; there are, however, different customs with regard to this latter practice.

Tefillah shel yad is put on first, being mentioned first in the Divine precept. The reverse order is observed in taking off the *tefillin*. Originally the *tefillin* were worn all day long,[2] but at present they are worn only during the morning prayer.

[1] The knot formed by the רְצוּעוֹת of the *tefillah shel rosh* has the shape of a *daleth*, that of the *tefillah shel yad* is like a *yod ;* these two letters added to the *shin* of the *tefillin shel rosh* read *shaddai,* "Almighty."

[2] In the evening it was but natural that *tsitsith* and *tefillin* should be laid aside, as the greater part of the night was devoted to sleep ; the rule was therefore generally adopted : "The night is not the proper time for laying *tefillin* " (לילה לאו זמן תפילין). The opposite principle, however, "The night is likewise a suitable time for laying *tefillin* " (לילה זמן תפלין), had also its advocates among Rabbinical authorities (Babyl. Talm. Menachoth 36*b*).

The *tefillin* are not worn on Sabbath or Festival. The observance of these days is " a sign for ever " of our belief " that in six days the Lord made the heavens and the earth." The very days of rest thus remind us of the truths of which the *tefillin* are " a sign." The *tefillin* became, therefore, unnecessary on those days.

The commandment of *tefillin* applies to all male persons from their thirteenth birthday.[1]

The performance of this commandment is preceded by the usual benediction (ברכת המצות), concluding להניח תפלין, " to place the *tefillin*," *scil.*, on the arm and on the head. According to the German rite, a second benediction is recited before placing the *tefillah shel rosh* on the head, viz., על מצות תפלין, " concerning the commandment of *tefillin*." [2]

In order to prevent a mere perfunctory observance of this commandment, we are taught to reflect on the importance and the object of the *tefillin*, and to declare that by placing the *tefillin* on the head and on the arm, near the heart, we indicate our consciousness of the duty to employ the thoughts that rise in our mind, and the desires of our heart, in the service of the Lord, who gave us the powers of thought and will.[3]

---

[1] With the completion of the thirteenth year a boy becomes of age in reference to the fulfilment of all religious duties. He is then called *Bar-mitsvah* (lit. " a son of the commandment "), a member of the Jewish community, upon whom devolve all such duties as a Jew has to perform. On the Sabbath following that birthday he is called to the Law, either to read a portion of the *Sidra* or to listen to its reading, and publicly acknowledge God as the Giver of the Law.

[2] Compare p. 329.   [3] See Daily Prayer Book, Morning Service

מזוזה *Door-post Symbol.*

The *Mezuzah* is a piece of parchment on which the two first paragraphs of *Shema* (Deut. vi. 4–9, xi. 13–20) are written. The parchment is rolled together, put into a small case, and fixed on the right-hand door-post. A small opening is left in the case, where the word שַׁדַּי "Almighty," written on the back of the scroll, is visible.[1]

The object of the *mezuzah*, commanded in the words, " And thou shalt write them on the door-posts of thy house and upon thy gates " (Deut. vi. 9 and xi. 20), is to remind us of the Presence of God, of His Unity, Providence, and Omnipotence, both on entering our home and on leaving it ; of the all-seeing eye that watches us, and of the Almighty who will one day call us to account for our deeds, words and thoughts. The *mezuzah* thus serves to sanctify our dwelling and protect it from being polluted by evil deeds.

Signs of God's Covenant.

Besides the signs mentioned above, there are two other signs of the covenant between God and Israel.

1. Sabbath is called " an everlasting covenant," and " a sign between God and the children of Israel for ever " (Exod. xxxi. 16, 17). See pp. 254 *sqq.* and 339 *sqq.*

---

[1] There are, besides, on the back of the scroll, just behind the names of God in the first line three words of a mystic character consisting of the letters following in the alphabet the letters of these divine names. The words have in themselves no meaning, and it may be that their object is simply to indicate from outside where the names of God are written, and to prevent a nail being driven through that part in fixing the *mezuzah* to the door-post.

2. The covenant of Abraham (ברית מילה "the covenant of circumcision"). God made a covenant with
Abraham, and said, "Thou shalt keep my covenant,
thou and thy seed after thee in their generations. This
is my covenant which ye shall keep between me and
you, and thy seed after thee : Every male child among
you shall be circumcised when eight days old" (Gen.
xvii. 9, 10, 12). If the eighth day happens to be on
a Sabbath, the circumcision takes place on that day ;
but if, because of illness, or from any other cause, the
rite has not been performed on the eighth day, it must
be done on some other day, but not on a Sabbath or
Festival.

NOTES.—1. In reference to the importance of these *mitsvoth,*
Maimonides, in Mishneh-torah, says as follows :—

"Although we are not commanded to get a *talith*, and to put it
on in order to join the *tsitsith* ("fringes") to it, a religious person will
not consider himself free from this duty, but will always endeavour to wear a garment to which fringes must be affixed. During
prayer we must be especially careful to provide ourselves with a
talith. It is a disgrace for a scholar (*Talmid chacham*) to say the
prayer without the *talith*. We must be particularly anxious to
perform this *mitsvah ;* it is of great importance with regard to all
the precepts, according to the words, 'And ye shall look upon it,
and remember all the commandments of the Lord'" (2nd Book,
Ahabhah, Hilchoth tsitsith iii. 12).

"The holiness of the *tefillin* is great, for so long as the *tefillin*
are upon the head and the arm of a man, he is humble and God-
fearing, keeps away from levity and idle talk, does not conceive
evil thoughts, but turns his heart exclusively to words of truth
and justice. We ought therefore to wear them all day long ;
this would be the proper way. It is said of Rab, the pupil of
Rabbi Jehudah, the Holy, that he was never seen otherwise than
with *torah* or *tsitsith* or *tefillin*.

"Although we ought to wear *tefillin* all day long, it is our special
duty to wear them during prayer. Our Sages said, 'He who

reads *Shema* without *tefillin* rejects, as it were, his evidence concerning the Almighty as false'" (ibid., *Hilchoth tefillin* iv. 26).

"We should be particular with regard to the *mezuzah*, which is a duty incumbent uninterruptedly on every one. Whenever we enter or leave the house our eye meets with the name of God ; we remember His love, and rousing ourselves from our torpitude, we are led to regret our foolish devotion to the vanities of the time, and recognise that nothing remains for ever except the knowledge of the Rock of the universe. We shall then at once devote ourselves to know Him, and walk in the way of uprightness. Our ancient Sages said, 'He who has *tefillin* upon his head and upon his arm, *tsitsith* on his garment, and *mezuzah* on his door, he is safe from sin, since he has many reminders of his duties, and these are the angels that protect him from going astray ; and to him the following verse applies : "An angel of the Lord encampeth round those who fear Him"'" (ibid., *Hilchoth mezuzah* vi. 13).

2. The great importance of the *tefillin*, as described by Maimonides, was not understood or recognised by all Jews. Various sayings occurring in the Talmud indicate the existence of laxity or even opposition with regard to the carrying out of this precept in its literal sense. When persons with *tefillin* on their head and on their arm showed by their conduct that their heart was not filled with the holiness and uprightness of which the *tefillin* are the symbol, it was but natural that not only were these persons accused of hypocrisy, but the Divine precept itself was discredited. But the greater the opposition by one section of the Jewish community, the more the enthusiasm of the other section grew in its favour. Hence the numerous Talmudical and Rabbinical utterances concerning the sanctifying force inherent in the *tefillin* (comp. *Tur Orach Chayyim* xxxvii.). Thus, when a Rabbi was cautioned not to be over joyous, as excess of joy led to sin, he replied, " I lay *tefillin ;*" *i.e.,* "The thoughts which the observance of this precept awakens protects me from sin." This idea of protection from sin may be the origin of the Greek name *phylacterion,* "protection."—In times of persecution, when the Jews were forbidden by their oppressors to perform any of their religious rites on penalty of death, the precept of *tefillin* was not included among those which they performed even at the risk of their life. To this circumstance Rabbi Simeon b. Elazar ascribes the laxity with regard to the *tefillin* (Babyl. Talm. Shabbath 130*a*).

Y

3. There occurs in the Midrash (Sifre on Deut. xi. 18), in reference to *tsitsith* and *tefillin*, the following passage : " Also when in exile deck yourselves with *mitsvoth*, in order that on your return to your own land the Divine precepts should not seem to you new and unknown." This passage has been misinterpreted as if the author of that passage were of opinion that precepts like *tsitsith* and *tefillin* did originally not apply to those who are outside the Holy Land. The meaning is rather this : Although a large portion of the laws is not in force outside Palestine, yet continue to wear these reminders in exile, in order that by this act your attention may constantly be turned to the whole Torah, to those precepts which are in force at present as well as to those which are not. Thus all the precepts will be familiar to you, and when the time comes in which the observance of all the laws will again be possible, none of the laws will appear to you new and strange.

4. There is, on the whole, no difference between men and women with regard to the obedience due to the Divine commandments. All Jews are equally bound to obey the Will of God expressed in the Law. This is absolutely the case with all prohibitions (לא תעשה). In the case of positive commandments (מצות עשה) the following rule has been laid down by our Sages : Women are exempt from the performance of such religious duties as are restricted to a certain period of time (מצות עשה שהזמן גרמא נשים פטורות). The object of the seeming anomaly is probably this : the principal duty and the privilege of women is to manage the household, a task that demands constant attention. Religious acts which are to be performed at a certain time might involve an interference with such of their household duties as demand immediate attention ; *e.g.*, nursing a patient, a task which generally falls to the lot of the female section of the family. Jewish women, nevertheless, zealously fulfil most of the duties from which the above rule exempts them. They thus are most eager to obey the laws concerning *shofar* on New-year, *lulab* on Tabernacles, and the like ; and some of them are named as having conscientiously laid *tefillin* (Mechilta on Exod. xiii. 9).

IV. Sabbath and Festivals.

The daily work which has chiefly the well-being of the body as its aim must be interrupted on certain days which the Almighty has appointed for the promotion of man's spiritual well-being. Sabbath and Festivals are the days thus appointed, and are therefore called מועדי יי "the seasons of the Lord," and מקראי קדש "holy convocations." The blessing derived from the observance of Holy-days in the true spirit is described by the prophet as follows: "If thou keep back thy foot because of the sabbath, from doing thy business on my holy day; and call the sabbath a delight, the holy of the Lord, honourable, and shalt honour it, not doing thine own ways, nor finding thine own business, nor speaking thine own words: then thou shalt delight thyself in the Lord: and I will cause thee to ride upon the high places of the earth, and feed thee with the heritage of Jacob, thy father" (Isa. lviii. 13, 14). To those who fail to observe the seasons of the Lord in the true spirit, the prophet says in the name of the Almighty: "Your new-moons and your festivals my soul hateth: they are a trouble unto me; I am weary to bear them" (*ibid.* i. 14).

Maimonides[1] comprehends the various duties and observances of the Holy-days in the following four terms: זכור "remember," שמור "take heed," כבוד "honour," and עונג "delight." The first two are found in the Pentateuch, and form the beginning of the fourth commandment in Exodus and Deuteronomy respectively; the other two occur in the above descrip-

---

[1] Mishneh-torah III., *Zemannim*, Hil. Shabbath, ch. xxx. § 1.

tion of the Sabbath quoted from Isaiah (lviii. 13, 14).
Following the example of our great teacher, we shall
likewise treat of the laws and customs of Sabbath and
Festivals under these four heads:[1]——

a. כ ר *"Remember."*

Remember the Sabbath-day; speak of it, of its holiness and its blessings. We fulfil this duty when
Sabbath comes in, by the *Kiddush,* "the sanctification
of the day," in which we praise the Almighty for the
boon bestowed upon us by the institution of the Sabbath; and when Sabbath goes out, by the *Habhdalah,*
in which we praise God for the "distinction" made
between the holy and the ordinary days. We have
both *Kiddush* and *Habhdalah* in a double form: (*a*)
as a portion of the *Amidah* in the Evening Service; the *Kiddush* being the middle section of the
Amidah, the *Habhdalah* consisting of a prayer added
to the fourth paragraph beginning אתה חנן; (*b*) as a
separate service especially intended for our homes.
It is this home-service that we generally understand
by the terms *Kiddush* and *Habhdalah,* and in this
sense they are employed in the following.[2]

Kiddush.

There is a traditional explanation of the term *zachor*:
זכרהו על היין "remember it over the wine." As "wine

---

[1] Maimonides applies these terms to Sabbath; but they apply
generally with equal force to the Festivals.

[2] We "remember" also the Sabbath or Festival by naming after it the
preceding day, the night following, and in the case of Festivals the day

gladdens the heart of man " and forms an important
element in a festive meal, it has been ordered that our
meal on the eve[1] of Sabbath and Festival should be begun
with a cup of wine in honour of the day, and that mention should be made of the holiness of the day before
partaking of the wine. The *Kiddush* consists of two
blessings (ברכות) : one over the wine,[2] and one that refers
to the holiness of the day. On Holy-days—except the
last days of Passover—a third blessing (שההינו) follows,
praising God for having granted us life and enabled
us again to celebrate the Festival. On Friday evening
a portion from Genesis (i. 31 to ii. 3) is added, which
contains the first mention of the institution of Sabbath.
If a Festival happens to fall on Sunday, we add part
of the *Habhdalah* to the *Kiddush* on Saturday evening,[3]

---

[1] following : the eve of Sabbath or Festival ערב יום טוב, ערב שבת ;
the night after Sabbath or Festival, מוצאי יום טוב ·מוצאי שבת ;
"the day after the Festival," אסרו (lit., " bind the Festival," with
reference to Ps. cxviii. 27).

[1] A similar ceremony takes place before the first meal in the morning. A cup of wine or other spirituous liquor is poured out, some
Biblical passages referring to the Sabbath are recited, and the usual
blessing is said before partaking of the beverage. The blessing containing the *Kiddush* is not said, and the ceremony has the name
Kiddush or *Kiddusha rabba*, " great *Kiddush*," only on account of its
similarity with the evening *Kiddush*. The passages recited are the
following : Exod. xxxi. 16, 17, xx. 8–11 ; Isa. lviii. 13, 14.

[2] ברוך אתה . . . בורא פרי הגפן. " Blessed art thou, O Lord, our
God, King of the universe, who hast created the fruit of the vine."
In the absence of wine, or if wine is disliked or injurious to health,
the blessing over bread is substituted for that over wine.—The blessings are generally preceded by the word סברי " Is it your pleasure, *scil.*,
that I read ? " whereby it is simply intended to call the attention of the
company to the prayer.

[3] See p. 352, on the difference between the holiness of Sabbath and
that of Festivals.—The last two ברכות, viz. בורא מאורי האש and

referring to the distinction between the holiness of the Sabbath and that of the Festivals.

The *Kiddush* is part of the Sabbath or Festival evening meal, and in the absence of the latter the *Kiddush* is omitted.[1] In Synagogues of the German and Polish *Minhag* the Reader recites the *Kiddush* at the conclusion of the *Maarib* Service. This custom is a survival of the ancient way of providing for the poor and the stranger. In the absence of better accommodation lodging and food were given to the needy in rooms adjoining the Synagogue, or even in the Synagogue itself. It was for these that the Reader recited the *Kiddush*, before they commenced the evening meal, as most probably wine was not served to all. Although circumstances have changed the mode of maintaining the poor, and the latter find no longer lodging and board in the Synagogue, the *Kiddush* has been retained as part of the *Maarib* Service, except on the first two nights of Passover, when there had never been an occasion for reading *Kiddush* in the Synagogue. The poor were treated on these nights with four cups of wine each, and they recited *Kiddush* by themselves as part of the *Seder*.

המבדיל are added; the second part of the latter is slightly modified order to suit the transition from Sabbath to Festival.—The *Habhdalah* on the night following the Day of Atonement consists of three ברכות, that over spices being omitted, except if *Jom-kippur* falls on Sabbath; in that case the *Habhdalah* includes all the four ברכות.

[1] *Habhdalah* is likewise omitted when Sabbath is closely followed by the Fast of *Ab*. On Sabbath night, eating and drinking being forbidden, only the one blessing, בורא מאורי האש is recited; that over spices is omitted, and the remaining two blessings are recited on Sunday evening after the fast.

Habhdalah הבדלה.

Habhdalah is recited in the evening following Sabbath or Holy-day, after the Evening Service. A cup of wine is raised, and the ברכה over wine is followed by another ברכה, in which God is praised for the distinction made between the holy and the ordinary day (בין קדש לחול), or between two kinds of holiness (בין קדש לקדש) in case Sabbath is followed by a Holy-day.—On Sabbath night we take a candle and a spice-box, and add two blessings after that over wine ; in the one we thank God for the enjoyment of the fragrance, in the other for the benefit He bestowed on us by the creation of light. A few verses from the Bible, especially the Prophets, precede the *Habhdalah*.

The origin of the introduction of the blessings for light and for spices in the *Habhdalah* may be the following :—The principal meal of the day used to be taken about sunset ; light and burning incense were essential elements of a festive meal. On Sabbath these could not be had, and were therefore enjoyed immediately after the going out of Sabbath. Although the custom of having incense after the meal has long ceased, it has survived in the *Habhdalah*, and has, in course of time, received another, a more poetical interpretation. The Sabbath inspires us with cheerfulness, gives us, as it were, an additional soul—נְשָׁמָה יְתֵרָה—traces of which are left on the departure of Sabbath, and are symbolised by the fragrance of the spices. For the use of the special light there has likewise been suggested a second reason, namely, that it is intended at the commencement of the week to remind us of the first product of Creation, which was light.

There are a few customs connected with the *Habhdalah* that may be noticed here.

(1.) The wine, when poured into the cup, is allowed to flow over, as a symbol of the overflowing Divine blessing which we wish and hope to enjoy in the coming week.

(2.) Some dip their finger in wine and pass it over their eyes, in allusion to the words of the Nineteenth Psalm (ver. 9), "The commandment of the Lord is pure, enlightening the eyes." The act expresses the love of the Divine commandments (חִבּוּב מִצְוָה).

(3.) Only male persons partake of the wine; they have more interest in the *Habhdalah* as the signal for the resumption of ordinary work and business.—The exclusion of women from the wine of *Habhdalah* may also have its origin in the fact that Jewish women generally abstained from taking wine, considering strong drink suitable only for the male portion of mankind. They only partake of the wine of *Kiddush* on account of its importance; to *Habhdalah* less importance was ascribed.

(4.) On reaching the words בֵּין אוֹר לְחשֶׁךְ, "between light and darkness," some hold their hands against the light, the fingers bent inside, in illustration of the words which they utter, showing darkness and shadow inside and light outside.—With the practice of these and similar customs we must take good care that we should not combine any superstitious motive, or join actions which are really superstitious, and did not originate in Jewish thought and Jewish traditions.

We further remember the Sabbath-day to sanctify it by increased devotion, by reading special Lessons from the Pentateuch and the Prophets, and by attending religious instruction given by teachers and preachers.

Besides various additions in the Service, and the substitution of one paragraph concerning Sabbath or Festival for the thirteen middle paragraphs of the Amidah, there is another Service inserted between the Morning and the Afternoon Services; it is called *Musaph*, " the Additional Service," and corresponds to the additional offering ordained for Sabbath and Festival (Num. xxviii. 9, *sqq.*).

An essential element in the Morning Service is the Reading from the Torah (קריאת התורה) and the Prophets (הפטרה). A periodical public reading from the Law was enjoined in the following words: " At the end of every seven years, in the solemnity of the year of release, in the feast of tabernacles, when all Israel is come to appear before the Lord thy God in the place which he shall choose, thou shalt read this law before all Israel in their hearing. Gather the people together, men and women and children, and the stranger that is within thy gates, that they may hear, and that they may learn, and fear the Lord your God, and observe to do all the words of this law; and that their children, which have not known anything, may hear and learn to fear the Lord your God " (Deut. xxxi. 10–13).

A seven years' interval would surely have destroyed the impression produced by the reading. The reading was probably repeated throughout the country at shorter intervals. Tradition ascribes to Moses the institution of reading the Law every Sabbath, Monday, and Thursday morning, in order that three days might never pass

without Torah.   Ezra is said to have added the reading
on Sabbath afternoon, and to have made various other
regulations with regard to the reading of the Law.

Quantity and manner of reading were at first, no
doubt, variable.   In the course of time certain systems
found favour and became the fixed rule.   Some completed the reading of the whole Pentateuch in three
years, others in one year.   The former mode was gradually displaced by the latter, and the attempts which
have lately been made to revive it have not succeeded.
Traces of the triennial reading may be noticed in the
number of *sedarim* contained in each of the five books
of the Pentateuch.   At present, however, the annual
course is followed in almost all our Synagogues.   The
section read on one Sabbath is called *sidra*; the first,
בראשית, is read the first Sabbath after the Feast of
Tabernacles, and the last *sidra* is read on *Simchath-
torah* (the 23rd of Tishri).

For the Festivals such sections were selected as contained either direct or indirect reference to the Festivals.
If these happen to be on a Sabbath, the ordinary reading
is interrupted, and that of the Festivals substituted for it.

The number of persons who were to take part in the
reading varied according as the people were likely to
devote less or more time to Divine Service : on week-
days and on Sabbath afternoon three, on New-moon
and *Chol-hammoed* four, on the Festivals five, on the
Day of Atonement six,[1] and on Sabbath seven.   Some
may have required the assistance of the *chazan*, and in

---

[1] Although the whole of the Day of Atonement is devoted to Divine
Service, less time is given to reading from the Law than on Sabbath,
in order to leave more time for Prayers, Confessions, and Meditations.
Rabbi Akiba, however, was of opinion that seven should be called up

some cases the *chazan's* voice was the only one that
was heard; gradually the *chazan* became the reader,
and the original reader became silent, being content
with reciting the *b'rachoth.* Only in the case of the
Bar-mitsvah, the *Chathan-torah,* and the *Chathan-
b'reshith* the original practice has been retained.

As regards the order of those who take part in the
reading of the Law, the first place is given to a *Cohen,*
i.e., a descendant of Aaron, the priest; the second to a
Levite, *i.e.,* a non-priest of the tribe of Levi; and then
follow other Israelites, that are neither Levites nor
Cohanim, without any prescribed order. The last who
concludes the reading from the Law on those days on
which a chapter from the Prophets is also read is called
maftir, "concluding;" and the lesson from the Prophets is called *haphtarah,* "conclusion."

In the selection of the *haphtarah* care was taken
that it should contain some reference to the contents
of the lesson from the Pentateuch, and as there was
not much choice, the *haphtarah,* once chosen, was as a
rule read again on the recurrence of the same *sidra.*
Different communities had different series of *haphtaroth.*
A few negative rules concerning the selection of the
haphtarah are mentioned in the Mishnah (Megillah iv.
10); Ezek. i. and xvi., 2 Sam. xi. and xiii., are to be
excluded. These rules, however, were not observed, as
Ezek. i. is the *haphtarah* for the first day of the Feast
of Weeks. There is an ancient rule about the nature of
the *haphtaroth* between the Fast of Tamuz and New-
year; viz., there should be three *haphtaroth* of "rebuke"

to the Law on the Day of Atonement, and six on Sabbath (B. Talm.
Megillah 23*a*).

and seven of "comfort" (דפרענותא 'ג, דנחמתא 'ז). The former are taken from Jeremiah (i. and ii.) and Isaiah (i.) ; the latter are selected from Isaiah (xl. to. lxvi.)

Various accounts are given of the origin of the *haphtarah*. One account traces its origin to a period of persecution, when the Jews were not allowed to read from the Torah, and the scrolls of the Law were either confiscated or concealed. In both cases it was easy to read from the Prophets, for this could be done by heart and in any place ; whilst for the reading of the Torah it was necessary to produce a copy of the Law. According to another account, the *haphtarah* served as a protest against the theory of the Samaritans, who recognised the Torah alone as holy. But it is more likely and more natural to suppose that the *haphtarah* was introduced as soon as the Prophets became part of the Holy Scriptures.

There was a tendency to have recourse to the Divine messages of future comfort and glory when the present was gloomy and sad. At the end of the Service or a religious discourse, just before leaving the Synagogue or the *Beth ha-midrash*, passages from the Prophets were read, in order that the people might carry away with them a strengthened faith in God and in the ultimate victory of their religion. On Sabbath morning the lessons from the Prophets were of greater importance, since a larger number congregated, and more time could be devoted to it. A *b'rachah* therefore introduced it, and *b'rachoth*, including a prayer for the restoration of Zion, followed it. The name *haphtarah* suggests this explanation ; it denotes literally "causing to leave," "departure," or "conclusion."

After the return of the Jews from Babylon they spoke the Chaldee dialect; the lessons from the Bible were accordingly accompanied by a Chaldee translation called *targum*. The translation was not always literal, but was frequently a paraphrase. It was given, as a rule, after each verse, by an appointed *methurgeman*.—In communities which only understood Greek the Greek version was read. A Spanish translation of the *haphtarah* is still added at present on the Fast of *Ab* in the Portuguese Ritual; but otherwise the practice of adding a translation to the text has long since been discontinued.

b. שמור   " *Take Heed.*"

The negative commandment concerning the Holydays is: לא תעשה כל מלאכה, " Thou shalt do no manner of work." The very name Sabbath (שבת, " rest ") implies absence of labour. We are commanded to rest on the Sabbath, but not to indulge in laziness and indolence, which are by no means conducive to the health of the body or the soul. The Sabbath rest is described in our Sabbath Afternoon Service as " voluntary and congenial, true and faithful, and happy and cheerful." Moderate exercise, cheerful reading, and pleasant conversation are indispensable for a rest of this kind.

What is to be understood by the term " labour " or " work " in the prohibition " Thou shalt not do any manner of work "? The Pentateuch gives no definition of the term. But the Israelites, when they were told that work was prohibited on Sabbath, and that any breach of the law was to be punished with death, must have received *orally* a full explanation of the prohibition. A case is mentioned of one who profaned the Sabbath by gathering sticks, and was put to death; this could not have been done if any doubt had been left in his mind whether the act of gathering sticks was included in the prohibition.

A few instances of work prohibited on a Sabbath-day are met with in the Bible. In connection with the manna, the prohibition of cooking and baking is mentioned; also the commandment, "Let no man go out of his place on the seventh day" (Exod. xvi. 29); *i.e.*, we must not travel or go beyond a certain distance [1] on the Sabbath. Another act distinctly forbidden is contained in the words, "Ye shall kindle no fire in all your dwellings on the day of rest" (*ibid.* xxxv. 3). The prophet Amos (viii. 5), in rebuking the Israelites for cheating their fellow-men, puts the following words into their mouth: "When will the new moon be gone, that we may sell corn? and the Sabbath, that we may open our stores of wheat?" This shows that the Israelites conducted no business on New-moon and Sabbath. Jeremiah (xvii. 21 *sqq.*) says as follows: "Thus saith the Lord, Take heed to yourselves, and bear no burden on the sabbath day, nor bring it in

---

[1] The distance allowed is called שבת תחום "a Sabbath-journey," and is 2000 cubits in every direction; it is reckoned from the outskirts of the place in which we live. If, however, a person desires to perform a *mitsvah*, such as *milah*, at a place distant about a double Sabbath-journey from his domicile, he may fix before Sabbath his abode for that day half-way between the two places, and then traverse on Sabbath the whole distance from the one place to the other. This change of abode is called *erubhe thechumin*, "combination of two Sabbath-journeys into one," by changing the centre from which they are measured.

by the gates of Jerusalem ; neither carry forth a burden out of your houses on the sabbath day, neither do ye any work, but hallow ye the sabbath day."—Nehemiah relates (xiii. 15): " In those days saw I in Judah some treading wine-presses on the sabbath, and bringing in sheaves, and lading asses ; as also wine, grapes, and figs, and all manner of burdens, which they brought into Jerusalem on the sabbath day : and I testified against them in the day wherein they sold victuals. Then I said unto them, What evil thing is this that ye do and profane the sabbath day ? " As a general rule, we may say that the work prohibited on Sabbath and Festivals embraces two classes : viz., (1) All such acts as are legally—*i.e.*, in the Oral Law—defined as מלאכה " work." It makes no difference whether we consider any of them as labour or not. Under thirty-nine different heads[1] they are enumerated in the Mishnah (Shabbath vii. 2). The following are a few of them :—Ploughing, sowing, reaping, threshing,

[1] They are called אבות מלאכות " principal kinds of work," and are those which directly or indirectly were wanted in the erection of the Tabernacle, and were therefore included in the prohibition of doing any work for this purpose (Exod. xxxi. 15 and xxxv. 2).

There are certain things which cannot be brought under any of these heads, and are nevertheless prohibited, because they frequently lead to a breach of the Sabbath laws ; *e.g.*, riding in a carriage or in any kind of conveyance ; playing music. These prohibitions are called שבות, *i.e.*, acts prohibited on Sabbath and Holy-days by our Sages ; or גזרה (lit., " decree "), safeguard against breaking the Law.

Divine precepts, however, ordained for the Sabbath—*e.g.*, sacrifices— or for a certain day, which happens to fall on a Sabbath—*e.g.*, initiation of a male child into the covenant of Abraham on the eighth day of its birth, or saving the life of a fellow-man in case of illness or any other danger—must be performed although they may involve any of the acts otherwise prohibited on the day of rest.

grinding, baking, hunting, killing an animal, tanning, sewing, writing, kindling light or fire, and carrying things abroad.

(2.) Everything which our conscience tells us to be inappropriate for the Sabbath ; acts which come neither under the head of מלאכה nor under that of שבות, but which would tend to change the Sabbath into an ordinary day ; *e.g.*, preparing for our daily business transactions, although such preparation does not involve an actual breach of any of the Sabbath laws.

Whatever we are not allowed to do ourselves, we must not have done for us by a co-religionist, who deliberately disregards the fourth commandment. Neither must we employ non-Israelites to do our work on Sabbath, except in case of need ; *e.g.*, in case of illness or fear of illness.

As regards Holy-days, there is the general rule that work (מלאכה) prohibited on Sabbath must not be done on Holy-days : " Save that which every man must eat, that only may be done of you " (Exod. xii. 16) ; that is to say, it is allowed on Festivals to cook, to bake, or to prepare food in any other way.[1] Of course, for the Festival that happens to fall on a Sabbath, the

---

[1] The preparation of food is only permitted on Holy-days if wanted for the same day, except when Sabbath follows immediately after the Holy-day. In that case it is allowable to prepare the food for Sabbath on the Holy-day, provided such preparation has commenced before and need only be *continued* on the Holy-day. The preparation made for Sabbath before the Holy-day comes in is called *erubh tabhshilin*, " combination of dishes," *i.e.*, of the dishes prepared for Sabbath on the eve of the Festival (ערב יום טוב) and of those prepared on the Festival itself ; it is accompanied by a blessing and a declaration of the significance of the *erubh*. The following is the blessing : ברוך . . . אשר קדשנו במצותיו וצונו על מצות ערוב " Blessed art thou . . . who hast

laws of Sabbath remain in force. The Day of Atonement is in this respect equal to Sabbath.

c. עֹנֶג " *Delight.*"

The principal and noblest delight yielded by Holy-days is the pleasure we feel in more frequent communion with the Divine Being, in the purer and holier thoughts with which we are inspired when at rest from ordinary work, and able to devote ourselves more fully

sanctified us by thy commandments, and hast ordained for us the *mitsvah* of *erubh*."

It may here be noted that there are, besides, three kinds of *erubh*, viz. :—

1. *Erubh techumim.* See above, page 350.

2. *Erubh chatseroth* (lit., "combination of the houses in a court "). According to the traditional law, we must not carry anything on Sabbath from a private place (רשות היחיד) into the street (רשות הרבים). The former is defined to be a locality belonging to one person or family, and separated from the public by a fence. The Jewish inhabitants of a court or a town closed on all sides combine to form one family, and thus turn the רשות הרבים into רשות היחיד. The symbol of such combination consists of some food kept in a room, to which all have access (*e.g.*, the Synagogue). This is the origin and meaning of the Passover-cake (מצה) which may still be noticed in some of the Continental Synagogues.

3. *Erubh par excellence.*—An opening left in a fence or wall round a רשות היחיד must at least have some token that indicates the closing of the space ; *e.g.*, a wire drawn through the open space from one part of the fence to the other. Such symbol is called *erubh*, "combination of the various parts of the fence or wall into one." Such *erubh* may likewise be noticed in some of the Continental towns. In all these cases the symbol was not introduced for the purpose of permitting the actual transgression of a law, but rather for the purpose of reminding us of what the law forbids us to do ; since, in fact, that which becomes permitted through these symbols is even in their absence no direct breach of any of the Sabbath laws.

Z

to the contemplation of the works and words of God. In this sense the day of rest is described in one of the hymns (זמירות) after supper as " a foretaste of the world to come " (מעין עולם הבא יום שבת מנוחה).

But *oneg shabbath* includes also delight of a less spiritual character. We are not commanded on the days of rest to forget altogether the wants of the body. On the contrary. Nehemiah, when on the first day of the seventh month, that is, on New-year, he perceived that his brethren were sad, addressed them thus : " Go your way, eat the fat and drink the sweet, and send portions unto him for whom nothing is prepared : for this day is holy unto the Lord : neither be ye grieved ; for the joy of the Lord is your strength " (Neh. viii. 10). The same conception of " the sabbath unto the Lord " is met with in Talmud, Midrash, and throughout the whole of the Rabbinical literature. In one of our Sabbath-hymns (זמירות) we say : " This day is for Israel, light and joy, a sabbath of rest ; " and in our prayers for Sabbath we glory in being *shom're shabbath ve-kor'e oneg*, " observers of the sabbath, and such as call it a delight."—With regard to the Festivals, the duty of rejoicing is repeatedly enjoined (Deut. xvi. 11, 14).

In our regulations, customs, and prayers for Sabbath and Festivals, this duty is clearly indicated. All fasting and mourning is prohibited. Care was taken that Divine Service should be free from such prayers as would be likely to create feelings of grief and sadness.[1] A special formula has also been introduced for the

---

[1] Comp. the two forms of the prayer השכיבנו in the Evening Service for week-days and for Sabbath, in the Spanish Ritual.

expression of our sympathy with the sick and the mourner on Sabbath and Festivals.[1]

When any of the obligatory fasts—except the **Day of Atonement**—happens to fall on a Sabbath, the fasting is put off (נדחה) till the next day, or kept, as in the case of the fast of Esther, on the preceding Thursday. Tradition has raised the taking of the three regular meals on Sabbath (שלש סעודות), viz., supper, breakfast, and dinner, to a religious act—a *mitsvah,* and the religious character of the meals is shown by the special prayers and hymns—*zemiroth*—which accompany them. A fourth meal is, according to some authority, likewise obligatory; whilst, according to another authority, it may be replaced by spiritual food, by reading and studying the Torah.

d. כבוד " *Honour.*"

We honour the day inwardly by considering it a holy, distinguished season, which ought to be devoted to higher objects than the wants of our body. Our mind should be entirely turned aside from our daily business, in order to be free for loftier and holier thoughts. For the purpose of effecting this inward distinction of the Sabbath, we honour it also outwardly by various things, which are partly a symbol, partly a reminder of the distinction claimed by the day. We honour the Sabbath, therefore, by giving a festive appearance to our meals, our dress, and our dwelling. The

---

[1] שבת היא מלזעוק ורפואה (ונחמה) קרובה לבוא ושבתו בשלום

"To-day is Sabbath and we must not lament, for recovery (comfort) is near to come ; now keep Sabbath in peace."

principal thing required is neatness and cheerfulness;
not luxury. On the contrary, we are guided in this
respect by the principle : Make rather thy Sabbath an
ordinary day—*i.e.*, omit the distinction in food and dress
—than render thyself dependent on the support of thy
fellow-men.[1]

It is customary to have two loaves on the table, over
which the blessing *ha-motsee* is said. They are to
remind us of the double portion of bread or manna
(לחם משנה, Exod. xvi. 22) given to the Israelites in the
wilderness on the sixth day because of the succeeding
Sabbath-day. The cloth spread beneath the loaves,
and the cover over them, represent symbolically the
dew which both lay on the ground under the manna
and also over it.[2] The origin of this custom of covering the bread may perhaps be found in the following
Talmudic law : " If a meal that has commenced on
Friday afternoon is continued in the night, it must be
interrupted when Sabbath comes in ; a cloth is to be
spread over the bread whilst the *Kiddush* is recited "
(Babyl. Talm. Pesachim, 100*a*). The spreading of the
cloth appears to be here merely a sign of the pause,
and the distinction between the ordinary meal and that
of Sabbath.[3] That which was at first ordained for

---

[1] עשה שבתך חול ואל תצטרך לבריות (B. Talm. Shabbath, 18*a*).

[2] Exod. xvi. 13, 14.

[3] Another explanation of this custom has been suggested. Bread and
wine being before us, it is doubtful which should have the preference
for the purpose of *Kiddush ;* the bread is therefore covered, so that no
choice is left (Tur Orach Chayyim 271). Bread being the ordinary
requisite at our meals, the use of wine for *Kiddush* is considered more
indicative of the distinction of the day. If, however, wine is disliked
or injurious, bread is used as its substitute.

special cases became in course of time a general custom.[1]

The loaves are called *birchoth* (ברכות), *taashir* (תעשיר), or *challah* (חלה). The first name they received as symbols of God's blessing, the double portion of manna which the Almighty sent to the Israelites on Friday because of the Sabbath (see Rashi on Gen. ii. 3). The verse, "The blessing of the Lord, it maketh rich" (תעשיר, Prov. x. 22), suggested the second name. *Challah* reminds us of the commandment to give the first part of the dough to the priest (Num. xv. 17–21). Although at present this commandment cannot be carried out, we separate a small piece, called *challah*, of the dough which we prepare for bread, and burn it, after having recited an appropriate blessing.[2] It is customary to prepare the dough for the Sabbath loaves at home, in order to be able to act in accordance with this custom. This is one of the religious acts which it is the special duty of women to perform, and some of the pious women of Israel (נשים צדקניות) have the praiseworthy custom to lay something aside for charity when performing this or similar religious acts.

Another act performed in honour of Sabbath and

---

[1] A peculiar ceremony may here be noticed. Some pass the knife over the bread before the *berachah* is said. The origin of this custom is this : the rule has been laid down that there should not be a long interval between the *berachah* and the partaking of the food. The knife and the bread are therefore kept ready, and originally an incision was made into the loaf in order to shorten that interval as much as possible.

[2] ברוך א' י' א' מ' ה' אשר קדשנו במצותיו וצונו להפריש חלה, "Blessed art thou, O Lord, our God, King of the Universe, who hast sanctified us by thy commandments, and commanded us to separate *challah*."

Festivals is the kindling of special lights before the holy day comes in, to indicate symbolically the approach of a day of light and cheerfulness. This duty is likewise the privilege of the housewife [1] or her representative. Before [2] kindling the lights the following blessing is recited: וצונו להדליק נר של שבת . . . . ברוך אתה "Blessed art thou . . . . and hast commanded us to kindle the sabbath lights." שבת ויום, or יום טוב, יום הכפורים, יום טוב שבת ויום הכפורים is substituted for שבת according as a Holy-day, the Day of Atonement, or these days when they happen to fall on a Saturday, come in. On Festivals, except the last days of Passover, the following blessing, called שהחינו, is added: שהחינו וקימנו . . . ברוך והגיענו לזמן הזה "Blessed art thou . . . who hast kept us in life, preserved us, and enabled us to reach this season."

NOTES.

1. The reading of the Law is preceded and followed by a blessing. In the first we praise God for having distinguished Israel by revealing the Law to them, and in the second for the benefit derived from the Law as the source of eternal life. The love and regard for the Law expressed in these blessings should be shown by the congregants in silent and respectful attention to what is recited by the Reader. Those who are called up to the Law consider this as an important event, and make it an occasion of special prayers for relatives and friends (*mi-shebberach*), accom-

---

[1] Comp. Mishnah Shabbath ii. 16.

[2] Some kindle the lights first, and then say the blessing whilst their hands are spread out before the lights. The origin of this latter practice is this : It happens sometimes that the housewife is not ready in time for kindling the lights, and lets another do it for her, she reserving to herself the privilege of saying the *berachah* later on. In that case the holding of the hands before the lights and withdrawing them after the blessing represents symbolically the kindling of the lights. What was originally done in exceptional cases became subsequently the rule.

panied by promises of contributions to communal and charitable institutions. On days of family rejoicing, as well as on days of mourning, the religious privilege of being called to the Reading of the Law is especially valued; in the former case offerings are vowed in honour of our living friends, in the other case *in memoriam* of those near and dear to us, who have departed from our midst. These additional prayers thus serve a double purpose; they help to preserve the bond of relationship and friendship, and secure a material support for the benevolent and other institutions of the community.

Objections have been raised to this in itself praiseworthy custom for two reasons : first, the *mi-shebberach* only concerns a few, and appears to the rest of the congregation a useless interruption in the reading of the Law ; secondly, it gives occasion to a display of vanity and pride.

As to the first objection, provision could and should be made that the interruption be not unduly long, and cause irritation among the congregants. Due regard should be shown to the fact that the Divine Book is open on the reading-desk, and everything should be avoided that might diminish the reverence proper to such an occasion. The second objection is based on a pessimistic estimate of our fellow-men ; if there is any one whose offerings are made from vain and ostentatious motives, he is certainly lost in the multitude of those who take a more serious and a more dignified view of their duties when standing before the open Torah.

2. There is an old tradition that we should recite daily a hundred benedictions. On Sabbath and Holy-days, when the Amidah contains only seven *berachoth* instead of eighteen, the deficiency is made up by seeking an occasion for *birchoth ha-nehenin.* Hence the *minhag* spread of partaking on these days of various kinds of fruit between the meals.

3. Tradition teaches us that on the holy days of rest we must not only abstain from actual work, but also from ordering anything to be done by those who refuse to recognise the Sabbath-laws as binding on them.—Circumstances force us to deviate at times from this rule. There were Jews who would not allow any work to be undertaken on Friday which would continue of its own accord after the Sabbath had set in. Thus they would not have light in their homes on Friday evening or warm food

on the Sabbath-day, although all necessary precautions had been taken before Sabbath came in to keep the light burning and the food warm for twenty-four hours. But the more these Jews insisted on excluding light and fire from their homes, the more did our Sages demand light and warm food as essential comforts of the Sabbath, and to them the Sabbath-candles and the warm food were a *mitsvah* of great importance. Much work is done on Sabbath for the public by non-Jews ; *e.g.*, in connection with railway-trains, steamboats, and other public conveyances. May the Jew avail himself of the work thus done for all alike without his bidding? He may in some cases—*e.g.*, for a long sea-voyage—in others not. But he must always bear in mind that Judaism depends on the adherence of the Jews to the noble principle, כל ישראל ערבים זה בזה "All Israelites are sureties responsible for each other." The meaning of this principle is this : If a certain act appears to one of us allowable, but at the same time our action might mislead others and cause them to break the Law, we must not do it. Thus if Jews were to avail themselves of the public conveyances, the whole aspect of the Sabbath would change, and the day would ultimately be forgotten.

4. When dire necessity compels a Jew to break the Sabbath, let him not think that the Sabbath is lost to him, or he to Judaism. So long as Jewish conscientiousness is alive within him, let him endeavour to keep as much of the Sabbath as he is able. He must not say, " I have broken the Sabbath. How can I join my brethren in the Sabbath Service !" Whatever he does conscientiously will be acceptable before God, and he will thus find himself exhorted to watch carefully, and to seize the first opportunity of returning to the full observance of Sabbath. The same principle applies to all the Divine Precepts.

THE JEWISH CALENDAR.

The Jewish Calendar [1] reckons the day from evening to evening, in accordance with the order observed in

---

[1] Calendar is derived from the Latin *Calendæ*, which signifies the first of the month. The Hebrew term לוח, used for "Calendar" or "Almanac," denotes "table" or "tablet." In the Talmud, *Sod* (or *Yesod*) *ha-ibbur* is used in the sense of "the theory of the Calendar :"

the verse, "And it was evening and it was morning, one day" (Gen. i. 5). Íne evening begins after sunset, at the moment when stars become visible under normal conditions of the atmosphere: at צאת הכוכבים "the coming forth of the stars," *scil.*, of at. least three stars of middle size.

The day is divided into evening, morning, and afternoon. With each of these periods is connected an appropriate prayer or service, viz., *Maarib* or Evening-prayer, *Shacharith* or Morning-prayer, and *Minchah* or Afternoon-prayer.

Seven days form a week. The days of the week are described in the Bible and the Talmud simply as the first day, the second day, &c. Only the seventh day has a second name, *Yom ha-shabbath* or *shabbath*, "the day of rest," or "the rest." In post-Biblical literature the sixth day is called *Erebh shabbath* or *Ma'ale shabbatha*, "the eve of Sabbath," or "the coming in of Sabbath." The evening following Sabbath is named *Motseë shabbath*, "the departure of Sabbath." Similarly the day preceding a Festival and the evening following it are called *Erev yom-tobh* and *Motseë yom-tobh*, "the eve of the Festival," and "the departure of the Festival."

Four weeks and one or two days make one month, חרש or ירח. The length of the month is determined by the duration of one revolution of the moon round the earth. Such revolution is completed in twenty-nine days and a half.[1] As, however, the calendar month

literally, the term denotes the fixing of the additional day to the month or the additional month to the year.

[1] Or more exactly, 29 days, 12 hours, 44 minutes, 3⅓ seconds. The technical formula in Hebrew is: כ"ט י"ב תשצ"ג 29 days, 12$\frac{798}{1080}$ hours.

does not commence in the middle of the day, but at the beginning of the evening, it was necessary to add half a day to one month, and to take off half a day from the next. The months have therefore alternately twenty-nine and thirty days.

The months are named according to their order, the first month, the second, &c.; the first being the first month in the spring. Other names, implying agricultural and climatic relations, were likewise in use, and the following four of them have been preserved in the Bible: the first month is called *Abib*, "ears of corn;" the second *Ziv*, "beauty;" the seventh *Ethanim*, "hardy fruit;" and the eighth, *Bul*, "rain."[1] Since the return of the Jews from the Babylonian exile, names of foreign origin have been in use, viz., *Nisan, Iyar, Sivan, Tammuz, Abh, Elul, Tishri, Cheshvan, Kislev, Tebheth, Shebhat* and *Adar*.[2] Roughly speaking, these months correspond to April, May, June, July, August, September, October, November, December, January, February, and March.

The year is either an ordinary year or a leap-year, the former consisting of twelve, the latter of thirteen months. The extra month is called *Adar-sheni*, "the second *Adar*," and is added between *Adar* and *Nisan*. It serves to adjust from time to time the lunar to the

---

[1] In the first month the barley becomes ripe; in the second the whole vegetation of the country stands in its full splendour; in the seventh the hardy fruit, which withstood the heat of the summer, ripens; and in the eighth the first rain of the season comes down.

[2] The meaning of most of these names is uncertain. The two names *Elul* and *Tishri* seem to denote "the disappearance" and "the beginning" of the year.

solar year ;[1] for there is between the lunar year—that is, the time of twelve revolutions of the moon round the earth—and the solar year, or the time of one revolution of the earth round the sun, a difference of about eleven days, the one consisting of about $354\frac{1}{3}$, the other of about $365\frac{1}{4}$ days. In nineteen years the difference amounts to about seven months. We have therefore seven leap-years in every cycle (מחזור) of nineteen years, viz., the 3rd, 6th, 8th, 11th, 14th, 17th, and 19th.

Neither the ordinary years nor the leap-years have a uniform duration ; the former fluctuate between 353, 354, and 355 days ; the latter between 383, 384, and 385 days. The following is the cause of this variety : There are certain days in the week which are never made the beginning of the new year (the 1st of *Tishri*). Whenever the astronomical beginning of the year happens to be on one of these days, a day is added to one year, and taken from the next. The addition in the former case is made in the month of *Cheshvan*, and the curtailing in the latter case in the month of *Kislev*. The length of the months is therefore as follows :—*Nisan*, 30 ; *Iyar*, 29 ; *Sivan*, 30 ; *Tammuz*, 29 ; *Abh*, 30 ; *Elul*, 29 ; *Tishri*, 30 ; *Cheshvan*, 29 or 30 ; *Kislev*, 30 or 29 ; *Tebheth*, 29 ; *Shebhat*, 30'; *Adar*, 29, in leap-year 30 ; *Adar-sheni* (in leap-year), 29 days.

The first day of the month is called New-moon-day

The adjustment is necessary for the right observance of Passover, which must be celebrated in the first month (Exod. xii. 2), the month of *Abib* (Deut. xvi. 1), that is, in the spring, when in Palestine the corn begins to ripen. Without the periodical insertion of a month, Passover would be celebrated in every succeeding year eleven days earlier than in the previous one, and in course of time at different seasons, contrary to the Law.

חדש [1] or ראש חדש, "beginning of the month." In those
months which have thirty days, the thirtieth day is
likewise kept as *Rosh-chodesh*.

The beginning of the astronomical month is the
moment of the conjunction of sun and moon,[2] when
the moon is exactly between the earth and the sun.
Nothing is then visible of the moon. Six hours at
least later a very small portion of the moon can, under
favourable conditions, be seen, and the day on which
this takes place is the first of the calendar month.

At first, from the earliest days down to Hillel II.
(about 360 C.E.), *Rosh-chodesh* was determined by direct
observation. The highest court, the great *Sanhedrin*,
examined the witnesses who had noticed the reappearance of the moon, and accordingly determined the first
day of the month by the solemn declaration, *Mekuddash*,
" sanctified ; " that is, the day is to be kept as *Rosh-
chodesh*. These proceedings took place on the thirtieth
day of the month. If witnesses presented themselves
who testified to the appearance of the new moon, and
after due examination their statement was found to be
correct, the same day was proclaimed as *Rosh-chodesh*,
and the preceding month had twenty-nine days ; if no
witnesses presented themselves, or the witnesses could
not sustain their evidence, the day was added to the
expiring month, and the day following was the first of
the next month. The decision of the *Sanhedrin* concerned only the thirtieth day of the month. As soon
as their decision was arrived at, Jewish congregations
located within a certain distance were informed by

[1] The Hebrew term חדש has a double meaning "beginning of the
month " and "month ; " comp. שבת, "day of rest," and also "week,"
or the period that passes between two consecutive Sabbaths.

[2] In Hebrew *molad*, "birth."

signal or by trustworthy messengers which day had been fixed as the first of the new month. The decrees of the *Sanhedrin*, the highest religious council of the nation, were accepted by all Jewish congregations as law, and the Festivals were celebrated in accordance with the New Moon thus appointed. There were, however, Jewish congregations in distant parts that could not be reached by the messengers in due time, and these were in doubt concerning the day on which a Festival had to be celebrated. Being anxious not to miss the day kept as a Festival on the authority of the *Sanhedrin* by their brethren at the religious centre of the nation, the Jews abroad observed two days as Holy-days instead of one; only the Fast of the Day of Atonement had no additional day, because, being a fast-day, the majority of the people were unable to abstain from food for two consecutive days. New-year, on the other hand, was, as a rule, everywhere observed two days, even in places near the seat of the *Sanhedrin*, and sometimes even in the very place where the *Sanhedrin* met, on account of the uncertainty whether the 30th of *Elul* or the day following would be fixed by the *Sanhedrin* as *Rosh ha-shanah*. Though, with regard to the most holy Festival, the uncertainty of the day admitted of no remedy, this circumstance did not prevent our pious ancestors from applying a remedy where it could be done.

It was not ignorance that led Jews outside Palestine to observe two Holy-days instead of one. A rough calculation of the time in which the various phenomena of the moon are to be noticed is not difficult, and could be made by many Rabbis and laymen long before Hillel II. framed the permanent Calendar. Nevertheless, two days were kept, because it was impossible to calculate or anticipate all the accidental circumstances that might cause the *Sanhedrin* to defer the fixing of *Rosh-chodesh* for the next day.

Nor was it a decree of the *Sanhedrin*, or of a Rabbinical assembly, that ordered the observance of יום טוב שני, "a second day of the Festival." This was done by the voluntary act of the nation, and their resolution was confirmed by continued usage. It was the outcome of genuine piety, of the earnest desire to be at one with the central authority of the nation. The observance of יום טוב שני is so old that no trace of its actual introduction can be discovered in the Talmud; wherever mention is made of it, it is represented as an institution already in existence. It may already have existed in the days of the prophets, and traces of the celebration of a second day of *Rosh-chodesh* may be recognised in the first book of Samuel (i. xx. 27).

This practice, which sprang from true fear and love of God, was spontaneously adopted by all the Jews outside Palestine, continued by generation after generation for more than two thousand years, and has, as a *minhag* of long standing, become law. It is not a precept commanded in the Written Law, or decreed in the Oral Law; it is only a *minhag* "practice," but a *minhag* that must be cherished and respected as a national institution. There may come a time when the institution of יום טוב שני will be abolished; this can, however, only be done by the national will, confirmed by a *Sanhedrin* which will be recognised by the whole nation as the only religious authority. Until then it is incumbent upon us to adhere firmly to the observance of the second days of the Festivals.

NOTES.

The following are the general principles upon which our Calendar is based :—

1. Twenty-nine days $12\frac{793}{1080}$ hours elapse between one *molad* and the next.[1]

2. An ordinary year must not have less than 353 or more than 355 days, nor the leap-year less than 383 or more than 385 days.

3. The 1st of *Tishri* is fixed on the day of the *molad* of *Tishri*. There are four exceptions (דחיות) :—

a. לא אד"ו ראש. If the 1st of *Tishri* falls on a Sunday, Wednesday, or Friday.

b. מולד זקן. If the *molad* of *Tishri* is at noon or later.

c. If the *molad* of *Tishri* in an ordinary year is on Tuesday $3\frac{204}{1080}$ A.M. or later (ג' ט' ר"ד).

d. If the *molad* of *Tishri* of a year succeeding a leap-year is on Monday $9\frac{589}{1080}$ A.M. or later (ב' ט' תק"פט).

The first of these four exceptions is to prevent the Day of Atonement from falling on Friday or Sunday, and *Hoshaana-rabba* from falling on Sabbath ; the third exception is to guard against having an ordinary year of more than 355, and the last from having a leap-year of less than 383 days.

4. The character of the year is described by three letters, the first of which indicates the day of the week for the 1st of *Tishri*, the last the day of the week for the 1st of *Nisan*, the middle letter, according as it is כ, ח, or ש (=כסדר "regular ;" חסרה "defective ;" שלמה "perfect"), indicates a regular year of 354 (in leap-year 384) days, a defective year of 353 (in leap-year 383), or a perfect one of 355 (in leap-year 385) days.

The present year (September 1890 to October 1891) is, according to Jewish tradition,[2] the year 5651 A.M. (of the Creation) ; its characteristics are ב' ח' ה' ; *i.e.*, the 1st of *Tishri* is on Monday ; the year is defective ; and the 1st of *Nisan* is on Thursday. The year is, besides, a leap-year, consisting of 13 months ;

---

[1] The *molad* of *Tishri* in the year 1 is assumed to have been on Sunday evening between eleven and twelve. (בהר"ד)

[2] In this tradition the period of the Persian rule in Palestine, which lasted over two centuries, is contracted to thirty-four years. It is possible that the years were counted according to the years of Release (שמטה) or the years of the Jubilee, and these were probably not kept immediately after the return of the Jews from Babylon.

it is the eighth year of the 298th cycle (of 19 years). It is the
first year of the Septennate, or the first year after the year of
release (שמטה. See Lev. xxv.).

THE FESTIVALS.

"The feasts of the Lord, even holy convocations,
which ye shall proclaim in their seasons" (Lev. xxiii.
4), are Passover, Feast of Weeks, Day of Memorial,
Day of Atonement, and Feast of Tabernacles. These
are divided into two groups called שלש רגלים and ימים
נוראים, "three festivals" and "solemn days." In the
Pentateuch the two groups are kept distinctly asunder.
Thus in Exod. xxiii. 14–17 and xxxiv. 18, and
Deut. xvi., only the former group is mentioned.

The name *shalosh regalim* derives its origin from
the following Biblical passage: "Three times thou
shalt keep a feast unto me in the year," שלש רגלים תחג
לי בשנה (Exod. xxiii. 14). Although in a parallel
passage the word רגלים has been replaced by פעמים
(*ibid.* ver. 17), of the same meaning, "times," *shalosh
regalim* has been preferred, because רגלים reminds one
also of "a journey on foot," "a pilgrimage," an important element in the celebration of these three festivals,
according to the Divine commandment, "Three times
every year shall thy males appear before the Lord thy
God, in the place which he shall choose, in the feast
of unleavened bread, in the feast of weeks, and in the
feast of tabernacles" (Deut. xvi. 16).

The name *yamim noraim* for the remaining two
feasts is not founded on a Biblical phrase, but on the
fact that these festivals are devoted more than the rest
to earnest reflection and solemn devotion.

I. *The Three Festivals* (שלש רגלים).

The three festivals have the following three characteristics in common :—

1. They refer to important events in our national history ; viz., Passover to the deliverance of the Israelites from Egyptian bondage ; Feast of Weeks to the Revelation on Mount Sinai ; and Tabernacles to the travels of the Israelites through the Arabian desert.

2. They mark the various stages of the harvest ; viz., Passover marks the season of the early harvest, Feast of Weeks the second harvest, and the Feast of Tabernacles the ingathering of the fruit.

3. They serve as a means for imparting essential religious truths ; viz., Passover embodies the principle of the Existence of God, the Feast of Weeks that of Revelation, and the Feast of Tabernacles that of Divine Providence.

The Distinguished Sabbaths (ד' פרשיות).[1]

There are in the months *Adar* and *Nisan* four Sabbaths distinguished by the circumstance that on them additional sections are read from the Pentateuch and special lessons from the Prophets. Two of them are connected with the celebration of Passover.

1. שבת שקלים " Sabbath of the shekels ; " *i.e.*, on which the law concerning the half-shekel contribution is read from the Pentateuch (Exod. xxx. 11–16), and also the account of the gifts for the repair of the Temple in the reign of King Joash (2 Kings xii.

---

[1] See Mishnah, Megillah iii. 4.

2 A

I—I7). Every male Israelite, twenty years old or upward, had to contribute annually one half-shekel towards the maintenance of the Temple and the Temple Service. The year commenced the 1st of *Nisan*, when public sacrifices had to be bought with money of the new contributions.[1] Every one was therefore expected to send his contribution before the 1st of *Nisan*. On the 1st of *Adar* proclamations were made throughout the country that the half-shekel was due.[2] Hence the custom to read the above-named sections on the Sabbath before the 1st of *Adar*, or on the 1st, if this happens to be on a Sabbath.

2. שבת זכור " Sabbath Remember " is the Sabbath on which the paragraph concerning the enmity of Amalek is read from the Pentateuch (Deut. xxv. 17—19), and the defeat of Amalek by King Saul from the Prophets (1 Sam. xv.). The Agagite Haman, one of the principal figures in the history of *Purim*, is believed to be a descendant of Agag, king of Amalek (*ibid.* ver. 8). And as the Law commands us to remember the hostilities of Amalek against Israel, it has been found appropriate to read the above sections on the Sabbath before *Purim*.

3. שבת פרה " The Sabbath of the Red Heifer," *i.e.,* the Sabbath on which the law concerning the sacrifice of the red heifer and the purification with its ashes is read from the Pentateuch (Num. xix.), and "the future purification of Israel" (Ezek. xxxvi. 17—38) from the Prophets. It is the Sabbath after *Purim*, or, when the 15th or 16th of *Adar* falls on Saturday, the second Sabbath after *Purim*. All Israelites had

---

[1] Talm. Jerush., Shekalim i. 1. [2] Mishnah, Shekalim i. 1.

to come to the Temple, and to offer the Passover-lamb on the 14th of *Nisan*, and this could not be done by any unclean person. By the reading of the above sections, all are, as it were, reminded to take the necessary steps for their purification, and thus prepare themselves for the celebration of Passover.

4. שבת החדש "The Sabbath of *ha-chodesh*," *i.e.*, the Sabbath before the 1st of *Nisan*, or on the 1st of *Nisan* if it falls on a Saturday, on which the law that fixes *Nisan* as the first month [1] and the commandment concerning Passover are read from the Pentateuch (Exod. xii. 1—20), and the description of the sacrifices of the 1st of *Nisan*, Passover, and other Festivals in the future Temple from the Prophets (Ezek. xlv. 16—xlvi. 18).

In addition to these four Sabbaths, the Sabbath preceding Passover is to be mentioned. It is not distinguished by any special lesson from the Pentateuch, but it has nevertheless received the title "the Great Sabbath," שבת הגדול [2] on account of the importance of

---

[1] According to Tradition, Exod. xii. 2 not only deals with the appointment of *Nisan* as the first month of the year, but implies also the rules for fixing ראש חדש, New-moon, or the first of the month; and this verse, with its traditional interpretation, was therefore considered as the basis of the Jewish Calendar. Hence the prominence given to this section of the Pentateuch by having it read on the 1st of *Nisan* or on the Sabbath before the 1st of *Nisan*.

[2] Various reasons are given for this title. According to Tradition, the 10th of *Nisan* in the year of the Exodus was on Saturday; it was considered a great event, a miracle, in fact, that the Israelites could on that day select a lamb for sacrifice without being molested by their Egyptian masters, who at other times would have stoned them for such daring (Exod. viii. 22). Another reason is this: The Sabbath before any of the chief Festivals was called the great Sabbath on account of

the approaching Festival. The last part of Malachi (iii. 4–24) is read as the *haphtarah* of the day, in which the ultimate triumph of the God-fearing is described by the Prophet.

פסח *Passover.*

Passover is the first of the Three Feasts, and is kept eight days, from the 15th of *Nisan* to the 22nd; the four middle days being half-Holy-days, called *chol ha-moëd* ("the week-days of the festival").

The name *Pesach*, "Passover,"[1] reminds us of the way in which the Israelites enjoyed the Divine protection before they left Egypt. Pharaoh, king of Egypt, kept the Israelites as slaves, and when asked in the name of God to let them go, refused to obey. But the ten plagues which consecutively afflicted his land without causing injury to the Israelites taught

the instruction sought and given respecting the importance and the observances of the coming Festival (see Zunz, Ritus. p. 9). This name has only been preserved in the case of the Sabbath before Passover.—It is, however, possible that "the great day," the predominant idea in the *haphtarah* of the day, suggested the name.

It is the custom in some congregations to read in the Afternoon-service of *Shabbath haggadol* part of the *Haggadah* instead of the Psalms (civ. and cxx.–cxxxiv.).

[1] The word פסח "Passover," signifies (1) the act of passing over or sparing (Exod. xii. 11); (2) the sacrifice of passover, especially as object to the verb עשה "to make" (*ibid.* 47, 48); (3) the time when the passover was offered and consumed; *i.e.*, the 14th of *Nisan*, afternoon and evening (Lev. xxiii. 5; Num. xxviii. 16); (4) the whole of Passover (Mishnah, and in all post-Biblical literature).

The day on which an Israelite brought a sacrifice was a Festival to him and his family; and no work was done on that day. Accordingly on the afternoon of the 14th of *Nisan*, ערב פסח, the time fixed for the Passover-offering, no work was done; some abstained from him the existence of a higher Power, to whose decrees the will of earthly rulers has to submit. It was especially the tenth plague, the slaying of the first-born, that convinced the king and his people of this truth. When the Lord smote all the first-born in the land of Egypt, "he *passed over* the houses of the children of Israel" (Exod. xii. 27).

The Feast has a second name, viz., "feast of unleavened bread," חג המצות, a name derived from the commandment to eat מצה "unleavened bread," instead of the ordinary חמץ "leavened bread," during the Festival. The purpose of this commandment is to commemorate the deliverance of the Israelites from Egypt as well as the mode of their actual departure. For when the tenth plague, the slaying of the first-born, had visited the Egyptians, they were overcome with fear, and urged the Israelites at once to leave the country. The Israelites therefore left Egypt hurriedly,

work the whole day (Mishnah, Pesachim iv. 1 ; comp. also *ibid.* 5).—
It is customary for the first-born to fast the whole or part of ערב פסח (Talm. Jerus. x. 1, and Masecheth Soferim xxi. 3). They might rather be expected to feast in memory of the deliverance of the first-born Israelites in Egypt. But the case is similar to that of *Purim*. Both the day of danger and the day of victory are celebrated ; the one by fasting (fast of Esther), the other by feasting (*Purim*). So here the 14th of *Nisan* was for the first-born the day of danger, the following night the season of deliverance. Hence the fasting during the day and the feasting in the evening. The day suggests thoughts like the following : Our forefathers were saved from danger : should we deserve to be saved if danger threatened us ? Such reflections may have been the origin of the fast of the first-born on the eve of Passover. Some also fast on this day, or at least abstain on it from a full meal, in order to do honour to the festive meal in the evening and approach it with appetite (לתיאבון). A similar custom obtains, though not to the same extent, on the eve of Sabbath and of every Festival (Mishnah, Pesachim x. 1).

and had no time for preparing the ordinary "leavened bread," and baked for themselves unleavened cakes (מצות) of the dough which they had made.

Passover thus commemorates two distinct moments in the deliverance of the Israelites from Egyptian slavery, viz. (1) the special protection which the Almighty granted them in Egypt, and (2) their departure from the house of bondage.

Two distinct observances, therefore, were ordained for the Feast of Passover, viz. (1) the sacrifice of the Passover-lamb, and (2) the eating of "unleavened bread" and the abstaining from "leavened bread."

1. *The Passover-lamb.*—A short time before their departure from Egypt the Israelites were commanded by the Almighty that on the tenth of the first month every family should procure a lamb, keep it four days,[1] kill it in the afternoon of the fourteenth, sprinkle of its blood on the "lintel and the two door-posts," and "eat in the evening the meat roast in fire, with unleavened bread and bitter herbs, in haste, their loins girded, their shoes on their feet and their staff in their hand" (Exod. xii. 3—11). Whatever the material benefit was which the Israelites, in the moment of starting for a long and uncertain journey, derived from the meal prepared and partaken of in this manner, there was a higher purpose in the Divine commandment; it was

[1] Within the four days there was ample time for examining the lamb, whether it was really תמים, without blemish, and fit both for sacrifice and for human food.—Some suggest that the keeping of the lamb for four days was to be a test of the faith of the Israelites, whether they would obey the Will of God in spite of the dreaded wrath of the Egyptians.

demanded that the lamb should be " a passover sacrifice unto the Lord " (*ibid.*). The proceedings should be an expression of faith in God,[1] and of gratitude to Him for His protection. Every house should thus form a place holy unto the Lord ; an altar, as it were, on which the blood of the sacrifice was sprinkled.

The Passover sacrifice first observed in Egypt was afterwards ordained as a permanent institution (*ibid.* ver. 24). This difference, however, was observed, that the Passover-lamb, like all sacrifices, had to be brought to the Sanctuary, to " the place which the Lord chose to place his name in " (Deut. xvi. 6). All who were prevented from performing their duty on the 14th of *Nisan* were allowed to offer the Passover on the 14th of the second month (*Iyar*). By way of distinction from the sacrifice on the first date, this offering was called " the second passover " (פסח שני,[2] Num. ix. 9–14). Since the destruction of the Temple all sacrificial service has been discontinued, and in accordance with the words, " We will compensate with our lips for the bullocks " (Hos. xiv. 3), prayers and recitals from

---

[1] Their faith in God had to be shown by their willingly going forth whither the command of God led them, without taking with them any provision for the journey. The lamb which they had prepared was to be consumed before they left Egypt, and whatever was left had to be burnt. This was probably also the object of the precepts that no bone of the lamb was to be broken, and no part of it was to be carried from one house to another ; for the breaking of the bones and the carrying part of the meat about from place to place would facilitate its being stored away for the journey.—Other precepts, which implied haste and readiness, *e.g.*, the roasting it with fire, eating it with loins girded, &c., were to teach the Israelites the lesson that they were to be always ready and willing to do God's bidding.

[2] An instance of Passover being put off because of the unfitness of the priests to offer up sacrifices is met with in the Second Book of

the Bible have taken the place of sacrifices, whilst psalms and hymns are added such as used to accompany the act of offering sacrifices. The Passover sacrifice has therefore been discontinued; but the law of eating unleavened bread and bitter herbs is still observed.

2. *The Unleavened Bread.*—" Seven days shall ye eat unleavened bread; even the first day ye shall have put away leaven out of your houses: for whosoever eateth leavened bread from the first day until the seventh day, that soul shall be cut off from Israel " (Exod. xii. 15). " Unleavened bread shall be eaten seven days; and there shall no leavened bread be seen with thee, neither shall there be leaven seen with thee in all thy quarters " (*ibid.* xiii. 7). " Seven days shall there no leaven be found in your houses " (*ibid.* xii. 19). The distinction between leavened and unleavened only applies to bread or any other form of food prepared out of any of the following five kinds of grain: barley, wheat, rye, oats, and spelt. Bread or cake prepared from any of these five kinds is called unleavened bread, or מצה, if the dough is baked immediately after it has been prepared, no time being left for fermentation.[1] It is not only forbidden during the

Chronicles (xxx. 2). It seems similar to the rule of *Pesach sheni*, but is in reality different from it. King Hezekiah did not put off the Passover sacrifice for a month on account of the uncleanness of the priests, but he made the preceding year a leap-year, and the month which would have been the second became the first, whilst the first was counted as the thirteenth of the past year (comp. Mishnah, Pesachim iv. 9).

[1] It is only the fermentation of any of these five kinds of grain that forms חמץ. Fermentation of grapes or other fruit constitutes no חמץ.

Festival to eat leavened bread, but it is not permitted to derive any benefit whatsoever from it.[1]   All leaven and leavened bread must be removed before Passover comes in ; and in accordance with the traditional interpretation of the precept, " Thou shalt not offer the blood of my sacrifice with leavened bread " (*ibid.* xxiii. 18), the leaven must be removed before the time in which the Passover was offered.[2]

The law forbidding חמץ " leavened bread," to be kept in the house during Passover is frequently and most emphatically repeated in the Torah.   Jews have therefore, as a rule, been very conscientious and zealous in the fulfilment of this Divine command.   In accordance with this law, the following observances have been ordained :—

(1.) בדיקת חמץ " the searching for leavened bread " on the eve of the 14th of *Nisan.*[3]   The head of the family, or his deputy, examines his residence thoroughly, and keeps the *chamets,* which he has found, in a safe place till the next morning.   This searching, like every other performance of a religious duty, is preceded by a blessing, viz., ברוך . . . אשר קדשנו במצותיו וצונו על ביעור חמץ " Blessed art thou . . . who hast sanctified us by thy

---

[1] חמץ is both אסור באכילה and אסור בהנאה (Mishnah, Pesachim ii. 1).

[2] It is now the custom to eat חמץ on *Erebh Pesach,* only during the first third of the day ; *i.e.,* till about ten o'clock in the morning (*ibid.* i. 4).

[3] *Ibid.* i. 1.—The evening was chosen for this task, because with a taper or lamp the corners and dark recesses can be better searched than by daylight.   Besides, in the evening, when every one has finished his day's work, people are more at ease to do the searching in a thorough manner.

commandments, and hast commanded us concerning the removal of the leavened bread."[1]

(2.) ‏ביעור חמץ‎, "the removal or the destruction or *chamets*." All the *chamets* that is left after the first meal on the 14th of *Nisan* must be removed, *i.e.*, sold or given as a present to a non-Israelite, or destroyed. In addition to the actual removal or destruction of *chamets*, a solemn declaration is made by the head of the family, that if any *chamets* should be left in his house without his knowledge, he would not claim it as his. The object of this declaration is to free the master of the house from all responsibility in case any *chamets* should be found on his premises, contrary to the Law.[2]

(3.) Utensils which have been used for *chamets* are put away, and replaced by new ones, or by such as have exclusively been kept for Passover. Some vessels used during the year may be used for Passover, after having undergone a certain process called *kasher;*[3] *i.e.*, "fitting" them as vessels for use on Passover.

---

[1] The formula with ‏על‎ is employed here, because we need not do the searching by ourselves; it may be done by a substitute.—Although we only *search* in the evening, we use the term ‏על ביעור חמץ‎ "concerning the *removal* or the *destruction* of the *chamets*," because this removal or destruction is the object of the searching.

[2] The declaration, printed usually on the first page of the *Haggadah*, is made twice : once in the evening after the searching of the *chamets*, and once in the morning after its removal ; with this difference, that in the evening only the *chamets* that has not been found is disclaimed ; in the morning all *chamets*, if left in the house, is disclaimed, whether it has been noticed in the course of searching or not.

[3] There are different kinds of the process of *kasher* : (1) by making the articles in question red hot—this applies to the iron oven and other iron vessels ; (2) by dipping the vessel in boiling water, or pouring boiling water over it, or letting the water in the vessel boil over. The object of this process is to free the vessel from any *chamets* it may have

(4.) Although the articles of food that are directly forbidden as *chamets* are very few, there are a great many things that contain an admixture of *chamets*, and those "who fear the word of the Lord" use during Passover only those articles of food concerning which there is no doubt whatever that they are perfectly free from *chamets*. Articles of food for Passover are therefore only bought of persons who can be trusted to hold these observances in respect.

In addition to the commandments of the Passover-offering and the unleavened bread, there is a special duty, mentioned four times in the Pentateuch, for the Israelite to relate to his children the history of the departure from Egypt, and to explain to them the meaning of the several rites connected with the celebration of Passover. This duty is called *haggadah*, "relating," and a service has been arranged for the purpose, called *Seder*, "the Order." The first two evenings of Passover are therefore called "*Seder*-evenings," and the book which contains this Service is generally called *Haggadah*.

The *Seder*-service contains four elements: (1) the relation of the deliverance of the Israelites from Egypt; (2) the festive meal, preceded by *Kiddush* and the partaking of bitter herbs and unleavened bread, and followed by Grace; (3) *Hallel* and other hymns; (4) the partaking of four cups of wine (*arba kosoth*).[1]

absorbed.—Before the process of *kasher* begins, the vessel must, of course, be thoroughly cleaned.

[1] The four cups of wine are not taken at once; but one serves for *Kiddush*, as on Sabbath and Holy-days; the second is taken at the conclusion of the first part of the *Seder*; the third after Grace, it being customary also on ord...ary days to take a cup of wine after Grace; the fourth at the conclusion of the second part of the *Seder*. The four cups

The head of the family or his substitute who reads the Service has before him on the table: (1) three unleavened cakes (*matsoth*);[1] (2) bitter herbs and

are also said to indicate our joy in reference to four elements constituting the redemption, and implied in the four terms: והוצאתי, והצלתי, וגאלתי, and ולקחתי, (Exod. vi. 6, 7), liberation from bondage, deliverance from service, redemption from all dependence on Egypt, and appointment as "the people of the Lord."—These four cups were considered of such importance for the *Seder*-evening that the poor were provided as of right with wine for the *arba kosoth* (Mishnah, Pesachim x. 1).—Although the number of the four cups of wine is sanctioned by the reference to the above four expressions of redemption, a fifth cup may, if needed, be interpolated before singing Ps. cxxxvi. (Tosaphoth, Pesachim 117*b*).

It is customary to pour in an extra cup and keep it ready for any new-comer that might join the company. The cup is called כוס של אליהו "the cup of Elijah," because his advent may be looked for at any time. Comp. Mal. iii. 23.

[1] Two of them are the "double portion," לחם משנה, of Sabbath and Holy-day. The third represents the לחם עני "bread of poverty," and is therefore broken into pieces, in order to be distinguished from the others as "bread of poverty." The bread of poverty is intended to remind us of the bread of poverty or affliction eaten by our forefathers when kept as slaves in Egypt. But *les extrèmes se touchent ;* it is remarkable that this very term לחם עני admits also of the meaning "bread of song," and has been interpreted to signify the bread eaten at a joyous meal, such as the Israelites in Egypt ate the night of their liberation. It is possible that the author of the opening paragraph of the *Haggadah* purposely employed the term לחמא עניא in this double sense (Pes. 115*a*).

Among some Israelites it is the custom to style the three unleavened cakes, Cohen, Levi, and Israel. The three *matsoth*, as a play upon words, are also called *mitsvoth*, "commandments ; " *i.e.*, *matsoth* employed in fulfilment of the commandment, "In the evening ye shall eat unleavened bread." These *matsoth* are distinguished from the rest by being baked especially for this purpose. Some are careful in regard to these *matsoth* to have every process in their preparation, from the cutting of the wheat to the baking of the *matsoth*, done for the express purpose of the *Seder*, and to have the wheat and the flour well guarded from moisture or any foreign admixture. *Matsoth* prepared in this way other vegetables;[1] (3) salt water, in which the vegetables (*karpas*) are dipped before they are eaten, and *charoseth*, a mixture of apples, almonds, various spices, especially cinnamon, and wine, in which mixture the bitter herbs are dipped;[2] (4) a bone with some meat on it and an egg,[3] both roasted.

The order of the Service is indicated in most

are called מצה שמורה, "guarded *matsoth.*" People still more particular have all their unleavened bread for Passover prepared in this way.

[1] The vegetables, that were ordinarily taken as a relish and a means of producing appetite for the meal, have only been introduced here (Pesachim 114*b*) for the purpose of attracting the attention of the children. According to the custom of those ancient days, the master of the house had before him a table covered with the different dishes required for the meal, and sent portions to every member of the company. When the meal was finished, before Grace, this table was removed. But on the *Seder*-evening the table was removed immediately after the partaking of a little parsley or other vegetables. The child, accustomed on ordinary evenings to have supper without such an introduction, asks expressly or implicitly why things are different to-night, adding also other questions. Instead of parsley, other vegetables, or even some of the bitter herbs, may be taken. This last act not being an essential element in the Service, and not being obligatory, is not preceded by the *berachah*, "Blessed art thou . . . who hast commanded us, &c.," but "Blessed art thou . . . who hast created the fruit of the earth."—At present the table is not removed, but the lifting up of the *Seder*-dish while reciting the first paragraph (כהא לחמא) is the survival of that custom.

[2] Two views are expressed in the Talmud concerning *charoseth :* (1) it is a medicinal protective against the evil effects of the bitter herbs ; (2) it is an essential part of the *mitsvah*, a symbol and reminder of the bricks and mortar with which the Israelites had to do the work imposed on them by their taskmasters (B. Talm., Pesachim 115*b*) ; it may also serve to suggest to us the idea that there is a means of softening the bitterness of oppression, viz., faith in God (Mishnah, Pesachim x. 3).

[3] The bone and the egg are symbols of two dishes that used in the time of the Temple to be on the table : the Passover sacrifice and the festive offering called חגיגה ; the latter was added when the company was large (*ibid.* vi. 3, and B. Talm., Pes. 114*b*).

editions of the *Haggadah* in rhymed Hebrew as follows :—

קַדֵּשׁ וּרְחַץ . כַּרְפַּס יַחַץ . מַגִּיד רָחַץ . מוֹצִיא מַצָּה .

שֻׁלְחָן עֹרֵךְ . מָרוֹר כֹּרֵךְ . צָפוּן בָּרֵךְ . הַלֵּל נִרְצָה :

The following is the explanation of these lines :—

1. קדש Say *Kiddush.*   See above, page 379.

2. רחץ " Wash," *scil.*, your hands.—Only the head of the family does so at this part of the Service.[1]

3. כרפס " Vegetables."   A piece of parsley or salad or bitter herb is dipped in salt water, and eaten after the recitation of the blessing : בָּרוּךְ . . . בּוֹרֵא פְּרִי הָאֲדָמָה " Blessed art thou . . . who hast created the fruit of the ground." [2]

4. יחץ " He divides."   Of the three *matsoth* before him, the head of the family breaks the middle one, part of which is laid aside, to be eaten at the end of the meal." [3]

5. מגיד " Relating," [4] *scil.*, the history of the de-

---

[1] The eating of anything dipped in water or in any other liquid was usually preceded by the washing of the hands.   But as the eating of vegetables at this point is not obligatory, the reader alone washes his hands, but without reciting the blessing, עַל נְטִילַת יָדִים.

[2] See p. 381, note 1.

[3] Comp. p. 380, note 1.   The part laid aside is called *afikuman,* a name of which many curious etymologies have been suggested.   The meaning is clear ; it is that which is eaten just before the table is removed (p. 381, note 1), or before the dishes are cleared away : the dessert.   The name is therefore a compound of two Chaldaic words, *afiku-man,* " dish-remover," *i.e.*, the dessert after which all dishes are removed and the company is ready for Grace (B. T. Pesachim 86a Rashi).

[4] The term is derived from the words of the Pentateuch, וְהִגַּדְתָּ לְבִנְךָ " And thou shalt tell thy son " (Exod. xiii. 8).   Hence also the name of the book *Haggadah.*

parture from Egypt. The reader, pointing to the broken מצה before him, exclaims, "Such was the bread of poverty which our forefathers ate in the land of Egypt;" as if to say, "We are all alike descendants of those who ate the bread of poverty in Egypt." In the same sense, the reader continues, "We all alike should rejoice in the kindnesses shown by the Almighty to our nation, and all alike should seek and find true comfort in the hope of the Messianic blessing promised by Him for the future."[1] One of the company, usually the youngest, puts to the reader four questions, as formulated in the paragraph beginning מה נשתנה "Why is different?"[2] Additions and alterations may, of course, be made by the inquirer according to his knowledge and intellect. The object of these questions is to obtain an explanation of the rites that distinguish this evening from others. In answer to these questions, the reader refers to the past history of Israel in three different forms,[3] viz. :—

(1.) The first answer begins, עבדים היינו, "We were

[1] The first paragraph is not an invitation sent forth to those whom it cannot reach, but an appeal to those present to join heartily in the Service and the succeeding meal; that none should feel ashamed of his poverty, none elated on account of his possessions; all having been brethren in past troubles, and in the deliverance from them, and all destined alike to share in the glories of the coming redemption.

[2] The questions have been arranged according to their importance; otherwise the third question might have been expected first (see p. 381, note [1]). The expression "dipping" (טבול) used in this question merely signifies "taking some relish," in distinction from the real and solid meal, and the meaning of the question is, "Why do we to-night partake twice of the vegetables before approaching the actual meal? It indicates a festive supper. What is the reason for this?"

[3] The three different forms correspond perhaps to the three characters or ages of the inquirers: the ignorant, the simple, and the sceptic;

slaves;" and ends, בשעה שיש מצה ומרור מונחים לפניך
"When unleavened bread and bitter herbs lie before
thee." Here the reader restricts himself, without any
comment, to the one fact that our forefathers were at
first slaves in Egypt, and were then delivered, and
illustrates the duty of speaking that night more fully
concerning the departure from Egypt, by precedent, by
the authority of the Mishnah, and by the Midrashic
interpretation of the law commanding us to tell our
children this event.

(2.) The second form of the answer begins, מתחלה
עבדי עבודה זרה היו אבתינו "Our forefathers were at first
worshippers of idols," and ends, מצילנו מידם "delivers us
out of their hand." Here the exodus from Egypt is
described as the fulfilment of the promise made by God
to Abraham, that his descendants would be delivered
out of the hands of their oppressors.

(3.) The passage from Deut. xxvi. 5–8 is recited
with its Midrashic interpretations,[1] and in conclusion
all the benefits received by the Israelites from the

whilst the answer to the wise has not been formulated, but depends
on his question, and the capacity of the father to instruct him. It
is only the general question as to the difference between the *Seder*-
evening and other evenings that is answered in these three forms.
Each of these forms was probably followed by the explanation of
Pesach, Matsah, and *Maror.*

[1] The Midrashic comparison of "finger of God" to "His hand"
and the multiplication of the number of plagues must not be understood as intended to gratify our feeling of revenge, but merely as a
simple and child-like illustration of the greatness of the Divine Power
displayed on those occasions.—Rabbi Jehudah, probably from a feeling of tender sympathies with the sufferers, would not mention even
the full names of the plagues, but merely indicated them by initial
letters.

departure from Egypt till the building of the Temple are enumerated, and our duty of gratitude is shown.

In all these three forms no notice has been taken of the particular questions. Rabban Gamaliel insists that this should be done, and a section is therefore added, containing the explanation why the Passover-offering, the unleavened bread, and the bitter herbs were to be eaten; this, like the three other sections, concludes with the emphatic declaration that we—after so many generations—are still bound to praise and to thank God for the benefits bestowed upon our nation so long ago. Hereupon follows the *Hallel*, of which the first two paragraphs, containing special reference to the departure from Egypt, are sung before supper; the first part of the Seder-Service concludes with a blessing, in which we praise God for our past deliverance and pray for the approach of our future redemption.

6. רחץ "Washing." All those who partake of the meal wash their hands, as is ordinarily done before meals.

7. מוציא מצה. Two pieces of מצה are taken; one piece, broken off the whole cake, representing the bread eaten at ordinary meals for מוציא, and the other piece taken from the broken one, representing the מצה we are commanded to eat on the Seder-night. Before eating the two pieces two blessings are recited . . . ברוך המוציא לחם מן הארץ "Blessed art thou . . . who bringest forth bread from the earth," and . . . ברוך . . . אשר קדשנו על אכילת מצה "Blessed art thou . . . who hast sanctified us by Thy commandments and hast commanded us to eat מצה." [1]

---

[1] It seems that in the time of the Talmud the one piece was eaten after the first blessing, and the other after the second. As, therefore,

8. מרור "Bitter herb." Bitter herbs dipped in *charoseth* are eaten, after the following blessing has been recited ברוך . . . אשר קדשנו . . . על אכילת מרור "Blessed art thou . . . who hast sanctified us by thy commandments and hast commanded us to eat bitter herbs."

9. כורך "Combining;" *scil.*, unleavened bread and bitter herbs; these are eaten together, just as formerly, in the time of the Temple, Hillel used to eat together meat of the Passover-offering, unleavened bread, and bitter herbs (Exod. xii. 8; Num. ix. 11).

10. שלחן עורך "Table laid." The evening meal is taken.

11. צפן "Laid aside." The meal is concluded with a piece of the half *matsah* that has been laid aside at the beginning of the Service. It is called *afikuman*, "dessert." [1]

the partaking of *matsah* has taken place before the second blessing, the formula על אכילת מצה is used (see p. 329, note 2). The same is the case with regard to the blessing before "eating bitter herbs," as it was not contrary to usage to partake of bitter herbs instead of *karpas* at the beginning of the Service.

[1] The *afikuman* has been reserved wrapped in a napkin (reminding of Exod. xii. 34), in order that the meal should finish up with *matsah*, just as in the time of the Temple it finished up with meat of the Pass-over-sacrifice.—In the Talmud (Pes. 109a) the rule is given וחוטפין מצה "We make haste to come quickly to the eating of *matsah*," before the younger members of the company become drowsy or fall asleep. The words וחוטפין מצה have erroneously been interpreted, "We should snatch away the *matsah*," and this interpretation caused the Service to be accompanied by a certain kind of childish amusement: some one of the company stealthily possesses himself of the *matsah* laid aside for *afikuman*, and does not surrender it until the master of the house promises him some present.—The custom is unseemly and ought to be discouraged.

I 2. ברך " Say grace." [1]

I 3. הלל " *Hallel.*"—The rest of *Hallel* is sung, followed by Ps. cxxxvi., and the whole of נשמת with the concluding blessing.—The fourth cup of wine is then taken, and the usual prayer after the partaking of wine is recited.

I 4. נרצה " Completed." [2] — The Seder-Service is

---

[1] After Grace a few verses from the Bible (Ps. lxxix. 6, 7, and Lam. iii. 66) have been added, beginning שפך חמתך and containing a prayer for God's wrath to be poured forth over the godless peo who seek the destruction of Israel. The cause of the addition is this : The season of Passover was, in the Middle Ages, a season of constant terror and danger to the Jews, because of the hostilities of their Christian neighbours against them. Helpless and defenceless, the Jews had no other way of meeting their foe than to cry to Him "who is near to all who call upon Him in truth." The conduct of their neighbours towards them hardly suggested thoughts of love, especially at that moment. For it frequently happened that several families met in one house for the purpose of hearing the Seder-Service. They dispersed after the first part of the Service, took their meals at home, and assembled later in the evening for the second part of the Seder. Sometimes another course was taken. One person read the Service in several houses consecutively for the benefit of those who were not capable of doing so for themselves ; then, after having had his meal, he began his circuit again for reading the second part of the Service. The return of the Reader or of the several families was anxiously waited for. The opening of the door before שפך חמתך, at present meaningless, had its origin in this circumstance. On returning to the second part of the Service, the guests had too often a sad tale to tell of their experiences in the street, and filled with indignation, they gave expression to their feeling in the above verses. We continue to read these verses now, but in a different spirit. We live in peace with our neighbours, protected by the laws of the country and unmolested in the performance of our religious duties. We have nothing but feelings and thoughts of love for our fellow-men, and in reciting these verses we merely condemn the wickedness of those who seek the destruction of the people of the Lord. Our Christian neighbours may certainly join us in this condemnation.

[2] Comp. Isa. xl. 2.

completed ; it concludes with a prayer for the rebuilding of the Temple and the restoration of Israel
to Zion. The prayer seems to have been originally
the conclusion of a *Piyyut* or liturgical poem on the
Passover Sacrifice.

The *Haggadah* contains, besides, several hymns and
songs, of which the following are found in the ordinary
editions of the work :—

1. ויהי בחצי הלילה " And it was in the middle of the
night." The author reflects on the various marvellous
events in our history that happened in the night-time.

2. ואמרתם זבח פסח " And ye shall say, It is a sacrifice of Passover." A song referring to wonderful
events which, according to Tradition, took place on
Passover.

3. כי לו נאה " To him praise is seemly." A praise
of God as the only Being worthy to be called King
and Ruler.

4. אדיר הוא " He is mighty." A praise of God, and
an expression of hope that He will soon rebuild the
Temple.

5. אחד מי יודע " One, who knows ? " A popular
song enumerating persons and objects in Jewish History and Tradition, as well as in Nature according to
numbers up to thirteen, with the object of emphasising
the Unity of God.

6. חד גדיא " One kid." A popular song that illustrates the working of Divine Justice in the history of
mankind.

Passover as an agricultural feast was kept " in the
season of the month of ripeness " (למועד חדש האביב),

when the barley sown in the winter had become ripe. On the second day of Passover an offering was brought of "the beginning of the harvest;" it consisted of an *omer* [1] of barley (Lev. xxiii. 9 *sqq.*). Before this offering was presented it was not allowed to eat of the new corn (*ibid.* 14).

From the bringing of the *Omer* to "the harvest feast" the days are counted, viz., forty-nine days, and the fiftieth day is the feast of harvest (חג הקציר), or "the day of the first-fruit offering" (יום הבכורים).

The counting commences on the second evening. It is done either immediately after *Maarib*, or later on during the Seder-Service; it is preceded by the following blessing: ברוך . . . אשר קדשנו . . . על ספירת העומר "Blessed art thou . . . who hast sanctified us by thy commandments and hast commanded us . . . to count the days of the *Omer*." The following is the way of counting: היום יום . . . לעומר "This day is the first day since the *Omer*." From seven upward the number of weeks is likewise expressed,[2] . . . היום יום . . . שהם שבועות . . . לעומר "This day completes . . . that is . . . weeks . . . since the offering of the *Omer*."

The celebration of Passover serves to inculcate into our hearts the first principle of our faith: the existence of God, the Supreme Being who rules the whole universe, in whose hand are the destinies of kings and peoples, whose power was recognised by the Egyptians when they were punished for their mis-

---

[1] An *omer* is, according to Tradition, equal to the space occupied by 43⅕ eggs of ordinary size; it is about half a gallon.

[2] Or . . . לעומר שהם . . . היום (Portug. Ritual).

deeds, and whose might was seen by the Israelites when He divided the Red Sea for them, and fulfilled the Divine promise made to the patriarchs, Abraham, Isaac, and Jacob.

The season of Passover, in which we celebrate our liberation from earthly taskmasters, is called זמן חרותנו "The season of our freedom." The deliverance from Egypt, the first step leading to the fulfilment of the promise, " And I will take you unto me for a people," has been poetically conceived as the betrothal of Israel to God, and in the *Piyyut* for Passover ample use has been made of this idea. It has further found expression in the custom of reading the Song of Solomon on the first *Sabbath* after the first two days of Passover, and by some also on the Seder-evening after the conclusion of the ordinary Service.

The Service is, in general outline, the same as on Sabbath. It consists of *Maarib, Shacharith, Musaph,* and *Minchah.* The Morning-Service includes *Hallel,* the reading of the Law, and Lessons from the Prophets (קריאת התורה and הפטרה). The following sections, containing description of, or reference to, Passover or to the departure from Egypt, are read consecutively on the eight days: Exod. xii. 21—51, on the Passover celebrated by the Israelites in Egypt; Lev. xxii. 26 to xxiii. 44, on " the seasons of the Lord ; " Exod. xiii., xxii. 24 to xxiii. 19, and xxxiv. 1—26: Num. ix. 1—14, on the second Passover; Exod. xiii. 17—xv. 26, the crossing of the Red Sea ; Deut. xv. 19 (on Sabbath, xiv. 22) to xvi. 17 contains laws referring to the three Festivals. On *Sabbath chol-ha-moëd,* Exod. xxxiii. 12 to xxxiv. 26.—In addition to these sections

verses from Num. xxviii.–xxix., referring to the sacrifices prescribed for each day of the Festival, are read
from a second *sefer*.

The Lessons from the Prophets are the following :—
Josh. v. (preceded in the German Ritual by iii. 5—7),
on the first Passover kept by the Israelites in Palestine ; 2 Kings xxiii. 1—9 and 21—25, on the Passover celebrated in the days of King Josiah ; 2 Sam.
xxii., the song of David after deliverance from his
enemies, a parallel to the Song of Moses ; Isa. x.
32—xii., on the defeat of Sennacherib, and the blessings of the Messianic days. According to Tradition
the defeat of Sennacherib took place on Passover ;
moreover, the celebration of the deliverance from
Egypt suggests the reflection on the final Redemption
of Israel. The Lesson from the Prophets chosen for
Sabbath chol-ha-moëd is taken from Ez. xxxvi. 1—14.
The prophet sees in a vision how the dry bones of the
dead are awakened to fresh life by the Will and the
Spirit of the Lord : a precious lesson for us, designed
to strengthen our hope of a revival of every good
and noble idea, though for the present it be dormant
within us. Nature around us awakening to fresh life
in the spring supplies a parallel to the vision of
Hezekiel.

The *Machzor* (lit. Cycle) or Prayer-book for the Holy-
days contains numerous additions to the ordinary prayers.
They are called *Piyyutim,* and vary according to the
custom and the taste of the congregation. The *Piyyut*
added in the second paragraph of the *Musaph-amidah* on
the first day of Passover is called *tal,* " dew," or prayer
for dew ; the rain season having come to an end, we

pray that the vegetation may, during the hot season, be refreshed by the regular descent of the dew. The praise for " sending down rain " in the same paragraph, viz., משיב הרוח ומוריד הגשם, " Thou causest the wind to blow and the rain to fall," is discontinued after the *shacharith* prayer of the first day of Passover. In the Portuguese Ritual the words מוריד הטל, " Thou causest the dew to fall," are introduced instead.

Similarly, there is an additional prayer for rain (גשם) in the *Musaf* of *Shemini-atsereth.* The time chosen for these prayers is in accordance with the meteorological conditions of Palestine. This custom, however, does not exclude the addition of prayers for rain or dew, according to the needs of the country in which we live.

The Days of the Counting of the Omer, ימי הספירה

The period from Passover to the Feast of Weeks is full of sad memories of massacres of Jews that took place in the days of the Crusades; also of the miseries that befell the Jews in Palestine in the days of the Emperor Hadrian. During the month of *Iyar,* the Jews abstain from rejoicings and weddings,[1] with the exception of the 18th of the month, which is the 33rd of the *Omer,* because, according to Tradition, a plague that had raged among the disciples of Rabbi Akiba ceased on that day. The 18th of *Iyar,* ל"ג בעומר, is therefore called " the scholars' festival."

---

[1] As the month of *Iyar* corresponds to some extent to May, some assert, without foundation, that the Jews hold no weddings this month, because May is held by non-Jews to be an unlucky season for marriages. Jews who refuse to celebrate marriages in May for this reason are guilty of gross superstition.

The Feast of Weeks, שבועות

The Feast of Weeks is celebrated on the fiftieth day [1] of the *Omer* (Lev. xxiii. 16); *i.e.,* the 6th of *Sivan.* It is, in the first place, "the feast of harvest," חג הקציר (Exod. xxiii. 16), especially of the wheat, and "the day of the first-fruit offering," יום הבכורים (Num. xxviii. 26). The first sacrifice of the new corn was offered: "the bread of the first-fruit," which was to serve as an expression of gratitude for the blessing of the harvest. In the absence of sacrifices in our days, the custom widely prevails of adorning the Synagogue and the home with plants and flowers, in order that the sight of these beautiful objects might awaken and strengthen feelings of gratitude toward the Almighty for His loving-kindness. Each one of the plants and flowers reveals a special form of the Creator's wisdom, power, and goodness.—The feast is called Feast of Weeks, חג השבעות (Deut. xvi. 10), on account of the completion of the seven weeks counted from the day of the *Omer.*

The Feast of Weeks, the 6th and the 7th of *Sivan,* commemorates also an historical event: the Law-giving on Mount Sinai. It is therefore called "the season of the giving of our Law," זמן מתן תורתנו.

As Passover has been poetically called the day of Israel's betrothal to God, the Feast of Weeks would

---

[1] According to the traditional interpretation of ממחרת השבת "from the morrow after the Sabbath," the term "Sabbath" signifies "day of rest" or "festival," and refers to the first day of Passover (comp. Lev. xxiii. 32). The Sadducees, and afterwards the Karaites, contested the correctness of this interpretation, but without success (see Babyl. Talm., Menachoth 65 ; and Ibn Ezra on Lev. xxiii. 15).

correspond to the wedding-day, and the counting of the *Omer* does thus not only connect two harvest-feasts, but represents the longing of the bride for the day of her complete happiness; *i.e.*, the longing of the Israelites for the Divine Revelation, which was to complete the work of their deliverance from Egypt.

The celebration of the Feast of Weeks thus involves the second principle of our faith : תורה מן השמים " The belief in the Divine origin of the Law," or " Divine Revelation."

On the first day we read Exod. xix.–xx., the account of the Law-giving on Mount Sinai, and Ez. i., the first vision of the prophet Ezekiel, in which the glory of God is revealed to him. On the second day Deut. xv. 19 (on Sabbath, xiv. 22) to xvi. 17 ; and Hab. iii., " the prayer of Habakkuk," in reference to God's Revelation as the Ruler of the universe.—There is also the custom to read the Book of Ruth, which contains the account of Ruth's embracing the true faith, and a description of the harvest and the treatment of the poor in the harvest-season.

There is a custom among some of our brethren to employ the first night of the Feast in preparing themselves for the coming celebration of the giving of the Law. The greater part of the night is spent in reading passages from the Scriptures and from the Talmudical books.[1] The custom has its basis in the preparation commanded by God to be made during " the three days of bordering " (שלשת ימי הגבלה) which preceded the Law-giving (Exod. xix. 10–12).

---

[1] The collection of these passages is called תקון לליל שבועות. A similar collection for the seventh night of Tabernacles is called תקון לליל הושענא רבא. See p. 398, note 1.

The Feast of Tabernacles, סכות

" **The** fifteenth day of this seventh month (*Tishri*) shall be the Feast of Tabernacles (סכות) for seven days unto the Lord " (Lev. xxiii. 34). The name has its explanation in the commandment, " Ye shall dwell in booths seven days " (*ibid.* 42) ; " that your generations may know that I made the children of Israel to dwell in booths, when I brought them out of the land of Egypt " (ver. 43). We are thus commanded to commemorate the travelling of the Israelites through the wilderness. They dwelt in tents, that gave them shelter to some extent ; but without the Divine protection this shelter would have proved insufficient. Of this twofold shelter and protection we are reminded by the tabernacle in which the Law commands us to dwell during the Festival.

In fulfilment of this commandment we make booths (סכות). The chief difference between a booth and an ordinary house consists in the mode and in the material employed for roofing the two structures. For the *succah* must not be covered with fixed boards and beams or with canvas, but with detached branches of trees, plants, flowers, and leaves, in such a manner that the covering is not quite impenetrable to wind and rain, or starlight. During the Festival the *succah* is our dwelling-house, in which we take our meals, study, receive our friends, and, if possible, enjoy rest and sleep. If, on account of the severity of the climate, the constant dwelling in the *succah* threatens to prove injurious to our health, we content ourselves with taking our meals in the *succah*. Before each meal

we recite the blessing ברוך . . . אשר קדשנו . . . לישב בסוכה
"Blessed art thou . . . who hast sanctified us by thy
commandments and hast commanded us to dwell in
the booth." The first time we are in the *succah* we
add the blessing, שהחינו (p. 358).

The Festival is, secondly, called "the Feast of
Ingathering," חג האסיף. The produce of the fields and
gardens have been gathered in, and the people rejoice
before the Lord in gratitude for the blessings which
He has granted to them. "And ye shall take unto
you on the first day the fruit of the goodly tree,
branches of palm-trees, and boughs of thick-leaved
trees, and willows of the brook; and ye shall rejoice
before the Lord your God seven days" (Lev. xxiii.
40). In accordance with the traditional interpretation of this verse, we take four kinds of plants
(ארבעה מינין), viz., אתרוג "the citron;" לולב, "a branch
of the palm-tree;" הדסים, three "myrtle branches;"
and ערבות, two "branches of the willow." According
to a *Midrashic* interpretation, they represent four
different types of plants, that which has a pleasant
fragrance and a beautiful form (*esrog*); the beautiful in
form, but without fragrance (*lulabh*); that which smells
pleasantly, but is inferior in form (*hadassim*); and that
which has neither a goodly form nor an agreeable
fragrance (*arabhoth*), as if to say that we are thankful to
God for all that He has given us, although to our mind
some of these seem imperfect in comparison with others.

In obedience to this commandment we take, every
day of *Succoth* except Saturday,[1] the above four kinds

---

[1] On Sabbath the *lulabh* is not taken, because it might be necessary
to carry it from place to place through the street (רשות הרבים), and

into our hands, hold them during the recitation of the
Hallel, and make with them a procession round the
Synagogue,[1] while singing the hymns called *hoshaanoth* (so called on account of the repeated occurrence
of the word *hoshaanah* in them).

Before taking the *arbaah minim* into our hands we
say the following blessing: . . . אשר קדשנו . . . ברוך
על נטילת לולב " Blessed art thou . . . who hast sanctified us by thy commandments and hast commanded
us to take the *lulabh*."[2] On the first day שהחינו is
added.

Succoth lasts seven days, the last five days being
half Holy-days, חול המועד. The seventh day is called
Hoshaana-rabba, because on that day many prayers
beginning with *hoshaana* are offered up, during the

this is forbidden (see Mishnah, Shabbath i. 1 and vii. 2). For the same
reason the *shofar* is not blown on the first day of New-year, if it happens
to fall on Saturday. In the Temple, however, there was no occasion
for the above apprehension ; the *lulabh* was therefore taken and the
shofar was blown on Sabbath (Mishnah, Succah iv. 1, and Rosh ha-
shanah iv. 1).

[1] In the Temple willow-branches were placed round the altar, the
shofar was blown, and the priests made then a circuit round the altar,
with the *lulabh* in their hands, and singing part of *Hallel.*—The *hoshaanoth* refer chiefly to the redemption of Israel and the rebuilding of the
Temple.—The circuit round the altar reminds us of the taking of
Jericho, and strengthens our hope that in future also the Almighty
will be with us, and help us through all difficulties to ultimate
victory.

[2] The *lulabh* alone is mentioned in the blessing, because it is the
most prominent, and the other three species seem to be its appendages.
—The form על נטילת is explained by the fact that we generally hold
the four species in our hand, and thus commence the *mitsvah,* before
the *berachah* (see p. 329, note 2).—The three species, palm-branch,
myrtle, and willow, are usually bound together by means of leaves
of the palm-tree. Some used to add golden bands to these leaves
(Mishnah, Succah iii. 8).

chanting of which seven processions round the Synagogue are made.[1]

The Feast of Tabernacles is closely followed by " the feast of the eighth day," שמיני עצרת,[2] which, like all other Festivals, is kept two days. The second day is, in addition, called " Rejoicing of the Law," שמחת תורה

---

[1] Mishnah, Succah iv. 5.—In the Temple the *shofar* was sounded during the priests' circuit round the altar. A similar custom exists in the Spanish and Portuguese Synagogues on *Hoshaana-rabba.*—Tradition attributed great importance to the Morning Service on *Hoshaana-rabba,* and made it a kind of sequel to the Service on the "Solemn Days," as if to give another opportunity of repentance to those who had not made full use of the means of grace afforded by the Day of Atonement, before the final sentence (נמר חתימה טובה) is pronounced. The preceding evening is therefore spent by many in devotional exercises (תקון לליל הושענא רבא). Comp. p. 394.

It is an old custom to take a few extra twigs of the willow-tree on this day and keep them in one's hand during the chanting of the *hoshaanoth.* These branches, when shaken or struck, lose their leaves one after the other ; so do the trees from which the branches have been cut, and so also all other trees. But the rain and heat sent by God in due time give them fresh life, and they produce new leaves. A similar experience is ours. The struggle for life reduces our strength and weakens our health ; cares and troubles discourage us. But faith in God and trust in His Providence renew our strength ; our health improves, our cares and troubles are diminished, and we feel ourselves restored to fresh life.

[2] Lit. "the eighth day, a festival."—A prayer for rain (גשם) is inserted in the *Musaf*-Service, and corresponds to the prayer for dew on the first day of Passover ; for fine weather we pray on the *first* day of the Festival, for rain on the *eighth* day. From *Shemini-atsereth* to the *Musaf* of the first day of Passover the words משיב הרוח ומוריד הגשם "Thou causest the wind to blow and the rain to fall," are inserted in the second paragraph of the *Amidah.* The words do not contain a direct prayer for rain, but a praise of Him who causes the rain to fall (גבורות גשמים), whilst the daily direct prayer for rain (ותן טל ומטר "Give dew and rain ") begins about two months later,—the time when the pilgrims that had come from distant countries to Jerusalem to the Festival were assumed to have reached their homes.

because on this day the reading of the Pentateuch is completed and recommenced.

The nine days of the Festival are called זמן שמחתנו "The season of our rejoicing," and it is the third principle of our faith, the belief in Divine Providence, that this Festival impresses on our hearts. On the one hand, we have the rejoicing and the four species of plants as proofs and tokens of Divine blessing; and, on the other hand, the *succah* is a symbol of human frailties and imperfections. Thus, in all our rejoicings we should remember that our abode on earth is not permanent, and that all earthly happiness is like the plants that easily fade away. In order to impress this idea on our mind, we read the book of *Koheleth* on *Sabbath chol-ha-moëd* or on *Shemini-atsereth*.

The following portions are read from the Pentateuch: Lev. xxii. 26 to xxiii. 44[1] (on the first two days); Exod. xxxiii. 12 to xxxiv. 26 (on *Sabbath chol-ha-moëd*); Deut. xiv. 22 to xvi. 7 (on the eighth day); Deut. xxxiii. to end of Pentateuch; and Gen. i. 1 to ii. 3 (on *Simchath Torah*). In addition, the paragraph of the sacrifices of the day (Num. xxix. 12—39) is read

---

[1] It has always been considered a special *mitsvah* and honour to be called to the reading either of the last or of the first section of the Pentateuch. Those on whom this honour is conferred are called respectively חתן תורה "Bridegroom of the Law," and חתן בראשית "Bridegroom of the first section of the Law." In the rejoicing with the Law special efforts are made to induce the younger members of the congregation to take part. They are usually invited to join the procession with the scrolls of the Law round the Synagogue, and have also the privilege of being called to the Torah, although they are not yet thirteen years old. This and similar things are done in order to inspire our children with love for the Torah and for the study of the Torah.

from a second *sefer*. The Lessons for *chol-ha-moed* are taken from the same passage.

The Lessons from the Prophets are the following: Zech. xiv., prophecy on the future of Israel and on the punishment of those who would not come to Jerusalem to celebrate there the *Succoth* Festival; I Kings viii. 2–21, on the opening of the new Temple; on *Sabbath chol-ha-moëd*, Ez. xxxviii. 18 to xxxix. 16, on the war with Gog; I Kings viii. 22–66, prayer of Solomon on the eighth day of the services for the consecration of the Temple; Jos. i., accession of Joshua to the leadership of Israel.

Solemn Days, ימים נוראים

By ימים נוראים "solemn days," we understand the first ten days of the month *Tishri*, especially their beginning and their end: ראש השנה, "New-year," and יום כפור "the Day of Atonement."[1]

It is customary to prepare for the "solemn days" during the month of *Elul*, by additional prayers, called סליחות "forgiveness," after or before the Daily Service, and by blowing the *shofar* at the close of the

---

[1] Whilst the three Festivals demanded great sacrifices of each individual Israelite—to undertake a pilgrimage to the Temple, and not to appear empty before the Lord—the "Solemn Days" demanded only abstention from work, and on one day also from food. The Sacrificial Service on the Day of Atonement concerned directly the High-Priest and the priests in the Temple, the public at large but indirectly; and if great multitudes assembled in the Temple, it was curiosity rather than duty that brought them there. More importance was therefore attached by chroniclers and historians to the three Festivals and the national gathering in and round the Temple on the Feasts of Pilgrimage than to the Day of Memorial or the Day of Atonement. The Law

Daily Service.[1] According to the Portuguese Ritual, the *Selichoth* begin on the 1st of *Elul*, and are continued

deemed it necessary to urge on the Israelites the celebration of the former more frequently than that of the latter. When Solomon at the dedication of the Temple celebrated with the Israelites twice seven days, the first seven days probably commenced the 1st of *Tishri* on the Festival (1 Kings viii. 2), and the second seven days on the 15th of the month; therefore they are reckoned separately (*ibid.* viii. 65; 2 Chron. vii. 9, 10). Ezra, who read the Law to the Jews on the 1st of *Tishri* (Neh. viii. 2), which was a Holy-day (*ibid.* 10), read it also on the second day, which may likewise have been a special day for reading the Law, probably the Day of Atonement, and here they learnt that they were commanded to build booths for the next Festival. They must therefore have heard Leviticus xxiii., which includes the commandment concerning the fasting on the Day of Atonement. It may also be noticed that, although the commandment concerning the Day of Atonement is not mentioned in Exodus, the day is referred to as a well-known institution (Exod. xxx. 10).

[1] The reason Tradition assigns for this observance is as follows: After the giving of the Law Moses ascended Mount Sinai on the 7th of *Sivan*, and descended on the fortieth day, the 17th of *Tammuz*, with the tables of testimony. On the 18th he ascended again, and spent forty days in prayer for forgiveness for Israel; and ascended for the third time on the 1st of *Elul*, and returned on the 10th of *Tishri* with the Divine message, "I have pardoned in accordance with thy words of prayer." Cherishing the hope that we may ourselves receive such a heavenly response on the Day of Atonement, we follow the example of Moses, and add these *Selichoth* or devotional exercises to our daily prayers, while the sound of the *shofar* aids in awakening us to earnest reflection and true improvement.

There are various names for these additional prayers: תחנונים "Supplications," and סליחות "Prayers for forgiveness," the latter being the general name for the early additional Service. Some of them have special names: פתיחה "opening" (*i.e.*, the first prayer); פזמון "psalm," a hymn sung or recited alternately by the Reader and the congregation; עקדה a composition referring to the binding of Isaac; תחנה "supplication," generally at the end of the *Selichoth*. Prominent among these prayers is the recitation of the Thirteen Attributes of Mercy (Exod. xxxiv. 6, 7) and the "Confession of sins" (וידוי).

2 C

morning and evening till the Day of Atonement. The German Ritual has *Selichoth* only in the Morning Service; they begin on the Sunday before New-year, and if the Festival is on Monday or Tuesday, on the second Sunday before, and end on the Day of Atonement. The blowing of the *shofar* takes place in the German Synagogues during the month of *Elul*, in the Portuguese during the penitential days.

ראש השנה *New-year.*

The first and the second days of *Tishri* are kept as New-year.[1] In accordance with the command, " The first of the first-fruits of thy land thou shalt bring unto the house of the Lord thy God " (Exod. xxxiv. 26), we devote the first ten days of the year as an offering to the Lord ; they are days of increased devotion, earnest self-examination, and new efforts to lead a good, virtuous, and godly life. They are called עשׂרת ימי תשובה " ten days of return " to God, or " ten penitential days."

We greet and congratulate each other on New-year, using the phrase, לש׳ ט׳ תכתבי, תכתבו or—לשנה טובה תכתב תכתבנה according as a male, a female, several males, or several females are addressed—" May you be inscribed for a happy year." It is a figurative expression, borrowed from the writing and signing of decrees by earthly judges.

[1] Although *Nisan*, the month of the departure of the Israelites from Egypt, is the first month, and Passover the first of the Festivals of the year, *Tishri*, though the seventh month, was in many respects the beginning of the year. In the month of *Tishri* the Jubilee year commenced, the slaves were liberated, and landed property returned to the original owners (comp. Mishnah, Rosh ha-shanah i. 1).

In the Bible the Festival is not called New-year,[1]
but יום תרועה "Day of blowing the *shofar*" (Num.
xxix. 1); and זכרון תרועה "Memorial of the blowing
of the *shofar*" (Lev. xxiii. 24); in our prayers the
names יום הזכרון and יום הדין "Day of Remembering"
and "Day of Judgment," are also used.

The first of these four names implies, according to
the traditional interpretation, the commandment of
blowing the *shofar*. As a rule the *shofar* is blown
during the Morning Service before the *sefer* is returned
to the Ark, and during *Musaf*.[2] The blowing of the
shofar is expressed by תרועה, which denotes the sound
of an alarm; hence we learn that the *shofar* is intended
to awaken us, and to call us forth to range ourselves
under our banner. It is an ideal banner, the worship
of God and faith in Him, that we are called upon
to protect and to defend from enemies without and
within.[3] Prominence is therefore given in our Service
for New-year to the proclamation of God as King of
the universe, and to our longing for the time when all
mankind will unite in the worship of the One God.

[1] The name does, however, occur in the Mishnah as a term long in
use and well known. It is impossible to decide when the name was introduced. The words ראש השנה in Ez. (xl. 1) denote the beginning of
the year, including ten days or more, but do not signify "New-year."

[2] The blowing of the *shofar* is preceded by the blessing : . . . ברוך
אשר קדשנו . . . לשמוע קול שופר "Blessed art thou . . . who hast
sanctified us by thy commandments and hast commanded us to hear
the sound of the *shofar*." This blessing is followed by שהחינו.

[3] According to Saadiah, the *shofar* reminds us of the following ten
things with which it is directly or indirectly connected :—(1) Creation; (2) Our duty to return to God; (3) Revelation on Mount
Sinai; (4) The exhortations of the Prophets; (5) Destruction of the
Temple; (6) The binding of Isaac for sacrifice; (7) Imminent danger;
(8) Day of Judgment; (9) Redemption of Israel; (10) Resurrection.

The name "Memorial of blowing the *shofar*" indi
cates that we are to remember some historical event
suggested by the sound of the *shofar*. We are reminded of the period when the Israelites, encamped
round Mount Sinai, on hearing the Divine message,
"Ye shall be my peculiar people," "a kingdom of
priests," and "a holy nation," joyfully replied, "All
that the Lord hath spoken we will do" (Exod. xix. 8).
The *shofar* thus awakens us to greater watchfulness
and activity in the purification and sanctification of
our heart.

The third name, "Day of Memorial," seems to be a
modification of the second; but it has a more general
meaning. The second name, that reminds us of our
duty as God's peculiar people, suggests also the idea
that God, who declared us to be His people, watches
over us; that what we do, we do in His presence.
He perceives, notes, and remembers all our deeds,
words, and thoughts. When, therefore, we appeal to
the goodness of Him, who remembers all His creatures
and provides for the wants of every one of them, we
must not forget that He is also just. This idea, again,
suggests the fourth name, יום הדין "Day of Judgment,"
the day on which we are judged according to our
deeds, both our merits and our shortcomings being
taken into account.

The essential elements in our Service are the three
sections in the *Amidah* of *Musaf:* מלכיות, זכרונות and
שופרות. They chiefly refer to the three fundamental
principles of our religion: (1) Existence of God, a
Being that is King of the universe; (2) Divine
Justice, and (3) Revelation. Ten passages are quoted

from the Bible in support of each of these principles.

Tradition has fixed the 1st of *Tishri* as the date of
several events in the history of Israel, *e.g.*, the birth of
Isaac, the binding of Isaac (עקדה), and the birth of
Samuel (B. T. Rosh ha-shanah 10*b*). Hence Gen.
xxi. and xxii. are read on the two days of New-year,
in addition to the paragraph on the sacrifices of the
Festival (Num. xxix. 1–6).

From the Prophets, we read on the first day 1 Sam.
i. 1 to ii. 10, on the birth of Samuel, and the prayer
of Hannah praising the justice of God ; on the second
day, Jer. xxxi. 2–20, a prophecy concerning the restoration of Israel.[1]

The Sabbath between New-year and the Day of
Atonement is called שבת שובה because the *haphtarah,*
taken from Hosea (xiv. 1 *seq.*), commences with the
word שובה and is an exhortation of Israel to return
to God.

יום כפור *" Day of Atonement."*

The tenth day of the seventh month, *Tishri,* is the
most important of all the Holy-days. It is the Day
of Atonement, on which " God will forgive you, to
cleanse you, that you may be clean from all your sins
before the Lord " (Lev. xvi. 30).

---

[1] In some congregations it is the custom to walk in the afternoon
of New-year along the banks of a river or the sea-shore, in order to
reflect on the purifying effect which water has on the body, and to be
reminded that even as the body is purified by water, so ought our
souls be purified by repentance and the appeal to the help and mercy
of God. An appropriate passage from Micah (vii. 18–20) is recited,
and the custom has received its name *tashlich* from the word ותשליך
" and thou wilt cast," which occurs in the passage.

"Ye shall do no manner of work; it shall be a statute for ever throughout your generations in all your dwellings. It shall be unto you a sabbath of rest, and ye shall afflict yourselves: in the ninth day of the month at even, from even unto even, shall ye celebrate your sabbath" (Lev. xxiii. 31, 32).

The Day of Atonement is therefore a day of resting, fasting, prayer, and spiritual improvement.

It is a day of rest, and the prohibition of work is the same as on the ordinary Sabbath.

The fasting begins the 9th of *Tishri*—ערב יום כפור—about sunset, and lasts till the beginning of night on the following day. The phrase, ועניתם את נפשתיכם "Ye shall afflict yourselves," is explained by Tradition to signify the total abstinence from all kinds of food and the gratification of other bodily desires (Mishnah, Yoma viii. 1). The reason of this commandment may be the following: The principal source of sin is the gratification of our bodily appetites; תשובה "return" to the right way must therefore include the earnest attempt to control, and when necessary to suppress, such appetites. Fasting is such an attempt. But it must be borne in mind that fasting is only one of the duties we have to fulfil on the Day of Atonement, and that the other duties are equally essential.

תשובה "return," is the principal object of the celebration of the Day of Atonement; it implies the following four steps:—

1. *Consciousness of sin*, ידיעת החטא. We must again and again examine ourselves and try to discover our failings; our actions and our words must pass in review, and we must remember that, however good we may

be, no man is righteous upon earth "that doeth good
and sinneth not" (Eccles. vii. 20).

2. *Confession of sin,* וידוי.[1] On the discovery of
sin, we must have the courage to confess our guilt
before him against whom we have sinned; if it is
against God alone that we have sinned, we make
silent confession before Him; if we find ourselves
guilty of an offence against our fellow-man, we must
confess our sin to him.

3. *Regret,* חרטה. Having discovered and confessed
our sin, we should feel pain and remorse, alike for the
evil we have done and for the good we have left
undone.

4. *Amendment,* עזיבת החטא. The regret should be
followed by a firm resolve to abandon the way of evil,
and not to sin again, even if occasion be given for a
repetition of the sinful act.

There are five Services on the Day of Atonement:

[1] The confession of sins (וידוי) as contained in our Prayer-book is
made by the whole community collectively; and those who have not
themselves committed the sins mentioned in the confession regret
that they were unable to prevent them from being committed by
others. The form of the confession is therefore in the plural: "We
have been guilty," &c. The words אבל אנחנו חטאנו "Indeed we
have sinned," would suffice for the purpose of confession. But the
long lists of various forms of sins in the sections beginning אשמנו,
על חטא or על חטאים and which are repeatedly recited during the Service, help us to remember our misdoings; what has escaped our attention
the first time may be revived in our memory, when we read the confession a second or third time. Especially numerous are the terms denoting
sins committed with our tongue; and indeed they are numerous! And
where is the person that could say that his tongue has never been
employed in falsehood, or slander, or self-praise, or hasty promises, and
similar offences? It is necessary that we should reflect over and over
again on these vices, and on the way in which to obtain better control over
our tongue, and thereby a fuller mastery over the passions of our heart.

(1) Evening Service, מעריב;[1] (2) Morning Service, שחרית; (3) Additional Service, מוסף; (4) Afternoon Service, מנחה; (5) Concluding Service, נעילה.[2]—The

[1] The Evening Service is preceded by a formal rescinding of previous vows. Of what kind were the vows which are thus annulled? None of those that were made by a member of the community individually. No one can by means of this formula free himself from the obligation to fulfil what he has promised to his fellow-man. The declaration concerns the whole congregation, and has probably its origin in the customs of former days, when those who refused to join in the communal work, or to submit to the law of the congregation, or shocked by any act of theirs the conscience of their brethren, or abandoned Judaism outwardly, were excommunicated and shut out from all contact with their co-religionists. Such transgressors, *abarjanim*, when desirous to pray in the Synagogue on the Day of Atonement, were admitted, and all opposition was silenced by the solemn declaration.

That such was the original object of *Kol-nidre* is sufficiently clear from its surroundings. It is preceded by the following announcement: "In the name of God, and in the name of the congregation, with the sanction of the Court above, and that of the Court below, we declare that it is permitted to pray together with those who have been transgressors (*abarjanim*)." *Kol-nidre* is followed by the verse, "And it shall be forgiven all the congregation of the children of Israel, *and the stranger that sojourneth among them;* seeing all the people were in ignorance" (Num. xv. 26).

The original object of this declaration does not apply at present; but it serves as a reminder of the following principles :—

1. We should always be disposed to forgive those who, in the heat of strife, acting under strong irritation, have offended us.

2. We should be careful with regard to vows, and before making them consider their effect.

3. We should reflect on human weakness, and consider that what we believe to be able to do to-day may prove impossible for us to-morrow. This reflection would remove every thought of pride from our heart and inspire us with humility.

[2] At the conclusion of the Service we once more proclaim the Unity of God (שמע ישראל), repeat three times the praise of His kingdom, and seven times that He alone is the Almighty. The sound of the *shofar* announces, as on the occasion of the Revelation on Mount Sinai, the conclusion of the Holy-day.

confession of sin, ודוי is the most essential and characteristic element in the Services of the Day of Atonement.

In the Morning Service we read Lev. xvi., and Num. xxix. 7–11, on the sacrifices on the Day of Atonement; in the Afternoon Service, Lev. xviii., on forbidden marriages. The Lessons from the Prophets are: in the morning, Isa. lvii. 14–lviii. 14, on our duties on the fast-day; in the afternoon, the Book of Jonah, illustrating the effect of sincere repentance, and Micah vii. 18–20, on Israel's repentance.

HISTORICAL FEASTS AND FASTS.

Besides the Festivals commanded in the Torah, we celebrate also in the course of the year anniversaries of certain days both of joy and of sorrow. Of the former, kind are חנוכה and פורים; of the latter, the 9th of *Ab* and four other fasts.

חנוכה *Feast of Dedication.*

On the 25th of *Kislev* we begin to celebrate eight days of חנוכה or Dedication, in commemoration of the victories of the Maccabees over Antiochus Epiphanes, king of Syria. Antiochus had attempted to force the Jews to idolatry, and to make them abandon the worship of the true God. The Jews, led by the Maccabees, resisted, and, armed with faith in God, gained the victory over large armies of the enemy. The Temple, which had been defiled by the heathen soldiers, was again purified, and the Service of God re-established.

For lighting the continual lamp (נר תמיד) pure oil was wanted, that had not been touched by the heathen. Only a small cruse of pure oil was found, which was believed to be sufficient for one night; but it sufficed for eight days, by which time a fresh supply could be procured.

The Feast of Dedication commemorates the victory of the faithful over the faithless, of the true religion over idolatry, of light over darkness, and is celebrated—

(1.) By lighting חנוכה lights, one on the first evening, and adding one light each successive evening, so that on the eighth evening eight lights are kindled.

(2.) By giving expression to our feeling of gratitude in psalms (הלל) and prayers of thanks (על הנסים).

In the Morning Service a few verses from Num. vii., on the dedication of the Altar, are read. On *Sabbath Chanuccah*, Zechariah's vision, Zech. ii. 10 to iii. 7, including the vision of the golden candlestick, is read as *haphtarah;* and if there happen to be a second *Sabbath Chanuccah*, 1 Kings vii. 40–50, a description of the various vessels and ornaments in the Temple of Solomon is read on that Sabbath.

NOTE 1.—The חנוכה lights remind us, in the first place, of the reopening of the Temple and the resumption of the regular Temple Service. But they are also intended to remind us of the light of our holy faith, which Antiochus Epiphanes attempted in vain to extinguish. For it shed forth its light again, and shone brighter and brighter every successive day. We thus learn that when our religion is imperilled, firmness against temptation or force is sure to lead to success and victory.

2. Before lighting the *Chanuccah* lights the following blessings are said : ברוך . . . אשר קדשנו . . . להדליק נר של חנוכה "Blessed art thou . . . who hast sanctified us by thy commandments and hast commanded us to kindle the lights of *Chanuccah*."

"Blessed ברוך . . . שעשה נסים לאבותינו בימים ההם בזמן הזה
art thou . . . who wroughtest miracles for our fathers in days of
old at this season." On the first night שהחינו is added.

פורים *Purim.*

פורים or "Feast of Lots," is celebrated on the 14th
and the 15th of *Adar* (second *Adar* in a leap-year), in
commemoration of the defeat of Haman's wicked plans.
Haman was chief minister to Ahasuerus, king of Persia,
and planned to kill all the Jews in the Persian Empire,
but the Almighty frustrated his designs through the
agency of Mordecai and his cousin Esther. The Feast
is called *Purim*, that is, "lots," because Haman had
cast lots in order to discover the day most favourable
to his plans.

We celebrate *Purim*—

(I.) By reading twice, once during the Evening
Service and once during the Morning Service, the
Book of Esther (מגלת אסתר), which contains the history
of Haman's plans and their frustration. The reading
is preceded by the following blessing: ברוך . . . אשר
קדשנו . . . על מקרא מגלה "Blessed art thou . . . who
hast sanctified us by thy commandments and hast
commanded us to read the *Megillah*." ברוך . . . שעשה
נסים לאבותינו בימים ההם בזמן הזה "Blessed art thou . . .
who wroughtest miracles for our fathers in days of
old at this season," and שהחינו.

(2.) By giving presents to our friends (משלוח מנות)
and gifts to the poor (מתנות לאביונים).

(3.) By a festive meal (סעודת פורים). Comp. Esth.
ix. During the Morning Service the account of the
war with Amalek is read from Exod. xvii. 8—16.

The 15th of *Adar* is called *Shushan Purim*, because
the Jews in *Shushan* continued to fight against the
enemy on the 14th of *Adar*, and kept *Purim* on the
15th. The 13th of *Adar*, being the day appointed
for the slaughter of the Jews, is now kept as a fast-
day, and is called תענית אסתר " the Fast of Esther."

The Four Fasts.

There are four days kept as fast-days in commemoration of events connected with the fall of Jerusalem.
They are called in the Bible (Zech. viii. 19) " the fast
of the fourth month and the fast of the fifth, and
the fast of the seventh and the fast of the tenth."
These days are the anniversaries of the commencement
of the siege of Jerusalem (10th of *Tebeth*), of the breach
made in the wall (17th of *Tammuz*), of the destruction
of the Temple (9th of *Ab*), and of the murder of
Gedaliah (3rd of *Tishri*). The 9th of *Ab* is kept as a
day of fasting and mourning for the destruction of the
Temple. According to Tradition, both the first and
the second Temple were destroyed on the same day.

The Lesson from the Pentateuch read in the Morning
and in the Afternoon Services on the fast-days is Exod.
xxxii. 11—14 and xxxiv. 1—10. On the 9th of *Ab*
this section is read in the afternoon only ; the Morning
Lesson being Deut. iv. 25—40 and Jer. viii. 13 to ix.
23 ; in the Afternoon Service on all fasts Isa. lv. 6
to lvi. 8 is read as *haphtarah*.

NOTE 1.—These fasts begin with daybreak, except the fast of
the 9th of *Ab*, which commences with the previous evening and
lasts twenty-four hours, and is in all respects like that of the

Day of Atonement. During the day the Lamentations of Jeremiah, various elegies called קינות, "Lamentations," and the Book of Job are read. On the Fast of *Ab*, as a sign of mourning, *talith* and *tefillin* are not worn during the Morning Service. They are, however, put on for the Afternoon Service.

2. The Sabbath preceding the Fast of *Ab* is called שבת חזון, and the Sabbath following, שבת נחמו because the *Haphtaroth* on these Sabbaths (ch. i. and ch. xl. of Isaiah) begin respectively with the words חזון and נחמו ; the one containing rebukes and threats, the other a message of comfort.

Besides these historical fasts, there are voluntary fasts observed by some as an expression of deep-felt piety ; *e.g.*, the three fasts of שני חמישי ושני of Monday, Thursday, and Monday, kept after the festive seasons of Passover and Tabernacles, in imitation of Job, who after the days of feasting sanctified his sons, and brought special sacrifices (Job i.). To this class of fasts may be reckoned the day before New-moon, called יום כפור קטן on which in some congregations the Afternoon Service is enlarged by propitiatory prayers.

V. Divine Worship, עבודה

In the Midrash the following legend is related : When, at the conclusion of the seventh day, the sun had set and darkness had spread over the earth, Adam was afraid that the world was now coming to an end. But the Almighty caused him to find two stones, by means of which he produced light. On seeing this Adam was full of joy, and although he had himself produced the spark, he felt that it was to his Creator and Master that thanks were due, and gave expression to his feelings in the words, " Blessed art Thou, O

Lord, our God, King of the Universe, who createst the light of the fire."

Thus the legend traces the beginning of Divine Worship to the first man; and, in fact, the desire to commune with the Creator and to give outward expression to the inner feeling of reverence and allegiance is so general that it seems to be part of man's nature.

In a different way this feeling was expressed by the sons of Adam, by Cain and Abel. They brought presents to the Lord, probably accompanied by words of praise and prayer. No essential difference is noticed by us in the offerings of the two brothers; each of them brought what seemed best in his eyes. And yet the offering of Cain was rejected, whilst that of Abel was received favourably. An important lesson it is that Scripture teaches here at the very threshold of the history of sacrifices. It is this: The value of an offering does not lie in its outward appearance, in that which is open to man's judgment, but in something that is known to the Omniscient alone, in the heart of him who approaches his Creator with a gift, in the motives which prompt him to do so, and in the feelings which accompany that act. From these beginnings the two forms of Divine **Worship,** Sacrifice and Prayer, gradually developed.

Sacrifice (קרבן, מנחה).

What was the main idea that prompted **man** to bring an offering to the Almighty? He felt, as it were, the existence of a higher Being, the Creator and Ruler of all things; he was conscious that his own life and welfare depended on the Will of the Being to whom in reality everything belongs that man believes himself to possess and to enjoy. In order to give expression to this feeling of allegiance man brought the first and best of what he had acquired to the true Owner, and thus introduced [1] himself by such gifts as a faithful subject who is anxious to merit the favour of his Master. That which was at first introduced by man voluntarily, was afterwards sanctioned and regulated by Divine command.

There were two kinds of sacrifices : bloodless sacrifices, *minchah* and *nesech*, " flour-offering " and " drink-offering," and blood sacrifices : animal-offerings. But no difference is discernible between these two kinds with regard to their importance, sanctity, and efficiency. As a rule, the animal-offering was supplemented by *minchah* and *nesech*. The treatment of sacrifices varied according as they were intended to express the feeling of reverence, rejoicing, gratitude, or repentance, and special rules had to be observed in each case, the various kinds of sacrifice being עולה " burnt-offering," or שלמים " peace-offering," or תורה " thanksgiving," or חטאת " sin-offering," or אשם "guilt-offering." The Law further fixed the place, the time, and the method of sacrificing, and appointed also the persons who alone were allowed to attend to this function, so that no strange element, no

---

[1] The idea of introduction is implied in the term *minchah*, "introduction" (from the root נחה "to lead," "to conduct ").—*Minchah*, originally denoting any present or offering, was the special name of flour-offerings, probably because flour or corn was the most common *minchah* offered by people to their sovereign.—Comp. " I will appease him with the present (*minchah*) that goeth before me, and afterwards I will see his face " (Gen. xxxii. 21).

idolatrous or superstitious customs, could be introduced
into the sacrificial service ordained by the Law.

Great stress is laid on the sprinkling of the blood
of the sacrifice upon the altar. " The blood," the Law
says, " is the soul of all flesh ; and I have given it to
you upon the altar to make an atonement for the
soul " (Lev. xvii. 11). We are thus reminded that, in
so far as the animal life is concerned, " the pre-eminence
of man over the beast is nought," and yet the Creator
gave us the right to shed the blood of animals in order
to save our life. Why ? Because man has a higher
mission to fulfil ; he has been created in the image of
God.

These and similar reflections were suggested by
the different elements constituting the sacrificial rite.
With the destruction of the Temple sacrifices ceased ;
with the Restoration of Israel and the Rebuilding of the
Temple the Sacrificial Service will likewise be resumed.
(Comp. Mal. iii. 4). There are persons who believe
that the Sacrificial Service, implying much of anthropomorphism, could not have been intended to be permanent, and that it was only a concession made to the
fashion and the low degree of culture of the age. Those
who reject sacrifices on this account must also reject
prayer, which is likewise based on a certain degree of
anthropomorphism, though less strikingly than sacrifice.
If the law concerning offerings were only intended for
a certain age, such limitation would have been indicated in the Law. In the absence of such indication
we have no right to criticise the Word of God, and to
think that we are too advanced in culture to obey the
Divine commands. It has been further argued that,

according to Maimonides and his followers, the laws
concerning sacrifices only served as a means of counter-
acting the idolatrous tendencies of the age. But Maimonides never went so far as to contend that these
laws have served their purpose, and are now null and
void. Even those laws which have been enacted by
human authority remain in force till they are repealed
in a regular and legal manner. But what human being
can claim a right to abolish laws given by the Almighty?
Whether any of the laws of the Torah will ever be
abrogated we do not know, but we are sure that, in
case of such abrogation taking place, it will be done
by a revelation as convincing as that on Mount Sinai.

On the other hand, the revival of the Sacrificial
Service must likewise be sanctioned by the divine
voice of a prophet. The mere acquisition of the
Temple Mount or of all Palestine by Jews, by war,
or political combinations, or purchase, would not
justify the revival. It is only the return of the Jews
to Palestine, and the rebuilding of the Temple by
Divine command and by Divine intervention, that will
be followed by the restoration of the Sacrificial Service.
And however contrary the slaughter of animals, the
sprinkling of their blood, and the burning of their
flesh be to our taste, we ought to look forward with
eagerness and pleasure for the revival of the full Temple
Service as an event that will enable us to do the Will
of the Almighty revealed in the Torah. Instead of
modelling the Divine laws according to our liking, we
ought rather to regulate the latter according to the
teaching of Scripture, and suppress it when contrary
to the express Will of God. We therefore give

2 D

expression to our hope "for the restoration of the Temple with its ancient Service" in frequent and fervent prayers, and in accordance with the exhortation of Hosea (xiv. 2) we read each day during the Service Scriptural passages referring to the sacrifice of the day.

"Sacrifices have been condemned by prophets and psalmists"! But in the passages which seem antagonistic to sacrifices only those sacrifices are referred to which are brought in a wrong spirit or from bad motives. (Comp. 1 Sam. xv. 22; Isa. i. 11–13, xliii. 24, lxvi. 2; Jer. vii. 21; Hosea vi. 6; Amos v. 25; Ps. l. 8.)

Prayers, תפלה [1]

Prayer is the general name for that form of Divine Worship which is expressed in words; it has a wider scope than sacrifices, for it is not limited to a special place, or to a certain time, or to one privileged family. It is accessible to all, in all places and at all times. All alike are addressed by the Psalmist, "Let everything that hath breath praise the Lord. Praise ye the Lord" (Ps. cl. 6).

There is no direct commandment in the Torah concerning prayer; it is rather assumed as a matter of course, and as inseparable from our belief in God. According to Tradition (Sifre on Deut. xi. 13), the exhortation to serve God with all the heart implies the duty of prayer. "What duty depends on the heart? It is the duty of prayer." (Comp. Maim. Mishneh-torah,

---

[1] תפלה from פלל "to judge," implies self-examination whether we are worthy of addressing the Most Holy. As to the purifying effect of prayer, see above, p. 183.

Hilchoth Tefillah i. 1.) The following are a few of the general rules laid down by our Sages with regard to Prayer :—

" Better little with devotion (כונה) than much without devotion " (Shulchan-aruch, Orach Chayyim i. 4).

" During prayer bear in mind before whom you stand " (Babyl. T., Berachoth 28*b*).

" The value of the words uttered with the lips is determined by the devotion of the heart " (Babyl. T., Berachoth 15*b*).

What is devotion ? The concentration of all our attention upon the words we utter, the banishment of all foreign thoughts from the mind, and the consciousness that we stand in the presence of the Almighty, whom it is our duty to love, fear, and obey. A prayer uttered in this frame of mind is called " a prayer without lips of deceit " (Ps. xvii. 1). Comp. Maim., *l. c.*, iv. 15.

It is a matter of course that indecorous conduct, unbecoming attitudes, and the like cannot harmonise with true devotion. With regard to language, form, time, and place of prayer nothing was fixed originally ; all was regulated by the momentary impulse of the heart of the worshipper. But people who considered themselves incapable of giving adequate expression to their devotional feelings borrowed the words of those more capable than themselves and followed their leading. Such a course was also necessary for common and united devotion. When a certain prayer or a certain order of Service was frequently repeated at the same season and in the same place, the form, the time, and the place of prayer became to a certain degree fixed by custom—

minhag—and that which had in the beginning been voluntary (רשות) was subsequently made law or duty (חובה or מצוה).[1]

The *minhag* is a most important element in Jewish religious life. What one has been accustomed to do for a long time, or even from his earliest youth, is deeply impressed on the heart, and is not readily surrendered. Such customs are sometimes more cherished and more firmly adhered to than express precepts.[2] It is the outcome of this respect for custom that in all countries the Jews pray in Hebrew. But nevertheless the general principle remains in force that it is not the language that determines the value of prayer but "the devotion of the heart," and those who do not understand Hebrew may give expression to "the devotion of their heart" in the language they understand and speak. Women, who as a rule were not expected to be Hebrew scholars, used to read translations of the Hebrew prayers in the vernacular instead of, or in addition to, the original; they had also prayers composed for them in the vernacular (תחנות). And in more ancient times, when the Jews of Babylon had adopted the Aramean dialect spoken in that country, and retained it also after their return to Palestine, many prayers were composed in the more familiar

---

[1] This was necessary for two reasons : it served to foster a disposition for devotion and to assist the multitude in their endeavour to give expression to their feelings ; it gave also uniformity to the prayers, which is indispensable in public Divine Worship (תפלה בצבור).—The free effusion of our heart before our Creator is by no means restrained, and is certainly not intended to be excluded by these regulations.

[2] מנהג עוקר הלכה "Custom overrules law," is a well-known saying that is frequently acted upon (Soferim xiv. 18).

language, although Hebrew was retained for the principal prayers. Hebrew has a special claim to privilege and distinction among the Jews. It is our national language, which our forefathers once spoke; it is the language in which the Almighty addressed the prophets, and through them the Israelites; the language in which God revealed His Will to the Israelites on Mount Sinai; the language in which the holy Psalmist sang the praises of the Creator, the priests blessed the people, and worshippers prayed in the Temple at Jerusalem. It must be the pride of every Jew to be enabled to pray at home, and especially in the Synagogues, in that same language, and if Hebrew be not the language of his every-day life, he should seek to perfect his knowledge of it to such an extent that he shall be able to understand the prayers and to pray with his whole heart. Those who seek the abolition of Hebrew in our Services aim, consciously or unconsciously, at the destruction of our nationality as the people of the Lord, by breaking asunder one important link which connects us with the wonderful past of our nation.

Equally indifferent with regard to the value of prayer are its length and its form. The Bible offers examples for all kinds and lengths of prayer. If one wishes to pray in a few words, he need only follow the example of Moses, who in the moment of anguish uttered nothing beyond the words, " O God, heal her now " (Num. xii. 13). If one prefers a long prayer, he may also take Moses as a guide, who prayed forty days for the forgiveness of the Israelites after they had made the golden calf (Deut. ix. 18, 25). Both prayers

were equally efficacious.   Miriam was healed, and the
Israelites obtained pardon.   With regard to the form,
we have in the Bible prayers in prose and in poetry;
some uttered in simple speech, others in song; some
with musical accompaniment, some without it.   All of
them seem to have been at first the response to a
momentary impulse, but were afterwards repeated on
similar occasions in the original or in a modified form.

Among the various motives that impel us to seek
communion with our Father, is the desire for certain
things which we have not, and the conviction that it
is solely in His hand to fulfil our wishes.[1]   A genuine
prayer of this kind—for the fulfilment of certain wishes
of ours—is impossible without the belief in the efficacy
of prayer.   We cannot with certainty expect that our
petition will be granted, but we hope that it will; we
submit our wishes to the Will of the Almighty.   The
Hebrew name for prayer תפלה implied the idea of
judgment, as if we judged that the concession of our
petition might fairly be anticipated.   Such judgment,
however, is not to be considered as decisive; and if
our request is to be granted, it will be as an act of
mercy and grace (רחמים ותחנונים), and not because it is
a claim fully proved (קבע).[2]   We hope that our prayer
will be granted, but never lose sight of the condition
"if it please God."   There are a few exceptional cases.
Prophets like Moses (Exod. viii. 6), Samuel (1 Sam.

---

[1] Comp. *supra*, page 183 *sqq.*, on the efficacy of prayer. Comp. page
280 *sqq.*

[2] This is one of the three explanations suggested in Babyl. Talm.,
Berachoth 29*b*: (1) A burdensome task, of which one desires to get
rid ; (2) a claim and not a supplication ; (3) fixed without any spon-
taneous addition.

xii. 17), Elijah (1 Kings xviii.), Elisha (2 Kings iv. 33 *sqq.*), and others, men inspired by the Almighty, were, on certain occasions, sure of the effect of their prayer. In the Mishnah (Taanith iii. 8) the case of Choni (חוני המעגל) is mentioned, who spoke with certainty of the result of his prayer. It must, however, in the latter case be added that the head of the Sanhedrin, Shimeon ben Shatach, blamed him for his conduct.

This we know for certain, that whenever and wherever we respond to an inner impulse by the utterance of a prayer, God is near us, for " He is nigh unto all them that call upon him, to all that call upon him in truth " (Ps. cxlv. 18); that we and the place on which we stand are hallowed by the Divine Presence. Places once hallowed by such devotion, whether of our own or of our fellow-men, we like to visit again and again for the same purpose. The spot of Jacob's first communion with God thus became " the house of God; " and even during the period when there was one central Sanctuary for the Sacrificial Service in Israel, at Gilgal, Mizpah, Shiloh, and later in Jerusalem, there were houses of God throughout the country for devotion unaccompanied by sacrifices. These were " the meeting-places of God " (Ps. lxxiv. 8), in which the Israelites assembled to meet their Creator. Such houses of God were established wherever Jews settled; their main purpose was united devotion; but they served also many other purposes—in fact, every holy, good, and noble cause. The house of God was the Assembly-house, Synagogue (בית הכנסת), in which the affairs of the community (צרכי צבור) were settled;

the young had there their school, adults came there for religious instruction, and found there opportunity for the study of the Law, and the poor and stranger received there support and hospitality.

In a Jewish Synagogue there were two important features, the platform (בימה) and an ark (תבה) containing scrolls of the Law. From the platform in the middle of the Synagogue, the lessons from the Pentateuch and the Prophets were recited, and everything else that was directly or indirectly addressed to the congregants. But prayers addressed to the Most High were offered up from a lower place near the Holy Ark,[1] in accordance with the words of the Psalmist (cxxx. 1), "Out of the depth have I cried unto thee, O Lord."

The Ark, or Holy Ark (ארון or ארון הקדש), in almost all modern Synagogues—in places west of Jerusalem—occupies the middle of the east side of the Synagogue. In the time of the Talmud the Synagogues were to some extent made to resemble the Tabernacle which the Israelites built in the wilderness or the Temple in Jerusalem. The entrance was from the east, and the Ark, which was to represent the Most Holy, was in the west. The Ark was, like the original one, movable. It was called *tebhah*, lit. "box," in order to distinguish it from the original. The recess in which it was kept was the *Hechal* or *Kodesh*, "The Holy." The *tebhah* seems to have served both as a

---

[1] Hence the phrases in the Talmud, "He went down toward the Ark" (*tebhah*), or simply "He went down" to read the *tefillah*. It was not so in all places of worship, because another phrase is sometimes used, "He passed toward the *tebhah*."

receptacle for the scrolls of the Law, and as a desk on which these were put whenever they were required for the reading of the Torah. On certain extraordinary occasions, when, on account of the absence of rain, a general fast was ordered, the *tebhah*, with a *Sefer-torah* on it, was carried into the street,[1] where a special service was held.

The reason why the entrance to the Sanctuary and to the Synagogues was from the east, and the worshippers consequently stood during prayer with their face toward the west, may, according to the Mishnah (Succah v. 4), be explained thus: The principal prayer of the day being that in the morning, the Jews, as a protest against the sun-worship of the idolaters, who at that hour were accustomed to greet the sun with their prayer, turned away from the east and offered up their prayer to the Almighty in the opposite direction. When sun-worship had ceased, probably after the destruction of the second Temple, the national grief and hope found expression in the custom of praying toward the Sanctuary in Jerusalem. Hence the Jews who live west of Jerusalem stand during prayer with the face toward the east, while those east of Jerusalem turn westward. This custom is, besides, supported by the following passage from the prayer of King Solomon: "And they pray unto thee toward their land, which thou gavest unto their fathers, the

---

[1] On such occasions a large congregation was expected, coming from the whole neighbourhood, and the Synagogue was considered too small. It is also possible that a prayer-meeting in the open air was intended to attract the indifferent, who did not attend the regular Services in the Synagogue.

city which thou hast chosen, and the house which I have built for thy name" (1 Kings viii. 48).[1]

In most Synagogues there is a continual lamp (נר תמיד) burning. It is a Biblical institution, but only designed for the Sanctuary; its presence in the Synagogue is of comparatively modern date. The *ner tamid* of the Sanctuary, however, is explained to be a lamp burning "from evening to morning" (Exod. xxvii. 21). A golden candlestick standing in the Sanctuary against the south side, with its seven branches arranged from east to west, served this purpose. According to Tradition it was the second branch, counting from east to west, which really burnt continually; but this was not considered as implied in the term *ner tamid*, which only meant "a continual lamp" in the sense of a lamp that burns *regularly* every night.

The *ner tamid* in the Synagogue, which burns continually day and night, is not mentioned by any of the earlier Rabbinical authors. It has been introduced as a symbol representing our conviction that from the Synagogue shall continually come forth the light of instruction, the light of comfort and blessing, and the light of love and peace.

In the Synagogue women are separated from men. There was also in the Temple an עזרת נשים "court of the women," distinguished from the עזרת אנשים "court of the men," to which women had no access. During the Feast of Tabernacles, when the great rejoicings in the Temple attracted a large assembly, special care was taken (תקון גדול היה שם) that the separation of the sexes should be maintained (Mishnah, Succah v. 2; and

---

[1] See Mishnah, Berachoth iv. 5, 6, and Babyl. Talm., Berachoth 30a.

Talm. B., Succah 5 1*b*). This precedent has been followed in the Synagogue, and has been accepted as law up to this day.

Reservedness and modesty (צְנִיעוּת) have always been the pride and ornament of Jewish women, both in their homes and in the Synagogue; hence also their taking a silent part in the public devotion is an honour to them, and by no means derogatory.

In addition to the above-mentioned points, a Synagogue ought to be distinguished by the greatest possible simplicity, by the absence of all kinds of images, portraits, or statues representing living beings, whether real or imaginary. The Jewish religion is void of every visible symbol; and the so-called *magen-david* (the double triangle) is probably not of Jewish origin, and has no connection with our holy religion. It is not a symbol of this kind, but some inscription of a passage from the Scriptures that in most houses of worship reminds us of the sacredness of the place. We enter it with due reverence, manifesting it outwardly, in our peculiar traditional manner, by keeping the head covered. It is our ancient custom to cover the head when engaged in prayers, in reading the Bible or Talmud and their commentaries. This outward sign serves to remind us that not only our Service but even our literature is something holy, and its study a religious act (מִצְוָה).[1]

Before we proceed to describe the details of our

---

[1] As our religion demands frequent recitations of *berachoth* in the course of the day, the custom spread among the Jews of keeping the head always covered. Comp. Babyl. T., Kiddushin 31*a*; Shulchan aruch, Orach Chayyim ii. 6.

ritual, we mention one important point in which the present Synagogal Service differs from the ancient Service in the Temple. From what we are told in the Scriptures and in the Talmud, we learn that instrumental music was an essential element in the Service, and that King David and his successors paid great attention to it, whilst, with a few exceptions, it is almost entirely absent from our Synagogues. The principal reason why instrumental music is excluded from the Synagogue is its prohibition on Sabbaths and Holy-days by Rabbinical law (Babyl. T., Erubin 104*a*). This prohibition, like many other enactments, did not apply to the Temple Service; for the sacrificial laws had to be obeyed, irrespective of the fact that they involved acts which, if performed apart from the Temple Service, would constitute a breach of the Sabbath laws. Apart from the Temple Service the Sabbath laws remained in full force for the priests as well as for the general public.

There were also other considerations that helped to keep instrumental music out of the Synagogue Service. Its absence, though not directly a sign of mourning, served to preserve the memory of the destruction of the Temple, and to strengthen our longing for its restoration. It is also urged that the introduction of instrumental music into the Service would not satisfy any real want of Jewish worshippers, but would merely be a concession to the desire to assimilate our Divine Service to that of our non-Jewish neighbours, contrary to the prohibition of *chukkoth haggoyim* contained in the words, " Ye shall not walk in their statutes " (Lev. xviii. 3), *i.e.*, in the statutes of the Gentiles. But, on the other hand, it has been argued that the feeling once expressed by the nation in the words " This is my God, and I will worship him in a beautiful manner" (Exod. xv. 2), still animates us. It is said that it is our duty to make our Service as beautiful and as attractive as possible. This argument deserves consideration, and might even outweigh some of the above-mentioned arguments against the introduction of music into our Service, if we were sure of the result of such introduction. But this is by no means the case, for the experiment, where tried, has not been successful if judged by the most practical test. The number of worshippers has not been increased, and discontent has not been removed. Whether the devotion of the worshippers has been improved, refined, or intensified by music is a question that cannot be answered with certainty. Even if the answer were satisfactory, it could only apply to the introduction of instrumental music into our Service on week-days, on Friday evening before the commencement of Sabbath, but not on Sabbaths and Holy-days.

The Ritual.

In the Bible there is no indication of a fixed ritual; there are, however, a few instances of forms of prayer prescribed for certain occasions. There is the priests' blessing (Num. vi. 24–26); the thanksgiving on bringing the first-fruit offering to the Temple (Deut. xxvi. 3–10); prayer on distributing the tithes which accumulated in three years (*ibid.* 13–15). David (Ps. lv. 18) says, " Evening, and morning, and at noonday do I pray ; " Daniel " kneeled upon his knees three times a day and prayed, and gave thanks before his God, as he did aforetime " (Dan. vi. 11); but nothing is said about the form and the contents of these prayers. The Mishnah first speaks of certain fixed forms of prayer: the " Eighteen " (שמונה עשרה), the reading of *Shema* (קריאת שמע), and Benedictions (ברכות). The composition of the *tefillah*, " Prayer " *par excellence*, is attributed to the Men of the Great Synagogue (אנשי כנסת הגדולה), but only in its outlines. The number of the paragraphs, the theme of each paragraph, and the formula by which it is concluded may then have been fixed, the rest being left to be filled up by each supplicant according to his capacity. It was but natural that prayers uttered repeatedly by men eminent for their piety should be eagerly copied by others, and gradually become, to some extent at least, fixed forms of prayer. The *tefillah*, however, in the time of the Mishnah was by no means identical with the *tefillah* of the Men of the Great Synagogue. The destruction of the Temple necessitated several changes ; *e.g.*, the prayers for the welfare of Jerusalem, for the prosperity of Israel and of the Holy Land, and for the acceptance of the Service in the Temple were altered in accordance with the new state of affairs.

The Mishnah speaks of the *tefillah* as a well-known existing institution ; it seems that it was the regular prayer in the Synagogue Service, and the discussion whether the *tefillah* should be repeated every day *in extenso* or in an abbreviated form (Mishnah, Berachoth iv. 3) refers probably to the prayer recited *privatim* (תפלת יחיד), and not to the Service in the Synagogue.

The prescribed " Eighteen Blessings " were the frame-work, into which each man was expected to fit in his peculiar, individual supplications ; whilst in the public Service the *tefillah* remained uniform. In the days of Rabban Gamliel of Jamnia, and with his sanction, an important addition was made by Samuel : a prayer for the discomfiture of those who by slander, denuncia-tion, or other wicked means attempt to undermine the existence of the Jewish religion and community (ברכת הצדוקים or ברכת המינים).[1] In some congregations two other paragraphs (את צמח and וְלִירוּשׁלם) were at the same time combined into one, in order to keep to the traditional " Eighteen Blessings." [2]

The reading of *shema* in the evening and in the morning, the three sections constituting the *shema*, and the order of these sections, are assumed in the Mishnah as fully established by law and usage. Only a few regulations are discussed concerning the time and the mode of the reading. There was this differ-ence between the custom of the Babylonian Jews and that of their brethren in Palestine, that the latter omitted in the evening the passage referring to *tsitsith*. Later on, however, the Palestine Jews conformed to the Babylonian custom. Suggestions have been made

[1] Attempts have been made to modify and to soften down the seemingly harsh words against those who design our ruin ; some even wish to have the whole paragraph expunged from the prayer. In these attempts it has been ignored that the prayer is not directed against certain persons or nations ; it is a petition for the protection of Israel from the wicked plans of evildoers.

[2] This fact is probably the source of the statement in Midrash Rab-both (Num. xviii.), that the *tefillah* before the *birchath ha-tsadukim* was added contained seventeen paragraphs.

to substitute other Biblical passages for *shema*, but they have been rejected. Several attempts have been made to introduce, as an addition to the three sections of *shema*, the reading of the Decalogue; the addition was disallowed, lest people should be misled to think that the Ten Commandments alone were to be observed, and that the other laws were not binding (Babyl. T., Berachoth 12a).[1]

The Benedictions which precede and follow the reading of *shema* were fixed in the time of the Mishnah as regards number, order, and form; but the contents were left unsettled for some time (Mishnah, Berachoth i. 4); in the Gemara their wording is still a subject for discussion. The same can be said with regard to the relative order of *shema* and *tefillah*. For the Evening Service the *tefillah* seems to have generally been considered as optional. As to Benedictions in general, their obligatory character is assumed in the Mishnah as admitted by all, and only their form seems to have been fixed by the regulations mentioned in Berachoth vi.–ix.

The Mishnah (Megillah iii. 4–iv. 10) includes a number of regulations concerning the reading of the Law, the Prophets, and the Book of Esther. Detailed rules were laid down for the reader and the translator (*methurgeman*), pointing out which passages should be omitted in the translation, and which should be omitted

---

[1] In the Temple the priests recited daily the Decalogue, and no objection was raised, because the congregation—priests, Levites, and general worshippers—constantly changed; and secondly, the very Service in the Temple sufficiently proved the existence of other Divine laws.—This ruling applies only to the addition of the Decalogue to the *shema*, not to its introduction into any other part of the Service.

even in the original. It seems that there was a regular, consecutive reading, which was interrupted on extraordinary days by the reading of passages referring to these days.

The ritual which was adopted for the priests in the Temple was an abridged form of the ritual then in general use. It was as follows : They commenced with a benediction—the first of those which precede the *shema* (יוצר אור) ; then they read the Decalogue, *shema* (the three paragraphs), and three further benedictions, אמת ויציב ,עבודה (corresponding to רצה in our prayer), and the blessing of the priests (Mishnah, Tamid v. 1).

A special ritual is also mentioned in the Talmud (Mishnah, Taanith iv. 2) for the *Maamadoth* and the Fast-days.[1] There were four Services daily, as on the Day of Atonement. The principal feature in the Service of the *Maamadoth* was the reading of the first chapter of Genesis.

At the conclusion of the Talmud (about 500 C.E.) the essential parts of our present ritual were already in a settled state ; the *shema* with the benedictions preceding and following, the *tefillah* with its variations for New-moon, Sabbath, and Holy-days, the reading from the Law and the prophets, and *Hallel*. The *Seder* evening Service was complete in its main parts.

---

[1] The priests were classed in twenty-four divisions ; they had to perform a week's active Service in the Temple by turns ; the same was the case with the Levites. The Israelites of the district of which it was the turn of the priests and the Levites to serve in the Temple sent a deputation (*Maamad*) to Jerusalem, who represented them in the Temple ; whilst they themselves held special prayer meetings, called *Maamadoth*.

Of the Benedictions (*Berachoth*) on various occasions both form and contents were fixed, and the rule was laid down by Rabbi Meir (Berachoth 40*a*) that he who uttered a *berachah* in a form different from that fixed by our Sages has not fulfilled his duty (or, according to Maimonides, Hilchoth Berachoth i. 5, is in error). Notwithstanding this rule, however, changes were made; new benedictions were introduced and old ones discontinued.[1]—*Kaddish* and *Kedushah* seem to have formed part of the Service; of the latter the Talmud mentions the name, of the former the response: "May his great Name be praised" יהא שמו הגדול מבורך or יהא שמיה רבא מ' (Comp. Babyl. Talm., Berachoth 3*a*).

In the next period, that of the *Geonim*, we meet with the complete *Siddur*, "Arrangement" or "Order" of Service for ordinary days, for Sabbaths and Festivals, Benedictions for all occasions, and *Piyyutim* as optional additions. Such a *Siddur* was arranged by the Gaon Rabbenu Saadia (892–942), and another by the Gaon Rabbenu Amram (about 880). Henceforth the principal prayers underwent only insignificant alterations. Of the next period the most important *Siddurim* are those included in the Mishneh-torah, at the end of the second book, and that contained in the *Machzor Vitry*.[2]

The additional prayers and *piyyutim*, being optional, varied according to the taste of each congregation and

---

[1] *E.g.*, the addition of הנותן ליעף כח to, and the omission of שלא עשני בור from, the ברכות השחר.

[2] *Machzor*, lit., "Cycle" of prayers, both the obligatory and the optional, or the ordinary *tefilloth* and the *piyyutim*, for the various seasons of the whole year. It is called *Machzor Vitry*, after its compiler, Simcha of Vitry (about 1100)

its leaders; in course of time these variations became permanent; the same was the case with minor changes, especially in the less essential elements of the Service, and thus the various *Minhagim* (Rites) of the various congregations came into existence. The principal *Minhagim* of importance for us are: the Polish, the Sephardic, the German, and the Italian Rites.[1] In the following description of the Ritual only the two rites adopted in the principal Synagogues of the Anglo-Jewish congregations in England will be noted.

Prayers at Fixed Times.

Although we constantly enjoy the blessings of God, the very breath we breathe being the gift of our Heavenly Father, yet certain seasons of the day, of the week, of the month, and of the year have been selected as especially fit for reminding us of God's kindness, and predisposing our heart to devotion. Thus in the day, morning, noon and evening have been fixed for prayer; in the week, Sabbath; in the month, New-moon; in the year, the Festivals.

We have three daily Services: *Maaribh*, " Evening prayer; " *Shacharith*, " Morning prayer,"[2] and *Minchah*, " Afternoon prayer." On Sabbath, New-moon. and Festivals an " Additional prayer," *Musaf*, is inserted

---

[1] As to the importance of *minhag* in our religious life, see above, p. 420.

[2] According to the Mishnah (Berachoth iv. 1), the time fixed for this Service is the first fourth of the day ; but the notions of "early" and "late" are now different from what they were in ancient times. An extension of the time has long been conceded, especially for the Public Service on Sabbaths and Festivals.

between the Morning and the Afternoon Services, and on the Day of Atonement, *Neïlah,* "Concluding Service," is added after *Minchah.*

The two most essential elements in these Services are : (1) the Reading of *Shema* (קריאת שמע), in the *Maaribh* and the *Shacharith;* (2) the *Tefillah* or *Amidah,* common to all the Services.

1. *The Reading of Shema.*

In obedience to the precept, "Thou shalt speak of them," *i.e.,* of "the words which I command thee this day—when thou liest down and when thou risest up," three sections of the Law are read daily in the morning and in the evening, viz., (1) Deut. vi. 4—9, beginning שמע "Hear;" (2) *Ibid.* xi. 13—21, beginning והיה אם שמע תשמעו "And it shall be if ye will diligently hearken;" (3) Num. xv. 37—41, beginning ויאמר " "And the Lord said." The first section teaches the Unity of God, and our duty to love this One God with all our heart, to make His Word the subject of our constant meditation, and to instil it into the heart of the young.—The second section contains the lesson of reward and punishment: that our success depends on our obedience to the Will of God. This important truth must constantly be kept before our eyes and before the eyes of our children.—The third section contains the commandment of *tsitsith,* the object of which is to remind us of God's precepts: "Ye shall see it and remember all the commandments of the Lord and do them, and that ye seek not after your own heart and your own eyes, after which ye use to go astray, that you remember and do all my commandments, and be holy unto your God."

The reading of the *shema* is preceded by two *berachoth*: (1) אור יוצר Praise of the Creator for the regular sequence of day and night, light and darkness; (2) אהבה רבה or עולם אהבת Praise of His goodness in giving us the Torah, and prayer for His assistance in the study of the Torah. The *shema* is followed by a *berachah* on the Redemption of Israel; it contains a reflection on the last words of *shema*, "I am the Lord your God," an expression of our faith in the truth of these words, which strengthen our belief in the future Redemption of Israel.[1] In the Evening Service a second *berachah* follows, beginning השכיבנו, and containing a prayer for protection during the night.[2]

2. *The Tefillah or Amidah.*

The *Tefillah*, "Prayer" *par excellence*, is called *Amidah* (lit., "standing"), because the worshipper stands during the time he offers it up. It is also called *Shemoneh-esreh*, "Eighteen," because it contains on most occasions eighteen (or nineteen, comp. p. 431) paragraphs, each concluding with a benediction.

[1] As to the principle expressed in these three *berachoth*, see *supra*, p. 170.

[2] In the German Ritual for week-days a third *berachah*, beginning לעולם יי ברוך and concluding מעשיו כל ועל, is added. This *berachah* seems to have been at first a substitute for the *Amidah*, which was optional in the *Maaribh* Service. The substitute became in many congregations an integral part of the *Maaribh*, and was retained even when the *Amidah* was generally adopted as obligatory. On the eve of Sabbath and Festivals the *Amidah* was always recited, and there was no need for the substitute. The third *berachah* is therefore absent from the *Maaribh* on these evenings.

The first three paragraphs contain praise of God's goodness to us, the descendants of the pious patriarchs (1), His omnipotence (2), and His holiness (3).

The next thirteen paragraphs are petitions for our individual and national well-being. For our individual well-being (4–9), namely, for reason and wisdom (4), assistance in our endeavour to return to God (5), forgiveness of our sins (6), deliverance from trouble (7), from illness (8), and from want (9).——For our national well-being (10–15), namely, for the gathering of those who are scattered (10), under good leaders (11), protected from the evil designs of our foes (12), for the support of the faithful (13), the rebuilding of Jerusalem (14), and the advent of Messiah (15). The sixteenth paragraph is a prayer that our petition may be accepted.——The last three paragraphs include a petition for the re-establishment of Divine Service in the Temple of Jerusalem (17), thanksgiving (18), and prayer for peace and prosperity (19). When the prayer is finished we express the wish that our lips, from which prayer to God has come forth, may not be defiled by unworthy language.

On Sabbaths, Holy-days, and in every *Musaph* the thirteen middle paragraphs are replaced by one in which reference is made to the characteristic feature of the day; in the *Musaph* of New-year three *berachoth* (p. 404) are substituted for the thirteen middle *berachoth* of the ordinary *tefillah*. The thirteen paragraphs have been eliminated in order that we should not be reminded on Sabbath and Holy-days of our failings, wants, and troubles; that those seasons should be

marked by a happier and more cheerful mood than
ordinary days (*supra*, p. 354).

There are two shorter forms of the *tefillah* for urgent
occasions: the one is a substitute for the "Eighteen,"
in which the middle thirteen paragraphs are contracted
into one; it is called הבינני (the first word of this middle
section), or מעין שמונה עשרה "abstract of the 'Eighteen.'"
The other is a contraction of the Friday evening
tefillah, and is called מעין שבע "abstract of the 'Seven'"
(*scil.*, paragraphs forming the *tefillah*), originally intended for those who were too late for the full Service.[1]

Each of the above Services ends with a prayer called
after its initial word *alenu*, "It is our duty." In this
prayer we thank God that we have the privilege of
proclaiming His Unity, and express our hope to see the
worship of the One God adopted by all mankind. It
is omitted between two Services following closely the
one upon the other.

In addition to the above, the Service contains the
following parts:—

(1.) ברכות השחר "Blessings of the Morning," forming
the first part of the Morning Service. It contains
benedictions, reflections, and prayers suggested by the
change from night to day, from sleep to wakefulness,
from rest to activity.

(2.) *Psalms.*—Our Service contains various groups
of psalms: chief among them the *mizmorim* or *pesuke
dezimrah* ("songs" or "verses of song"), and *shir shel
yom* ("song of the day"), in the Morning Service. The
former include Ps. cxlv. to cl., some other psalms, and

---

[1] See note 2 on p. 446 *sq.*

the song of Moses (Exod. xv.). The latter correspond
to the songs of the Levites in the Temple, and consist
of Ps. xxiv. (for Sunday), xlviii. (for Monday), lxxxii.
(for Tuesday), xciv. (for Wednesday), lxxxi. (for Thursday), xciii. (for Friday), and xcii. (for Saturday).—The
repetition of Ps. cxlv. three times a day, twice during
Shacharith and once during *Minchah*, is an old *minhag*
(Babyl. Talm., Berachoth, p. 4*b*).

(3.) *Supplications* (תחנונים) added in the Morning
and the Afternoon Services after the *tefillah*.

(4.) Readings from the Bible and Post-Biblical
Sacred Literature, such as Num. vi. 22 *sqq.* (priests'
blessing); Gen. xxii. (binding of Isaac); Exod. xvi.
(manna); Mishnah, Peah i. 1, and Babyl. T., Shabbath
127*a*, in the earlier part of the Morning Service; and
words of comfort (beginning ובא לציון) from the Prophets
after the "Supplications." Originally an exposition of
the Written and the Oral Law followed the "Supplications," and concluded with Messianic prophecies, recited in Hebrew and in the Chaldee Version.

(5.) Biblical and Post-Biblical passages referring to
the Sacrificial Service, in the Morning and the Afternoon Services.

In addition to the above Services, read either in the
Synagogue or privately at home, there is a special
prayer read by us before retiring to rest. The chief
element in it is the first section of *shema*; hence the
name קריאת שמע שעל המטה "Reading of *shema* before
going to bed." Some psalms and supplications are
generally added.

Public Service, תפלה בצבור.[1]

The following points mark off the Public Service from the various forms of private prayer :—

(1.) *Kaddish,* "Sanctification," a prayer for the universal sanctification of God's name, which will distinguish the age of Messiah. In the second part of the *Kaddish* we pray for the Messianic peace, and in the last sentence express our hope that it may soon be granted.

Formerly the *Kaddish* concluded the Service; at present it is recited at the end of the Service in its full form (קדיש שלם "the whole *Kaddish*"); the first half (חצי קדיש "half-*Kaddish*") has its place at the end of a section of the Service—*e.g.,* after the פסוקי דזמרה in the Morning Service; a third form is recited by mourners after עלינו and after special hymns or psalms; it is the whole *Kaddish* with the omission of the sentence beginning תתקבל. It is called קדיש יתום "*Kaddish* of the orphan," and is intended to express the mourner's faith in God and his resignation to His Will.—Sometimes a special *Kaddish,* called *Kaddish dirabbanan,* is recited after the reading of some Talmudic or Midrashic passages. It is the same as *Kaddish shalem,* except that the sentence beginning תתקבל is replaced by a prayer for the welfare of the scholars, the Rabbis, and their pupils.

[1] As to the merits of Public Service, see above, p. 284. Ten male persons of thirteen years and upwards constitute a congregation, צבור (or מנין "number" or "quorum"), and their united devotions form Public Service (תפלה בצבור), into which the additions enumerated above are introduced.

(2.) Repetition of the *tefillah* by the Reader, with the addition of *Kedushah* before the third paragraph, and the Priests' Blessing before the last paragraph, of the *tefillah*. The *Kedushah*, " Proclamation of the Holiness of God," is based on the visions of Isa. vi. and of Ezek. iii., with citation of three verses, Isa. vi. 3, Ezek. iii. 12, and Ps. cxlvi. 10, in which the Holiness, Glory, and Kingdom of God are proclaimed.

The Priests' Blessing, originally spoken by priests, descendants of Aaron, is now in most Synagogues included by the Reader in the *tefillah* by way of quotation; only on Holy-days it is pronounced by the priests.

(3.) קריאת התורה " the Reading of the Law," and the " Lessons from the Prophets " (הפטרה), with the benedictions preceding and following (*supra*, p. 348).

Occasional Prayers—Benedictions, ברכות.

The feeling of our dependence on the goodness of God must constantly be present to our mind. Whatever we enjoy, be it in the form of eating or drinking, or some pleasing or remarkable sight, an agreeable smell, a festivity on a joyful event, or the performance of a Divine commandment (מצוה); whatever befall us, whether it be pleasant or unpleasant—all this we consider as sent to us by the Will of the Almighty, and we express our conviction by a suitable *berachah*. The general rule is thus laid down by our Sages: It is unlawful for man to enjoy anything on earth without previously acknowledging by a *berachah* that God is the source whence the enjoyment is derived. For different cases different forms of " blessings " have been fixed by our Sages. In some cases the enjoyment is also followed by a prayer of thanksgiving, the most important being the prayer after meals, called ברכת המזון " Benediction for food or Grace." [1] In the Mishnah it is called " Three Blessings " (שלש ברכות), because it consisted originally of three paragraphs, each ending with a benediction. The three paragraphs are the following : (1) ברכת הזן (" Benediction commencing הזן "), in which we praise God's providential care of all creatures. (2) הודאה " Thanksgiving," or ברכת הארץ (Benediction referring to Palestine). In this paragraph we offer thanks for our individual sustenance, as well as for our national gifts : Palestine, the Covenant, and the Law. (3) Prayer for the restoration of Zion and the rebuilding of the Temple (בנין ירושלם).—Subsequently a fourth paragraph was added (הטוב והמטיב " who is good and causes His creatures to be good ") in commemoration of the relief given to the Jews after the close of the war with Hadrian.[2]—On certain occasions, *e.g.*, at a wedding repast, suitable additions are made. Besides these, various supplications have been added in later times.

There are various short forms of this ברכת המזון ; the shortest is that for children, " Blessed be the Merciful, the Giver of this bread." [3]—When three grown-up male persons or more have their meal to-

---

[1] Before meals we wash our hands, say the blessing, על נטילת ידים, and eat a piece of bread after having said the *berachah*, המוציא.—Some wash their hands a second time (מים אחרונים) before Grace. See Shulchan-aruch, Orach-chayyim clxxxi.

[2] Comp. Babyl. Talm., Berachoth, p. 48*b*.

[3] ברוד שאכלנו משלו or בריך רחמנא מריה דהאי פיתא.

gether, a special introductory form is used, called זמון "summons to prayer," one of the company acting as Reader, and the rest forming the congregation.

Another form of thanksgiving is the "Abstract of the Three Blessings" (מעין שלש), consisting of one paragraph which contains the whole of the Grace in a contracted form, and is used after cake, wine, and the like.

No restriction is enforced upon us if we desire on our part to give expression to our feeling of gratitude and reverence toward the Almighty in our own words on occasions not provided for in the ancient forms of benedictions and prayers. In order, however, to make a distinction between the forms of obligatory *berachoth* fixed by our Sages and the optional ones introduced by ourselves, we do not employ the words, "O Lord, our God, King of the Universe," which are essential in the former.

NOTES.

1. *On Page 424 sqq.*

Among the different *minhagim* observed in the Synagogue the following are noteworthy :—The head is kept covered, the hands uncovered ; gloves are generally taken off before the beginning of the Service. It was customary to spread forth the hands during prayer, and the phrase "spreading forth the hands " is used in the Bible in the sense of "praying." The priests still raise their hands when pronouncing the blessing. Isaiah, rebuking those who prayed to God without seeking purification from evil deeds, says, "And when you spread forth your hands I will hide mine eyes from you ; yea, when ye make many prayers I will not hear ; your hands are full of blood" (Isa. i. 15). Following the example of the Psalmist, "I will wash my hands in innocency, so will I compass thine altar" (Ps. xxvi. 6), we wash our hands before prayer, as a symbol of the duty of purifying our conscience from guilt before approaching the Almighty with our petitions. We thus uncover our hands as if to say, " The reproach of Isaiah does not apply to us ; we have tried to free our heart and our hands from guilt."

A custom frequently animadverted upon is the habit which many Jews have adopted of swinging their bodies forward and backward during prayer. We consider it a more decent way to stand or sit still when communing with the Supreme Being. Both ways find support in the Talmud (Babyl. T., Berachoth 31a, and Shabbath 10a) ; whilst the one stands like " a servant in the presence of his master," the other gives way to his emotions and excitement. The *Magen Abraham,* on chap. xlviii. 4, says : " He who follows the one example is right, and he who follows the other is likewise right : all depends on the devotion of the heart." Rabbi Jehudah ha-Levi in his *Cuzari* (Book II. chap. xli.) mentions and explains the custom of shaking during prayer. The habit of accompanying the emotions of our heart by corresponding motions of our body has produced the custom of raising the whole body upwards when uttering the word " holy " in the *kedushah.*

During *tefillah* we remain standing in the same place ; at the end, when we have finished our petition, we retire slowly a few steps backward ; the same is done by the Reader during the last paragraph of the *kaddish.* It is as if, our petition ended, we reverently withdrew from the heavenly King who has given us audience during the prayer.

We bend the knee, incline our head, and bow down on certain occasions during the Service, but we do not kneel during prayer. —It has perhaps been avoided as an idolatrous practice, with reference to Judges vii. 5.

When the Ark is opened and the *Sefer* is taken out or put back, we stand and show our respect for the Word of God in various ways. Some bow the head ; others, considering this as worship, kiss the *Sefer,* or otherwise express their reverence.

The traditional way in which the *kohanim* proceed to bless the people is this : they remove their shoes, as the priests did who ministered in the Temple ; water is then poured over their hands by the Levites, the ablutions of the ancient priests being thus imitated to some extent (see Exod. xxx. 20). It is a holy act, and is done in the Synagogue generally in front of the Ark.

The priests ascend the steps of the *hechal* and wait till called upon by the Reader to pronounce the blessing. They turn toward the congregation, spread forth their hands in the traditional manner, and cover head and face with the *talith*, in order not to be disturbed in their devotion by the sight of the congregation before them ; the Reader dictates the words of the benediction to them to guard against any mistakes being made by them. The congregation, giving special importance to each word, add Biblical quotations and special supplications during the interval between one word and the other. Of greater importance, however, is respectful listening to the words uttered by the priests, and chanted by them is a peculiar traditional tune. The priests turn to all directions while pronouncing the blessing, expressing thereby that they would have no one excluded from the blessing.

Some *kohanim* refuse to perform this duty, pretending or believing that they are unworthy to bless the congregation. This is a mistake. Those who feel that they are unworthy must try by improved conduct to render themselves worthy, but disobedience to the direct commandment of the Divine Law is certainly not the beginning of improvement. Others object to the singing, in which they are unable to join ; others to taking off their boots. The excuses are certainly insufficient. But as these two elements are less essential, they might, if necessary, be dispensed with if the fulfilment of the commandment is secured thereby.

2. *On Page* 439.

There are various parts in our Service which originally seem to have formed a substitute, under certain circumstances, for a section of the Service or for the whole of it, but were subsequently, when the circumstances altered, embodied as an integral part of the Service in addition to the sections which they had replaced.

In the Morning Service there is in the section called ברכות השחר a prayer beginning לעולם יהא אדם and concluding לעיניכם אמר יי. This prayer, preceded by an exhortation to be God-fearing in secret—when persecution prevented public worship of God—contains an expression of pride in our history, and of gratitude to God that we have the privilege to proclaim the

Unity of God in the words, " Hear, O Israel," &c., and a petition for the fulfilment of the Messianic prophecies.

In the *Maaribh* the part beginning ברוך יי לעולם and ending על כל מעשיו was originally a substitute for the *Amidah*, and the conclusion of the Evening Service for those who considered the *tefillah* in the evening optional. Similarly, on Friday evening the contracted *tefillah* was originally a substitute for the *tefillah* for those who came late. In both these and similar cases the substitute and its original have been retained as integral parts of the Service.

3. *On Page* 442 (2).

In the public Service the *tefillah* is repeated by the Reader after the silent prayer (בלחש) of the congregation This *minhag* must have been introduced very early. In the Talmud (end of *Rosh ha-shanah*) it is spoken of as a regular institution, its purpose is discussed, and the reason stated why we should not dispense with the Reader's repetition or with the silent *tefillah*. It seems that there was, on the one hand, a desire on the part of the congregants to have an uninterrupted silent *tefillah* in which they could give suitable expression each one to his personal and peculiar wants and wishes. On the other hand, there was also a desire felt by many to be guided in their devotions by the Reader. Our *minhag* satisfies both requirements. But it is a grave error to think, as unfortunately many do, that, while the Reader repeats the *tefillah*, the congregants may turn their heart and mind to other things, however holy these be. The congregation and the Reader must be united in devotion during תפלה בצבור, and where the continued concentration of thought during the *tefillah* and its repetition seems unattainable, it would be better to sacrifice the *minhag* of repeating the tefillah rather than to have the repetition of the prayer without the participation of the congregants, or even without decorum.

In the repetition of the *tefillah* the *kedushah* forms an important addition. The essential idea of the *kedushah* is repeated thrice during the Morning Service, viz., in the first of the benedictions preceding the *shema*, in the *tefillah* or *Amidah*, and in the concluding section commencing ובא לציון.

In the first *kedushah* (called קדושה דיוצר), while praising God

as the Creator of light and of the heavenly luminaries, we introduce these, as proclaiming, as it were, the holiness and glory of
God in the words of the Prophets. In the last *kedushah* (called
סידרא דקדושה or קדושה דסידרא) we merely read, among other
passages from the Prophets, those verses of Isaiah and Ezekiel
which contain the chief sentences of the *kedushah.* In the *kedushah* of the *tefillah* the Reader summons the congregation to proclaim the sanctification of God in the manner of the angels above ;
it has therefore its place only in Public Worship, whilst as to the
other two *kedushoth* there is no difference whether a person prays
by himself or in a congregation of worshippers.

As regards קדיש וברכו, two prayers generally united, it must
be remarked that in their meaning they are disunited : the half-
kaddish is the conclusion of the *mizmorim* or *pesuke dezimrah*, and
ברכו is the commencement of the next section : *shema*, with its
benedictions. The half-*kaddish*, wherever it occurs, concludes
some section of the Service. In *shacharith*, after *Amidah*, or after
"Supplications," or after the Reading of the Law ; at *Musaf*,
Minchah, *Neïlah*, and *Maaribh* after the introductory psalms.
The half-*kaddish* before the *Amidah* in the *Maaribh* is probably
a remnant of the whole *kaddish* that used to be said when the
Service ended there and the *Amidah* was considered optional
(רשות).

4. *On Page* 442 (3).

An important element in the Service is religious instruction.
The means adopted were the reading of the Torah and Haphtarah, the introduction of moral lessons, principles of faith,
exposition of Divine precepts into the Service, and lectures containing various lessons, exhortations, and explanations of the
Biblical and Post-Biblical Sacred Literature. These lectures
are an ancient institution. The prophets instructed the people,
especially on New-moon and Sabbath (2 Kings iv. 23) ; the
Scribes and the Rabbis of the Talmudic age expounded the Torah
and other Biblical and Post-Biblical writings ; they were followed
by *darshanim* and *maggidim*, the modern preachers and ministers.
The aim of these lectures is to create, maintain, or intensify the
fear of God and the love of the Torah (אהבת תורה ויראת שמים).

The Sermon has lost much of its original force and influence.
The cause of this fact is probably to be sought chiefly in the

materialism and scepticism of the age, but to some degree also in the character of the sermon. It cannot be denied that the pulpit, instead of being made a place from which Love of Torah and Fear of God receive life, encouragement, and strength, is frequently turned into a platform for discussing communal or personal quarrels or theological controversies, or creating a discontent with existing institutions, without sufficiently considering the result of such discontent. Themes like these are not outside the province of the preacher, but they must not be the staple of his discourses, which must principally seek to foster אהבת תורה ויראת שמים in the hearts of the congregants. As to the history and literature of this branch of the Service, see Zunz, *Die Gottesdienstlichen Vorträge der Juden.* Berlin, 1832.

5. *On Page* 420.

The question is frequently asked whether special meetings and Services may be arranged with a view of improving the religious status of the Jewish community. There is no reason why attempts should not be made in this direction. By all means let everything be done that is conducive to a revival of religious feeling and religious practice. But in such attempts care must be taken that nothing be done that is contrary to the precepts of the Law, both Written and Oral; that the teachers, preachers, or lecturers do not themselves display a disregard for recognised religious authority, and by such conduct undermine the existing reverence for the inherited traditional Religion.

On this basis meetings on Sabbath for the purpose of reading the Bible, praying, and singing, in whatever language this be done, and special Services for the pupils of Religion Classes at the close of the session, must be welcome to all who have a love for our holy Religion.

6. *On Page* 420.

A question of equal importance that frequently disturbs the peace of the congregation is this: whether and in how far the established Ritual or *minhag* of a Synagogue may be altered. The Ritual is not the work of one man or of one age; it is the product of the thoughts and the feelings of our nation through many

2 F

centuries. Its foundation was laid by the Men of the Great Synagogue in the time of Ezra. Generation after generation were busy in the construction of the building ; storey was added to storey ; from time to time new wings made their appearance. Reverence and piety made successive builders reluctant to pull down what the same feelings of preceding generations had reared. The whole formed a Sanctuary every single stone of which was cherished and guarded against desecration. Notwithstanding the storms and tempests to which it was exposed, and which certainly caused a breach here and there, our Sanctuary stands still on its ancient foundations, and its walls retain their power of resistance.

What is the duty of the present generation with regard to this structure ? Architects or would-be architects examine it minutely from foundation to top-stone ; but they come to different conclusions. We will examine these conclusions, *sine irâ et studio,* assuming that the examination has been conducted *bonâ fide,* with a view of strengthening the Sanctuary, and that the reports are in accordance with truth and the examiners' innermost conviction.

(1.) Some declare "the Building no longer *attractive;* there are so many other edifices full of points of attraction both without and within ; these must in course of time draw away the visitors from our Sanctuary, and estrange those who used to fill it." We admit the force of the argument. It has always been the aim of those who had the management of the Synagogue in their hands to make the Service attractive ; there is no reason why it could or should not be done at present. Means of attraction are mostly of an external character : the art and luxury displayed in the building and its furniture, the eloquence of the preacher, the voice of the reader, the singing of the choir, introduction of novelties, such as instrumental music (*scil.,* on weekdays) and prayers in the vernacular. In themselves these things are harmless, and although they are not the essence of the worship, they may lead to it ;[1] and, for this reason, it must be considered a condition *sine quâ non,* that the style of singing, reading, and preaching should be such as to please the majority, if not every one, of the congregants.[2] But there is this to be feared and guarded

---

[1] מתוך שלא לשמה בא לשמה.

[2] The Reader must be שליח צבור the real representative of, and acceptable to the congregants (Shulchan-aruch I. liii. 4).

against : viz., that the husk be mistaken for the fruit, and true devotion be lost. Besides, the experiment has been made, and the desired result has not been obtained. There are plenty of places for the enjoyment of vocal and instrumental music, with which the Synagogue would vie in vain in point of attractiveness, and novelties, as novelties, soon wear away, and bring no real improvement. Let the leaders of the Synagogue strengthen the faith of their brethren in God and His Word, maintain, by good example, their reverence for our ancient traditions and customs, and be themselves earnest and devout worshippers ; they will then surely be more successful in drawing others to the House of God.

(2.) Another critic says : "The Synagogue Services are discordant ;" that is, the feelings expressed in our prayers have no echo in the hearts of the worshippers. "Education and general progress have so entirely changed the whole life of man that he can no longer be edified by the prayers and method of devotion followed by our forefathers." Those who assert this, of course, only assert it of themselves, and so far their statement may be accepted as correct. But on examining it more closely we find that there must be something misleading in it. For what is the central idea of the ancient prayers and hymns ? The conviction that we address our Heavenly Father, who is the Creator and Ruler of the Universe ; who is just, good, and holy ; who alone can fulfil the wishes which we utter in our prayers, and "who is near to all those who call upon him in truth." Does progress of education force us to abandon this principle ? Certainly not. Those who do abandon it cannot be said to do so by force of education, for they are found among the educated and uneducated alike ; and we should be false to our own Faith if we were to abandon this fundamental principle of our Divine Service.

The second of the fundamental Principles of our Faith, though less general than the preceding, is yet equally essential in Judaism, viz., the belief in Revelation, in the Integrity and the Divine origin of the Torah, and the truth of the Divine messages sent through the prophets. The Ritual is replete with references to this belief, and it would amount to a rejection of this essentially Jewish Principle, if we were to expunge such references from the Ritual in order to please a few unbelievers.

References to the Sacrificial Service, and especially prayers for its restoration, are disliked by some, who think such restoration undesirable. Let no one pray for a thing against his will; let him whose heart is not with his fellow-worshippers in any of their supplications silently substitute his own prayers for them, but let him not interfere with the devotion of those to whom "the statutes of the Lord are right, rejoicing the heart; the commandment of the Lord pure, enlightening the eyes; the judgments of the Lord true and righteous altogether" (Ps. xix. 9, 10), and who yearn for the opportunity of fulfilling Divine commandments which they cannot observe at present.[1] Prayer, in the true sense of the word, is impossible without the recognition of God as our Master, whom we are willing to serve, and whose commands we desire to do, whether the act implied in them be in other respects agreeable to us or not.

(3.) The Ritual contains many sections which owe their existence to particular circumstances that have passed away, and to local conditions which are different from those prevailing in the countries in which we live. Have these a right to be kept perpetually in the Ritual? Certainly not. There is no reason why prayers which have become obsolete and meaningless should not be modified or discontinued. But as a rule our prayers are free from references to the particular causes of their composition, and there is no need to expunge from the Service petitions, thanksgivings, or praises which were originally intended for a special occasion, if they are expressed in general terms, and have become in the Synagogue a source of devotion and edification. But as to the latter condition, it is difficult to decide whether a liturgical composition has become, and is still, an aid to devotion. Much depends on the individual character of the particular congregation in which the question has been raised, and each case should be decided on its own merits by a competent and responsible authority.

Many of the *Piyyutim* [2] and *Selichoth* belong to this class; also a few sections in the ordinary Ritual (see note 2), and the repetition

---

[1] See above, page 417.

[2] *E.g.*, נשם and טל, in the *Musaph* of the first day of *Pesach* and the eighth day of *Succoth* are based on the climatic conditions of Palestine.

of the *Amidah*, and the *Kiddush* in the Synagogue on the eve of Sabbaths and Festivals.

(4.) It is further asserted that the Ritual was formulated in bygone times ; our wants and tastes are different from those of former ages. We can neither pray for the same things nor in the same way as our ancestors. But what did our ancestors pray for ? For the well-being of their body and of their soul ; for the realisation of our national hopes and the ultimate triumph of our holy Religion. Just the same ends we wish to obtain at present, and these objects form the substance of our Ritual.—There are some petitions which seem to many out of place, and out of date. Such are petitions against cruel oppressors. Our fathers had good reason to cry to the Almighty for relief, for they were oppressed, whilst we, living in a free country, in the enjoyment of all the rights of citizens, have no cause whatever for complaint. If we were to separate ourselves from our brethren in distant countries, we could expunge all such petitions from the Ritual. This is, however, not the case ; we feel deeply grieved at the sufferings of our brethren. We should like to see them relieved from oppression and persecution, and pray to God for His interference in behalf of the persecuted. When we use the term "revenge" (נקם) we do not associate with it any base desire to see the enemy crushed or annihilated ; we use it rather in the sense of a just and merited penalty for evil-doers, and associate with it the idea of the ultimate victory and triumph of our holy Religion after long periods of oppression and persecution. It is their Faith for which our fathers suffered, and our brethren in some countries still suffer, and the triumph of which forms the centre of these petitions. Intense grief and sorrow sometimes suggested harsh expressions, such as "Destroy our enemies," "Put an end to them," but these are figurative expressions, and are used in the sense explained by Beruria, the wife of Rabbi Meir : " May the sinners cease from sinning, and sinners will be no more." Similarly we pray in the *Amidah :* " Let our slanderers have no hope of success, so that evil-doers may soon vanish and disappear ; break the power of the presumptuous, and humble them." In these words we give expression to our feeling of indignation against the slanderers of our holy Religion, the revilers of Judaism, such, *e.g.*, as from time to time renew the blood-accusations, or by false and deceptive arguments or other means entice Jews to abandon their faith.[1]

(5.) We hear frequently the complaint that the Public Service is too long. This complaint is of a relative character; it is different from the feeling of joy expressed in the words, " Blessed are those who dwell in thy house ;" it is different from the sentiment of those *chasidim* (Mishnah, Berachoth v. 1) who sat still a while before the commencement of the prescribed prayer, or those who after the conclusion thereof sit down again, saying, " Surely the righteous shall give thanks to thy name ; the upright shall dwell in thy presence " (Ps. cxl. 14). As regards the length of the Service, we should bear in mind the principle of our Sages : It makes no difference whether the Service is long or short : only be devout. It is provocative of irreverence to protract the Service unnecessarily until it becomes wearisome ; but it is equally unbecoming to hurry over it as though it were an unpleasant task. On the whole the Services, especially when they are well regulated, are not too long, unless too much time be spent in singing or in unnecessary interruptions.

In all cases in which a modification seems advisable and lawful it must be borne in mind that the Ritual is a Sanctuary every element of which is holy, and that hasty reforms may be less effective than is hoped. It may perhaps be easy to pull down, but it is not so easy to build up. Devout members of a congregation may easily be alienated, but not so easily will new members be attracted, or if attracted, permanently retained.

7. *On Page* 424.

Rabban Gamaliel said, " Provide thyself a teacher, and be quit of doubt" (Aboth i. 16). The rule laid down in these words for every individual applies also to the whole community. Questions like those mentioned in the preceding note frequently arise in Jewish congregations, and cause dissension where union is so much needed. A teacher must be appointed in every com-

---

[1] Those who fear that the seemingly harsh expressions might imply or suggest ideas and feelings of a baser kind can easily modify them and remove the sting.—Similarly, expressions contrary to our taste and sense of propriety ought to be removed.

munity, who shall be able to guide and to instruct it as to what is right and wrong. In fact, such a teacher has, as a rule, been appointed in Jewish congregations ; he is known by various names : Haham (חכם), Rav (רב) "Teacher"), Rabbi (רבי) "My teacher"), Teacher of righteousness (מורה צדק), and Judge (דין). The weight of his authority is less to be determined by the nature of his office or by written conditions than by his learning, piety, and personal influence. According to the rule, "Judge not alone" (*ibid.* iv. 8), he is generally assisted by two councillors (*dayganim*), with whom he forms a court of judgment—*Beth-din* —when questions of more than ordinary importance have to be decided. The congregation must accept his decisions as final, and must have confidence that he, like the high-priest of old, will give his answers according to "light and integrity."

VI. The Dietary Laws.

"Thou shalt not eat any abominable thing" (Deut. xiv. 3); that is, according to our traditional explanation, everything that the Word of God declares to be abominable (Sifre, *ad locum*). One of the sections of the Dietary Laws concludes thus : "For I am the Lord that brought you up out of the land of Egypt, to be your God : ye shall therefore be holy, for I am holy" (Lev. xi. 45).

Holiness is therefore the only object of these laws that is distinctly mentioned in the Pentateuch. But what is the nature of the holiness which they are intended to produce or to promote? "The Dietary Laws," says Maimonides, "train us in the mastery over our appetites; they accustom us to restrain the growth of desire, the indulgence in seeking that which is pleasant, and the disposition to consider the pleasure of eating and drinking the end of man's existence" ("The Guide," III., chap. xxv. p. 167). And, indeed, wherever the Law commands restraint of some bodily enjoyment, or restriction of any of our appetites, such commandment is followed or preceded by the exhortation to be holy, or the warning not to defile oneself.

Is there any secondary object in these laws besides the motive distinctly mentioned? It has frequently been observed that Jews have enjoyed a certain degree of immunity from epidemics that raged among their non-Jewish neighbours. It has further been noticed that they have a lower rate of mortality and a greater longevity. These facts are generally explained to be the result of a temperate life, regulated by the Divine Law. Finding that such is the consequence of obedience to the Dietary Laws, we may fairly assume that in distinguishing certain things from the rest, in prohibiting some and permitting others, the Lawgiver aimed at the health and the well-being of man's body. Our conception of the goodness of God compels us to believe that in recommending certain things for our use He intended thereby to promote our well-being, and to show us what is good for our health, and what is injurious. But we must take care that we do not on that account consider these precepts exclusively as sanitary regulations, however important such regulations may be. We must not lose sight of the fact that Holiness is the only object of the Dietary Laws, mentioned in the Pentateuch.

But what difference can it make to the Almighty whether we eat this or that? Surely it makes no difference to the Almighty; but we have faith in His Goodness and Wisdom, and are convinced that He knows by what means we may best attain to that holiness which we are so frequently exhorted to seek, and that the Divine Laws which He revealed to us for this very purpose show the shortest and the safest road to this aim.

With the following exceptions, the Dietary Laws concern only animal food :—

(1.) ערלה " Forbidden fruit," *i.e.*, the fruit of a tree during the first three years after its planting (Lev. xix. 23).—The fruit of the fourth year (נטע רבעי) was formerly, in the time of the Temple, brought to Jerusalem, and consumed there amidst praises and thanksgiving to Him who is the source of all blessing (*ibid.* v. 24). Those who lived far from Jerusalem were allowed to redeem the fruit of the fourth year with silver, and to spend the latter in the holy city.

(2.) חדש " New corn."—The Omer of barley offered on the second day of Passover is called " the first of your harvest" (Lev. xxiii. 10), and it was enjoined, " Ye shall eat neither bread, nor parched corn, nor fresh ears,[1] until this selfsame day, until ye have brought the oblation of your God " (*ibid.* 14).

These two laws (ערלה and חדש) seem to have their source in the dictum, " The first of the first-fruits of thy ground thou shalt bring into the house of the Lord thy God" (Exod. xxiii. 19).

(3.) כלאים.—Mixture of different kinds. " Thou shalt not sow thy field with two kinds of seed " (Lev. xix. 19).[2] " Thou shalt not sow thy vineyard with

---

[1] *I.e.*, of the new corn. This law of חדש applied to the corn sown during the year preceding the festival of Passover and beginning with the previous Passover (Babyl. Talm., Menachoth 69).

[2] The grafting of two species of trees one upon the other is included in this prohibition.

two kinds of seed" (Deut. xxii. 9). In the former case only the sowing of divers kinds is prohibited, but the produce of such sowing is not forbidden; in the latter case, if the law is transgressed, the produce of both the vine and the seed is not to be used for any purpose whatever (אסור בהנאה), for the law is followed by the words, "lest the whole fruit be forfeited, the seed which thou hast sown and the increase of the vineyard."

Although these and similar [1] precepts are introduced by the words "Ye shall keep my statutes (חקתי)," and no reason is given for the enactment of these statutes, it seems, from the position occupied by these laws in a section of moral precepts, that they serve as reminders of the important lesson that our conduct should be regulated by the principles of contentment and simplicity of life, principles which are the best safeguard against undue desire for luxury and superfluity. The prohibition of sowing divers kinds of seed further reminds us of the importance of preserving our heart in a state of simplicity and purity; that twofold weights, twofold measures, and especially a twofold heart are an abomination to the Lord.

In reference to animal food the following principles are observed :—

---

[1] *E.g.,* "Neither shall there come upon thee a garment of two kinds of stuff mingled together." Such mixture is called שעטנז, and applies only to the mixture of wool and linen (Deut. xxii. 11). Another commandment belonging to this category is this: "Thou shalt not plow with an ox and an ass together" (*ibid.* 10). Ibn Ezra, in his Commentary on the Pentateuch (*ad locum*), suggests the following reason for this commandment, "The Almighty has mercy upon all His creatures; the strength of the ass being inferior to that of the ox, an unfair demand would be made upon the strength of the former when drawing the ploughshares together with the latter."

1. The killing of animals and the consuming of their flesh must not tend to create savage and cruel habits. It is therefore forbidden—

(*a.*) To cut off a piece of flesh from a living animal for our food (אבר מן החי "a limb of a living animal").

(*b.*) To kill the parent with its young on the same day (Lev. xxii. 28; comp. Deut. xxii. 6).

(*c.*) To give unnecessary pain to the animal in killing it. The various regulations for the lawful killing of animals, שחיטה, handed down by Tradition as Mosaic, הלכה למשה מסיני, are not only in harmony with this principle, but seem in many instances to have been dictated by it.

(*d.*) To eat the blood of beasts and birds (Lev. xvii. 12, 14). The blood contained in the meat is removed as far as possible by having the meat soaked in water for half-an-hour, and then kept covered with salt for an hour, the salt being again removed by rinsing. This process is called *kasher;* that is, preparing the meat so as to make it *kasher* (כשר "fit for food").

2. The flesh of beasts and birds that have died from any other cause than having been killed in the manner prescribed is forbidden. The flesh of animals that have been killed in the prescribed manner, but are found to have been affected with some dangerous disease, is also forbidden as *t'refah* (טרפה).[1]

3. With regard to the distinction between animals allowed for food and those forbidden, all animals are

---

[1] טרפה originally designated meat of animals torn by wild beasts, but it is used to designate food, especially meat, forbidden by the Law. All permitted food is called *kasher* (כשר).

divided into בהמה and חיה "cattle and beast," עוֹף "bird," דג "fish," and שרץ "creeping thing."

(*a.*) With regard to cattle and beasts, the rule is given, "Whosoever parteth the hoof and is cloven-footed and cheweth the cud, that you may eat" (Lev. xi. 3).—The clean cattle (בהמה טהורה) and the clean beasts (חיה טהורה) are enumerated in Deut. xiv. 4 and 5 respectively.

(*b.*) A number of *birds* are enumerated (Lev. xi. 13–19) as forbidden, but no general characteristics of the clean or the unclean birds are given; and as we are uncertain as to the exact meaning of the names of many of the birds, we only use for food such birds as are traditionally known as "clean birds."

(*c.*) *Fish* that have scales and fins are permitted; others—*e.g.*, the eel—are "unclean" (*ibid.* xi. 9–12).

(*d.*) "All winged animals that creep (שרץ העוף), going upon all four, shall be an abomination unto you. Yet these may ye eat of, every flying creeping thing that goeth upon all four, which have legs above their feet, to leap withal upon the earth; even these of them ye may eat; the *arbeh* with its kind, and the *soleam* with its kind, the *chargol* with its kind, and the *chagabh* with its kind" (*ibid.* 20–22). These are certain kinds of locusts that satisfy the above condition. (Comp. Maimonides, Mishneh-torah, *Hilchoth maacha-loth asuroth* i. 21–23.)

(*e.*) "And every creeping thing that creepeth upon the earth shall be an abomination; it shall not be eaten" (Lev. xi. 41). In this prohibition are included all kinds of worms such as are found in fruit, and mites, snails, oysters, lobsters, crabs, &c.

4. The milk of "unclean" cattle or beasts (*e.g.*, asses' milk), the eggs of "unclean" birds, and the roe of "unclean" fish (*e.g.*, caviare prepared of the roe of the sturgeon) are likewise forbidden.

5. "Ye shall eat no manner of fat, of ox, or of sheep, or of goat" (Lev. vii. 23). From the context we learn that only those portions of the fat of cattle are forbidden which in the case of sacrifices were burnt upon the altar as an offering made by fire unto the Lord," viz., "the fat that covereth the inwards, and all the fat that is upon the inwards, and the fat that is upon the kidneys which is by the flanks" (*ibid.* iii. 3, 4). The forbidden fat is known by the name חלב, *chelebh*, whilst the fat permitted as food is called שומן, *shuman*.

6. "Therefore the children of Israel do not eat of the sinew which shrank, which is upon the hollow of the thigh, unto this day: because he touched the hollow of Jacob's thigh in the sinew that shrank" (Gen. xxxii. 33). This law is designed to remind us of the wrestling of Jacob with the man who attacked him, which struggle forms a type of Israel's fight against the evil threatening him from within and from without, and teaches us the lesson that, despite temporary troubles and struggles, Israel will ultimately be victorious. The hind-quarters of cattle are not eaten unless the forbidden fat and "the sinew that shrank" (גיד הנשה) have first been removed from them.

7. "Thou shalt not seethe the kid in its mother's milk" (Exod. xxiii. 19). Tradition explains this law as forbidding all mixture of meat and milk (בשר בחלב). In its literal sense the verse in which this law is

mentioned seems to point to the duty of self-restraint, as if to tell us that we should not greedily devour the first ripe fruit, or the young immediately after their birth.

The significance of the law may be learnt from the fact that it is mentioned three times in the Pentateuch. Hence the strictness with which this commandment is observed in Jewish homes. In a Jewish household, established in accordance with Jewish law and tradition, there are two separate sets of utensils, the one to be used for the preparation of meat-diet, the other for the preparation of milk and butter diet.

The flesh of fish is not considered as meat in this respect, nor are fish subject to the laws of *shechitah*.

NOTES.

I. *On Page* 459—1a.

The prohibition of eating meat taken from the body of an animal whilst alive is based on the words אך בשר בנפשו דמו לא תאכלו "But flesh, when the blood thereof is in its soul, shall ye not eat" (Gen. ix. 4). The phrase "to be in the soul" means to be surrounded and animated by the soul, to be in the midst of active, living organs of the animal. "The blood of an animal is in the soul thereof" may therefore be paraphrased thus, "The blood hath its vital powers and the animal is alive." (Comp. Lev. xvii. 11.)

This prohibition is one of the שבע מצות בני נח "the seven Noachide commandments," *i.e.*, commandments which, according to Tradition, were already in force in the days of Noah, and are binding on all his children or all mankind, and not on the Israelites alone ; viz., (1) the prohibition of idolatry (עבודה זרה), (2) of murder (שפיכות דם), (3) of adultery (גלוי עריות), (4) of blasphemy (ברכת השם), (5) of robbery (גזל), (6) of eating meat taken from a living animal (אבר מן החי), and (7) the institution of courts of justice (דינין). See Babyl. Talm., Sanhedrin 56a.

2. *On Page* 459—1c.

The existence of certain rules concerning killing animals for food included in the oral teaching of the Torah is derived from the following passage : " Thou shalt kill of thy herd and of thy flock which the Lord hath given thee as I have commanded thee" (Deut. xii. 21). In the Commentary of Rashi, *ad locum*, we read : " Here we see that certain commandments have been given with regard to the killing of animals, how this should be done. These commandments are comprised in *Hilchoth Shechitah*, which form part of the Oral Law, revealed to Moses on Sinai." They are fully discussed and explained in the first chapter of the treatise *Chullin*.

Any deviation from these rules in the act of killing the animal renders the *shechitah* unlawful (פסולה). The killing of cattle, beasts, or fowl for food is therefore entrusted only to such persons as possess a knowledge of the rules of *shechitah* and are skilled and trustworthy. The *beth-din* or the Chief-Rabbi decides whether a person has duly qualified himself for the office of *shochet* (שוחט), and whether he may kill animals for *kasher* food.

It is the duty of the *shochet* to examine the animal before killing it, and to satisfy himself that it is not in a dying condition ; after the *shechitah* of any cattle or beast (בהמה or חיה) he must examine the lungs to assure himself that they are in a normal condition. If he finds them in a diseased state he declares the flesh of the animal as *t'refah* (טרפה) and unfit for food. In the case of poultry the examination is not made by the *shochet ;* but if any deviation from the normal state is discovered in the lungs or in any other part, the meat must not be used as food unless the animal has been examined by a competent person (Rabbi or *dayyan*), and declared by him to be *kasher*.

As to the beneficial influence of these examinations on the general condition of health in the Jewish community, see Dr. H. Behrend's articles in *Jewish Chronicle*, November 12, 1880, and October 24, 1890, and *Nineteenth Century*, October 1890.

3. *On Page* 459—1d.

The following particular rules are to be observed in *kashering* meat :—

(*a*.) The meat is first soaked in water for half-an-hour ; this must be done within three days after the killing of the animal. It is then taken out of the water, placed on a slanting board or in a wicker-basket, and after a few minutes, when the water has sufficiently run off, sprinkled on all sides with salt. After the lapse of an hour the salt is again removed by soaking and rinsing.

(*b.*) In case of urgency, when, *e.g.*, the meat is wanted for a patient, or when on Friday afternoon there would not be left time enough for cooking or roasting the meat, it need only be kept in water for fifteen minutes and in salt for half-an-hour.

(*c.*) In *kashering* poultry all the inner parts of the animal must be taken out and salted separately ; the rest must be sprinkled with salt both within and without.

(*d.*) Liver is salted a little and roasted on fire, not in the oven or in any vessel. This done, the liver may be cooked or roasted in any way.

(*e.*) The heart is cut open before the salting, and a piece is cut off at the apex, in order that the blood may run off more easily.— For the same purpose the horny part of the legs is cut off.—The head must be opened and sprinkled with salt on both sides, after the brain has been taken out ; from the latter the skin is drawn off, and then it is salted.

(*f.*) Eggs found in poultry are treated as meat, but must be salted separately.

(*g.*) The vessels used for soaking and salting the meat should not be used for other purposes.

4. *On Page* 459—1c.

The law of *shechitah* applies only to cattle, beasts, and birds (בהמה, חיה and עוֹף) ; there is no commandment as regards the killing of fish. Tradition supports this exception by reference to the distinction made in Num. xi. 22 : "Shall the flocks and the herds be slain (יִשְׁחֵט) for them, to suffice them ? or shall all the fish of the sea be gathered together (יֵאָסֵף) for them, to suffice them ?" Although the latter term (יֵאָסֵף) is also used of quails (*ibid.* 32), no such inference is made with regard to birds, because in ver. 32 the term יֵאָסֵף is not contrasted by יִשְׁחֵט ; besides, the verb שָׁחַט is frequently applied in the Law to birds, but never to fish. Comp. Babyl. Talm., Chullin, p. 27*b*.

There is this difference to be observed between בהמה on the

one hand, and חיה and עוף on the other. In the case of the latter two the *shechitah* must be followed by the covering of the blood (כסוי דם Lev. xvii. 13). The object of this law is, according to some, to prevent the blood being used for idolatrous and superstitious purposes, as birds and beasts were generally hunted in the fields, mountains, and woods, places frequently associated in the imagination of the ancients with evil spirits and the like. (Comp. Commentary of R. Obadiah Seforno on the Pentateuch, *ad locum.*) The law was perhaps intended to impress the lesson on the mind of the hunter that the blood shed of a living being presents a ghastly sight that offends the eye of man. He will accustom himself to think that taking away the life of another being, even of an animal, is an act of grave responsibility, and will not be led to misuse his weapons against any of his fellow-men.

5. *On Page* 460—3*b*.

Comp. Mishnah, Treatise Chullin, iii. 6.—The characteristics of the clean and the unclean cattle and beasts are given in the Pentateuch, but the characteristics of the clean or the unclean birds are not mentioned in the Law. Our Sages, however, declared every bird of prey—or every bird that seizes its food with its claws, and lifts it up from the ground before eating it (Rashi) to be an unclean bird ; while all birds are clean that have a projecting claw (אצבע יתרה a claw longer than the rest) and a crop (זפק), and whose stomach has a membrane that can easily be peeled off (קרקבנו נקלף). Another rule is this : Birds that dwell and associate with unclean birds are unclean. "Not without reason does the starling go to the raven : they are of the same species" (Babyl. Talm., Chullin 65*b*). The sentence serves also as a moral lesson (*ibid.*, Baba Kama 92*a*). At present, however, only those birds are killed for food which are known traditionally to have always been considered as "clean birds" (Maimonides, Mishneh-torah, *Hilchoth maachaloth asur th*, i. 14–20 ; Tur Joredeah, chap. lxxxii.).

6. *On Page* 461—7.

Onkelos translates this commandment : לא תיכול בשר בחלב "Thou shalt not eat meat in milk," in accordance with the Oral Law. The threefold repetition of the commandment forbidding

the seething of a kid in its mother's milk is explained traditionally to indicate a threefold prohibition : that of boiling meat and
milk together, that of eating such mixture, and that of deriving
any benefit whatever from it (איסור בישול, איסור אכילה, ואיסור
הנאה). In obedience to the principle, "Make a fence round the
Law," we abstain from milk or butter for some time after having
partaken of meat.

7. On Page 461—4.

The honey of bees is an apparent exception from the rule that
the products of the unclean animals are forbidden. The honey
mentioned in the Bible is mostly the juice of fruit, especially of
dates ; but the honey of bees is also mentioned (Judges xiv. 8).
It is assumed that honey does not contain any part of the bee
itself, but is merely the juice of the flowers sucked and again
discharged by the bees. (See Babyl. Talm., Bechoroth 7*b* ; Maim.,
Mishneh-torah, *Hil. maachaloth asuroth* iii. 3.)

Note 8.

In addition to the things enumerated in this chapter as forbidden, there is the prohibition of "wine of libation" (יין נסך).
Everything used in the worship of idols was condemned, and could
not serve as food, drink, or any purpose ; it was אסור בהנאה.
Wine was frequently used by heathens in libations to their idols.
The wine of a heathen was therefore always suspected of having
been employed in idolatrous libaticns, and was consequently
forbidden as יין נסך. Since, however, such libations have ceased
this prohibition has also lapsed.

It has, however, not lapsed in its entirety. It is only the
אסור הנאה that is no longer in force. The prohibition of using
wine prepared by non-Jews (סתם יין) as a beverage still continues. This and similar prohibitions were intended as a barrier
against the increase of mixed marriages among the Jews. (Comp.
Babyl. Talm., Shabbath 17*b*.)

VII. JEWISH LIFE.

The first paragraph of the *Shulchan-aruch* runs thus: "'I have set the Lord always before me' is one of the most important principles of our holy Religion;" and, indeed, the more the actions of the Jew conform to this principle, the nearer does he approach the ideal of a true servant of God, who is faithful in the service of his Master, and whose life is the expression of genuine recognition of God's sovereignty (קבלת עול מלכות שמים) with unconditional obedience to His Will (קבלת עול מצות). Neither attendance at Public Service, nor the regular recitation of prayers, nor the study of the Law, nor the performance of certain religious acts, constitute by themselves Jewish Life, but the supreme influence which the Word of God—the Torah—is constantly made to exercise over man's doings. Every movement of his is regulated by the Law, and wherever he turns he is met by a Divine precept that elevates his heart towards Him who gave us the Law. The very garments he wears, though not different from those of his fellow-men,[1] except by the

---

[1] In accordance with the traditional explanation of the commandment, "Thou shalt not destroy the corners of thy beard" (Lev. xix. 27), a razor is not employed, and shaving is avoided; the hair of the beard and the face is clipped with scissors. This prohibition, like that of "rounding the corners of the head" (*ibid.*), belongs to a group of precepts which aimed at keeping the Israelites away from the idolatrous customs of their heathen neighbours. The second prohibition has led to the fashion noticeable among Russian and Polish Jews of letting the hair of "the corners of the head" (in Hebrew *peoth*) grow very long.—In the Mishnah (Kethubhoth vii. 6) it is mentioned as a distinctively "Jewish custom" that married women have their head covered when going out. Many Jewish women observe also this

absence of *shaatnez* (combination of wool and linen),
include the *arba kanfoth*, "the four-cornered garment,"
with *tsitsith;* his house, the same in every other respect as
those of his neighbours, is distinguished by the *mezuzah*
on the doorposts. These distinctive characteristics,
however, are not intended to attract the attention of
others; they only concern the man himself; they
serve him as reminders of God and His Will. Within
the house the furniture and the whole arrangement
are in accordance with the custom and fashion of the
place;[1] there is simplicity or luxury, taste or want
of taste, according to the individual character of the
occupier. Only the kitchen and the table have a
distinctly Jewish aspect; these must be adapted to the
requirements of the Dietary Laws. The most striking
feature is the double set of kitchen utensils and of
vessels for the table, the one set for meat, the other
for butter and milk.

In the choice of his occupation, trade, or profession,
the Jew, like all his fellow-men, is influenced by his

custom within the house.—With these exceptions there is nothing
in his dress and appearance that need distinguish the Jew from the
Gentile, only that sometimes Jews are more conservative with regard
to fashion than their neighbours, and old-fashioned style is then mistaken for "Jewish fashion."

[1] Some people leave on one of the walls of the house a certain piece
unpapered and unpainted as a sign of mourning for the destruction of
Jerusalem and the Temple. From the same reason, in some congregations, the bridegroom on the wedding-day has ashes strewn on his
head. In accordance with Ps. cxxxvii. 6 we remember Jerusalem
on various occasions. We recite Ps. cxxxvii. on week-days, and
Ps. cxxvi. on Sabbath and Holy-days, after every meal. Again,
when we give expression to our sympathy with mourners we pray
that God may comfort them together with those who mourn for the
Destruction of Jerusalem.

inclination, capabilities, and opportunities; but, in addition to these, there is another important factor that must ultimately determine the choice—his religion; and such occupation as would be likely to compel him to abandon any of the Divine precepts, cannot be chosen. No manner of labour or trade is in itself derogatory; on the contrary, all labour is honourable, unless man degrades it by his conduct, and by the object he aims at achieving by means of it. Thrift, economy, and temperance are essential conditions of success. But success, however desirable, and however sweet when obtained, leads only to the material well-being of man. As to his spiritual well-being, the Jew, though busy with urgent work, will try to find some spare moments in which to turn his attention to "the three things upon which the world is based · Study of the Torah, Divine Service, and Charity" (Aboth i. 2).

Before the work of the day commences, and when it is finished, attention is paid to *torah* and *abhodah*. The Service, especially the Morning Service, contains various sections which are not prayers, but rather lessons for study. In addition to these, the Jew, according to his capacity or opportunity, should read the Bible, the Mishnah, and the Talmud. For those who have no opportunity at home, the *Beth ha-midrash* is open with its library. Synagogue and *Beth ha-midrash* are the places of spiritual recreation where the Jew refreshes his mind, elevates his heart, and gathers new strength, courage, and hope for the battle of life.

Charity in its various branches, *tsedakah* and *gemiluth chasadim*, is a virtue practised by the wealthy and the poor alike. Any heart or house from which this virtue is absent does not deserve to be called Jewish. Some Jews have charity-boxes in their houses, and whenever any member of the family has something to spare or is moved by a special impulse of charity, these boxes receive an addition to their contents. Others imitate the law of *maaser* (" tithe "), and set aside a tenth part of their earnings and profits for charitable purposes. Hospitality (הכנסת אורחים) is another method of charity, and it forms one of the ornaments of a true Jewish house. Although societies and public institutions do at present what was formerly considered to be the duty of the members of the community, individual hospitality has by no means become superfluous, and there is ample opportunity for its practice. Hospitality graces especially the lady of the house; it is her duty to provide for the comfort of the guests, and to act according to the rule, " Let the poor be the children of thy house " (Aboth i. 5).

This is one of the privileges possessed by women. According to the principle of division of labour, woman rules supreme in the house: " The King's daughter is all glorious within " (Ps. xlv. 14); whilst man is more in contact with the outer world, devotes himself to labour, trade, or profession in order to provide the necessities of life for those who are dependent upon him. There are, however, many exceptions to the rule, and there is scarcely any trade or profession in which women have not been engaged. Women were not excluded even from the highest honours. The Jews had their prophetesses, and women were entrusted with judgeship and even with sovereignty. There are instances of women distinguished by learning, experience, wit, and especially by piety. Women of piety (נשים צדקניות) were never wanting in Israel; and many a scholar owes the success he has attained in the field of learning to the piety of his wife, who willingly undertook her husband's burdens and cares in trade and business in order to facilitate his devotion to study. No sacrifice is too great for a true Jewish mother to have her children instructed in the Word of God, and nothing adds more to the happiness and pride of the mother than the progress her son has made in the knowledge of the Torah. "What is the great merit of women? They have the merit of making their children attend the school, and of encouraging their husbands to study the Talmud" (Babyl. Talm., Berachoth 17a).

The moral and the intellectual as well as the physical training of the children is in its earliest stages almost exclusively in the hands of the mother. If we add to this the responsibility for having the food prepared according to the requirements of the Dietary Laws, we easily understand the reason why Jewish women are exempt from various religious duties incumbent on the other sex. The rule is this: "Women are exempt from the fulfilment of all precepts which are restricted to a certain time" (Mishnah, Kiddushin i. 7), in order to prevent any collision between these and her principal and most important duties in the house. Thus it happens that there are Jewish women who faithfully cling to the inherited religion, and yet are rare visitors of the Synagogue. On week-days the Synagogue is only in exceptional cases attended by women.

From this reason women are disqualified for forming the quorum (*minyan*) required for public worship (*tefillah batsibbur*). This and similar disqualifications are based on the principle of regard for women and their home-duties, and by no means on a belief in their inferiority. Passages in the Talmudical and Midrashic Literature which ascribe to women vanity, levity, and other shortcomings are outweighed by sayings which evidence a sense of high regard for the virtues and accomplishments of women. The following sentences are a few examples; "Woman has been endowed by the Creator with greater intelligence than man" (Babyl. Talm., Niddah 45*b*). "Who is rich? He who possesses a wife fair in her doings" (*ibid.*, Shabbath 25*b*). ' It was through the merit of pious women that the Israelites were redeemed from Egypt" (*ibid.*, Sotah 11*b*).[1] Modesty and reservedness (צניעות) are the distinguishing virtues of Jewish women. The principle, "The daughter of the King is all glorious within," was applied literally. In the fulfilment of her home-duties the daughter of Israel seeks her

---

[1] The above-mentioned exceptions, and the fact that the woman is passive in the marriage ceremony as well as in the case of a divorce, have been erroneously interpreted as evidence of the low estimate in which she is held by the Jewish Law. How the Jews were taught to honour their wives may be gathered from the Jewish marriage document, in which the husband promises "to honour his wife in accordance with the rule in practice among Jews, that every husband honours his wife." There are, unfortunately, also bad Jews who ill-treat, neglect, or entirely abandon their wives; but these cases are exceptions, and proportionately less numerous than among non-Jews. On the whole, Jewish women are treated by their husbands with love and regard, and the good relations that exist between husband and wife ensure the comfort and happiness of both.

happiness and her pride. It used to be opposed
to the sense of propriety of Jewish ladies to speak,
sing, or act in public.[1] This צניעות was the main
cause of the preservation of the sanctity of the Jewish
home and the purity of Jewish family life, a treasure
and a blessing which ought to be well guarded.

The working days of the week are divided between
labour and devotion. Three Services are attended daily
either in the Synagogue or at home, and every meal
is preceded and followed by prayer. Jewish women
have, in addition to the Prayer-book, a small volume
of supplications (תחנות) in the vernacular for every
day, every season, and every occasion.

Mondays and Thursdays, on which days a Lesson
from the Law is read during the Morning Service, are
considered as special days for earnest devotion. There
have been pious Jews who fasted the whole or part of
these days.—Tuesday is looked upon as a favoured
day, because it is distinguished in the account of the
Creation (Gen. i. 10, 12) by a repetition of the phrase,
" And God saw that it was good." It is therefore
called " the day with double *ki-tobh* (that it was
good)." This circumstance may be the cause of the
belief that it is not advisable to begin a new undertaking on Monday or Wednesday;[2] preference should be

---

[1] To this respect for feminine modesty is due the arrangement made
in the Synagogue for female worshippers (see p. 426). It is also the
reason why girls have no ceremony corresponding to the celebration of
the *bar-mitsvah*.

[2] Women do not like to do needlework on Saturday evening immediately after the close of Sabbath ; it was considered a *mitsvah*
to prolong the Sabbath, just as it is a sign of love and esteem if we
induce a friend to defer his departure. The saying that only shrouds

given to Tuesday. But this belief, although seemingly founded on a Biblical phrase, is contrary to Jewish principles, and is included in the prohibition, " Ye shall not observe times " (Lev. xix. 26), to declare a particular day as lucky or unlucky.

Friday is an important and busy day in a Jewish house. It is not only the circumstance that food is being prepared for two days [1] that causes greater activity, but also the anticipated pleasure at the approach of a beloved guest. The same is the case when a Festival is near. Each Festival has its own particular wants and pleasures. In some houses the activity in preparing for Passover may be noticed a whole month before, although the actual clearing of the *chamets* is done in a very short time. Before *Succoth* all hands are busy with preparing and ornamenting the Tabernacle, and selecting *esrog* and *lulabh*. It is genuine religious enthusiasm [2] in the fulfilment of Divine duties that inspires this kind of activity, and gives to the house a peculiarly Jewish tone and Jewish atmosphere. We feel in it " the season of our joy " before and during the Three Festivals, and " the season of solemnity and earnest reflection " during the penitential days; grief when the 9th of *Ab* ap-

---

are to be sewn on Sabbath evening may perhaps be traced to Mishnah, Shabbath xxiii. 4.

[1] In order to have warm food on Sabbath without breaking any of the Sabbath laws, the food is put in an oven which is heated in such a manner that the fire continues to burn without requiring to be stirred or rekindled, or in which the heat is otherwise retained. Such food is called *chalet*, which is probably a French word, corresponding to the Hebrew חמין " warm."

[2] Or חבוב מצוה " love of *mitsvah*."

proaches, and hilarity when *Purim* is near. Twice
a year we are invited by law and custom to give
ourselves up to gladness and merriment : on *Simchath-
torah* and on *Purim.* Although even a certain excess
of mirth is considered lawful on the latter occasion,
there are but very few that indulge in this license.

All the seasons of rejoicing are also occasions for
mitsvoth—charity, and for strengthening the bond of
love between husband and wife, between parents and
children, and the bond of friendship between man and
man. Every *erebh shabbath* and *erebh yom-tobh* afford
the opportunity of giving *challah*,[1] kindling Sabbath
or Festival lights,[2] and inviting strangers[3] (הכנסת
אורחים) to our meals. On Sabbaths and Festivals children, even when grown up, come to their parents and
ask for their blessing.[4] Before *Kiddush* the husband
chants the section of Prov. xxxi. beginning אשת חיל,
in praise of a good wife. The *Shabbath shalom* or
Good *shabbath, Shabhua tobh* or Good *woch*, Good *yom
tobh*, and similar salutations, remind us that we ought
to have only good wishes for each other. Sabbath
and Festivals afford suitable occasions for home-
devotion, in which all the members of the family,
males and females, should take part. The meals are
preceded and followed by the usual *berachoth*, but it

---

[1] See p. 357.

[2] See p. 357 *sqq.*

[3] Jews consider it a duty to have guests (אורחים) at the table on
three occasions, viz., the *Seder*-evening, *Purim*, and *Succoth*.

[4] The blessing generally consists of the priestly benediction, and the
words of Jacob, "God make thee like Ephraim and like Manasseh"
(Gen. xlviii. 20) ; Sarah, Rebeccah, Rachel, and Leah being substituted
for Ephraim and Manasseh when females are addressed.

is customary to add extra psalms and hymns (*zemiroth*) in honour of the day, and those who are gifted should add to these, or even substitute for them, compositions of their own in any language they like *in gloriam Dei.* A second kind of home-devotion which ought not to be neglected, but should rather be revived where it is neglected, is the reading of the Scriptures. On Friday evening the pious Jew reads the *Sidra* twice in the original and once in the *Targum;* but all should at least read *Sidra* and *Haphtarah* in the vernacular.

The moon by its gradual increase in light from its minimum to full-moon, and the subsequent decrease from full-moon to its minimum, has in Agadic and Midrashic Literature frequently served as a symbol of the history of Israel, of his rise and his fall. The last day of the decline, the eve of New-moon, is kept by some as a special day of prayer and fasting,[1] while the first day of the rise, New-moon, is distinguished by *Hallel* and *Musaph.* If people, as a symbol of happiness (סימן טוב), prefer the middle of the month for marriage, their choice is harmless; but if they hold that season as more lucky than the rest of the month, they are guilty of superstition. As at the sight of other natural phenomena, so also has a benediction been fixed on observing the reappearance of the moon in the beginning of the month. For the above-mentioned reason, importance is attached to this *berachah*, and prayers are added for the redemption of Israel. The *berachah,* which is generally recited in the open air, is the chief element in the ceremony; the additional prayers and reflections are non-essential.

[1] A special Service of the day is called יום כפור קטן.

In the foregoing, Jewish Life has been described as it appears at the various seasons of the year; in the following, it will be given as it appears at the various periods of man's existence.

The first important moment is, of course, the moment of birth. The father, friends, and relatives are filled with anxiety for the life of both mother and child. Prayers are daily offered up for the safety and recovery of the patient and the well-being of the child. The Twentieth Psalm is sometimes written on a tablet placed in the room where the confinement takes place, probably as a reminder or an invitation for visitors to pray to the Almighty; in this sense the custom is to be commended; but if the tablet is filled with meaningless signs, letters, and words, and is used merely as a charm, the custom should be discontinued, being a superstitious practice. In some parts it has been the custom that during the week preceding the *Berith-milah* friends visited the house to pray there for the well-being of the child, and boys recited there Biblical passages containing blessings, such as Gen. xlviii. 16.[1] The night before the *berith* was spent in reading Bible and Talmud, so that the child might from the beginning breathe, as it were, the atmosphere of *torah*.[2]

[1] Friday evening was especially selected for this purpose; the visitors were treated with fruit and sweets; and this secondary element in the custom became in course of time the principal thing. The custom received the name *Shalom-zachar*, probably from the usual greeting, "*Shalom!* ("Peace," corresponding to our "How do you do?") O male child!"

[2] In different countries there were different ways of expressing this sentiment. In some congregations a band (*mappah*), with the name and birthday of the child inscribed on it, and ornamented with verses expressive of various good wishes, is presented to the Synagogue.

On the eighth day the male child is initiated into the covenant of Abraham (Lev. xii. 3). Circumcision is one of " those *mitsvoth* which the Israelites in times of religious persecution carried out notwithstanding imminent danger to life." The performance of this Divine precept is therefore made the occasion of much rejoicing. In some congregations the operation, as a sacred act, takes place in the Synagogue after the Morning Service; in others the privacy of the home is preferred. In ancient days mothers circumcised their sons, but now the operation is only entrusted to a person who has been duly trained, and has received from competent judges a certificate of his qualification for the functions of a *mohel*.[1] Although, according to the Law, any person, otherwise capable of doing it, may do the *mitsvah*, preference is given, and ought to be given, to a person of genuine piety and of true enthusiasm for our holy Religion, who performs the act *in gloriam Dei*. Not only the *mohel*, but all who assist in the act do a *mitsvah*, and the meal which is prepared for the occasion is a סעודת מצוה (a meal involving a religious act).[2] Immediately after the operation a name is given to the child.[3]

---

[1] *I.e.*, a person who circumcises.

[2] Of those who assist in the *mitsvah*, the *sandek* (godfather), who holds the child during the operation, is the most prominent, and is called בעל ברית ("who is in possession of the covenant," *i.e.*, of the child to be initiated into the covenant). The religious enthusiasm required for the performance of this *mitsvah* is symbolically represented by "the chair of Elijah" (כסא של אליהו), upon which the child is placed before the operation; Elijah in Jewish Tradition being the type of religious zeal.

[3] The Service for the occasion is included in the **Daily Prayer-book**, by Rev. S. Singer, p. 304.

The next important moment in a boy's life is the "Redemption" (פדיון הבן) in case of the first-born male child (Exod. xiii. 13, 15), which act is likewise made the occasion of a סעודת מצוה. A *cohen* (descendant of Aaron) receives the redemption-money to the amount of five shekels (or 15s.), according to Num. xviii. 16.[1]

In the case of a female child the naming generally takes place in the Synagogue on a Sabbath, when the father is called up to the Law. In many congregations this takes place when the mother has sufficiently recovered to attend again for the first time the Service in the Synagogue on Sabbath. Those who live at a great distance from the Synagogue pay the first visit to the place of worship on a week-day. A special Service has been arranged for the occasion.[2]

Great care is now taken by the parents for the physical well-being of the child, without entirely ignoring its moral and intellectual development. "At five years the child is fit to be taught *Mikra*, *i.e.*, reading the Bible" (Aboth v. 21), so the Mishnah teaches. But long before this the child is taught to pray, and to repeat short Biblical passages or prayers in Hebrew. It must, of course, be borne in mind that children are not all alike, and that each child must be taught, according to its own capacities and

---

[1] For the Blessing and Prayers on this occasion, see Prayer-book, p. 308.

[2] The chief element in this Service is ברכת הגומל, the thanksgiving for the Divine protection enjoyed in the moment of danger. This Blessing is pronounced by (1) those who have crossed the sea, (2) or a desert, (3) or have recovered from a serious illness, (4) or have been released from prison. (Comp. Ps. cvii.)

strength. The knowledge must be imparted in such a manner that the child should seek it as a source of pleasure and happiness.

As to the subjects which are to be taught, there is no branch of general knowledge from which Jewish children are debarred by their Religion, nor is there any branch of knowledge that is more Jewish than the rest. Jewish children must learn like other children, as far as possible, that which is considered necessary and useful, as well as that which is conducive to the comfort and happiness of life. But *Religion, Scripture*, and *Hebrew* must never be absent from the curriculum of studies of a Jewish child. The instruction in Religion need not occupy much time, for the best teaching of Religion is the good example set by the parents at home and the teacher in the school. The religious training of a child should begin early; the surroundings and associations must teach the child to act nobly, to speak purely, to think charitably, and to love our Religion. "Train up a child in the way he should go; and when he is old, he will not depart from it" (Prov. xxii. 6). Early practical training (חנוך) is also of great importance with regard to the observance of religious precepts. Children should be accustomed to regard with reverence that which is holy, to honour Sabbath and Festivals, and to rejoice in doing what the Almighty has commanded. Twice a year we have special occasion for the fulfilment of this duty, viz., on *Simchath-torah* and on the *Seder*-evening.

In teaching our children Hebrew our aim must be to make them understand the holy language, to enable them to read the Word of God in the original, and to pray to the Almighty in the language in which the Prophets and the Psalmists gave utterance to their inspirations, and in which our forefathers addressed the Supreme Being in the Temple.

A special ceremony used to introduce the child into the study of the Bible in the original.[1] Teacher and pupil went to the Synagogue, took a *sepher* from the *Hechal*, and the pupil was made to read the first lesson from the *sepher*. This and similar ceremonies were intended as a means of impressing on the pupil the great importance of studying the Word of God in the original language. After having acquired a sound knowledge of the Bible, the study of other branches of Hebrew literature, of Talmudical and Rabbinical works, is approached.

As a rule, boys devote more time to Hebrew studies than girls, only because girls are considered physically more delicate and not capable of doing so much work as boys. Girls are by no means excluded from acquiring a sound Hebrew knowledge; on the contrary, every encouragement should be given to them, if they are inclined to study Hebrew beyond the first elements.[2]

The boy when thirteen years old is *bar-mitsvah* (lit., " a son of the commandment "), bound to obey the Law, and responsible for his deeds. On the Sabbath following

---

[1] Leviticus was generally taken first.

[2] A misinterpretation of the dictum of Rabbi Eliezer, " Whoso teaches his daughter *torah*, teaches her, as it were, levity " (Mishnah, Sotah iii. 4), led many to believe that the Rabbis did not wish the daughters of Israel to know the Law. The dictum refers to a discussion which immediately precedes on the efficacy of the " bitter waters." Rabbi Eliezer holds that it is dangerous to the morality of a woman to engage her thoughts with the details of the Law concerning a wife suspected of adultery (Num. v.).

his thirteenth birthday the boy is called up to the Law ;
he reads the whole of the *Sidra* or a section of it, and
declares in the blessings which precede and follow the
lesson his belief in the Divine origin of the Torah, and
his gratitude to God for having given us the Law.[1]

The school-years come gradually to a close, and the
practical preparation for life begins. A vocation has
to be determined upon. From a moral and religious
point of view all kinds of trade, business, and profession are equal. They are honourable or base according as they are carried on in an honourable manner or
not. Whatever course is chosen, the moral and religious training must continue with unabated energy.
When the school-years are over, when the youth is no
longer under the control of the master, and is sometimes left even without the control of the parents, he
is exposed to various kinds of temptation, especially
through the influence of bad society. The vices against
which the youth must guard himself most at this
period of life are sensuality, excessive desire for pleasure, gambling, and dishonesty, which bring about his
moral, social, and physical ruin. Self-control, acquired
through continued religious training, is the best safeguard against these dangers. It is therefore advisable
that those who have left the school should continue
attending some religious class, or otherwise devote
part of their free time to Talmud-torah, to the study
of the Torah, and of works relating to it.

" At the age of eighteen years one is fit for marriage " (Aboth, *ibid.*) is an ancient dictum, but which

---

[1] The feast in honour of the *bar-mitsvah* is סעודת מצוה only when
it is accompanied by דברי תורה (" Words of the Law ") spoken by
him.

could never have been meant as an absolute law. For there are other qualifications equally important, and even more essential than age. Maimonides (Mishneh-torah, *Hil. Deoth* v. 11) says: " Man should first secure a living, then prepare a residence, and after that seek a wife. But fools act otherwise: they marry first, then look out for a house, and at last think of the means of obtaining a livelihood." (Comp. Deut. xx. 5—7 and xxviii. 30.)

Marriage is called in the Bible " a divine covenant" (Prov. ii. 17), or " the covenant of God." God is, as it were, made witness of the covenant; in His presence the assurances of mutual love and the promises of mutual fidelity are given by husband and wife (Mal. ii. 14). To break this covenant is therefore not only an offence of the one against the other, but an offence against God.—In addition to this religious basis of marriage, conditions of a more material nature were agreed upon. The maiden has been long of use in the house of her parents, and he who sought the privilege of taking her to his house and making her his wife had to give to the parents " dowry and gift " (מהר ומתן, Gen. xxxiv. 12). Later on, in the time of the Mishnah, all that the husband promised to his wife was made the subject of a written document (כתובה), signed by two witnesses. In this document he guarantees to her 200 *zus* (or half the sum if she is a widow), the value of her outfit and dowry (in Hebrew נדוניא), and a certain amount added to the afore-mentioned obligatory sum (תוספת כתובה). He further promises to honour her, work for her, maintain her, and honestly provide her with everything necessary for her comfort.

The marriage was preceded by the betrothal (אירוסין or קידושין), the solemn promise on his part to take her after a fixed time to his house as his wife, and on her part to consider herself as his wife and to prepare herself for the marriage. Legally she was already his wife, and infidelity was visited with capital punishment. The interval between the betrothal and marriage used to be twelve months; at present the two events are united in the marriage ceremony, and are only separated from each other by an address or by the reading of the *kethubhah*. That which is now called betrothal or engagement is merely a preliminary settlement of the conditions of the marriage (תנאים "conditions"). The conditions used to be written down, including a fine (קנס) for breach of promise; the agreement used to be concluded by the breaking of a glass [1] and by a feast.

The actual betrothal takes place on the wedding-day, and consists mainly of the following significant words addressed by the bridegroom to his bride: הרי את מקודשת לי בטבעת זו כדת משה וישראל "Behold, thou art consecrated (betrothed) to me by this ring according to the Law of Moses and of Israel." While saying this he places a gold ring [2] on the second finger of the

---

[1] At festivities a glass was broken in order to remind those present of the transient nature of all earthly things, and thus warn them against excess of joy (Babyl. Talm., Berachoth 31a).—The same is done after the wedding ceremony.

[2] In the Talmud the custom of the ring is not mentioned; anything could be used, provided it had the value of a *perutah*, a small coin, and was the property of the bridegroom. Among Jews the use of the ring is a modern fashion. The ring must not contain any jewel or precious stone, the value of which can in many cases not easily be estimated, and which might therefore lead to misunderstanding and dispute.

right hand. This act is preceded by a *berachah* over wine, read by the celebrant while holding a cup of wine in his hand, and the *birchath erusin* ("blessing of betrothal"), in which God is praised for the institution of Marriage. Bride and bridegroom, who during the ceremony stand under a canopy (חופה), taste of the wine.

The canopy or *chuppah* [1] represents symbolically the future home of the married couple, which they have to guard as a sanctuary, and to render inaccessible to evil deeds, words, and thoughts that would pollute it. The top of the canopy, which is formed of a curtain (פרכת) of the *Hechal*, or of a *talith*, expresses the idea of sanctity.

After the *birchath erusin* the bridegroom makes the solemn declaration [2] mentioned above: "Behold, thou art consecrated (betrothed) unto me by this ring according to the Law of Moses and of Israel," [3] whereupon the *kethubhah* is read in Aramaic [4] or in English,

---

[1] There are, besides, various explanations of the term *chuppah:* (1.) The wreath on the head of the bride when led to the marriage ceremony (הינומא, Mishnah, Kethubhoth ii. 10). (2.) A cover over the head of the bride; in some countries, therefore, instead of erecting a canopy, a *talith* is held over the bride and bridegroom during the ceremony; in others a separate ceremony of covering the head of the bride takes place before the actual marriage (comp. *supra*, p. 467, note 1). (3.) A private chamber into which bride and bridegroom retire for breakfast when the ceremony is over.

[2] In order to prevent mistakes the minister reads the formula slowly, and the bridegroom repeats it; the minister omits the word לי "unto me," and the bridegroom inserts the word by himself, or assisted by some one else.

[3] "And of Israel" signifies: "According to the Jewish traditional interpretation of the Law of Moses;" these words are added because the rules of *kiddushin* are not directly mentioned in the Torah.

[4] The *kethubhah* is in its essential elements very old, and dates probably back to the time when the Jews in Palestine spoke Aramaic. The

and an address is sometimes given. Then follow the ברכות נשואין ("Blessings of Marriage"), called also after their number שבע ברכות "Seven Blessings."[1] The ceremony concludes with the breaking of a glass and the mutual congratulations of friends and relatives, expressed in the words *Mazzal-tobh* (מזל טוב "Good luck").[2]

A banquet (סעודת נישואין) follows, which is a סעודת מצוה. It is introduced by the usual *berachah* (המוציא), and followed by Grace and the "Seven Blessings."

The following are a few of the various customs connected with a Jewish marriage without being essential elements of the marriage ceremony:—

(1.) On the Sabbath previous to the wedding-day the bridegroom, his father, and the father of the bride are called up to the Law, and offerings are made (*mi shebberach*) in honour of the bride and the bridegroom. In some congregations Gen. xxiv. is read after the Service, on the morning of the wedding-day.

(2.) Bride and bridegroom enter upon a new life; the wedding-day is to them a day of rejoicing, but also a day of great solemnity. It is kept as a day of earnest reflections, of prayer and fasting, till after

---

settlement described in this document should be made to correspond with the actual deed of settlement legally executed. On the other hand, even the poorer bridegrooms should be induced to make a real settlement corresponding to the promises made in the *kethubhah*. The system of life insurance facilitates such a course. Otherwise the *kethubhah* has no importance.

[1] The contents of these Blessings are : (1) Benediction over wine ; (2) praise of God as the Creator of the Universe, (3) as the Creator of man, (4) and of woman ; (5) prayer for the comfort of Zion, (6) for the rejoicing of the young couple, and (7) for their united happiness.

[2] *Lit.*, "Good planet." The term has entirely lost its original meaning, and denotes simply "hearty congratulation."

the ceremony, when the fast is broken and the rejoicing begins. The bridegroom adds in the *Minchah amidah* the Confession (ודוי) of the Day of
Atonement.

(3.) The good wishes of friends and relatives are
variously expressed. Rice, wheat, or similar things
are thrown over the bride and the bridegroom as a
symbol of abundance and fruitfulness.

(4.) The feast is accompanied by speeches in praise
of the bride and bridegroom ; it was considered a
special merit to speak on such an occasion (אגרא דהלולא
מילי, Babyl. Talm., Berachoth 6*b*). The bridegroom
used to give a discourse (דרשה) on some Talmudical
theme, if he was able to do so. He received presents
for it (*derashah*-presents).

(5.) In the time of the Bible and the Talmud the
feasting lasted seven days.—The first day after the
wedding used to be distinguished by a fish dinner
(סעודת דגים), in allusion to Gen. xlviii. 16.

In spite of all blessings and good wishes the marriage sometimes proves a failure, husband and wife
being a source of trouble and misery the one to the
other, instead of being the cause of each other's happiness. In such a case a divorce may take place, and
man and wife separate from each other. Divorce is
permitted (Deut. xxiv. 1–4), but not encouraged; it
is an evil, but the lesser of two evils. A written
document was required (נט, ספר כריתות), and later
legislation made the writing and the delivery of the
document difficult and protracted, in order to facilitate
attempts at reconciliation; the fulfilment of the conditions agreed upon in the *kethubhah* also tended to

render divorce a rare event. The number of cases of divorce among the Jews is therefore comparatively smaller than among other denominations, but still unfortunately far too large, owing to want of foresight and reflection in the choice of a companion for life.

There is a kind of obligatory marriage (יבום) and or obligatory divorce (חליצה), viz., with regard to the widow of a deceased brother who has died without issue (Deut. xxv. 5–10). Since the abolition of polygamy[1] by Rabbenu Gershom (eleventh century) the obligatory marriage has almost disappeared, and the obligatory divorce (חליצה) must take place before the widow can marry again.[2]

We acknowledge the principle laid down in the Talmud, "The law of the country is binding upon us" (דינא דמלכותא דינא), but only in so far as our civil relations are concerned. With regard to religious questions our own religious code must be obeyed. Marriage laws include two elements—civil relations and religious duties. As regards the former, we abide by the decisions of the civil courts of the country. We must, therefore, not solemnise a marriage which the law of the country would not recognise; we must not religiously dissolve a marriage by גט, unless the civil courts of law have already decreed the divorce. On the other hand, we must not content ourselves

---

[1] In the Torah polygamy is not forbidden, but not encouraged. It was a luxury inaccessible to the multitude, and the king is distinctly told that he must not have many wives (Deut. xvii. 17). The principle of monogamy is implied in many Biblical passages, as, e.g., Gen. ii. 20 sqq.; Mal. ii. 14; Ps. cxxviii. 3; Prov. v. 18 sqq.

[2] A woman divorced from her husband by גט or from her brother-in-law by חליצה cannot marry a kohen.

with civil marriage or civil divorce; religiously, neither civil marriage nor civil divorce can be recognised unless supplemented by marriage or divorce according to religious forms. Furthermore, marriages allowed by the civil law, but prohibited by our religious law —*e.g.*, mixed marriages; that is, marriages between Jews and non-Jews—cannot be recognised before the tribunal of our Religion; such alliances are sinful, and the issue of such alliances must be treated as illegitimate. Those who love their Religion and have the well-being of Judaism at heart will do their utmost to prevent the increase of mixed marriages.

"To every thing there is a season, and a time to every purpose under the heaven: a time to be born, and a time to die" (Eccles. iii. 1, 2). Life is a precious gift the Creator has given us; while there is breath in our nostrils we thank Him for it, we pray to Him for its prolongation, do everything in our power to preserve it, and consider its wilful destruction a criminal act. But notwithstanding all this "there is a time to die." Life and death are equally mysteries to us; we trust in the mercy of Him who has ordained life and death, that both are for our good. Death is, therefore, not to be regarded with dread and horror; it is the transition to another state of life, the real nature of which is unknown to us. But it is our belief that the future life (העולם הבא) is infinitely superior to the present life (העולם הזה); hence the saying in the Midrash that the words "exceedingly good" (Gen. i. 31) applied to death. The only fear of death that can reasonably be justified is the fear of departing from this life before we have completed our task, before we have sufficiently strengthened "the breaches of the house" caused by our own dereliction of duty. Our Sages advise, "Return one day before thy death" (Aboth ii. 15); that is, every day, the day of death being concealed from our knowledge. In this manner we constantly prepare ourselves for death without curtailing our enjoyment of life. "Rejoice, O young man, in thy youth; and let thy heart cheer thee in the days of thy youth, and walk in the ways of thine heart, and in the sight of thine eyes: but know thou, that for all these things God will bring thee into judgment. Therefore remove sorrow from thy heart, and put away evil from thy flesh: for childhood and youth are vanity" (Eccles. xi. 9, 10). When passion overcomes us and evil inclinations invite us to sin, we are told by our Sages to remember the day of death, which may suddenly surprise us before we have been able by repentance to purify ourselves from our transgressions (Babyl. Talm., Berachoth 5*a*).

When death approaches, and announces itself through man's illness, we do everything that human knowledge and skill can suggest to preserve and prolong the earthly life with which God has endowed us; in addition, the patient himself and his friends invoke the mercy of God for his recovery.[1] Even when death appears invincible, when "the edge of the sword touches already man's neck, we do not relinquish our hope in God's mercy, and continue to pray to the All-merciful." The patient is asked to

---

[1] In every congregation there is a special society of those who devote themselves to the needs of the sick (חברת בקור חולים). See above, p. 302.

prepare himself for the solemn moment, although it may in reality be as yet far off.[1] The preparation consists of prayer, meditation, confession of sin, repentance, and of the profession of our Creed, especially of the Unity of God, in the words, " Hear, O Israel, the Lord is our God, the Lord is One." [2] To visit the sick, to comfort them by kind words and deeds, to pray with and for the patient, are acts included in the duty of " visiting of the sick " (בקור חולים).[3] In the moment of death those present testify their faith in God by proclaiming the Dominion, the Omnipotence, and the Unity of God in the same way in which we make this declaration at the conclusion of the Day of Atonement. Although Prayer-books contain certain forms of prayer for this purpose, the patient and those present should rather follow the impulse of their heart, and commune with the Almighty in any form their heart suggests.

When life has come to an end friends and relatives give free expression to their grief; [4] to check it by comforting words at this moment is useless (Aboth iv. 18). The mourners,[5] father, mother, son, daughter, brother, and sister, have now to direct all their atten-

---

[1] " Many have made confession and have afterwards recovered " are the very words to be addressed to the patient according to the Shulchan-aruch, *Jore deah* cccxxxviii.

[2] See *Sefer ha-chayyim,* and Daily Prayer-book, p. 314 *sqq.*

[3] See *supra,* p. 302.

[4] Those present exclaim : ברוך דין אמת " Blessed art thou . . who art the true Judge." The same is done by those who are not present on hearing the sad news. Relatives rend also their garments (קריעה).

[5] In Hebrew אוננים and אבלים ; the former term is applied to the mourners during the time between the death and the interment of their relatives ; the latter after the interment during the whole period of mourning.

tion to the deceased relative, in order that nothing be neglected in the last honours shown to him ; they are therefore free from all other religious obligations till after the burial. In Palestine and neighbouring countries, where, in consequence of the higher temperature, decomposition of the body begins soon after death, the burial takes place on the same day.[1] In colder climates two or three days elapse between death and burial. The mourners abstain during the interval from wine and meat.

Every act of piety in honour of the deceased is a meritorious religious act, a *mitsvah,* an act of kindness and truth (חסד ואמת), and in every congregation there exists a society, called חברא קדישא " holy society," whose members devote themselves to the fulfilment of these pious duties.

According to the principle that death equalises all, that " the small and great are there " (Job iii. 19), the greatest simplicity and equality is observed in all matters connected with the obsequies[2] of the dead. Friends and relatives follow to the burial-ground ; the הלוית המת, or attending the dead to their last resting-

---

[1] Some consider it a dishonour to the departed to leave the corpse unburied over night, since the Law does not allow even the body of a criminal to be treated in this way. The practice may also have commended itself on sanitary grounds.

[2] The shroud is made of white linen. The *kittel* or *sargenes* is part of the raiment in which the dead are clothed. It is the custom in some countries that the bride presents the bridegroom with this article on the wedding-day ; and it is worn by the husband on New-Year's Day and on the Day of Atonement, and on the *Seder*-evening during the Service. Some think that the object of wearing it is to remind us of death, and thus turn our thoughts away from the vanities of earthly life.—The custom has probably its origin in the fact that the white *kittel* was the festive garment of the day.

place,[1] is one of those *mitsvoth* " the fruits of which a man enjoys in this world, while the stock remains for him for the world to come."

Burying the dead is a very old custom, to which the Jews adhered firmly at all ages. The custom of the Greeks, who burnt their dead, found no advocates among the Jews. In the Written and the Oral Law only the burying of the dead is mentioned. To leave a human body unburied and unattended was considered by Jews, as by other nations, an insult to the deceased person, and whoever found such a body was bound to take charge of it and to effect its burial.[2]

In the Burial Service we acknowledge the justice of God, and resign ourselves to the Will of the Almighty (צדוק הדין). When the burial is over our attention is directed to the living; words of comfort are addressed to the mourners[3] who return home and keep שבעה " seven days of mourning." A certain degree of mourning is then continued till the end of

[1] In Hebrew בית החיים or בית עלמין " the house of life " or " the house of eternity."

[2] The case is known by the name of מת מצוה " the corpse which claims attention as a *mitsvah.*"

[3] The usual formula is, " May the Almighty comfort you together with those who mourn for Zion and Jerusalem." These words are addressed to the mourners when they return from the grave to the Hall, while passing the line (שורה) formed by those present, and are repeated during the week of mourning, especially on Friday evening when the mourners enter the Synagogue. When the Service is over, the mourners return home, and partake of a meal prepared for them by friends or neighbours (סעורת הבראה). In days of old wine was taken on that occasion (Kethubhoth 8*b*), but this custom, like several others, has dropped into oblivion. In the Grace the section which begins ובנה " And build," is modified during the week of mourning in order to give expression to the sentiments of the mourners.

the year by the children of the deceased, and till the end of the month (שלשים "thirty days") by other relatives.[1]

Our regard for the deceased (יקרא דשכבי) and our sympathies with the mourners (יקרא דחיי) are expressed in different ways.

The funeral oration (הספד) occasionally spoken at the grave, or in the house of mourning, or in the Synagogue, generally combines both elements; it contains a eulogy upon the deceased and words of sympathy and exhortation for the living.

The special prayers offered up on such occasions likewise include these two elements: petitions for the well-being of the soul of the deceased, that it may find Divine mercy when appearing before the Supreme Judge, and petitions for the comfort and relief of the mourners. The *Kaddish* of the Mourners, however, does not contain such prayers, but merely expresses their resignation to the Will of the Almighty, their conviction that He is the only Being that is to be worshipped, and that He alone will be worshipped by all mankind in the days of Messiah, and their wish that the arrival of those days may be hastened.

There are, besides, the following customs, the object

[1] During the week of mourning the mourners (1) remain at home, with the exception of Sabbath; (2) abstain from work and business; (3) hold the Morning and the Evening Services at home, and add appropriate psalms (such as xvi. and xlix.), prayers, and meditations; (4) sit on the floor or on low chairs; (5) listen to no music, avoid play, and all kinds of amusement, and (6) let the hair grow long.—During the rest of the month—or of the year, in case of mourning for father or mother—the last two observances are followed; the hair is only cut when it has become cumbersome as well as unsightly, and a banquet is only attended when it is a סעודת מצוה.

of which is to express our regard for the memory of the deceased : (1.) A tombstone (מצבה) is set up in front of or over the grave with the name of the deceased, the date of his death, and such words of praise as are dictated by the love and the esteem in which the deceased was held by the mourners. (2.) A lamp is kept burning [1] during the week, or the month, or the year of mourning, and on the anniversary of the day of death (*Jahrzeit*). (3.) By observing the anniversary of the death as a day devoted to earnest reflection, and to meditation on the merits and virtues of the deceased; we keep away from amusements, and say *Kaddish* in the course of the Services of the day. Some observe the anniversary as a fast-day. (4.) By doing some *mitsvah* [2] in commemoration of the deceased. (5.) By regarding with respect and piety the wishes of the departed relative or friend, especially those uttered when death was approaching. Our Sages teach : " It is our duty to fulfil the wishes of the departed." [3] The absence of this inner respect and piety makes all the outward signs of mourning, however conscientiously observed, valueless and illusory.

---

[1] A symbol of the soul of the departed, in reference to Prov. xx. 27.

[2] The three principal *mitsvoth* are : Study of the Law (תורה), Divine Service (עבודה), and Charity (גמלות חסדים). As regards the first, a section of the Mishnah is studied daily ; as regards the second, the bereaved, during the year of mourning, or on the *Jahrzeit*, acts as Reader in the Synagogue for the whole or part of the Service ; and as regards the third, relief is given to the poor *in memoriam*.

[3] Babyl. Talm., Gittin 14*b*.

NOTES.

In addition to the customs already mentioned, there are a few calling for some observation, customs which might seem superstitious, but are not so if properly understood.

When life is extinct the eyes of the deceased are closed, and in some cases also the mouth is kept shut. This is probably done out of regard for the dead, that their face should not present a too ghastly and repulsive appearance. The custom is mentioned in the Mishnah, Shabbath xxiii. 5, and is also alluded to in the words, " And Joseph shall put his hands upon thine eyes" (Gen. xlvi. 4).

From the house in which there was a dead person, and from the houses in its immediate neighbourhood, the water was poured out. According to Num. xix., everything in the house—and, under certain conditions, also in the neighbouring houses—was unclean ; the water was poured out, from fear lest it be used in preparing holy food, such as *terumah* (" heave-offering "). Furthermore, a *kohen* is not allowed to enter such a house, and the pouring away of the water served as an indication that a dead person was in the house.

An important element in the preparation for the burial is the " cleaning " and robing of the body (טהרה) ; the cleansing of the body before it returns to the earth is to be a symbol of the purification of the soul by the mercy of God.

It is customary that those who came into contact with the deceased during his lifetime express regret for any offence they may have committed, knowingly or unknowingly, against him —a good custom, that might serve as an exhortation to us all to be careful in our actions towards our living fellow-men.

Whenever we mention the name of a deceased friend or relative we add, as a mark of respect, עליו (עליה עליהם עליהן) or השלום, (abbreviated, נוחו (נוחה) עדן or זכר צדיק לברכה, זכרונו (זכרונה) לברכה or ע"ה, ז"ל, זצל or נ"ע), " Peace be to him (her or them)," " his (or her) memory be for a blessing," " the memory of the righteous be for a blessing," or "his (or her) rest be Eden." Comp. Zunz, *Zur Literatur u. Geschichte.* Similarly we add to the names of living friends and relatives the wish שיחיה (שתחיה), or נרו יאיר " May he (or she) live," or " May his light continue to shine."

APPENDIX.

——

I.

THE THIRTEEN PRINCIPLES OF FAITH.

אנו מאמין באמונה שלמה

א—שהבורא יתברך שמו הוא בורא ומנהיג לכל הברואים והוא לבדו
עשה ועושה ויעשה לכל המעשים:

ב—שהבורא יתברך שמו הוא יחיד ואין יחידות כמוהו בשום פנים
והוא לבדו אלהינו היה הוה ויהיה:

נ—שהבורא יתברך שמו אינו גוף ולא ישינוהו משיני הגוף ואין לו
שום דמיון כלל:

ד—שהבורא יתברך שמו הוא ראשון והוא אחרון:

ה—שהבורא יתברך שמו לו לבדו ראוי להתפלל ואין ראוי להתפלל
לזולתו:

ו—שכל דברי הנביאים אמת:

ז—שנבואת משה רבנו עליו השלום היתה אמתית ושהוא היה אב
לנביאים לקודמים לפניו ולבאים אחריו:

ח—שכל התורה המצויה עתה בידינו היא הנתונה למשה רבנו עליו
השלום:

ט—שזאת התורה לא תהי מחלפת ולא תהי תורה אחרת מאת
הבורא יתברך שמו:

י—שהבורא יתברך שמו יודע כל מעשי בני אדם וכל מחשבותם
שנאמר היצר יחד לבם המבין אל כל מעשיהם:

יא—שהבורא יתברך שמו גומל טוב לשומרי מצותיו ומעניש לעוברי
מצותיו:

21

ב–בביאת המשיח ואף על פי שיתמהמה עם כל זה אחכה־לו בכל
יום שיבוא:

יג–שתהיה תחית המתים בעת שתעלה רצון מאת והבורא יתברך
שמו ויתעלה זכרו לעד ולנצח נצחים:

NOTE.—שתעלה רצון "when it will be decreed," lit. "when it—the
resurrection—will ascend into the will." Comp. the Talmudical
סלקא דעתך "you think," lit. "it ascends into your mind."

II.

The Jewish Calendar.

1. *Nisan.*—The Sabbath before Passover is called שבת
   הגדול "the Great Sabbath," on account of the im
   portance of the approaching festival.

   14th : ערב פסח "the Eve of Passover." Fast of the
   First-born.

   15th to 22nd פסח "Passover."

   16th : "Beginning of counting the Omer," ספירת העומר

   17th to 20th : חול המועד "Half-holydays."

   23rd : אסרו חג "Farewell to the Festival."

2. *Iyar.*—14th : פסח שני "Second Passover" (Num. ix.
   9 *sqq.*).

   18th : ל״ג בעומר the 33rd of the Omer. "Scholar's
   feast."

   שני חמישי ושני Fasts kept by some, on the first Monday,
   Thursday, and Monday succeeding each other in
   the beginning of the month, in order to atone for
   sins they may have committed on the Holydays.

   Sivan.—3rd, 4th, and 5th : שלשת ימי הגבלה "The three
   days of bordering" (Exod. xix. 10–12).

   5th : ערב שבועות "The eve of the Feast of Weeks."

   6th and 7th : שבועות "Feast of Weeks," also called
   "Pentecost."

8th : אסרו חג " Farewell to the Festival."

4. *Tammuz.*—17th : " Fast of Tammuz," שבעה עשר בתמוז

5. *Ab.*—"Sabbath before the Fast," שבת חזון (see p. 413)

9th : " Fast of Ab," תשעה באב

" Sabbath after the Fast," שבת נחמו (*ibid.*).

15th : חמשה עשר באב " 15th of Ab." Reconciliation of the Benjamites with the other Israelites (Judges xxi.).

6. *Ellul.*—ימי הסליחות " Days of propitiatory prayers," beginning on the first day of the month according to the Spanish Rite, and according to the German Rite, on the Sunday (or 2nd S.) before ראש השנה

29th : ערב ראש השנה " The eve of New-year."

7. *Tishri.*—1st and 2nd : " New-year," ראש השנה

3rd : " Fast of Gedaliah," צום גדליהו

1st to 10th : " The ten penitential days," עשרת ימי תשובה

" The Sabbath after New-year," שבת שובה (see p. 405).

9th : ערב יום כפור " The eve of the Day of Atonement."

10th : יום הכפורים or יום כפור " The Day of Atonement."

14th : ערב סכות " The eve of Sukkoth."

15th to 21st : סכות " Feast of Tabernacles."

17th to 21st : חול המועד " Half-holyday."

21st : הושענא רבא " The Great Hoshana Service."

22nd and 23rd : שמיני עצרת " Feast of the eighth day.

23rd : שמחת תורה " Rejoicing of the Law."

24th : אסרו חג " Farewell to the Festival."

Heshvan.—שני חמישי ושני "The Fast of ' Monday, Thursday, and Monday,' kept by some in the course of the month."

9. *Kislev.*—25th to 2nd (or 3rd) of *Tebeth :* חנוכה " Feast of Dedication."

10. *Tebeth.*—10th : עשרה בטבת " The Fast of Tebeth."

11. *Shebhat.*—15th : חמשה עשר בשבט " New-year for trees."

The last Sabbath in the month (or the first of Adar, if on Saturday) is שבת שקלים "The Sabbath of She-kalim." Exod. xxx. 11–16 is read in addition to the weekly section.

12. *Adar.*—7th : Anniversary of death of Moses.

Sabbath before Purim, שבת זכור (Deut. xxv. 17–19).

13th : תענית אסתר "Fast of Esther."

14th : Purim, פורים "The Feast of Lots."

15th : שושן פורים "Purim of Shushan."

The last Sabbath but one, שבת פרה Num. xix. is read as an extra lesson.

The last Sabbath in the month, or the first of Nisan, if on Saturday, is שבת החודש Exod. xii. 1–20 is read as an extra lesson.

[13. *Adar Sheni.*—פורים, תענית אסתר, שבת זכור, שושן פורים, שבת פרה, and שבת החדש which in an ordinary year are observed in Adar, are in a leap-year kept in Adar Sheni ; and שבת שקלים either on the last Sab-bath in Adar, or on the first of Adar Sheni, if on Saturday.]

NOTE.—The 15th of Shebhat is, according to the opinion of the Hillelites (Mishnah, Rosh ha-shanah i. 1), "New-year for the trees ; " *i.e.,* in reference to tithes, and to the fruit of the fourth or fifth year (Lev. xix. 24, 25) ; the fruit that begins to grow on a tree between the 15th of Shebhat of one year and the same date next year is reckoned as the fruit of one year.

Various reasons are given for the distinction of the 15th of Ab : (*a.*) The punishment decreed against the Israelites in the wilderness in connection with the spies (Num. xiv. 29) was discontinued from the 15th of Ab. (*b.*) The posts set up by Jeroboam on the borders of his kingdom for the purpose of preventing Israelites from going up to Jerusalem were removed on this date. (*c.*) The preparation of the wood for the altar was completed on the 15th of Ab. (*d.*) On this day the Israelites obtained permission to bury the bodies of those killed in the war against Hadrian. (*e.*) The reconciliation between the Benjamites and the other Israelites took place on the 15th of Ab (Judges xxi. 21 *sqq.*).

The Mishnah (Taanith iv. 8) states that the 15th of Ab and the Day of Atonement were to the Israelites once days of the greatest national rejoicings for all alike, rich and poor. In memory of these general rejoicings the daughters of Jerusalem wore on these days borrowed white garments, in order that those poor who had none of their own should not feel ashamed. The Mishnah then describes the causes of the rejoicings ; namely, the dancings in the vineyards (Judges, *l. c.*) for the 15th of Ab, and the giving of the Law (*i.e.*, the giving of the second tables, which, according to Tradition, took place on the 10th of Tishri), and the building of the Temple (*i.e.*, the rearing of the Tabernacle, which, according to Tradition, was commanded on the 10th of Tishri for the rejoicings on the Day of Atonement).

III.

RELIGIOUS EDUCATION.

Professor Lazarus in his recent work "Die Ethik der Judenthums" made the following observations : "In the continuity of the spirit of our nation we discover the solution of the riddle, which puzzled so many thinkers, viz. : how the small tribe of the Jews managed to outlive great and mighty nations." This continuity of the spirit has been secured by our religious education. It has been said that education aims at producing in the younger generation the capacity of receiving, preserving and developing the culture we have acquired ; this applies pre-eminently to religious education. That such continuity exists in our religious education, is evident from the fact that up to the present day the chief text-book for religious instruction has remained the same :—the Torah, or in a wider sense, the Bible, that everflowing fountain of living waters, not only for us Jews, but for almost all civilised nations. Our duty to preserve this continuity by handing over to the next generation the religious principles inherited from our predecessors is frequently insisted upon in Holy Writ, and emphasized on every occasion. We have in this respect a double duty to perform : Every parent is bound to secure as far as possible the well-being of his children ; religious education is indispensable for the children's well-being. The Torah, the source of our religious education, is besides, our National treasure and inheritance, and every member of our community has as such the duty to guard and protect this treasure, that the rising generation receive it in its integrity. It is therefore not sufficient for any one of us to provide for the religious instruction of his own children, it is his duty to contribute his share towards the maintenance of the public schools or classes established for the religious instruction of the young. The Israelites in the wilderness joyfully received the National treasure, and solemnly declared " the Law which Moses commanded us, has been handed to us as an inheritance," to be transmitted from generation to generation. These very words form the beginning of the religious education of our children, for as soon as they are able to speak, they are taught to recite and to understand the verse תורה צוה לנו משה מורשה קהלת יעקב " The Law which Moses commanded us, O congregation of Jacob, is an inheritance." (Deut. xxxiii. 4.). In accordance with this principle, the Torah, the reading of the Torah in its original language, in the Hebrew, the translation and the understanding of the Torah, must form the basis of Jewish Religious Education, both in private and public instruction. The Torah is the essential element in the curriculum of Jewish Institutions for Religious instruction·

Our Sages therefore teach (Aboth v. 2) : " Read the Torah again and again, for everything is in it, and in it thou wilt see everything ; and even when thou art old and worn out, remain faithful to it, and from it do not move away, for there is no better measure for thee than the Torah."

There are other important subjects which Jewish children of both sexes are expected to learn and to know: The principles of Religion, Scripture History, Jewish History and Literature, Geography of Palestine and Hebrew Grammar. None of these subjects should be excluded from the curriculum of a Jewish School. They must be taught, but must be taught in such a way that they help to illustrate the lessons of the Law, and to facilitate its study. It is certainly of great importance that our children should acquire as much knowledge as possible of our History and Literature ; of far greater importance, however, is the training of the heart in the faith of God, the inculcation of reverence for the Torah and the creation of a desire to live a pure, good and holy life, based on the fear and love of God. Text-books of Religion, though useful both to teacher and pupil, must by no means supersede the original, the Torah. Where for some cogent reason a minimum of time is spared for religious instruction—as is *e.g.* the case in many Religion Classes connected with Public Schools and Colleges, special care should be taken that the Torah receive its due attention. The best method must be employed, the best possible teachers must be engaged, who are well trained in the art of teaching, and possess a thorough knowledge of our holy religion and our history. If in addition to these qualifications, the teacher devotes himself to his profession with love and enthusiasm, his words, coming from the heart, will find their way into the heart of the pupil. No time can be spared for metaphysical speculations or for problems of Bible criticism. Besides, " The hidden things belong to the

Lord our God, but the things which have been revealed are for us and our children for ever : to do all the words of this Law." (Deut. xxix. 28). According to the teaching of Aboth, (v. 22) " one moment of victory over sin and temptation in this life surpasses all the blessings of the future life," and to train our youths in the way leading to such bliss, is the aim and motive of all Religious teaching.

IV.
PRAYER FOR BARMITZVAH.

Prayer which the young Candidate, having previously undergone a religious examination, should recite, when called to the Law, before the Blessing.

אֱלֹהַי וֵאלֹהֵי אֲבוֹתַי

בֶּאֱמֶת וּבְתָמִים אֶשָּׂא אֵלֶיךָ אֶת עֵינַי בַּיּוֹם הַגָּדוֹל

וְהַקָּדוֹשׁ הַזֶּה הַוֶּה לֵאמֹר: הִנֵּה יַלְדוּתִי חָלְפָה הָלְכָה לָה

וְאָנֹכִי הָיִיתִי לְאִישׁ: עָלַי לִשְׁמוֹר אֶת כָּל־חֻקֵּי רְצוֹנֶךָ

וְעָלַי לַעֲנוֹת בְּיוֹם פְּקֻדָּתִי כַּאֲשֶׁר תִּגְמוֹל לִי כִּפְרִי

מַעֲלָלִי: מִיּוֹם הִוָּלְדִי בֶּן יִשְׂרָאֵל אֲנִי · אָמְנָם בַּיּוֹם הַזֶּה

בָּאתִי שֵׁנִית בַּקָּהָל לָךְ · וְלִפְנֵי כָּל־הָעַמִּים אֶתְפָּאֵר עַל

שִׁמְךָ אֲשֶׁר נִקְרָא עָלֵינוּ:

וְעַתָּה אָבִי שֶׁבַּשָּׁמַיִם שְׁמַע אֶל הַתְּפִלָּה וְאֶל הַתְּחִנָּה

הַזֹּאת · שְׁלַח עָלַי שִׁפְעַת בִּרְכוֹתֶיךָ · גֶּשֶׁם נְדָבוֹת

וּבְרְכוֹת הָנֵף עָלַי · לְמַעַן יָמַי יִשְׂבְּעוּן וְיִרְוְיוּן מִדֶּשֶׁן

עֲדָנֶיךָ · הוֹרֵנִי נָא דֶּרֶךְ חֻקֶּיךָ · הַדְרִיכֵנִי בִּנְתִיב מִצְוֹתֶיךָ

תֵּן בְּלִבִּי לְאַהֲבָה וּלְיִרְאָה אֶת שְׁמֶךָ · הַחֲזֵק בְּיָדִי וְאַל

תַּרְפֵּנִי וְלֹא אֶכָּשֵׁל עַל דַּרְכִּי אֲשֶׁר אָנֹכִי הוֹלֵךְ עָלֶיהָ

הַיּוֹם בָּרִאשׁוֹנָה: הַצִּילֵנִי מִיֵּצֶר הָרָע וְתֶן בִּי כֹחַ לִשְׁמוֹר

אֶת תּוֹרָתְךָ הַקְּדוֹשָׁה וְאֶת פִּקּוּדֶיךָ אֲשֶׁר יַעֲשֶׂה אוֹתָם

הָאָדָם וָחַי בָּהֶם: וּבְכָל־יָמַי אֶקְרָא בְּקוֹל גָּדוֹל וְלֹא אֵבוֹשׁ

שְׁמַע יִשְׂרָאֵל יְיָ אֱלֹהֵינוּ יְיָ אֶחָד:

IV.

O MY GOD AND GOD OF MY FOREFATHERS!

On this solemn and sacred day, which marketh my passage from boyhood to manhood, I humbly venture to raise my eyes unto Thee, and to declare, with sincerity and truth, that henceforth I will observe all Thy commandments, and undertake and bear the responsibility of all mine actions towards Thee. In my earliest infancy I was brought within Thy sacred covenant with Israel, and to-day I again enter as an active responsible member, the pale of Thine elect congregation, in the midst of which I will never cease to glorify Thy holy name in the face of all nations.

Do Thou, O Heavenly Father, hearken unto this my humble prayer, and vouchsafe unto me Thy gracious blessings, so that my earthly life may be sustained and made happy by Thine ineffable mercies. Teach me the way of Thy statutes, that I may obey them, and faithfully carry out Thine ordinances. Dispose my heart to love Thee and to fear Thy holy name, and grant me Thy support and the strength necessary to avoid the worldly dangers which encompass the path lying before me. Save me from temptation, so that I may with fortitude observe Thy holy Law, and those precepts on which human happiness and eternal life depend. Thus I will every day of my life trustfully and gladly proclaim:

"HEAR, O ISRAEL, THE LORD IS OUR GOD, THE LORD IS ONE!"

V.

BIBLIOGRAPHY.

Religious books for the use of children at home or in school were unknown in olden times. The Torah was taught, and with it every thing else. A great part of the Book of Proverbs and many of the Psalms may have been intended for the education of the young. In the early post-Biblical time we meet with books like The Wisdom of Solomon, The Wisdom of Joshua, son of Sirach, and Sayings of the Fathers, which may have served the same purpose. To these may be added "The Duties of the Heart," by Bachya ibn Pekuda, "The Examination of the World" (Bechinath Olam), "The Choice of the Pearls," by Ibn Gabirol, Abraham ibn Ezra's "Foundation of the Fear of God, and Principle of the Law," and "The Book of the Righteous," by Rabbenu Jacob Tam, and "The Moral Lessons" (Toaliyyoth) by Rabbi Levi ben Gerson, and "The Shulhan Aruch" of R. Judah Aryeh di Modena. All these works are excellent books for the instruction of the young. They inculcate religious lessons, and shew the way to a pious life, but they are not text books of religion in the modern sense of the term. This branch of literature began to develop in the last century, with the exception of Abraham Jaghel's *Lekach-tob*, which was written in the beginning of the seventeenth century, and was the first Catechism of Jewish Religion. It was composed in the Hebrew Language aud subsequently translated into Latin and English. Since last century, however, religious books of all sizes, forms and tendencies have been produced in all countries, especially in Germany. The following list contains such books as are included in the Jews' College Library :—

English—

Albu, I., חק לישראל London, 1860.

Asher, B. H., Initiation of the Youth. London, 1850

Asher, D., Outlines of Jewish Religion. Manchester, 1845.

Cahen, M., Catechism of Religion. Liverpool, 1890.

Cahun, B., The Thirteen Articles of Faith. English and French. London. 1835.

Cohen, M. R.. Principles of Judaism. Sydney, 1855.

Cohen, S. I., Elements of Jewish Faith. Philadelphia, 1813

Cohen, S. I., Elements of Hebrew and English. London, 1815.

Davidson, M., Moral and Religious Guide. London, 1855.

Early lesson in the Jewish Religion, adopted from the Catechism of Giuseppi Levi. London, 1869.

Festivals of the Lord. London, 1839.

Friedlander, M., Text book of Jewish Religion London. 189⸱.

Goodman, T., Faith of Israel. 1835..

Joseph, N., Religion: Natural and Revealed. London, 1879.

Kley, E., Catechism. translated from the German by I. Lutomirski. Oxford. 1842.

Lesser, Isaac, Instruction in the Mosaic Religion. Philadelphia, 1830.

Meldola, R., Way of Faith. London, 1848.

Mendez, A. P., The Law of Moses. London, 1861.

Moss, Ph., Calendar, Hebrew and English. London, 1853.

Van Oven, J., Manual of Judaism, London, 1835.

Picciotto, M. H., Translation of Reggio's Guide for the Religious Instruction. London, 1855.

In German—

Arnhein, A., Leitfaden. Glasgow, 1829.

P. Beer,   Prague, 1818.

Ben-Zev, יסודי הדת. Wien, 1806.

Bing, A., Hanptlehren des Judenthums. München, 1827.

Bock, M. H., Catechismus. Berlin, 1814.

Brück, M., Ceremonialgebräuche. Breslau, 1857

Büdinger, A., מורה לתורה. Cassel. 1830.

Fassel, H. B., Mosaisch-rabbinische Religionslehre. Gross Kanisza, 1858.

Feilchenfeld, W., Systematisches Lehrbuch der israelitischen Religion. Posen, 1878.

Friedenthal, M. B., עקרי אמונה Prag, 1827.

Funk, B., Die Zehngebote. Breslau, 1816.

Grünbaum, E., Die Sittenlehre des Judenthums. Manheim, 1867

Dr. Heinemann, תורת אמונת בית ישראל(Hebrew and German). Cassel, 1812.

Dr. Herxheimer, Glaubens-und Pflichtenlehre. Bernburg, 1843.

Hirsch, R., חורב Israel's Pflichten. Altona, 1837.

Hochstädter, B., Glaubenslehre. Ems, 1862.

Johlson, I., Leitfaden, אלומי יוסף Pf. a/M. 1839.

Kaufmann D., Catechismus. Pest, 1884.

Kohn, S., Religionslehre. Wien, 1853.

Landau, T., Das Levitenhaus, Häusliche Ritual-Gesetze. Fkft. a/M. 1859.

Lash, G., Die göttlichen Gesetze. Halberstadt, 1857.

Prof. Lazarus, Die Ethik des Judenthums. Berlin, 1898.

Lehrbuch der israelitiscden Religion. Stuttgart, 1837.

Leimdoerfer, D., Religionslehre. Nordhausen, 1876.

Loewenheim, Die mosaische Religion. Licsnach, 1864.

Mannheimer, I., Gebetbuch und Religions Unterricht. Darmstadt, 1881

Mira, H., Leibfaden. Breslau, 1839.

Neuman, M. S., Religionslehre. Pest, 1826.

Philippson, L., Israelitische Religionslehre. Leipzig, 1861.

Philippson, S., Catechismus. Leipzig, 1843.

Plessner, S., Jüdish-Mosaischer Religions unterricht. Berlin, 1839

Stein, L., Torah u. Mizwa. Fkft. o/M. 1850.

Stern, M. E., Handbuch zum jüdischen Religions-unterrichte. Wien, 1861.

French and Italian—

Bloch, S., La Foi d'Israel.   Paris, 1859.

Lambert. L. M., Catéchisme Hebreu, Allemand et Français.   Paris 1837.

Loeb, H., Chemin de la foi.   Paris, 1859.

Vogue, L., La guide du croyant Israelite.   Metz, 1857.

Castiglioni, I. V., Dottrina Religiosa.   Trieste, 1861.

Tremellius, Imm., Dottrina Religiosa.   English   translation. London, 1818.

Modena, D. Z., Catechism.   Reggio, 1825.

Judaeo-German—

חינוך הילדים Warsaw, 1852.

טהנה יששכר Moral lessons, illustrated by tales from Talmud and Midrash.   Rödelheim, 1837.

Collections of Moral Sayings—

Maier, J., Sprüche.   Texts for Moral Lessons.   Tf o/M: 1830.

Steinschneider, M., אמרי בינה Berlin, 1847.

Mocatta, M., Sayings from Proverbs and Ecclesiastes.   London, 1837.

Josh. Steinberg, משלי יהושע Wilna, 1871.

Edelmann, H., דרך טובים London, 1852.

INDEX

OF

QUOTATIONS FROM BIBLE, MISHNAH, TALMUD, AND POSEKIM.

———◆———

* The numbers refer to pages in the Authorised Daily Prayer-book, with a new translation by the Rev. S. Singer.

GENERAL INDEX.

INDEX OF NAMES.

INDEX OF HEBREW TERMS.

ERRATA.

Page 329, note 2.—Doubt has been expressed as to the rule in the case of Mezuzah. The rule certainly does apply. We must bear in mind that the form of the blessings is determined by the general circumstances of the Mitsvah, and not by the exceptional conditions. As a rule the owner of the house, or a member of his household fixes the Mezuzah, whilst in the case of SHOFARL, MILAH, and the like the Mitsvah is as a rule performed by a substitute.

Page 300, note 4.—This note refers to the cases of a Jew being compelled by the laws of the State to do n Sabbath what the Divine Law forbids. The remark applies also to those who, in seeking a living, yield to the force of the circumstances, and break the Sabbath laws. Every possible opportunity should be seized to remind them of the existence of Sabbath and to inspire them with a desire to keep the Fourth Commandment. Care should, however, be taken that the means employed for this purpose should not cause the Sabbath to be utterly ignored, and Judaism utterly forgotten. Such would, *e.g.*, be the result if Jewish congregations were to institute special Sunday services for those who are unwilling to attend the Synagogue on Sabbath, or to join their brethren in the ordinary morning or evening Services.

Page 411.—In the Portuguese Synagogues no Haphtarah is read on Fast-days during the Minchah service, except on the 9th of Ab, when Hosea xiv, 2-10, and Micah vii, 18-20 is read.

Page 441.—In the Portuguese rite the prayer " *alenu* " is preceded and not followed by a " Kaddish of the Orphans."